CAMPUS CRIME

Second Edition

CAMPUS CRIME

Legal, Social, and Policy Perspectives

Edited by

BONNIE S. FISHER

Division of Criminal Justice
University of Cincinnati

and

JOHN J. SLOAN, III

Department of Justice Sciences
University of Alabama-Birmingham

CHARLES C THOMAS • PUBLISHER, LTD.
Springfield • Illinois • U.S.A.

Published and Distributed Throughout the World by

CHARLES C THOMAS • PUBLISHER, LTD.
2600 South First Street
Springfield, Illinois 62794-9265

©2007 by CHARLES C THOMAS • PUBLISHER, LTD.

ISBN-13: 978-0-398-007736-5
ISBN-10: 0-398-07736-3
ISBN-13: 978-0-398-07737-2 (pbk.)
ISBN-10: 0-398-07737-1 (pbk.)

Library of Congress Catalog Card Number: 2006048899

Printed in the United States of America
MM-R-3

Library of Congress Cataloging in Publication Data

Campus crime : legal, social, and policy perspectives / edited by Bonnie S.
 Fisher and John J. Sloan III. – 2nd ed.
   p. cm.
 Includes bibliographical references and index.
 ISBN-13: 978-0-398-07736-5
 ISBN-10: 0-398-07736-3
 ISBN-13: 978-0-398-07737-2 (pbk.)
 ISBN-10: 0-398-07737-1 (pbk.)
  1. College students–Crimes against–United States. 2. Universities and col-
leges–Security measures–United States. 3. Campus police–Legal status, laws,
etc.–United States. I. Fisher, Bonnie, 1969– II. Sloan, John J.

HV6250.4 S78F57 2007
364.973--dc22   2006048899

ABOUT THE CONTRIBUTORS

Catherine Bath is the Executive Director of Security On Campus, Inc. (SOC), the only national nonprofit organization devoted exclusively to assisting the victims of violence on college campuses, and to improving campus security. Cofounded by Connie and Howard Clery in 1987, SOC has been the driving force behind the federal *Clery Act* and nearly thirty other state and federal laws addressing campus crime reporting and victims' rights. Catherine became an advocate for change in postsecondary institutions' campus alcohol policies after the death of her son at Duke University in November of 1999 of aspiration pneumonia, a condition he contracted after a night of heavy drinking. Her advocacy focuses on educational efforts to reduce college students' alcohol and other drug consumption, and to encourage healthy lifestyle choices. An accomplished artist, Ms. Bath studied painting at the University of Illinois in Champaign-Urbana.

Joanne Belknap is a Professor of Sociology and Women's Studies at the University of Colorado at Boulder. She received her doctorate in criminal justice from Michigan State University in 1986. The third edition of her book, *The Invisible Woman: Gender, Crime and Justice* (2007), is an overview of research on women and girls as victims and offenders, and women as workers in the criminal legal system. Dr. Belknap has published extensively on female offenders and female victims. She is a past recipient of the "Inconvenient Woman of the Year" Award from the Division on Women & Crime of the American Society of Criminology and has also received numerous teaching and service awards.

Kristie R. Blevins is an Assistant Professor of Criminal Justice at the University of North Carolina at Charlotte. She received her Ph.D. in Criminal Justice from the University of Cincinnati. Dr. Blevins is coeditor of, and a contributor to, *Taking Stock: The Status of Criminological Theory* (2006). Her research interests include correctional rehabilitation, victimization, and the occupational reactions and attitudes of employees in the criminal justice system. She is currently involved in field research exploring the attributes, drug habits, and motivations of solicitors of prostitutes in a southern metropolitan area.

Max L. Bromley is an Associate Professor of Criminal Justice and Director of the Masters Program in Criminal Justice Administration in the Department of Criminology at the University of South Florida. Previously, he was Associate Director of Public Safety at the University of South Florida and worked in the criminal justice field for almost twenty-five years. He received his B.S. and M.S. in Criminology from Florida State University, and a Doctorate in Higher Education with an emphasis in Criminal Justice from Nova University. Dr. Bromley is the author of *Department Self-Study: A Guide for Campus Law Enforcement Administrators,* which has been used at over 1,000 institutions of higher education in the U.S. He is also coauthor of *Crime and Justice in America* (6th Ed.) (2004), *Hospital and College Security Liability* (1987), and *College Crime Prevention and Personal Safety Awareness* (1990). His work has appeared in *Policing, Police Quarterly, Criminal Justice Policy Review, and Journal of Contemporary Criminal Justice.* His research interests involve police administration, police organizational change, and specialized police agencies.

S. Daniel Carter is the Senior Vice President of Security On Campus, Inc. (SOC) the only national nonprofit organization devoted exclusively to assisting the victims of violence on college campuses and to improving campus security. Cofounded by Connie and Howard Clery in 1987, the organization has been the driving force behind the federal *Clery Act* and nearly thirty other state and federal laws addressing campus crime reporting and victims' rights. Carter has been working on improving victims' rights and campus safety for more than fifteen years, beginning his work while a student at the University of Tennessee from which he graduated in 1994 with a B.A. in Political Science. He has worked on every amendment to the Clery Act since 1992, including the *Campus Sexual Assault Victims Bill of Rights,* and serves as SOC's lead Crime Victim Advocate.

Francis T. Cullen is Distinguished Research Professor of Criminal Justice and Sociology at the University of Cincinnati. His recent work includes *Combating Corporate Crime: Local Prosecutors at Work* (1998), *Criminological Theory: Context and Consequences* (2007), and *Criminological Theory: Past to Present–Essential Readings* (2006). His research focuses on the impact of social support on crime, the measurement of sexual victimization, public opinion about crime control, and rehabilitation as a correctional policy. He is a Past President of both the American Society of Criminology and the Academy of Criminal Justice Sciences.

Leah E. Daigle is an Assistant Professor of Justice Studies in the Department of Political Science at Georgia Southern University. She received her Ph.D. in Criminal Justice from the University of Cincinnati. Her research interests include the development of offending over time, and gender differences in the antecedents to, and consequences of, criminal victimization and participation in offending across the life-course. Her most recent research has examined innovative responses to college women who have suffered sexual assault victimization, including self-protective action and acknowledgment. Dr. Daigle's work has appeared in *Justice Quarterly,* the *Journal of Interpersonal Violence,* and *Criminal Justice and Behavior.*

George W. Dowdall is Professor of Sociology at Saint Joseph's University. His books include *The Eclipse of the State Mental Hospital* (1996) and *Adventures in Criminal Justice Research* (2004). His research has focused on college student binge drinking, including one paper commissioned by the National Institute of Alcohol Abuse and Alcoholism Task Force on College Drinking. A graduate of Holy Cross, he received the Ph.D. in Sociology from Brown University and was an NIMH Postdoctoral Fellow at the UCLA School of Public Health. He has been a faculty member at Indiana

University, Buffalo State, and Saint Joseph's, and held visiting appointments at UCLA, Penn, Brown, and Harvard. In 2000, he was the American Sociological Association's Congressional Fellow. Dr. Dowdall also serves on the Board of Directors of Security on Campus, Inc.

Edna Erez is a Professor and Head of the Department of Criminal Justice at the University of Illinois at Chicago. She holds a law degree (LL.B.) from the Hebrew University of Jerusalem and Ph.D. in Sociology from the University of Pennsylvania. She is the current Coeditor of *International Review of Victimology* and an Associate Editor of *Violence and Victims*; she is also a past editor of *Justice Quarterly,* the official publication of the Academy of Criminal Justice Sciences. Professor Erez has published extensively on victims and women in the criminal justice system, and violence against women, including immigrant women. Among her current projects is a study of women involved in terrorism.

Bonnie S. Fisher is a Professor of Criminal Justice in the Division of Criminal Justice at the University of Cincinnati, and a senior research fellow at the Criminal Justice Research Center. She has been Principle Investigator on four national-level grants funded by the U.S. Department of Justice to examine issues concerning the victimization of college students, the sexual victimization and stalking of college women, violence against college women, and responses by colleges and universities to a report of a sexual assault. Her research interests include the correlates of victimization, fear of victimization, and attitudes toward criminal justice policy. Her most recent work has examined the extent and nature of repeat sexual victimization among college women and the efficacy of the protective action-completion nexus for sexual victimization.

Dennis E. Gregory is an Associate Professor of Higher Education at Old Dominion University and serves as Program Director for the Higher Education Graduate Programs. He has served in student affairs positions at schools in the Southeast between 1974 and 2000 and is a past President of the Association for Student Judicial Affairs. He has also served in a variety of professional leadership positions, including currently serving as Associate Editor of the *NASPA Journal* and on the Board of Directors of the Council for the Advancement of Standards in Higher Education (CAS). Dr. Gregory has presented over 100 programs, speeches, teleconferences, seminars and keynote addresses on student affairs and legal topics throughout the United State. He has authored or coauthored over fifty articles, book chapters, monographs and other publications, including *The Administration of Fraternal Organizations on North American Campuses: A Pattern for the New Millennium* (2003).

Timothy C. Hart is an Assistant Professor in the Department of Criminal Justice at the University of Nevada–Las Vegas (UNLV) and Director of the State of Nevada's Center for the Analysis of Crime Statistics. He received the Ph.D. in Criminology from the University of South Florida in 2006. His research interests include survey research, applied statistics, geographic information systems, and victimization. Prior to joining the UNLV faculty, Dr. Hart was a Statistician for the Bureau of Justice Statistics, a Program Analyst for the Drug Enforcement Administration and a Research Analyst for the Hillsborough County (FL) Sheriff's Department.

Steven M. Janosik is an Associate Professor and Senior Policy Analyst in the Department of Educational Leadership and Policy Studies at Virginia Tech. He received the B.S in Business Administration from Virginia Tech, an M.A. in Counseling and Student Personnel Services from the University of Georgia, and the Ed. D. in Educational Administration from Virginia Tech. Dr. Janosik has more than twenty years experience in college administration, and is the author or coauthor of two books, eleven book chapters, and fifty-four journal articles on such topics as campus crime, college administration, and higher education law. He has received the "Outstanding Research Award" from the American College Personnel Association's Commission III, the "D. Parker Young Award" for outstanding scholarship and research in the areas of higher education law and judicial affairs from the Association for Student Judicial Affairs, and the "Outstanding Contribution to Student Affairs Through Teaching Award" from National Association of Student Personnel Administrators, Region III.

Heather M. Karjane is Gender Issues Coordinator at the Massachusetts Administrative Office of the Trial Court. Dr. Karjane has specialized in the fields of violence towards women, violence prevention, traumatic stress, and survivorship for over twenty years. She has served as an advisor to the U.S. Air Force, the U.S. Department of Defense, the Children's Safety Network, the National Suicide Prevention Resource Center, and the Media Education Foundation. Her research has been funded by the National Institute of Justice and the Centers for Disease Control and Prevention. She is a founding member of the Greenbook National Demonstration Initiative and has been a member of the Massachusetts Governor's Commission on Sexual and Domestic Violence since 2002. Dr. Karjane holds a Ph.D. from the University of Massachusetts at Amherst, an M.A. from Simmons College, and a B.A. from Rutgers University.

Mark M. Lanier is an Associate Professor of Criminal Justice in the Department of Criminal Justice and Legal Studies at the University of Central Florida. He earned an interdisciplinary social science doctoral degree from Michigan State University in 1993 and formerly taught at Eastern Michigan University. Dr. Lanier has published numerous articles in a variety of interdisciplinary journals, including those in public health, criminal justice, criminology, law, and psychology. His funded research has examined youth and HIV/AIDS, and community-oriented policing (COP). In 1997, the College of Health and Public Affairs at the University of Central Florida named him one of its "Distinguished Researchers of the Year." He is coauthor (with Stuart Henry) of *Essential Criminology* (1998; 2004) and the *Essential Criminology Reader* (2006), and is coeditor (with Stuart Henry) of *What Is Crime?* (2001). In 2006, he was recognized as the Educator of the Year by the Southern Criminal Justice Association.

Samuel C. McQuade, III, Ph.D. currently serves as the Professional Studies Graduate Program Coordinator at the Rochester Institute of Technology. He is a former Air National Guard security officer, deputy sheriff and police officer, police organizational change consultant, National Institute of Justice Program Manager for the U.S. Department of Justice, and Study Director for the Committee on Law and Justice at the National Research Council of the National Academics of Sciences. Professor McQuade holds a Doctoral Degree in Public Policy from George Mason University and a Masters Degree in Public Administration from the University of Washington. He teaches and conducts research at RIT in areas inclusive of computer crime, security technology administration, and career options in Technology-oriented societies. Dr. McQuade also oversees a professional concentration of graduate courses pertaining to Security Technology, which are now offered through RIT's Professional Studies Masters of Science Degree. His new textbook titled, *Understanding and Managing Cybercrime,* was published by Allyn & Bacon/Pearson Education in 2006.

Elizabeth Ehrhardt Mustaine is an Associate Professor of Sociology at the University of Central Florida. She earned the Ph.D. in Sociology from the Ohio State University. Her research centers on issues of criminal victimization risks, domestic violence and stalking, and sex offender registration. Dr. Mustaine is active in both community organizations and numerous academic associations.

Matthew B. Robinson is an Associate Professor of Criminal Justice at Appalachian State University. He earned the Ph.D. in Criminology from Florida State University. He is author of *Justice Blind?: Ideals and Realities of American Criminal Justice* (2005), *Why Crime? An Integrated Systems Theory of Antisocial Behavior* (2004), and coauthor of *Spatial Aspects of Crime: Theory and Practice* (2004). His forthcoming books include *Lies, Damned Lies, and Statistics: A Critical Analysis of Claims Made by the Office of National Drug Control Policy* (2007) and *Death Nation: The Experts Explain American Capital Punishment* (2007). He is a Past President of the Southern Criminal Justice Association. His main areas of interest include criminological theory, crime prevention, the death penalty, the war on drugs, and injustices occurring in the legal system.

Sunghoon Roh is an Assistant Professor of Criminal Justice at Appalachian State University. He is a former Commander and Chief Officer assigned to the Crime Prevention Division, Criminal Investigation Unit and Combat Police Force Unit in

Busan, South Korea. He has published several articles and book chapters in the areas of community policing, spatial aspects of crime, and theories of crime. His main areas of interest include policing, race and crime, and crime mapping.

Shannon A. Santana is an Assistant Professor of Criminal Justice at Florida International University. She received the Ph.D. in Criminal Justice from the University of Cincinnati. She conducted the content analysis of data collected for the National Campus Sexual Assault Policy Study. Her work has appeared in the *Justice System Journal* and the *Security Journal.* She has also coauthored book chapters that have appeared in *Violence at Work: Causes, Patterns, and Prevention, Restorative Justice on the College Campus: Promoting Student Growth and Responsibility,* and *Reawakening the Spirit of Campus Community, and Changing Attitudes to Punishment: Public Opinion, Crime and Justice.* Her research interests include violence against women, the effectiveness of self-protective behaviors in violent victimizations, workplace violence, and rehabilitation.

Linda K. Shafer earned her Ph.D. in Political Science from the University of Oregon. A former academic, Dr. Shafer now lives and works on the West Coast. She works for the judicial branch of state government but remains involved in various victims' and women's rights causes.

Jessica Shoemaker is a candidate for the M.S. in Criminal Justice at the University of Alabama at Birmingham, where she earned her B.S. with Honors in Criminal Justice in 2005. Her thesis research examines the correlation between an inmate's readiness to change and his participation in faith-based correctional programs. Her research interests include faith-based inmate rehabilitation and the effect of extra-legal variables on sentence outcomes.

John J. Sloan, III is an Associate Professor of Criminal Justice and Chairman of the Department of Justice Sciences at the University of Alabama at Birmingham. He earned the Ph.D. in Sociology from Purdue University. His work has appeared in such journals as *Criminology and Public Policy, Justice Quarterly, Social Forces,* and *Criminology.* For over a decade, he has collaborated with Bonnie Fisher and others on numerous projects that examined victimization patterns, fear of victimization, and security issues on college and university campuses in the U.S.

Megan Stewart is a doctoral student in the Division of Criminal Justice at the University of Cincinnati. She holds a B.A. in Psychology from Miami University of Ohio and an M.S. in Criminal Justice from the University of Cincinnati. Prior to pursuing her Ph.D., she worked for the University of Cincinnati Police Department, and was a hotline counselor and rape crisis advocate for the Community Counseling and Crisis Center in Oxford, Ohio. Her current research interests include crime prevention, repeat victimization, sexual victimization, stalking, fear of crime, environmental criminology, and psychopathology.

Richard Tewksbury is a Professor of Justice Administration at the University of Louisville and Research Director for the National Prison Rape Elimination Commission. He holds a Ph.D. in Sociology from the Ohio State University. He is author/editor of eleven books and more than 150 scholarly articles and chapters. In 2006, he received the American Correctional Association's "Peter P. Lejin's Correctional Research Award," and in 2005, was named the Southern Criminal Justice Association's "Educator of the Year." He actively works with a number of local, state, and federal criminal justice and social service agencies. Dr. Tewksbury's research focuses on issues of risks of criminal victimization, sexual violence, men's sexuality, and sex offender registration.

*For T.A.H.S., T.S.M., and my family with thanks
for the support and the understanding.*

J.J.S.

*To Nick, Olivia, and Camille with many thanks
for their endless encouragement and patience.*

B.S.F.

PREFACE

This volume is the second edition of *Campus Crime: Legal, Social and Policy Perspectives.* The demand for a second edition is evidence that interest in the legal, social, and policy contexts of campus crime has not waned since publication of the first edition in 1995. Congress and state legislators have maintained continued interest in campus crime and security through passage of, and amendments to, laws addressing these issues. Researchers from a variety of disciplines have published numerous studies that examined a wide range of campus crime and security topics from the extent and nature of student victimization to compliance by postsecondary institutions to federal and state legislation. Law enforcement professionals have made progress reforming the organizational structure and tactical practices of campus police departments. Despite these continued actions, concerns about campus crime and security persist among students and their parents, administrators, faculty, staff, and student advocacy groups.

Among our purposes in assembling a second edition of *Campus Crime: Legal, Social and Policy Perspectives* is to share with readers the advancements that have been made to better understand campus crime, especially student victimization, and effectively address security issues. For the sake of continuity with the first edition, we maintain the three section divisions found there: The Legal Context of Campus Crime, The Social Context of Campus Crime, and The Security Context of Campus Crime. Within each section, contributors address what we believe, given our knowledge and expertise, constitute the most pressing crime and security issues that continue to face post-secondary administrators and their students, faculty, and staff.

Some chapters included in this second edition address "long-standing" topics such as the sexual victimization of college women and the role of campus police departments in securing the campus. The remaining chapters address "new" topics emerging since publication of the first edition. First, over 15 years have passed since passage of the first ever federal-level campus crime legislation, now known as the *Jeanne Clery Disclosure of Campus Security Policy and Campus Crime Statistics Act* (20 U.S.C. 1092[f]). Its requirements have generated numerous critical discussions and empirical analyses that raise questions about the legislation's effectiveness and on campus crime impact. Second, researchers have completed and published the results of at least five national-level and numerous smaller scale victimization studies since 1995. Together, they have filled gaps (some of which we identified in the Postscript of the first edition) in researchers' understanding of the extent, nature, and spatial aspects of student victimization. Beyond estimating victimization rates, these studies offer insight concerning how students' routine activities and lifestyles, including alcohol use and abuse, contribute to their victimization risk. Third, since 1995, legislatures have criminalized two "new" behaviors, stalking and "high-tech" abuses such as computer hacking and identity theft, which pose unique victimization risks and perpetration opportunities for students, and create security and policing challenge for campus administrators far different from "traditional" types of violence and property theft. Finally, implementation of community-oriented policing on many campuses has ushered in a new era of campus policing and which gives rise both to new practices and challenges.

Section I of the book examines the legal context of campus crime by presenting five chapters focusing on the *Jeanne Clery Disclosure of Campus Security Policy and Campus Crime Statistics Act (Clery)*. From a legal standpoint, *Clery* and its state-level counterparts have created important obligations for postsecondary institutions, including annually reporting campus crime statistics and publicly reporting institutional processes designed to enhance campus security and provide assistance to campus crime victims. The chapters acquaint the reader with: (1) the genesis and evolution of *Clery,* (2) the current state of research concerning public awareness of *Clery* and its impact, (3) results and implications of the only national-level evaluation of the sexual assault reporting requirements of Clery, the National Campus Sexual Assault Policy Study, (4) inherent limitations of *Clery's* goals and their effect on the "true" extent of gendered violence on campus and resulting ineffective institutional responses, and (5) a national-level comparative analysis of state-based *Clery*-style legislation.

Part II examines the social context of campus crime. The six chapters in this section present both descriptions of, and explanations for, the extent and nature of college student victimization, addressing a range of salient topics that are of interest to researchers and administrators. Four of the chapters address issues such as whether student victimization rates differ from non-students', the utility of routine activities and lifestyle theories for explaining college student victimization patterns, the role of alcohol use and abuse in understanding college student victimization, and the spatial distribution on campus of frequently occurring offenses, such as alcohol and drug violations, and vandalism. The remaining two chapters focus on crimes typically committed primarily against women. One chapter offers a comprehensive overview of the growing body of research into sexual harassment, rape, and intimate partner abuse of college women. The second chapter discusses the extent, nature, and impact of stalking behaviors committed against and by college students.

Section III of the book focuses on security issues on campus. Two chapters focus on the organization and practices of campus police by examining the evolution of campus policing over the past four decades and the administrative and operational models of campus police, including the recent implementation of community-oriented policing and the application of community-based strategies on campuses. The third chapter examines the rise of high-tech abuses and crimes on campus and offers suggestions for how postsecondary institutions can address these new forms of illegal behavior.

Although we added new topics to and updated others for the second edition, we remain committed to providing a timely compilation of topics to an audience of students, parents, academicians, practitioners, and college administrators. In compiling these chapters, our goal was to bring together works designed to provide readers a current picture and critical analysis of issues concerning the legal, social, and policy contexts of campus crime and security. We believe the collected works of this volume offer insightful discussions and raise relevant questions. The authors also provide plausible responses to addressing campus crime and security, a social problem that continues to affect students, their parents, and postsecondary institutions on a daily basis.

BONNIE S. FISHER
JOHN J. SLOAN, III

ACKNOWLEDGMENTS

We again thank our editor, Michael Payne Thomas, for his guidance and patience with us in putting together this second edition. We also are grateful to our contributors, both returning and new, for producing high-quality chapters and adhering to our deadlines with a sense of humor. Their enthusiasm for this volume and dedicated efforts give us hope that future research can better inform the development and implementation of effective proactive and prevention responses to campus crime.

John thanks Tavis for her support of this project, and Dr. Tennant S. McWilliams, Dean of the School of Social and Behavioral Sciences at UAB, for release time from administrative duties that allowed him to complete this project. Finally, he thanks his parents, John and Christine, and his siblings, Timothy and Kathleen, for their support over the years.

Bonnie thanks Nick for encouraging her to follow her passion for engaging in college student victimization research. She thanks her daughters, Olivia and Camille, for helping her understand how the world works from a girl's perspective and for making her laugh and think critically every day. She thanks her colleagues for their guidance and support throughout the years, especially her coauthors, Frank Cullen and Leah Daigle. Many thanks also to her students who provided her ideas and insights into *why* and *how* student victimization occurs.

John and Bonnie are already looking forward to working on a third edition of the book, although next time, we won't let ten years pass between editions! Mark your calendars for 2011—we've already marked ours!

CONTENTS

CAMPUS CRIME

Chapter 1

CAMPUS CRIME POLICY: LEGAL, SOCIAL, AND SECURITY CONTEXTS

BONNIE S. FISHER AND JOHN J. SLOAN, III

INTRODUCTION

In 1990, Congress passed and President George H.W. Bush signed into law the *Student Right-to-Know and Campus Security Act of 1990* (20 U.S.C. 1092[f]), renamed in 1998 the *Jeanne Clery Disclosure of Campus Security Policy and Campus Crime Statistics Act* (20 U.S.C. 1092[f]; henceforth the *Clery Act*), in remembrance of Jeanne Clery, who was murdered by a fellow student while she slept in her dorm room at Lehigh University in 1986. Concurrently, colleges and universities began being held liable for "foreseeable" criminal victimizations occurring in dormitories or other on-campus locations, state legislatures began passing their own "*Clery* style" legislation, and postsecondary institutions struggled to professionalize their campus security and law enforcement agencies. Additionally, social science researchers began systematically studying crime and security issues on post-secondary institutions. Their findings revealed sometimes-startling realities about life in "the ivory tower."

These events form the backdrop of what we call the legal, social, and security contexts of campus crime and are the basis for campus officials to develop, implement, and evaluate policies and programs that address campus crime. Importantly, a change in one of these contexts affects the others, making them inextricably linked. For example, research shows that a sizable portion of college students are crime victims, in particular that college women suffer sexual victimization at high levels (the social context). This was, in part, the rationale for legislation that was passed requiring postsecondary institutions to create both prevention programs, procedures and services for specifically dealing with these victims (the security context). Another example is research conducted (the social context) that examines postsecondary institutional compliance with state and federal legislation relating to campus crime and security (the legal context). Thus, while one can examine each context separately, it is also important to keep in mind the linkages among them and their relationship to campus crime policy.

In this chapter, we present an overview of the legal, social, and security contexts of campus crime. In doing so, our two goals are: (1) to give readers a broad-based overview of key issues relating to each context, and (2) to show readers important linkages among the contexts.

We organize the chapter as follows. We first present discussion of the legal context of campus crime, which includes both the judicial and legislative arenas. Here, we discuss postsecondary institutional liability for criminal victimizations occurring on campus property, as well as explore important legislative developments focusing on campus crime and security issues. Next, we examine the social context of campus crime, that is, important social scientific studies of campus crime and security. Following this, we examine the security context of campus crime, which includes discussing the development of professional campus police agencies, issues relating to their development, and the increasingly important role that information technology security plays on college campuses. We conclude the chapter by presenting important linkages across the three contexts and suggest that policy–federal, state, or on a single campus–is implicitly or explicitly an overarching theme that also ties together the contexts.

The Legal Context of Campus Crime

Generally, the legal context involves two separate but related branches of government: the judicial and the legislative. In the former arena, precedent-setting court decisions arising from lawsuits filed by students and their parents continue to shape campus crime security policy. Through these cases, courts have held institutions liable for foreseeable victimization against their students occurring on their campuses as a breach of express or implied contract. In the legislative arena, general sentiment during the early 1990s in Congress and state legislatures was that campus administrators and staff, lax in the enforcement of campus security, led to college and university students being at high risk for violent victimization, including murder. Media reports, victims' testimony at Congressional hearings, and campus advocacy groups fueled this perception (see Fisher, Hartman, Cullen, & Turner, 2002; Fisher, Sloan, Cullen, & Lu, 1998). Legislative reaction was to pass new laws or amend existing statutes to require college and universities to annually report and disseminate information about crime on their campuses. Mandates also included that campuses provide to interested parties, descriptions of security policies, protocols and programs, such as the availability of crime prevention education and victim services, incident reporting, filing criminal complaints, and initiating student disciplinary procedures.

These federal and state laws, as discussed below, created among some observers not only the perception of improved campus safety, but also increased institutional liability for crimes committed on campus. To understand better these issues, we review developments in the judicial and legislative arenas in the following discussion.

The Judicial Arena: Institutional Liability

Campus crime victims and their parents have repeatedly sued postsecondary institutions for damages resulting from injuries incurred during the commission of criminal incident. Smith (1995) described how the late 1970s first saw these lawsuits arising, but that postsecondary institutions did not feel their impact until the early 1980s. By the end of the 1980s, according to Smith (1995), this type of litigation had become more frequent because plaintiffs were winning their lawsuits. By the 1990s, colleges and universities were systematically responding to the threat of these lawsuits and newly passed congressional and state-level reporting mandates relating to campus security by upgrading security procedures and warning the campus community about crimes occurring on campus.

THEORIES OF LIABILITY. For some time, the courts have ruled that a third party (e.g., a college or university) is liable for damages incurred by the victim only under very specific circumstances (Burling, 2003). Within the context of an educational setting, to establish liability, a plaintiff must prove: (1) the postsecondary institution *owed a duty* to the plaintiff, (2) the institution *breached that duty,* (3) the *plaintiff suffered injuries,* and (4) if the *school had not acted (or failed to act) as it did,* the plaintiff would not have been injured. Burling (2003, p. 21) argued that decisions determining when and under what circumstances a postsecondary institution will be legally liable for damages suffered by an on-campus crime victim constitute "a maze of conflicting and inconsistent analysis." Burling (2003, p. 21) further noted that "What is worse, there is no clear line of cases leading to a coherent analysis."[1]

Burling (2003) suggested that three theories of liability have evolved that define possible relationships and therefore, certain duties owed by a postsecondary institution to its students. The first, known as the "special relationship" theory, is defined within the specific context of the parties' relationship such that one party (the postsecondary institution) has a duty to act. For a college or university, this relationship exists because students and parents expect the school to have a commitment to its students' well-being. The second theory recognized by the courts is the "landowner-business invitee" theory, and involves a relationship in which the property owner (the postsecondary institution) owes a duty to the business invitee (the student). Under this theory, colleges and universities have the same legal duty to students as any proprietor has to an invitee to the premises: use of reasonable care in inspecting for possibly dangerous conditions, warning invitees of these conditions, and protecting them against foreseeable dangers. Drawing from the business invitee relationship, the third theory of liability, "landlord-tenant," states a property owner must warn a tenant of any known risks or foreseeable dangers and take reasonable actions to protect against such risks or dangers. In this instance, the postsecondary institution is the landlord while the student is the tenant; such a theory would seem particularly applicable to university owned housing (e.g., dorms or apartments) in which students reside.

According to Burling (2003), courts have generally relied on the laws of negligence and contract law in cases arising from student victimizations. Under the laws of negligence, for courts to hold a postsecondary institution liable, the plaintiff must prove the criminal incident was "foreseeable," and if the crime was foreseeable, the institution had failed to provide "reasonable" security procedures to protect possible victims. Plaintiffs have proved "foreseeability" by providing evidence of a "history of crime" at or near the crime scene or of the existence of other dangerous factors, such as college policies allowing males 24-hour access to female residence halls. Establishing "reasonable" security protection is more difficult, with the courts generally making this determination once the foreseeability issue is settled. In other words, given the foreseeability of the crime, what actions, if any, did the school take to reduce the likelihood of future victimization?

Another interesting, if infrequently used, basis of liability arises when a postsecondary institution breaches an express or implied contract by "promising" students (and others) to "protect" them from criminal victimization by their policies or provisions. Promises of this type may be found in college catalogs or brochures, student codes of conduct handbooks, and/or annual security reports or campus housing contracts (e.g., a university says its residence halls are locked every night). Given these circumstances, in effect, the courts may construe such a promise of security as a contract between the institution and the student. Failure on the part of the school to provide protection, such as lax or poorly implemented security measures, may constitute a breach of contract and thus make the institution legally liable for that breach.

The Legislative Arena: Campus Crime and Security Acts

The legislative component of the legal context of campus crime involves federal- and state-level statutes. Some of these supplement court rulings on postsecondary institutional liability, or require campuses to "break the wall of silence" and "come clean" by reporting how much crime is reported on their campuses each year and outline what they are doing about it, from incident reporting to disciplinary procedures.

The *Clery Act* and *Clery*-like state-level legislation share a common goal: to increase student and parental awareness about, and discussion of, crime on campus (see Carter & Bath, 2007; Sloan & Shoemaker, 2007). As the chapters in Part I of this volume show, the *Clery Act* requires postsecondary intuitions who participate in federal student financial aid programs to prepare, publish, and distribute annual reports about campus crime and security to current and prospective members of the campus community so they can possess useful information about safety and security on the campus. The legislative intent behind these statutes was to force campus administrators to take appropriate steps (ranging from increased police patrols to Web-based crime incident reporting systems) for the express purposes of lowering the risk of criminal victimization happening on campus and providing effective services to victims.

Student advocacy and campus watchdog groups have hailed these legislative efforts to make campuses safer. Their continued activism, especially directed at the *Clery Act,* has focused primary on three main issues: (1) passage of amendments to legislative mandates to increase the crime reporting requirements of postsecondary institutions, (2) passage of additional legislation, and (3) compliance with the stated mandates.

First, *The Student-Right-To-Know and Campus Security Act* (20 U.S.C. 1092[f]) was originally passed by Congress in 1990 so that the campus community would have access to annual basic crime statistics and security polices (as mentioned above, the legislation was renamed the *Clery Act* in 1998). Subsequent amendments to the legislation eliminated loopholes and expanded postsecondary institutional reporting requirements by adding new categories of crime (arson and negligent homicide) for which statistics had to be compiled, requiring that schools break down their crime statistics by geographic location on campus (e.g., residence halls), and by providing a daily crime log to the public.

Second, Congress and the states passed additional legislation, including state-level mandates and new federal legislation, since 1988 when Pennsylvania became the first state to enact crime/security reporting legislation. The federal *Buckley Amendment Clarification* (1992) states that records kept by campus police and security for law enforcement purposes are not confidential "education" records under federal law and thus can be made public (see Carter & Bath, 2007). Also in 1992, Congress enacted the *Campus Sexual Assault Victims' Bill of Rights* as a part of the *Higher Education Amendments of 1992* (Public Law: 102–325, §486(c)).[2] The law mandates that colleges and universities provide to campus sexual assault victims specific rights, including their options to report the incident to law enforcement and change their academic and living situation if they desire. Additional mandates are found in the Foley Amendment passed in 1998 and the *Campus Sex Crimes Prevention Act* passed in 2000 (Public Law 106–386, §1601) that provide for the tracking of convicted sex offenders enrolled as students, or working or volunteering at postsecondary institutions (see Carter & Bath, 2007). There are also several campus crime bills currently pending in committees in both the House and Senate.

Third, the *Clery Act* contains very specific reporting mandates. Monitoring compliance with the *Clery Act* has become a primary concern of interested parties, especially the U.S. Department of Education (ED) charged with overseeing the Act's implementation. Concern by the ED recently prompted it to publish the *Handbook for Campus Crime Reporting,* designed to guide campus administrators through *Clery Act* regulations by explaining their meaning and what they require (United States Department of Education, Office of Postsecondary Education, 2005).

The ED has established administrative procedures for filing complaints and investigating allegations of noncompliance with the *Clery Act.* As part of their watchdog tasks, Security On Campus, Inc., assists, free of charge, the filing of a complaint alleging violations of *Clery Act* requirements (How to File a *Jeanne Clery Act* Complaint, 2006). Since 1994, the ED has conducted 375 audits and 184 program reviews arising from alleged violations of the *Clery Act.* The Department of Education has levied fines on some of these schools, including in one instance, levying a fine of $200,000 against a postsecondary institution (Complying with the *Jeanne Clery Act,* 2006).

Despite the good intentions of Congress in passing the *Clery Act* and the laudable efforts of the ED, campus advocacy groups, and student victims, to implement and monitor compliance, academicians interested in campus safety and student victimization issues identified limitations inherent to the *Clery Act* mandates. These researchers provided empirical evidence that question both the usefulness and the effectiveness of the *Clery Act* to actually increase safety on several dimensions (see Part I in this volume).

Several researchers, based on national-level studies, have questioned the ability of the *Clery Act's* crime statistics reporting mandates to provide valid and reliable information about the "true" occurrence of crime on campus because *Clery* does not require postsecondary institutions to compile and report statistics on commonly occurring offenses such as theft, simple assault, and stalking. Fisher et al. (1998) reported, based on results of the first ever national-level study of student victimization, that rates of student victimization involving personal larceny without contact/theft, and vandalism were much higher than were rates of rape/sexual assault, robbery, and aggravated assault. Hart (2003, 2007), using data collected by the National Crime Victimization Survey, showed that simple assaults were the most frequently occurring type of violent crime committed against college students, with rates much higher than those of rape/sexual assault, robbery, and aggravated assault. Further, Fisher, Cullen, and Turner (2000) reported results from the National College Women Sexual Victimization (NCWSV) study indicating that 13 percent of college women experienced a stalking victimization during an academic year–approximately seven months. Yet, statistics on none of these crimes–personal larceny without contact/theft, vandalism, simple assault, or stalking–that a large portion of college and university students have experienced are mandated by *Clery* to be included in the required annual security report prepared by postsecondary institutions (Fisher et al., 2000). Because campus crime reporting requirements do not require postsecondary institutions to compile and report statistics for these common crimes, interested parties are receiving, at best, incomplete information that does not include the actual types of crimes most likely to touch a student's daily life.

Aside from omitting various crimes, for a crime to be included in the annual security reports, victims must first report the offense to campus officials or law enforcement. Considering the types of crime that *Clery* mandates must be included in annual campus crime reports, a sizeable body of victimization research repeatedly shows that substantial numbers of college students *do not* report their victimizations to campus officials or law enforcement authorities for a variety of reasons (see Belknap & Erez, 2007; Hart, 2007; Shafer, 2007). As a result, such incidents are *not* included in reported campus crime statistics.

To illustrate the magnitude of this issue, using data collected from a national-level study of college student victimization, Sloan, Fisher, and Cullen (1997) reported that 75 percent of the on-campus burglaries went unreported to either campus police or other campus officials. Further, Hart (2003) reported that 1995–2000 NCVS data revealed that 47 percent of all robberies and 52 percent of all aggravated assaults involving college students were *not* reported to police. Using data collected in the NCWSV, Fisher et al. (2000) showed that *95 percent of rapes involving college students were not reported to the police,* an estimate comparable to the 1995–2000 NCVS's estimate of 86 percent of rape/sexual assault incidents not being reported to police. The important point here is that publicly reported postsecondary crime statistics (mandated by *Clery*) most likely significantly underreport the "true" amount of campus crime.

Additionally, researchers, including Janosik and Gregory (2007), have questioned whether students and parents, specifically targeted by *Clery,* are even *aware* of *Clery*. Should this be true, it is especially important because some *Clery Act* supporters have claimed that students and their parents use the information in the mandated annual campus crime and security report to decide which school to attend. Research has also shown that even those who work closely with student victims have reservations that students actually read the annual security reports (see Gregory & Janosik, 2007). Collectively, results of these and other studies suggest that more work needs to be done to make all interested parties, including campus personnel, aware of the availability of (and the limitations to) campus crime statistics, policies, and programs.

Student, faculty member, and staff awareness of the amount of campus crime, of the availability of crime prevention or safety education programs, or of campus security policies and protocols at a particular campus, is not enough to make that campus safe. Since current legislation does not mandate postsecondary *evaluation* of the effectiveness of crime prevention or education programs, or of safety and security protocols, students and their parents can only know *if* a school has such programs, policies, or protocols, but cannot know if these are *effective* in reducing or responding to campus crime.

In summary, there are significant flaws and limitations with current legislation mandating postsecondary institutions to "come clean" with their crime statistics and to report what they are doing to address campus crime. These problems seriously hamper the potential impact of federal and state legislation on campus crime and security. There is, however, some good news: interest and activism by campus advocates, watchdogs groups, and researchers with an interest in campus crime and student victimization is not waning, but growing. Their sustained interest, as evident by the chapters in Part I of this volume, has led to several evidence-based recommendations to address the noted limitations (and others not specifically identified) and weaknesses of the *Clery Act* and state-level *Clery* legislation. Lawsuits filed by campus crime victims or their parents continue, and have resulted in advances in the development of liability law for postsecondary institutions. Each effort has helped focus attention on and created the impetus for the analysis of pertinent issues concerning the legal context of campus crime and develop recommendations for change, and we hope, enhancement of campus security, the third context of campus crime.

The Social Context of Campus Crime

For our purposes, the social context of campus crime refers to social scientific research that has described and explained why campus crime happens and to evaluations of the effectiveness of campus-level programs and policies designed to address campus crime. Here, we present an overview of this context.

The Evolution of Interest in Student Victimization

Academic interest in college student victimization was initially sparked by two path-breaking sets of studies: Kirkpatrick and Kanin's (1957) initial and Kanin's subsequent (1967, 1970, 1977) research into sexual aggression by college males against women, and Koss, Gidycz, and Wisnieski's (1987) first ever national-level study of the sexual victimization experiences of female college students in the early 1980s. During the 1970s and 1980s, narrowly focused research, particularly that examining the extent and nature of violence against college women, continued.

It was not until the 1990s, however, influenced by several factors–the momentum of the feminist movement, rape law reforms, successful civil lawsuits files against colleges and universities, student activism, and federal crime reporting mandates–that academics from different disciplines began conducting large-scale and significant research on the victimization experiences of college and university students. For example, during the mid-1990s, the U.S. Department of Justice funded three national-level studies that examined general student victimization patterns, sexual victimization and stalking among college women, and nonfatal violence, including rape and sexual assault, against college women (Fisher et al., 1998; Fisher et al., 2000).

Additionally, during the 1990s, the National Crime Victimization Survey (NCVS), one of two official sources of national-level data on crime in the U.S., added a question to its main survey that asked respondents whether they were a college student for the express purpose of developing average annual victimization rates for college students compared to nonstudents of similar ages (Hart, 2007). Published results of numerous case studies and studies using small samples of college campuses also appeared during the 1990s and focused on student victimization experiences (see Mustaine & Tewksbury, 2007).

Interest in student victimization has not waned today. Researchers continue to publish studies examining the extent and nature of student victimization, including general levels of violent victimizations, theft victimization, stalking, intimate partner violence, identity theft, and computer crimes. Other studies have explored fear of victimization, including differences in fear levels by sex, and of temporal and spatial aspects of fear (see Part II of this volume for representative scholarship).

Classifying the Research

We divide published campus crime research into three categories: (1) studies that *describe the extent and nature of student victimization,* (2) studies that *explain the correlates and causes of victimization* among students, and (3) studies that *evaluate the effectiveness of responses to campus crime, including education or pre-vention programs.* Each category has produced a substantial body of research, which, in turn, has begun informing campus-level crime prevention, education, and policing programs and practices.

DESCRIPTIVE STUDIES. Descriptive studies *describe* the amount and type of student victimization and the nature of their experiences. These studies address fundamental issues such as developing improved measures of victimization, as well as exploring how much of which types of victimization happened among members of the campus community and where and when these victimizations occur. While these studies are important because they produce reasonable estimates of the extent and nature of crime against students, because they are descriptive, they cannot answer basic questions about possible causal forces at work that result in increased levels of risk or fear of victimization.

EXPLANATORY STUDIES. Explanatory studies generally use existing theory to guide *empirical tests of hypotheses about why student victimization* occurs. Using theories such as lifestyle and routine activities, and advanced quantitative statistical techniques, researchers have modeled the dynamics of student victimization and presented a fuller understanding of why students are at risk of experiencing different types of victimization (Dowdall, 2007; Fisher & Stewart, 2007; Mustaine & Tewksbury, 2007). These studies have not only identified individual-level factors associated with different types of victimization, but present statistical models predicting students' risk of experiencing different types of victimization. Coupled with these studies have been studies examining "hot spots" on campus, that is, identifying specific places on campus where most crime occurs and explaining these spatial patterns (Robinson & Roh, 2007).

EVALUATION STUDIES. Evaluation studies assess program processes or program outcomes (or both) of policies designed to reduce victimization, increase campus safety, or reduce levels of fear of victimization. Studies of this type are infrequently published in academic journals, partly because few evaluations of campus programs or polices have occurred. In the late 1990s, Congress attempted to remedy this situation by commissioning a national-level evaluation, the *National Campus Sexual Assault Policy Study* (see Karjane, Fisher, & Cullen, 2002, 2005) to assess how America's postsecondary institutions have responded to reports of sexual assaults. The study also evaluated institutional compliance with *Clery Act* mandates directed at sexual assault (see Fisher, Karjane, Cullen, Blevins, Santana, & Daigle, 2007).

Examples of each study type—descriptive, explanatory, and evaluation—appear in Part II of this volume, and some of the chapters represent more than one type of study. Regardless of study type, we believe each chapter contributes to the growing body of social scientific research on campus crime. The body of knowledge that has accumulated has produced a better understanding of the correlates of, and causal mechanisms underlying, student victimization; this knowledge can then be used (and is being used) to inform policies and programs to address crime on campus.

The Security Context of Campus Crime

As discussed above, postsecondary institutions face possible liability concerning foreseeable victimizations resulting from security lapses which institutions fail to address in a timely manner. Liability issues relate directly to the third context of campus crime we explore in this volume: campus security.

As shown in Figure 1.1, campus security is a subcomponent of the larger context of "campus safety." Campus security specifically encompasses three related sets of activities: those relating to physical security (such as controlling who has keys to buildings and access to parking lots or garages, closed circuit television (CCTV) monitoring), those relating to law enforcement activities (the campus police), and those relating to information technology security (such as infrastructure protection and construction of firewalls to prevent hackers from gaining entry to on-campus networks). Part III of this volume presents chapters addressing campus policing and information system security, with some reference made to physical security.

As per requirements of the *Clery Act,* postsecondary institutions must annu-

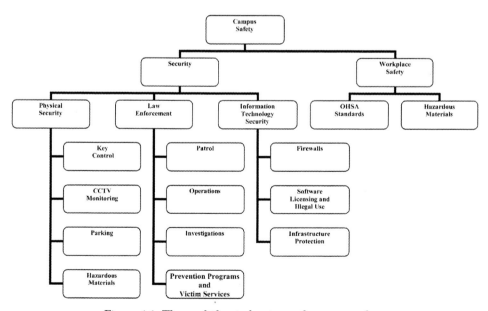

Figure 1.1. The multifaceted nature of campus safety.

ally report not only their campus crime statistics, but also their security policies and the power and authority of their campus security/police departments. *Clery* has thus put an even greater onus on colleges and universities to
develop modern security/law enforcement departments that can adequately
protect and respond to the security needs of the campus community.

The Professionalization of Campus Security

The past 20 or so years has seen a key development in the context of campus security: the *professionalization* of the individuals and departments
charged with the sometimes daunting task of reducing opportunities for on-
campus victimization, responding to calls for assistance, and providing services to crime victims. This professionalization has touched almost all aspects
of campus security and has resulted in significant changes in, and upgrades
to, security policies.

When one looks back at the history of campus security, one finds that for
most of the past century, universities primarily geared security toward protecting property—preventing and responding to break-ins, addressing vandalism, or insuring doors were locked. As a result, until very recently, an
organized police presence on college campuses was an unknown. Rather,
"night watchmen" (so-called because women did not occupy such roles)
would "patrol" campus in search of physical plant problems, violations of
student codes of conduct, etc. and address the problems discovered.

During the early 1970s, changes occurred when college and university
administrators realized that the campus unrest of the late 1960s and other
issues would likely result in the presence of armed, local police officers on
their campuses if they did not take action to deal with the problems confronting them. The action they took was to create a new department on the
campus, the campus police department.

Campus administrators typically put these early departments in the charge
of an experienced police officer with extensive experience in the realm of
municipal policing, who usually had occupied an upper rank in the department (e.g., precinct commander or deputy chief). Campus administrators
gave these individuals the responsibility of first designing, and then staffing
and overseeing an on-campus operation whose mission not only was to protect property and person, but to enforce the law. Made possible by state-level
enabling legislation, campus police departments with sworn officers soon
became common.

During the 1980s, these operations sought legitimacy from their municipal
police colleagues by largely "copying" existing organizational, tactical, and
operational components of city agencies. Campus agencies also sought legitimacy by requiring new recruits to complete POST (Peace Officer Standards

Training) training offered at the same academies attended by municipal police recruits.

Because the organizational "model" available to campus police agencies was municipal police departments, early campus agencies emphasized the same sort of activities as those emphasized by municipal departments. In particular, rapid response to calls for service, quick clearance of calls received so the responding officer could resume patrol, and random "preventive patrol" in automobiles designed to deter prospective offenders because they never knew when a patrol car would appear in their area, were "hallmarks" of this model. At the same time, campus departments never really abandoned their roots, and used foot patrol and involved officers in much more interaction with members of the campus community than was the case with their municipal counterparts. While agencies did not overly stress these tactics, agencies viewed them as a "normal" aspect of policing a college or university campus.

As the chapters by Bromley (2007), and Sloan and Lanier (2007) report, recent years have seen campus agencies slowly adopting a "new" model for campus policing. Called Community-Oriented Policing (COP), this new model fundamentally alters the organizational, administrative, tactical, and philosophical aspects of policing. Stressing community partnerships and problem solving, COP involves the police in a variety of activities designed to enhance police/community relations, empower officers, and prevent crime. In entering this new era that stresses partnerships with students, faculty, and staff members, the need for officers to "get out of their cars" and interact with people, engage in foot and bicycle patrol, and develop new programs such as "campus watch," campus police departments are now partnering with the campus community to identify and eliminate common crime and security problems.

In summary, campus police have evolved over the past 100 years from "watchmen" who were a part of the physical security department of the university, to a highly trained, problem-oriented, professional group of law enforcers whose focus is on preventing crime and building strong rapport with the campus community. An additional area creating interest for both law enforcement and security personnel has accompanied the explosion in information-based technology the past 20 years. We now discuss this increasingly important aspect of campus security.

Information Security and Infrastructure Protection

The past decade has seen an explosion of new information technology. Computers and other information storage and communication devices, perceived as the stuff of science fiction as recently as 25 years ago, are now commonplace on college campuses. Campus-based computer networks that link hundreds if not thousands of personal computers together are standard. Students "surf the net" to conduct research, while faculty use supercomputers which process millions of commands in seconds to explore new research problems in the disciplines of science, medicine, mathematics, and social science.

These fundamental changes in information technology have created enormous problems for colleges and universities. Because of computer-based networks, it is now possible for intruders ("hackers") to access the names and social security numbers of students and employees stored in large-scale databases. Students can "pirate" software from various sources on the Internet and can "stalk" fellow students or send them obscene or threatening email messages. Unscrupulous individuals send "junk" email ("spam") to students and employees that may contain hidden programs designed to "take control" of one's personal computer. Thus, both sides of the "new technology" are encapsulated on the college campus and campus administrators face tremendous challenges in the realm of information security.

Increasingly, colleges and universities must be both *reactive* and *proactive* in their information technology security efforts. They must quickly react to threats or actual attacks on information technology infrastructures while simultaneously developing strategies that allow them to keep "one step ahead" of those seeking to misuse the technology, including students, faculty members, and staff (as well as outsiders).

The stakes are enormous by any measure. Consider the following scenario: A hacker is able to penetrate the firewalls at State University and gains access to all of the student records stored in the registrar's database. This individual now has access to thousands of social security numbers and he or she can use them for a variety of illegal purposes. The implications of such an event are overwhelming; such an event also raises a host of institutional liability issues.

Additionally, there are "crossover" implications of the misuse of technology that directly involve campus law enforcement. For example, a student is using a university-issued computer to "capture" and store social security numbers of other students by hacking into university-based databases. Campus law enforcement is informed of this situation and must now respond, which means the department must have appropriate expertise in computer forensics to identify, retrieve, preserve, and present the evidence from the personal computer to press charges and ultimately obtain a conviction. Information security must address these scenarios. McQuade (2007) and others have described the challenges that campus information security face.

In summary, the security context of campus crime not only involves physical security and law enforcement, it also involves "cyber security." Not only must colleges and universities address traditional kinds of security issues, such as burglaries and thefts, but must now also address the abuse of information technology for monetary gain or other reasons. While campus law enforcement agencies wrestle with a "new model" of policing, information security professionals wrestle with new and increasingly more dangerous threats by "cyber criminals" to computer networks and electronic databases housed on university campuses. In both, law enforcement and cyber security, professionals must develop both reactive and proactive responses to the challenges they face. No longer is campus security solely a matter of insuring that doors to research laboratories and faculty offices are locked. Increasingly, campus security involves not only the protection of property and person, but the protection of information as well.

Campus Crime Policy:
Linking the Legal, Social, and Security Contexts

This chapter has explored the legal, social, and security contexts of campus crime. It presented a broad-based overview of where campus crime and security have been during the past 20 or so years and where both issues are going. Included in this overview were glimpses into each of the three contexts: the legal, including the judicial and legislative; the social, including social science research that has attempted to describe, explain, or evaluate campus crime and security; and the security, including campus law enforcement and the increasingly important area of information technology security.

As we observed earlier in the chapter, there are important linkages across the three contexts: the *Clery Act* mandates annual reporting of campus crime statistics, but social science research shows the common forms of student victimization, theft, stalking, and simple assault, are not included in the reporting requirements. Social science research into the victimization of college students leads to the development of new institutional protocols for providing law enforcement and related services to victims, especially victims of sexual assault. Enabling legislation at the state level of government allows colleges and universities to create campus police agencies, staffed by sworn officers with wide-ranging arrest powers.

Throughout this and the remaining chapters comprising this volume, there is an implicit acknowledgement of the fact there is a circular relationship between the legal, social, and security contexts of campus crime and campus crime policy: each context influences policy and policy influences each context. This is true whether the policy context is national, state, or that found on a single campus. Federal or state legislation requires colleges and universities to develop policies to address crime victimization; successful lawsuits filed by students or their parents result in new policies concerning security on the campus; threats to the campus information technology infrastructure lead to new policies concerning student, staff, or faculty member access to key databases.

Policy, in short, is the overarching concept that not only links the individual contexts—legal, social, security—of campus crime examined in this volume, but which also serves as an instrument of change. Without policy changes, the contributions made by researchers, administrators, law enforcement and security personnel, and others concerned about campus crime would count little toward making campuses safer. Thankfully, that has not been the case, and the policy aspects of campus crime and security continue to remain "front and center."

Notes

1. For a comprehensive overview of case law of when a college or university has been held liable for crime occurring on its campus, see Burling, 2003.
2. According to Security On Campus, Inc., *The Campus Sexual Assault Victims' Bill of Rights* exists as a part of the campus security reporting requirements of the federal law that establishes all student aid programs, the *Higher Education Act of 1965*. It has not been amended since its enactment, except for a citation change to accommodate 1998 amendments to other requirements found in the campus security section.

REFERENCES

Belknap, J., & Erez, E. (2007). The acquaintance and date rape, sexual harassment, and intimate partner abuse of college women. In B. S. Fisher & J. J. Sloan (Eds.), *Campus crime: Legal, social, and policy perspectives* (2nd ed.). Springfield, IL: Charles C Thomas.

Bromley, M. (2007). The evolution of campus policing: Different models for different eras. In B. S. Fisher & J. J. Sloan (Eds.), *Campus crime: Legal, social and policy perspectives* (2nd ed.). Springfield, IL: Charles C Thomas.

Burling, P. (2003). *Crime on campus: Analyzing and managing the increasing risk of institutional liability* (2nd ed.). Washington D.C.: National Association of College and University Attorneys.

Carter, S., & Bath, C. (2007). The evolution and components of the Jeanne Clery Act: Implications for higher education. In B. S. Fisher & J. J. Sloan (Eds.), *Campus crime: Legal, social and policy perspectives* (2nd ed.). Springfield, IL: Charles C Thomas.

Complying with the Jeanne Clery Act (2006). Security On Campus, Inc. Retrieved February 13, 2007, from http://www.securityoncampus.org/schools/cleryact/index.html.

Dowdall, G. (2007). The role of alcohol abuse in college student victimization. In B. S. Fisher & J. J. Sloan (Eds.), *Campus crime: Legal, social and policy perspectives* (2nd ed.). Springfield, IL: Charles C Thomas.

Fisher, B., Hartman, J., Cullen, F., & Turner, M. (2002). Making campuses safer for students: The Clery Act as a Symbolic Legal Reform. *Stetson Law Review, XXXII*(1), 61–89.

Fisher, B., Karjane, H., Cullen, F., Blevins, K., Santana, S., & Daigle, L. (2007). Reporting sexual assault and the Clery Act: Situating findings from the National Campus Sexual Assault Policy Study within college women's experiences. In B. S. Fisher & J. J. Sloan (Eds.), *Campus crime: Legal, social and policy perspectives* (2nd ed.). Springfield, IL: Charles C Thomas.

Fisher, B., Cullen, F., & Turner, M. (2000). *Sexual victimization of college women.* Washington, D.C.: Department of Justice Statistics, National Institute of Justice, Bureau of Justice Statistics.

Karjane, H., Fisher, B., & Cullen, F. (2001). *Campus sexual assault: How America's institutions of higher education respond.* Final Report. Washington, D. C.: National Institute of Justice, United States Department of Justice.

Fisher, B., Sloan, J., Cullen, F., & Lu, C. (1998). Crime in the ivory tower: The level and sources of student victimization. *Criminology, 36,* 671–710.

Fisher, B., & Stewart, M. (2007). Vulnerabilities and opportunities 101: The extent, nature, and impact of stalking among college students and implications for campus policy and programs. In B. S. Fisher & J. J. Sloan (Eds.), *Campus crime: Legal, social and policy perspectives* (2nd ed.). Springfield, IL: Charles C Thomas.

Gregory, D., & Janosik, S. (2007). The research on the Clery Act and the impact of the Act on higher education administrative practice. In B. S. Fisher & J. J. Sloan (Eds.), *Campus crime: Legal, social and policy perspectives* (2nd ed.). Springfield, IL: Charles C Thomas.

Hart, T. (2003). *National Crime Victimization Survey, 1992–2000: Violent victimization of college students.* Washington D.C.: Bureau of Justice Statistics. Retrieved September 12, 2006, from http://www.ojp.usdoj.gov/bjs/pub/pdf/vvcs00.pdf.

Hart, T. (2007). The violent victimization of college students: Findings from the National Crime Victimization Survey. In B. S. Fisher & J. J. Sloan (Eds.), *Campus crime: Legal, social and policy perspectives* (2nd ed.). Springfield, IL: Charles C Thomas.

How to File a Jeanne Clery Act Complaint. (2006) Security On Campus, Inc. Retrieved February 13, 2007, from http://www.securityoncampus.org/students/clerycomplaint.html.

Kanin, E. (1967). An examination of sexual aggression as a response to sexual frustration. *Journal of Marriage and the Family, 29,* 428–433.

Kanin, E. (1970). Sex aggression by college men. *Medical Aspects of Human Sexuality, 4,* 25–40.

Kanin, E. (1977). Sexual aggression: A second look at the offended female. *Archives of Sexual Behavior, 6,* 67–76.

Karjane, H., Fisher, B., & Cullen, F. (2002). *Campus sexual assault: How America's institutions of higher education respond.* Final Report, NIJ Grant No. 99–WA–VX–0008. Retrieved February 13, 2007, from http://www.ncjrs.org/pdffiles1/nij/grants/196676.pdf.

Karjane, H., Fisher, B., & Cullen, F. (2005). *Sexual assault on campus: What colleges and universities are doing about it.* United States Department of Justice, NIJ Research for Practice Series. Retrieved February 13, 2007, from http://www.ncjrs.gov/pdf files1/nij/ 205521.pdf.

Kirkpatrick, C., & Kanin, E. (1957). Male sex aggression on a university campus. *American Sociological Review, 22,* 52–58.

Koss, M., Gidycz, C., & Wisniewski, N. (1987). The scope of rape: Incidence and prevalence of sexual aggression and victimization in a national sample of higher education students. *Journal of Consulting and Clinical Psychology, 55,* 162–170.

McQuade III, S. (2007). High tech abuse and crime on college and university campuses: Evolving forms of victimization, offending, and their interplay in higher education. In B. S. Fisher & J. J. Sloan (Eds.), *Campus crime: Legal, social and policy perspectives* (2nd ed.). Springfield, IL: Charles C Thomas.

Mustaine, E., & Tewksbury, R. (2007). The routine activities and criminal victimization of students. In B. S. Fisher & J. J. Sloan (Eds.), *Campus crime: Legal, social and policy perspectives* (2nd ed.). Springfield, IL: Charles C Thomas.

Robinson, M., & Roh, S. (2007). Crime on campus: spatial aspects of campus crime at a regional comprehensive university. In B. S. Fisher & J. J. Sloan (Eds.), *Campus crime: Legal, social and policy perspectives* (2nd ed.). Springfield, IL: Charles C Thomas.

Shafer, L. (2007). Women, gender, and safety on campus: Reporting is not enough. In B. S. Fisher & J. J. Sloan (Eds.), *Campus crime: Legal, social, and policy perspectives* (2nd ed.). Springfield, IL: Charles C Thomas.

Sloan, J., Fisher, B., & Cullen, F. (1997). Assessing the Student Right-to-Know and Campus Security Act of 1990: An analysis of the victim reporting practices of college and university students. *Crime and Delinquency, 43,* 148–168.

Sloan III, J., & Lanier, M. (2007). Community policing on university campuses: Tradition, practices, and outlook. In B. S. Fisher & J. J. Sloan (Eds.), *Campus crime: Legal, social and policy perspectives* (2nd ed.). Springfield, IL: Charles C Thomas.

Sloan III, J., & Shoemaker, J. (2007). State level Clery Act initiatives: Symbolic politics or substantive policies? In B. S. Fisher & J. J. Sloan (Eds.), *Campus crime: Legal, social and policy perspectives* (2nd ed.). Springfield, IL: Charles C Thomas.

Smith, M. (1995). Vexatious victims of campus crime. In B. S. Fisher & J. J. Sloan (Eds.), *Campus crime: Legal, social and policy perspectives.* Springfield, IL: Charles C Thomas.

United States Department of Education, Office of Postsecondary Education (2005). *The Handbook for Campus Crime Reporting.* Washington, D.C.: United States Department of Education.

Part I:

THE LEGAL CONTEXT
OF CAMPUS CRIME

Part I

THE LEGAL CONTEXT OF CAMPUS CRIME

INTRODUCTION

O ver 15 years have passed since Congress enacted the *Student-Right-to-Know and Campus Security Act of 1990* (20 U.S.C. 1092[f]) in response to concerns expressed by students, their parents, campus crime victims, and well-meaning advocates about perceived increases in campus crime and lax security. Requiring postsecondary institutions to "come clean" and report their campus crime statistics and security policies, supporters of the legislation believed this information would prove useful to both current and prospective members of the campus community, especially students and their parents. Given the frequency by which the statute has since been amended (most recently in 2000), Congressional interest in campus crime and safety has apparently not waned.

The combined activism of advocacy groups, such as Security on Campus, Inc., and student victims and their families has been the momentum behind Congressional action, including substantial amendments that have expanded the reporting requirements for postsecondary institutions. The most visible change, however, was to the name of the statute. Now known as the *Jeanne Clery Disclosure of Campus Security Policy and Campus Crime Statistics Act* (or the *Clery Act*), the change remembers freshman Jeanne Ann Clery who was raped and murdered by a fellow student while asleep in her Lehigh University dorm room on April 5, 1986. In keeping with Congressional concern about campus crime and safety, several state legislatures followed suit and passed their own *Clery*-like statutes.

In Part I, we present five chapters that address the *legal context* of campus crime by focusing on the *Clery Act*. Chapter 2, "The Evolution and Components of the *Jeanne Clery Act:* Implications for Higher Education," by Daniel Carter and Catherine Bath, documents the genesis and evolution of the *Clery Act* from its inception by providing a firsthand account from those who were involved from the beginning. Given the importance of the *Clery Act's* mandates for postsecondary institutions, the authors present thorough outlines of the *Clery Act* requirements and amendments to it, and companion legislation including the *Campus Sexual Assault Victims' Bill of Rights* and the *Campus Sex Crimes Prevention Act.*

A reasonable amount of time has passed since the initial passage of federal campus crime legislation. During this period, academicians have questioned, observed, and measured the implementation of the *Clery Act* and its effects on campus safety. Researchers from a variety of disciplines–sociology, political science, education, criminology, and women's studies–with different perspectives have critically questioned whether the *Clery Act* has had any substantial or measurable effects on campus crime and security. Three chapters in this section critically question the mandates of the *Clery Act* and offer data that suggest inherent weaknesses in the statute likely compromise the *Clery Act's* ability to address, in any substantive manner, the extent of campus crime and create effective security efforts.

Chapter 3, "Research on the *Clery Act* and Its Impact on Higher Education Administrative Practice," by Dennis Gregory and Steven Janosik, presents results from an analysis of legal, popular press, and several scholarly bibliographic sources containing what has been published about the impact of the *Clery Act.* Given their interests in higher education administration, the authors present results from their own studies of the perceptions of various campus personnel concerning the effectiveness of the *Clery Act.* They conclude that it has not had the overall impact its sponsors had hoped. Some good news, however, is their conclusion that the *Clery Act* has had some marginal effects on postsecondary student affairs practice and personnel. While Gregory and Janosik's overall results may disappoint *Clery Act* proponents, they also identify where changes are needed.

In Chapter 4, "Reporting Sexual Assault and the *Clery Act:* Situating Findings from the National Campus Sexual Assault Policy Study Within College's Women's Experiences," Bonnie Fisher, Heather Karjane, Francis Cullen, Kristie Blevins, Shannon Santana, and Leah Daigle critically question the validity of reported campus crime statistics, in particular those relating to sexual victimization occurring on campus. Using results from past victimization research of college women and their *National Campus Sexual Assault Policy Study,* they discuss on-campus barriers to victim reporting and explain how these barriers contribute to institutional underreporting of sexual victimizations. They also offer policy and response recommendations that campus administrators and campus safety advocates should consider implementing.

Linda Shafer, a political scientist and activist, wrote Chapter 5 entitled, "Women, Gender, and Safety on Campus: Reporting Is Not Enough." Shafer, like other authors in this section, takes a critical view of the *Clery Act.*

Her perspective, however, is unique from the other critics on two dimensions. First, she discusses what the *Clery Act's* requirement and its supporters have failed to take into account in assessing its impact and questions why legislators and campus administrators are unwilling to challenge the *Clery Act.* Second, she argues that a large body of scholarly research examining men's sexual violence and predatory behaviors against women on campus has been woefully ignored in postsecondary institutions' quest to "do something" about crime.

We conclude this first section on the book with John Sloan and Jessica Shoemaker's chapter, "State-level *Clery Act* Initiatives: Symbolic Politics or Substantive Policy?" which analyzes the content of state-level campus crime and security legislation and compares state-level requirements to those found in key *Clery* provisions. Their analyses lead Sloan and Shoemaker to conclude that state-level *Clery* initiatives offer little substantive impact and, as a result, constitute symbolic public policy in legislative efforts to address campus safety and security.

In summary, Part I of the book presents the legal context of campus crime by describing the evolution and requirements of the *Clery Act* and comparable state-level initiatives. The section provides insights into the evolution of the *Clery Act* and describes its mandates. The contributors also identify and critically discuss how weaknesses and limitations inherent in the *Clery Act* and state-level *Clery*-like statutes undermine their potential effectiveness at making campuses safer. Together, the chapters in Part I show how campus safety likely remains compromised even with the passage of well-intended campus crime legislation.

Chapter 2

THE EVOLUTION AND COMPONENTS OF THE *JEANNE CLERY ACT:* IMPLICATIONS FOR HIGHER EDUCATION

S. Daniel Carter and Catherine Bath

INTRODUCTION

How colleges and universities confront campus crime changed forever with the brutal rape and murder of Lehigh University freshman Jeanne Ann Clery in the early morning hours of April 5, 1986. Ms. Clery, asleep in her dorm room, was unaware of fellow Lehigh student, Josoph Henry (whom Ms. Clery did not know) as he crept into her room through a series of propped open and unlocked doors with the intention committing a burglary. When Ms. Clery awoke, Mr. Henry brutally raped and tortured her before strangling her to death in her own bed. During pursuant litigation, evidence accumulated showing that Lehigh University knew about propped open doors and other security lapses in campus dorms, yet failed to warn students about the potential dangers the lapses posed. The tragic death of their daughter proved the impetus for Howard and Connie Clery to create Security On Campus, Inc. (SOC) and begin a tireless effort to insure that lapses in sharing important security information, such as what occurred at Lehigh, never happened again on any college or university campus in the U.S.

In the early days of SOC, Senator Edward Kennedy's (D-MA) speech supporting SOC-backed legislation deeply impressed Connie Clery. Mrs. Clery says, "his use of the expression, 'sunshine is the best disinfectant,'" nicely summarized the whole intent of SOC's crusade, from beginning to end. Further, according to Mrs. Clery, "There is no way that campuses and their students can be safe unless institutions tell the truth about campus crime" (personal communication with Connie Clery, September 7, 2006).

Crime on college and university campuses has been an acknowledged reality for some time. As recently as 2001, Terry Hartle, Sr. Vice President of the American Council on Education, conceded:

> [College] campuses are far different places with respect to safety than they were 10 years ago. No college deals with crime the way they did before. All colleges have made security improvements in the last decade, often very significant and expensive ones. No college presidents thought much about this issue a decade ago, but they all do so now . . . Much of this change is solely attributable to the Clerys and their tireless efforts. (personal communication with Terry Hartle, August 3, 2001)

During the late 1980s, campus crime was "one of the best kept secrets in the country" (H. Clery, U.S. House of Representatives, March 14, 1990). The Clerys and the SOC staff had the distinct impression that campus officials were more concerned about protecting the image of their institutions, than they were with informing students of criminal incidents occurring there. Additionally, as recently as 15 years ago, out of some 8,000 postsecondary institutions participating in federal student aid programs in this country, only 352 of them voluntarily provided campus crime statistics to the government through the FBI's *Uniform Crime Reporting Program* (Public Law S. 580, 101st Cong., 136 Cong. Rec. H9947) (1990) (enacted). Thus, few schools bothered to report their crime statistics and even fewer advertised that fact. Further, few schools publicly reported their security policies, including whether the school had a campus police department and the extent of such an organization's power and jurisdiction. As a result, assessing the level of crime on, and specific security policies of, any particular college campus became extremely difficult for prospective students and their parents. The Clerys and SOC set out to change that reality.

In this chapter, we examine the evolution of the *Jeanne Clery Disclosure of Campus Security Policy and Campus Crime Statistics Act* (20 U.S.C. 1092[f]) (henceforth, the *Clery Act*) and its impact on campus crime policy through the eyes of Connie and Howard Clery. We begin by discussing why the *Clery Act* was necessary. We then review various stipulations of the *Clery Act* requiring postsecondary institutions to annually report their campus crime statistics to the U.S. Department of Education (ED) and make that information and their security policies available to current and prospective students and their parents, as well as current and prospective faculty members and staff. We also discuss related legislation designed to insure: (1) the protection of on-campus sexual assault victims' rights; (2) that federal student record privacy laws do not protect outcomes of campus disciplinary proceedings involving violent crimes under certain circumstances; and (3) that registered sex offenders notify colleges and universities of their presence on campus as students, workers, or volunteers. We conclude the chapter by describing the ongoing efforts of SOC to insure that students are safe while on campus.

The Need for the *Clery Act*

To say that the senseless murder of their daughter devastated Howard and Connie Clery fails to capture the depth of their grief. Both Security On Campus, Inc. and the *Clery Act* arose from the despair they felt over their daughter's death.

During Josoph Henry's criminal proceedings, the Clery family learned about not only his history of violence and substance abuse, but also a pattern of violent crimes at Lehigh about which students had not been informed. Ironically, Jeanne Clery had planned to follow her brothers' example and attend Tulane University, until her parents learned of the murder of a female student there. As a result, Jeanne's parents decided instead to send Jeanne to Lehigh University in Bethlehem, Pennsylvania because the campus seemed safe.

In 1987, Howard and Connie Clery announced the formation of Security On Campus, Inc. as a nonprofit organization, funded in part by settlement money from a civil suit the Clerys had brought against Lehigh. SOC was devoted to educating students and their parents about the dangers of campus crime, while their mission was to protect other families from experiencing the tragic loss of a child to campus crime. The Clerys made numerous appearances in the national media to raise awareness about campus safety issues and were intent on informing the public that postsecondary institutions were hiding their crime information. This led the Clery family, with the help of other families who had experienced campus violence, to push for state legislation requiring colleges to publish their crime statistics and security policies. The Clerys began working for the legislation in their home state of Pennsylvania and quickly worked their way to other states across the country, including California, Tennessee, and Florida. By 1990, campus crime reporting laws were either in effect or were being considered by nearly half of the states. The Clerys and the volunteers they mobilized traveled extensively throughout the U.S. to make this happen. During this period, Connie realized, "I knew I wouldn't live long enough to get legislation passed in every state. So I decided to start working for a federal law" (personal communication with Connie Clery, September 7, 2006).

The *Jeanne Clery Act*

The *Crime Awareness and Campus Security Act of 1990* (Title II of Public Law 101–542) was signed into law by President George H.W. Bush on November

8, 1990. For the first time, students and their parents had easy access to campus crime information when deciding where to go to school and, most importantly, a guide to use when deciding what safety precautions to take once enrolled.

All institutions, both public and private, eligible to participate in any federal student aid program under Title IV of the *Higher Education Act of 1965,* are subject to these reporting requirements stipulated in the *Clery Act.* The U.S. Department of Education (ED) has been enforcing the *Clery Act* since its inception.

In May of 2006, Congressional leaders questioned the ED's competence in enforcing the *Clery Act.* "I question whether the Department of Education is committed to enforcement and whether the department is capable of enforcement," Senator Arlen Specter (R-PA) told a Senate Judiciary Committee hearing gathered at the National Constitution Center in Philadelphia. "Many colleges and universities have failed to comply with the Act, but few were fined," Specter noted. "This seems to be a persistent problem" (McCaffrey, 2006).

Congress has amended the *Campus Security Act* several times, most notably in 1998, when it expanded the Act's reporting requirements and renamed the law, in memory of the student who inspired it, as the *Jeanne Clery Disclosure of Campus Security Policy and Campus Crime Statistics Act.* Throughout, highly paid lobbyists of postsecondary institutions and the American Council on Education fought the Clery family's efforts every inch of the way, trying to prevent these bills from becoming law (personal communication with Connie Clery, September 7, 2006).

Key Requirements of the Clery Act

In its current form, the *Clery Act* contains three key requirements, including:

- Disclosure of an annual security report with crime statistics and security policy;
- Disclosure of timely information through a public crime log and warnings issued about ongoing threats;
- Insuring the protection of certain basic rights for both the accuser and the accused in sexual assault cases dealt with on campus.

ANNUAL SECURITY REPORT. By October first of each year, each institution must publish an annual "campus security report" that contains crime statistics for the three most recent calendar years, certain security policy statements including sexual assault policies which assure basic victims' rights and details about the law enforcement authority of campus security officers, and where students should go to report crimes. The institution must make this report available automatically to all current students and employees, and notify prospective students and employees of its existence and afford them an opportunity to receive a copy. Under regulations published by ED in 1999 (section 668.41), schools can comply with the annual report obligation using an Internet website so long as the required recipients are notified and provided the exact URL address where the report can be found and afforded the opportunity to request a paper copy if they desire.

Each institution's crime statistics are to be reported in the following seven major categories, with several sub-categories: (1) homicide broken down by murder and non-negligent manslaughter and negligent manslaughter; (2) sex offenses broken down by forcible (including rape) and nonforcible offenses; (3) robbery; (4) aggravated assault; (5) burglary; (6) motor vehicle theft; and (7) arson. Schools are also required to report the following three types of incidents if they resulted in either an arrest or a disciplinary referral: liquor law violations, drug law violations, and illegal weapons possession. If both an arrest and a referral occur, the institution counts only the arrest.

To insure uniformity from state-to-state and between individual schools, each institution must use guidelines and definitions found in the Federal Bureau of Investigation's Uniform Crime Reporting Program (*Uniform Crime Reporting Handbook,* pp 7–74). In 2005, at the request of SOC and with the help of Senator Specter, ED issued *The Handbook for Campus Crime Reporting* and made copies available to every college and university in the country. This comprehensive, "plain language" guide to the *Clery Act* resolved some of the complications and varying interpretations that had been serving as excuses used by noncompliant institutions during ED investigations of *Clery Act* complaints.

The statistics are broken down geographically into "on campus," "residential facilities for students on campus," "noncampus buildings," or "on public property," such as streets and sidewalks immediately adjacent to or running through the campus. Schools can, but do not have to, use a map to denote these areas.

Prior to the 1998 Amendments, one of the major problems with the annual crime statistics had been the exclusion of crimes occurring on public streets and sidewalks running between campus buildings or immediately around the periphery of campus. This had been an issue especially for schools in urban settings. The original intent of Congress had been to exclude major highways and other areas unrelated to the campus, but the law had been interpreted by many schools and ED to exclude areas most people considered part of the campus—areas adjacent to the campus where there is frequent student pedestrian activity.

The law now mandates that crime statistics published by schools in their annual report must include crimes occurring on public property areas, specifically streets, sidewalks, and parking garages—inside the campus and immediately adjacent to it. As was the intent when Congress first enacted the law, the requirement excludes major thoroughfares like interstate highways. Properties owned by the institution but operated by a third party, such as a food vendor, must be included as well. In the past, some schools had excluded this type of property.

The security report must also indicate if any of the reported incidents or any other crime involving bodily injury to the victim was a "hate crime." The institution must then break these incidents down by the following categories of motivation, including race, gender, religion, sexual orientation, ethnicity, or physical disability.

Schools must gather these crime statistics from campus police or security, local law enforcement, and other school officials who have "significant responsibility for student and campus activities" such as student judicial affairs directors. Although nonlaw enforcement school officials with "significant responsibility for student and campus activities" have been required to report statistics and make timely warnings since the regulations implementing the original law took effect in 1994, the current rules strongly reinforce this requirement (in the past, some schools ignored this requirement and reported only police statistics). The regulations specify that "campus activities" include, but are not be limited to, "student housing . . . and campus judicial proceedings."

Additional guidance offered indicates that "a dean of students . . . a director of athletics, team coach, and faculty advisor to a student group" would be required to report crimes, but due to numerous titles currently in use across the country, the rules do specify exact job titles. ED rules stipulate that current "definitions and guidance reflect the reality that on college campuses, officials who are not police officials or acting as event security at student or campus events, nevertheless are responsible for students' or campus security" (Student Assistance General Provisions; Final Rule, 64 Federal Register 59063, November 1, 1999). This means schools cannot merely report their campus police or security office's crime statistics without making an effort to collect them from other offices on campus that may have dealt with a crime, such as student affairs. Schools must also make and then document a "good faith" effort to obtain statistics from local law enforcement agencies.

The rules exempt professional mental health and religious counselors from all reporting obligations when functioning in those capacities, but they may refer clients to a confidential reporting system (which the school must indicate whether it has). The exemption of these professionals occurred because of a 1998 change in the law that specifically prohibits the re-disclosure of any "privileged information." Apparently, some counselors had argued that campus officials were requiring them to disclose detailed information to tabulate their statistics, but if victims knew counselors could reveal this information, they would be reluctant to seek counseling.

Once it has compiled all this statistical information, the institution must provide a copy of the statistics to ED. ED will then include the information in an electronic database that it will make available to the public on an ED website (see http://ope.ed.gov/security). Members of the public can then search this database and review the statistical information for schools of interest.

CAMPUS CRIME LOGS. In addition to the crime statistics, one of the most significant requirements of the *Clery Act* is that public and private institutions with a campus police or security department maintain "public crime logs." Schools are required to disclose in this log, any crime that occurred on campus or within the patrol jurisdiction of the campus police or security department and reported to them. Schools that already maintain a police log under state law may use that log to comply with this requirement as long as all of the minimum requirements of *Clery* are met, and they may use state crime definitions in their log. Because the crime log provisions took effect in October 1998–before the ED had issued regulations–ED expected schools to make a "good faith" effort to comply with the public crime log requirement before it issued regulations that required schools to make public their crime logs.

The log is required to include the "nature, date, time and general location of each crime," as well as its disposition, if known. Incidents are to be included within two business days, but police or security departments may withhold certain limited information to protect victim confidentiality, ensure the integrity of ongoing investigations, or keep a suspect from fleeing.

Departments may withhold only the most limited information necessary but must release the information "once the adverse effect . . . is no longer likely to occur." The requirements do not mandate the release of names, but a school may include them at its discretion or under the stipulations a state-level law concerning crime logs.

The log must be available to the public during normal business hours. This means that, in addition to students and employees, the public, such as parents or members of the local press, may access it. Logs remain open for 60 days; after 60 days, logs must be available within two business days of a request. In 2005, as a part of *The Handbook for Campus Crime Reporting,* ED issued rules stating institutions must keep all archived crime log entries on file for at least seven years.

Because many students rely on the news media, especially campus media, for their crime information, media access to and reporting of this log is a critical public safety measure. The Clerys felt it dangerous for students to rely on rumors about crime and insisted that the open log provisions be included in the 1998 amendments; they felt only the truth about campus crime could enable campus security forces to address problem areas and allow students to take effective precautions. To illustrate this point, as late as 2006, the Clery family was very concerned about private schools belonging to the Association of Independent Colleges and Universities of Massachusetts (AICUM) refusing to disclose complete crime report information, like public colleges with police departments do. As a result, the Clerys felt the schools were unnecessarily endangering the safety of the Massachusetts' college students by depriving them of important knowledge about what crimes were occurring and where they were taking place on their campuses (personal communication with Connie Clery, September 7, 2006).

TIMELY WARNINGS. Schools also have an obligation to issue "timely warnings" to the campus community if they believe a reported crime poses an "ongoing threat" to students and employees. Unlike the crime log requirement, this reporting is not limited to a police or security department and should occur in less than two business days. These warnings, however, are restricted to the list of crimes that schools must report in their annual statistics, and the criteria used by a school for determining what poses a threat can be subjective. Institutions may use e-mail, flyers posted around campus, or other means to comply with the "timely warning" requirement. Schools do need to embrace the intent of the *Act* though, and if a potential threat exists, they should issue a timely warning.

An NBC 17 report from March 24, 2004 illustrates why "timely warnings" are so important:

> Duke University students rallied Wednesday and screamed for closer attention to the problem of rape on the school's campus. Student Allesandra Coloianni organized the 'Scream-In Protest,' which included several minutes of collective screaming by the participants following two sexual assault incidents over the past weekend. One student was raped in a wooded area Friday night near Duke Chapel. Another female student was assaulted in her west campus apartment Sunday. Coloianni said the screams were meant to represent women who have been silenced. 'People really stepped up, which is an indicator of how big an issue this is on campus,' Coloianni told NBC 17. Many students are upset with Duke's administration, saying they weren't told of the two sexual assaults until late Monday or Tuesday via e-mail. 'It's something that really affects all of us every day, and we really feel like we should be informed every minute when (such incidents) occur,' Illana Jacobs said (http://www.nbc17.com/educa-tion//2947237/detail.html).

Thus, the *Clery Act,* by requiring postsecondary institutions to provide detailed crime statistics; information on the power, authority, and jurisdiction of campus security agencies; daily crime logs; and timely warnings of offenses of high concern to the campus community, seeks to make not only students, but faculty members and staff safer. Through the information provided, both current and prospective members of the campus community can make informed decisions about the relative dangers they face and, importantly, take action to reduce their chances of becoming crime victims.

As discussed in the following sections, the *Clery Act* and related laws seek additional protection of members of the campus community by insuring that postsecondary institutions protect sexual assault victims' rights, that results of campus disciplinary proceedings are available and communicated to interested parties, and that convicted sex offenders cannot prey upon unsuspecting members of the campus community.

Campus Sexual Assault Victims' Bill of Rights

The *Clery Act* also requires postsecondary institutions to develop and make available policy statements dealing with on-campus sexual assault. Congress enacted the *Campus Sexual Assault Victims' Bill of Rights* in 1992 as a part of the *Higher Education Amendments of 1992* (Public Law: 102–325, section 486[c]) which President Bush signed into law in July of 1992. This law, which is now part of the *Clery Act*, requires that all colleges and universities, both public and private, participating in federal student aid programs afford sexual assault victims certain basic rights:

- The accuser and accused must have the same opportunity to have others present at campus disciplinary hearings;
- The institution shall inform both parties of the outcome of any disciplinary proceeding;
- The institution shall inform survivors of their options to notify law enforcement and assist them in doing so, if requested;
- The institution shall also notify survivors of available counseling services;
- The institution shall notify survivors of options for changing academic and living situations.

The late Frank Carrington, then Chief Counsel to SOC, developed this legislation to combat the revictimization of on-campus rape survivors at colleges across the country. The impetus for this legislation was Carrington finding that schools were more concerned with protecting their images than with seeing justice done.

In 1991, Frank was on an airplane reading his rough draft of the *Sexual Assault Victim's Bill of Rights.* Congressman Jim Ramstad (R-MN) was sitting next to him and asked what he was reading, which started a conversation between the two men about campus victims of sexual assault, which greatly interested Congressman Ramstad. He then asked if he could read Frank's draft of the law. The intent of the law so impressed Congressman Ramstad that he wanted to help get it passed. He and Congresswoman Susan Molinari (R-NY) worked passionately along with the Clerys and their staff at SOC to obtain passage of this important law in 1992. Frank Carrington tragically died in a fire at his home on New Year's Day in 1992 and did not live to see the legislation passed (personal communication with Connie Clery, September 7, 2006).

Many acquaintance rape victims contacting SOC complain that not only were they victimized by the rapist, but also by their school's response to the incident. Sexual assault survivor and former Ohio State University (OSU) student Stacy Bogart sued the university in 2004 for the way university officials handled her 2002 rape complaint. As she tells it:

> I was victimized once by the rapist and again by the university's inaction. Throughout all this, I realized that it takes a lot of pain to make change. I believe it is my obligation to stand up against the injustice and fight for the victims that OSU administrators have ignored, neglected, or silenced (personal communication with Stacy Bogart, December 2005).

In an NBC News *Dateline* segment that aired on December 11, 2005, Stacy said about her ordeal, "I know that this nightmare will follow me for the rest of my life." Stacy described her harrowing ordeal for the broadcast as follows:

One of the men Stacy "hung around" with her first year was Jeremy Goldstein, a wrestling star from her high school in Cleveland. Stacy acknowledges she had consensual sex with Jeremy once in October of that year. However, she says, what happened the night of February 22, 2002 was completely different. That night, Stacy came back from an off-campus bar–a little buzzed, she says, but not drunk–and met Jeremy for a smoke outside his dorm. Stacy says he had forgotten his cigarettes upstairs, so she agreed to go to his room to get them. She also says she told him she "wasn't interested in anything physical." She said, "We are not hooking up, right? You know that right?" Goldstein said, "Of course. My roommate's up there." His roommate, however, was "passed out cold." Jeremy started to kiss Stacy and initially she let him, but she says the former wrestler soon turned violent, pulling down her pants, penetrating her with his hand, and biting her neck, all while he had her pinned down. Stacy says she yelled so loud his roommate stirred and Jeremy got off her. She says she walked back to her dorm, feeling numb.

The next day, she went to a university official and reported she had been raped. In June of 2002, four months after she says she was raped, she decided to go to police and file a criminal complaint. As the criminal investigation of Jeremy Goldstein began, Stacy says she wanted the university to take action against him too–to have him expelled.

Beginning the fall of her sophomore year, she says, she had several conversations with the official in charge of campus disciplinary hearings, but she says "those talks went nowhere. " She asked for a school hearing but the head of judicial affairs at OSU told her, "If I were you it would be in your best interest to wait until the criminal proceedings were over." But justice was moving slowly through the courts and at Ohio State, no further action was taken on Stacy's case the remainder of her sophomore year.

At the end of her sophomore year, a Columbus grand jury indicted Mr. Goldstein on the charge of rape. Stacy says she returned to school the following fall, a full year-and-a-half after the alleged assault, determined to push for Mr. Goldstein's expulsion. She says that is when a rape counselor mentioned something university officials had never told her.

Just three weeks before Stacy says Mr. Goldstein assaulted her, another student had filed a complaint against Jeremy Goldstein. Her name was Jamie and during her first year at Ohio State, she lived in Baker hall, where Jeremy Goldstein also lived. Jamie says she and Jeremy had never even kissed, but she says as she was getting ready one evening to go to a party with him, Jeremy suddenly attacked her. The next day, Jamie reported the incident to her resident advisor. She also filed a police report, but decided not to press charges. Dorm officials met with Jeremy and Jamie and determined that Jeremy was responsible for sexual misconduct. The officials put Jeremy on disciplinary probation and moved him to another co-ed dorm next door. That location is where Stacy says Jeremy assaulted her, just three weeks later.

Soon, there was another complaint by three women a few weeks after Stacy says the rape occurred. Ohio State officials then removed Jeremy from university housing on an alcohol violation. He moved into an off-campus apartment building and was still free to go to classes, parties, and into OSU dorms.

According to Stacy, that is how things stayed for the next year and a half until her junior year. She says the whole time she lived in fear of her classmate Jeremy Goldstein while campus officials point out that in the end, they did take decisive action against Jeremy Goldstein. On September 23, 2003, some 18 months after Stacy and Jamie reported Jeremy Goldstein had sexually assaulted them and with a criminal rape charge pending against him, the university held a one-day hearing in the Judicial Affairs Office. That same week, Ohio State expelled Jeremy, nearly 18 months after Stacy and Jamie filed sexual assault reports against him. Stacy Bogart told *Dateline NBC* she feels that Ohio State could have prevented her rape by taking stronger action against Jeremy after it became aware of the first sexual assault allegation against him.

In late 2004, Jeremy Goldstein pleaded guilty in Stacy's case to "sexual imposition," a misdemeanor described in the state code as having sex when "the offender knows that the sexual contact is offensive to the other person" or when "the other person is so impaired she can't appraise the situation." Following state sentencing guidelines, the judge sentenced Jeremy to two years probation and ordered him to undergo an evaluation for sexual aggression.

That is not the end of the Jeremy Goldstein case. In fact, the story ends where it began, on a co-ed college campus. In 2004, Jeremy applied to, and was accepted by, Bernard Baruch College in New York City. Officials at Ohio State told *Dateline* the transcripts they had sent to Jeremy's new school included no information about his expulsion or about the reports filed against him by female students. Campus officials reported that OSU's policy is not to release disciplinary records unless the new school specifically asks for them. Stacy says, "[It] scares me because in my mind it's a whole new batch of women that don't know him or his history." Stacy's lawsuit against Ohio State was still pending in late 2005 at the time of the Dateline broadcast (*Dateline NBC,* November 11, 2005).

Family Educational Rights and Privacy Act (FERPA)

For years, colleges and universities have used their own system of "campus courts," known as student disciplinary proceedings, to address student violations of school codes of conduct involving such behavior as plagiarism, copyright infringement, or underage drinking. They also handle on-campus violent student misconduct like sexual assault and hazing.

Schools often claim these hearings provide the institution, victims, and offenders an easier and faster means than the criminal justice system for dealing with a violent incident. Schools have also claimed for years that results of student disciplinary proceedings constituted "educational records" and therefore FERPA was applicable and prohibited disclosure of the records to third parties without written consent of the student involved.

We continue to see administrators quoted in newspapers saying FERPA "does not allow" them to release this type of information. As a result, many crime prevention advocates and media organizations argue that keeping these proceedings secret denies the parties involved due process rights and deprives other students and their parents of information about campus crime and justice. Connie Clery says, "The problem with FERPA is that colleges and universities use it to 'muzzle victims' from sharing the truth with families and communities, the truth which could help to protect lives" (personal communication with Connie Clery, September 7, 2006).

Institutions attempting this tactic are incorrectly interpreting FERPA because both the Buckley *Amendment* clarification of 1992 and the *Foley Amendment* of 1998 addressed these issues and clarified that FERPA's confidentiality protections do not apply to law enforcement and certain student disciplinary records. The *Foley Amendment,* named after its sponsor Congressman Mark Foley (R-FL), changed FERPA rules to permit postsecondary institutions to publicly disclose the results of a campus disciplinary hearing in cases of violent crime where there is a finding of responsibility. Victim and witness names remain confidential unless they authorize the release in writing; the law is a bit ambiguous, however, saying that schools *may*–but are not *required* to–release the records upon request from third parties. The disclosure of disciplinary proceedings' results must include only the name of the offender, the violation committed, and any sanction imposed by the institution against the student (H. Amdt. 603 to H.R.6, 1998).

According to the Clerys, one of the problems with these "campus courts" is they are not equipped to deal with cases involving violence, such as sexual assault. To illustrate, one of the greatest examples of injustice to victims with which we are familiar is the death of David Schick at Georgetown University in 2000.

Although the D.C. Metropolitan Police Department ruled his death a possible homicide, authorities never sought prosecution in the case. A Georgetown student implicated in the incident was sanctioned by the university as follows: he had to write a ten-page reflection paper and endure a semester-long suspension (deferred on appeal), and the student graduated in 2002. The University asked Schick's parents, Jeff and Debbie, to sign a nondisclosure agreement before learning the disciplinary sanctions given the student. They refused, and only learned the results after a civil settlement with Georgetown ("Congress Cites GU in Privacy Reforms," 2005).

ED clarified the ambiguity of "proper disclosure, at least in sexual assault cases, in a July 16, 2004 letter to Georgetown in response to Georgetown's policy of requiring sexual assault victims to sign nondisclosure agreements. Specifically, before victims could learn the results of disciplinary action taken against the alleged assailant(s), Georgetown required victims to sign documents agreeing not to talk about the outcomes of the hearing. ED held that Georgetown's policy violated the *Clery Act's* victim's rights requirements and the letter states:

> Both the accuser and the accused must be informed of the outcome of any institutional disciplinary proceeding brought alleging a sex offence. Compliance with this paragraph *does not* constitute a violation of FERPA. Under the University's policy, a student who refused to execute an agreement would be barred from receiving judicial outcomes and sanctions information.

As a result, a key aim of the *Clery Act*–providing access to information to be used by affected persons in the recovery process–is defeated (ED determination letter, 7/16/04).

Campus Sex Crimes Prevention Act

The *Campus Sex Crimes Prevention Act* (§1601 of Public Law 106–386) or CSCPA was enacted on October 28, 2000 and provides for the tracking of convicted, registered sex offenders enrolled as students at institutions of higher education (IHEs) or working or volunteering on campus. SOC's support for this law occurred when Connie and Howard were speaking at a California College and University Police Chiefs Association conference in South Lake Tahoe in the spring of 2000. After the conference, the Clerys were having dinner with Detective Sally Miller and Chief of Police Terry Stewart of the Santa Rosa Junior College who asked the Clerys to help with legislation geared to protecting their campus from sexual predators by extending sex offender registration requirements to colleges. What really struck the Clerys and piqued their interest was when the officials told them they had approximately 200 sex offenders on their campus (personal communication with Connie Clery, September 7, 2006).

The CSCPA amended federal sex offender registration requirements to provide that any registrant already required to register in a state must also provide additional notice of each IHE where the person is employed, carries on a vocation, or is a student. The legislation requires that states ensure sex offender registration information is promptly made available to law enforcement agencies whose jurisdiction includes postsecondary institutions and is entered into appropriate state records or registry databases. If a college or university has a police department, the state must provide this information to them.

The Campus Sex Crimes Prevention Act amended the *Clery Act* to require IHEs to issue a statement, in addition to other required disclosures, advising the campus community where to find the information concerning registered sex offenders who are on campus (*Campus Sex Crimes Prevention Act,* §1601, Public Law 106–386).

Clery Act Complaints

The ED rules indicate citizens must file complaints regarding alleged violations of any *Clery Act* reporting obligations with the ED's regional office overseeing jurisdiction in the state where the school allegedly breaking the law is located. SOC has suggested several steps that citizens should take in filing such a complaint (How to File a Jeanne Clery Act Complaint, 2006).

First, SOC suggests that one obtain a copy of the institution's crime security disclosures. Next, SOC recommends that one review these disclosures to verify that all required crime statistical disclosures and security policies are present. If statistical or policy disclosures are missing, SOC recommends recording the violations by their regulatory citation. It is also important, according to SOC, to verify whether the disclosed policies are in fact routine practice at the school; if not, that is a violation of the Act. The *Clery Act* also provides that postsecondary institutions are to accord certain rights to survivors of sexual assaults on campus. If an institution has not accorded a survivor these rights and or the school does not have appropriate policies in place, the institution is in violation of the *Clery Act* (How to File a Jeanne Clery Act Complaint, 2006).

Third, while it may not be possible to verify that statistical disclosures include every covered incident for the required reporting periods, if one has knowledge of incidents that institutions have omitted from the disclosures, SOC recommends compiling all available evidence of these incidents or incident. In addition, if one can obtain an accounting of each specific incident used to arrive at the disclosed statistics, this will be helpful and verify whether the incident(s) were included.

Fourth, one should compile each of the regulatory violations into a list and forward it to the appropriate regional office of ED for the state in which the specific school is located. A Case Management Team at the regional office will handle the complaint; SOC provides a list of the various regional offices and the states over which they have jurisdiction.

SOC also provides the formal ED procedure for the filing complaints:

- An individual desiring to file a complaint alleging that an institution is not complying with these regulations should contact the Director of the Regional Office that serves the State in which the institution is located.
- When a complaint is filed against an institution alleging noncompliance with the campus security regulations, the Department will assess the complaint and determine the appropriate response.
- If an institution has difficulties administering a provision of these regulations, the Department will provide technical assistance so that violations can be corrected.
- If, however, an institution flagrantly or intentionally violates the campus security regulations, or fails to take corrective action, when appropriate, the Secretary will take action against the institution by imposing sanctions against that institution.
- The type of sanction will depend upon the severity of the violations; possible sanctions include the assessment of fines and in very severe violations, the limitation, suspension, or termination of the institution from participation in the Title IV, HEA Programs.

The ED Regional Office provides complainants an acknowledgment of the letter of complaint, but SOC recommends complainants send the complaint by certified-return receipt requested postal mail or by other means (e.g., courier) which provide some form of tracking procedure. Even though the individual is the complainant in the ED's investigation, that person has to file a *Freedom of Information Act* request to obtain copies of all subsequent documentation, including a copy of the initial inquiry of the "participating institution." The "Program Review" documentation will then become a matter of public record under the Federal Freedom of Information Act (FOIA), but ED does name the complainant in this document because the action is an "administrative review" of statutory compliance. Depending upon the degree of noncompliance found, if any, during the initial review, the ED may perform a "Program Review" on the institution's compliance with the *Clery Act*. ED may also perform a less intensive "informal review." Depending upon which process ED selects, it can conclude the investigation in just a few weeks or the investigation could last more than a year.

Based on results of its investigation, ED can fine institutions violating any of the *Clery Act's* provisions up to $27,500 per violation or impose other enforcement action including suspending the institution from participating in federal student aid programs. As of October 2005, ED has found over 400 institutions in violation of the *Clery Act*. Among these, ED conducted 185 "program reviews" of the institutions, including at least 14 campus security focused program reviews, but ED fined only three institutions for violations: Mt. St. Clare College in Clinton, Iowa ($15,000), Salem International University in Salem, West Virginia ($250,000), and Miami University of Ohio in Oxford, Ohio ($27,500) (see Security On Campus, Inc., 2006).

Conclusion

At Security On Campus, Inc., we have personally seen how the *Clery Act* transformed campus security since its passage in 1990. Campus crime has gone from an issue that frequently went unaddressed to one that is now addressed extensively, including at incoming student orientations, in campus newspapers, and in the local and national media both print and television. A study of incoming students and their parents has shown that campus crime is the most considered characteristic by students headed to public institutions and the third most important characteristic looked for by students headed to private institutions (Sevier & Kappler, 1996). Additional scholarly research found that, "criminal activity does dissuade [potential] new students" from attending a particular school (Depken, 1998).

Because of the efforts of Howard and Connie Clery, postsecondary institutions are doing more to help prevent crime on college and university campuses. While the struggle has now gone on for nearly two decades, the original goal of the Clerys to make institutions "come clean" with their crime statistics has been realized. U.S. Secretary of Education, Rod Paige summed up the spirit of the *Clery Act* when he said:

> I applaud the tireless efforts of Jeanne's parents, Connie and Howard Clery, and the thousands of other parents and crime victims who have worked with them. They have turned their grief into advocacy for a law that opens the book on the safety of our college campuses. Now the American people are empowered with the information they need to make informed decisions about campus safety." (United States Department of Education Releases Latest Campus Crime, SOC Update, 2001)

Notes

1. The Uniform Crime Reporting Program involves state and local law enforcement agencies voluntarily sending to the FBI, statistics on crimes known to them and arrests made on an annual basis. These statistics are then compiled into a report called *Crime in the United States: The Uniform Crime Reports*. Readers may obtain complete information on this program and a copy of the latest statistics by visiting the Federal Bureau of Investigation's website: http://www.fbi.gov.

REFERENCES

The Campus Sex Crimes Prevention Act. Public Law 106–386, § 1601 (2000).

Depken, C. A. (1998). College demand and the Campus Security Act of 1990. *American Economic Journal, 26,* 326.

Dateline, NBC (2005). "Rape on Campus." December 11, 2005, Producer, Julie Cohen.

Duke students rally against rape on campus. (2004). Retrieved September 7, 2006 from http://www.nbc17.com/education/2947237/detail.html.

Education Department determination letter, 7/16/2004.

How to File a Jeanne Clery Act Complaint. (2006). Retrieved September 16, 2006 from http://www.securityoncampus.org/students/clerycomplaint.html.

Howard K. Clery, Jr. Congressional Testimony of March 14, 1990. Retrieved September 7, 2006 from http://www.securityoncampus.org/congress/03141990. html.

Jeanne Clery Disclosure of Campus Security Policy and Campus Crime Statistics Act, 20 U.S.C. § 1092 [f] (1998).

Mccaffrey, J. (2006). Senators call for help in Clery Act enforcement. *The Philadelphia Evening Bulletin,* May 21. Retrieved September 16, 2006, from http://www.the eveningbulletin.com.

Mendoza, M. (2005). Congress Cites GU in Privacy Reforms. Retrieved September 7, 2006 from http://www.thehoya.com/news/030105/news2.cfm.

NBC-17 (March 24, 2004). Duke students rally against rape on campus. Retrieved September 7, 2006 from http://www.nbc17.com/education/2947237/detail.html 3/24/2004.

Sevier, R. A., & Kappler, S. D. (1996). *What students say: Results of two national surveys on how students choose a college.* Cedar Rapids, IA: Stamats Communications, Inc.

Regulations to revise the current Student Assistance General Provisions, 34 CFR, § 668 (1998).

Security On Campus, Inc. (2006). Retrieved September 6, 2006 from http://www.securityoncampus.org.

Student Assistance General Provisions: Final Rules. Federal Register, 64, 59063, November 1, 1999.

U.S. Department of Education releases latest campus crime statistics for more than 600,000 colleges, universities, and career schools. (2001). Security On Campus Update, 1, 18. Retrieved September 7, 2006 from http://www.securityoncampus.org/update/v01n18.html.

Un-covering crime. *Student Press Law Center Report, 24,* 36. Retrieved September 7, 2006 from http://www.splc.org/report_detail.asp?id=978&edition=24.

Chapter 3

RESEARCH ON THE *CLERY ACT* AND ITS IMPACT ON HIGHER EDUCATION ADMINISTRATIVE PRACTICE

DENNIS E. GREGORY AND STEVEN M. JANOSIK

INTRODUCTION

Are college and university campuses in the United States safe today? Are campuses safer than the communities that surround them? Are campus officials hiding campus crime? Do parents and/or students use campus crime data to make college choices? Are admissions offices including required notifications in the documents that they produce for prospective students? Do students use the campus crime data provided by campus officials to change their own habits and as a result increase their safety? Has the *Jeanne Clery Disclosure of Campus Security Policy and Campus Crime Statistics Act* (2000) or its predecessors (henceforth the *Clery Act* or the *Act*) changed the way in which campus police and student affairs officials on American campuses go about protecting students on their campuses? How does the press report on campus crime and efforts by campuses to solve problems related to crime? These and many other questions are of concern to college administrators, faculty, staff, students, parents, researchers, lawmakers, and others around the country.

While we do not provide unequivocal answers to all these questions in this chapter, we review studies that have addressed them and summarize for readers their major findings. We also compare the results of several studies that examined these issues. The purpose of this chapter is to provide readers a review of the state of the research literature on the *Clery Act* and describe several studies which demonstrate how the *Act* and its impact have been perceived by student affairs officials–judicial and housing officers, victim advocates, campus police–as well as students, parents, and admissions professionals. Several of the studies presented in the chapter provide readers a different and, we think, a more accurate, way to compare crime on American campuses than methods currently used by the press and advocacy groups, as well as by the U.S. Department of Education (ED).

The *Clery Act* in the Literature

The *Clery Act* sprang from the death of Jeanne Clery who was raped and murdered in her residence hall room on the Lehigh University campus. The Clery family received an out-of-court settlement in its suit against the university and pushed to have campus safety legislation passed first in Pennsylvania, and ultimately by Congress in 1990–*The Student Right to Know and Campus Security Act of 1990* (renamed the *Jeanne Clery Act* in 1998). Congress passed the *Act* not only because of this tragedy, but because legislation was viewed as a necessity due to perceived increases in juvenile crime in society as a whole, and a perceived increase in crime on college campuses. There were, however, no means at the time to determine whether this presumption about campus crime was accurate (Gregory & Janosik, 2003).

With the concern among the public, the press and watchdog groups, such as Security on Campus, Inc., about the safety of college campuses, it is surprising that little formal research has been completed on how the *Act* has been implemented, how campus officials have perceived its impact, and how effective it has been. In fact, the "literature" on the topic is replete with news stories and law review articles that opine about the *Act's* level of importance and enforcement. Most of the source material one finds is popular press-based, largely because the media appear fascinated by lurid reports of crimes including the murder of Virginia Commonwealth University student Taylor Behl (Bardsley & Huff, n.d.; Doolittle, 2005); allegations of rape and other criminal acts committed by members of the Duke Lacrosse team ("A Timeline of Bad Press," 2006; "From Lacrosse To Redick," 2006); and other high-profile crimes. While these crimes are certainly troubling and indicate that higher education faces many challenges, there is little evidence that such crimes are the norm on American campuses, particularly when one compares campus crime with that in larger society.

Gregory and Janosik (2002) described the tone and content of much of the literature related to the *Clery Act* that arose during the 1990s. This content included media commentary about the results of campus crime, reports of institutions that failed to accurately report crime, and criticisms of campuses that failed to be adequately open about the crime on and around their campuses. This literature also included legal journal articles that described the Act, its content, its strengths, and its weaknesses as well as several books on the topic (e.g., Fisher & Sloan, 1995; Gregory & Janosik, 2002; Smith, 1988,

1989; Smith & Fossey, 1995).

Method

To examine the number, content, and variety of published material relating to the *Clery Act* and review that material, we conducted Google™ and Google Scholar™ searches, followed by searches of Lexis-Nexis™ Academic and ProQuest™ databases. These sources provided us a broad overview of recent writing concerning the *Clery Act* and its impact. The databases we selected are both available to, and understandable by, people seeking information about the *Act* such as parents, students, police officials, and scholars. While not exhaustive, our review provides a reasonable summary of what consumers and others with an interest in the *Act* might find.

We first conducted a Google™ search using the term "Clery Campus Safety Act" that returned 170,000 citations. We reviewed the first thirty pages of citations returned and found the vast majority included references to electronic versions of campus security reports and related documents from various colleges and universities in the United States. The remainder of the citations were primarily electronic postings relating to Security on Campus, Inc., an advocacy group involved with insuring colleges and universities properly implement the *Clery Act* (see Carter & Bath, 2007; ED; and news reports from campus and other newspapers covering crimes on specific campuses). While we expected such a search would likely provide such sources, with 170,000 citations returned, we also expected to find citations to research, including master's theses and doctoral dissertations posted online.

We next conducted a search of Google Scholar™ using the same search term and found 117 "hits." Of these, we found Gregory and Janosik and their coauthors mentioned in 12 of the first 15 references returned and another reference mentioned one of the editors of this volume and her colleagues (Fisher, Hartman, Cullen, & Turner, 2002). Besides those noted above, only three of the 117 "hits" included quantitative or qualitative research on issues that in any way related to the *Clery Act* or campus crime more broadly. Google Scholar™ returned references for research on related issues, such as sexual assault on campus, alcohol abuse, fraternal organization violence and the like, but most of the references were for reports similar to those found in the Google™ database.

Using the same term, we next conducted a search of popular news sources for the last two years found in the LexisNexus™ Academic Database using the "Quick News" search. We undertook this search specifically to examine how the popular and legal press has covered the *Clery Act.* Our search returned 125 citations from campus and commercial newspapers. We examined the articles and found the majority described campus crime statistics, while others referred to specific criminal acts that had occurred on campus, were articles resulting from the inclusion of one of the words within the search phrase that were not related, or were articles which examined campus safety as an element of homeland security. As noted above for the Google™ database, this database contained sources almost exclusively from the popular and legal press and as a result, we did not expect the database to yield academic research articles.

We followed our search of popular press sources with a search of law journals/law reviews using the LexisNexis™ Academic Database, using the search term "Clery Campus Safety Act." The search produced no returns, so we revised it using the term *"Clery Act"* and located seven citations; four came from a *Stetson Law Review* 2002 issue containing a campus crime symposium and two of those articles were research studies. Two other articles dealt with sexual assault, and the final article dealt with student privacy in campus judicial proceedings related to crime committed on campus. A search of that database using the *Jeanne Clery Disclosure of Campus Security Policy and Campus Crime Statistics Act* yielded eight citations, including the seven noted above and one on federal jurisprudence (Clery, 1990).

The final search we conducted was of the ProQuest™ Electronic Database for Education Theses and Dissertations using the search term "Clery Campus Safety Act." Search results provided only three dissertations specifically related to the *Act.* We found several theses and dissertations that addressed the *Clery Act* and/or related campus crime issues.

Although the searches we conducted were not exhaustive, such as what is required for a doctoral dissertation, searching several databases readily available to the casual user and to scholars we found relatively little content that could be reasonably be considered research—analytical, qualitative, or quantitative—on *Clery.* As a result, we suggest that people inside and outside of higher education view campus crime based on anecdotal information collected in interviews and views espoused by the press—not academic research.

Below we review the results of our database searches. A small group of scholars, including the authors of other chapters in this volume and us, has conducted much of the research we review.

Clery Act Research

As mentioned, scholars have conducted limited scientific research on the *Clery Act* and on its impact on campus crime. Below, we discuss the content of the dissertations, theses, articles, and reports we found in our search for research material on the *Clery Act.* We arrange these by type of publication rather than by content focus for ease of reference. Finally, our review does not reveal a single set of conclusions from these studies as a whole, since their focus, methodologies, subjects, and research questions differed widely. There are, however, common themes we describe in the concluding section of this chapter.

Doctoral Dissertations

Our search of the *ProQuest*™ Electronic Database found dissertations by Kerr (2001), Greenstein (2002), and McGuire (2002). They examined various aspects of the Act and particularly focused on whether colleges or universities complied with the portions or aspects of the *Act* under study (e.g., crime statistics, timely warnings, reports of policies and procedures) and whether they were effective at reducing campus crime and increasing safety.

Kerr (2001) analyzed the extent of compliance with, and perceptions of the effects of, annual crime reports published by campus law enforcement. Kerr reported that while most of the campus security officials indicated institutional compliance with the *Clery Act,* he found (p. iv) that "a majority of the institutions did not comply with the content requirements of the law, including the requirements established in the 1998 amendments to the law." Kerr also noted that his subjects did not believe that the legally mandated methods of policy and procedure distribution as well as crime statistics were not effective ways to improve campus safety.

Greenstein (2002) examined perceptions of the "timely warning" requirements of the *Clery Act.* Greenstein reported that students and staff found timely warnings useful and wished to receive them. She found some perceptual differences between men and women in terms of the impact of the warnings. Female staff members and both male staff and students indicated that the warnings "made them feel informed and provided an opportunity to take precautions" (p. xiii). Female students, on the other hand, indicated that they felt "more fearful" (p. xiii), and that rather than hearing of incidents through formal channels, "that they received information in larger numbers through informal communication channels" (p. xiii).

McGuire (2002) "investigated the procedures three Illinois public residential universities followed to collect and distribute campus crime statistics and information in compliance with the federal law" (n.p.n.). He also examined campus policies, reports, and other literature related to campus safety and sought to examine administrative perceptions of campus safety as well as compliance with the law. He found a variety of methods by which institutions distributed the *Clery* report, and indicated several potential misapplications of the law by staff.

Master's Theses

In addition to the dissertations, we found two master's theses related to the

Clery Act. These include studies by Parkinson (2001) and Cohen (2005). Both studies examined a topic related to the purpose of the *Clery Act* or its implementation. For instance, Parkinson (2001) studied whether the crime rates on particular campuses affected a student's decision to attend and Cohen (2005) examined admissions literature to determine if the literature of study campuses complied with the requirements of the *Clery Act.* These studies, as was the case for the dissertations, had no common theme and used different research methodologies.

Parkinson (2001) found that campus crime statistics in particular and the *Clery Act* in general had no impact on decisions by prospective students to attend a set of small, private liberal arts colleges in the Midwest. In fact, Parkinson (2001) found no indication that the *Act* had any influence on students at all.

Cohen (2005) examined whether "a random sample of institutions were complying with all aspects of the *Clery Act* and if the required information was readily accessible to those who wish to view it" (p. 3). To make this determination, Cohen chose ten institutions randomly from across the U.S. She examined the "Admissions viewbook" and "Crime Statistics Report Handbook" from each institution, along with each campus's websites. Her results showed that nine of the ten institutions were not fully compliant with *Clery Act* requirements. Cohen recommended that each institution provide a map showing where crimes had taken place, the institution conduct an annual training workshop on the *Clery Act* for campus staff (particularly Admissions staff), and that each campus offer a program on campus safety for new students at the beginning of each academic year. Finally, Cohen suggested that the admissions information provided to students include a statement the institution was in compliance with the *Clery Act.*

Journal Articles, White Papers, Research Reports, and Proceedings

In addition to these dissertations and theses, researchers have conducted studies on various aspects of the *Clery Act* that have appeared in professional journals and other forums. There are several themes running through much of this research, which is not surprising since a small group of scholars has produced much of this work. Further, surveys conducted by some of the scholars contained common items. In general, the studies found that large percentages of study populations believed their campuses and the surrounding areas to be safe or very safe. Students, parents, and administrators indicated they did not study *Clery Act* crime statistics, and even when they did review the statistics, they did not use them to decide which school to attend. Only very small percentages of the administrative groups believed that campus officials were intentionally hiding crime on campus, and few among any study group reported that the *Clery Act* had had any appreciable affect on lowering crime rates or making campuses safer.

JOURNAL ARTICLES. One of the earliest studies on *Clery Act* related topics was by Gehring and Callaway (1997), which examined the impact of the Act on campus admissions decisions. This study, similar to the later study by Parkinson (2001), found little or no impact by the crime statistics reports on decisions about which institution to attend. Gehring and Calloway (1997), Janosik (2001), and Janosik and Gehring (2003) studied whether *Clery Act* crime statistics changed students' safety-related behaviors. Of particular interest were the results of Janosik and Gehring (2003), who found the great majority of students remain unaware of the *Act,* do not read the mandated reports, and do not use crime information in their personal decision-making on which college to attend.

Sloan, Fisher, and Cullen (1997) conducted another early study. Sloan et al. conducted a national victimization study of over 3,400 college students and from these data described the situation that they found regarding the *Clery Act* and campus crime. They stated that the key assumption related to the development of the *Act* was that it would produce crime reports that would be "valid and reliable" (p. 149). They go on to report that because the *Act* concentrates upon crimes of violence rather than theft-related crimes, it may foster an underreporting of crime on campus. Another reason why the *Act* results in underreporting of campus crime is because the statistics found in the reports are based upon crimes reported to campus police and much crime goes unreported for a variety of reasons.

Sloan et al. (1997) noted that there are three primary purposes of the *Act* that include (a) provision of information about campus crime and security policies to students and parents, (b) provision of information helpful to parents and students making admissions decisions, and (c) creation of a common system for crime reporting on all campuses. Sloan et al. indicated that only certain types of crime are included in statistical reports required by the *Act.* They noted ". . . the statistics may make campuses appear more dangerous than researchers have found them" (p. 153). Sloan et al. (1997, p. 153) cited earlier research by Seng and Koehler (1993) and Seng (1995) critical of the *Act* because its mandates resulted in the presentation of raw crime data, rather than as a "rates per some population unit [resulting in] inappropriate and misleading comparisons . . . of the volume of crimes known to police at campuses having different student populations, sizes, and locations." Sloan et al. (1997) concluded that statistics reported in compliance with the *Act* do not provide an accurate picture of campus crime because some crime goes unreported and the *Act* overemphasizes violent crime. Thus, "The [A]ct should be viewed as a symbolic attempt to 'do something' about the perceived 'crime wave' on college campuses" (p. 163).

Furthering this theme, Fisher, Hartman, Cullen, and Turner (2002) also argued that the *Clery Act* constituted a "symbolic" attempt at reform. Fisher et al. reported the "main goal" of the *Clery Act* was "to assure that parents and student applicants could secure accurate and official statistics about crime to make rational admissions decisions, while a secondary goal was to force campuses to be "safer social domains–to take crime and student safety more seriously" (p. 64). They also characterized the *Clery Act* as a "symbolic legal intervention of questionable value" (p. 64) to students and parents. Fisher et al. questioned whether the *Clery Act* as an unfunded federal mandate, is appropriate given the fact that "it is not clear that campuses are particularly dangerous social domains" (p. 79) and cited a study which showed that students were safer on campus than off. Fisher et al. also argued, "[C]ampuses are not the 'hot spots' of routine violence that the media has led the public to believe" (p. 82).

WHITE PAPERS. One of the most informative documents we found was a 2005 "white paper" by Carr. While not specifically about the *Clery Act*, the report did question current crime statistics. The American College Health Association sponsored this white paper, within which the author described research that reported issues related to campus violence. The paper used the World Health Organization (WHO) definition of violence:

> The intentional use of physical force or power, threatened or actual, against oneself, another person, or against a group or community, that either results in, or has a high likelihood of resulting in injury, death, psychological harm, maldevelopment or deprivation. (Krug, Dahlberg, Mercy, Zwi, & Lozano, p. 4 cited in Carr, 2005, p. 1)

Carr (2005) described problems with the accuracy of current crime reporting statistics and used a variety of sources during the period 1995–2005 from which she drew data regarding violence affecting college students. Carr (2005, p. 1) noted that, "college students ages 18–24 were victims of approximately 479,000 crimes of violence annually" and that "overall, the violent crime rate declined by 54%." Further, she indicated that, during this eleven-year period, students experienced crimes at a lower average rate than non-students age 18–24, except for rape/sexual assault" (p. 2). Among the items reported were that "approximately 93% of crimes against students occurred off-campus" and that "most (72%) of the off-campus violence against students was between 6 p.m. and 6 a.m." while "most on-campus violence (56%) occurred during the day, 6 a.m. to 6 p.m." (p. 2) (see also Hart, 2007).

CLERY ACT STUDY SERIES. Beginning in 2002, we began a series of studies to identify the perceptions of a variety of student affairs and related professionals about the effectiveness of the *Clery Act*, and determine whether the *Act* had any impact on their practice or student behaviors. To date, our colleagues and we have conducted several studies of campus law enforcement professionals, judicial officers, chief housing officers, senior student affairs professionals, parents, victim advocates, and admissions officers and registrars. We review these studies and compare their findings below (see Table 3.1).

Janosik and Gregory (2003a) studied perceptions of campus law enforcement administrators regarding the effectiveness of the *Clery Act*. The study surveyed 371 members (39% response rate) of the International Association of Campus Law Enforcement Administrators (IACLEA) and examined the perceptions of the respondents regarding the effectiveness of the *Clery Act*. Among the findings of this study were that a majority (57%) of campus police officials believed that the *Act* had improved the quality of campus crime reporting procedures, one of the primary purposes of the legislation. Janosik and Gregory (2003a) also found that all the respondents were keeping campus crime logs and making them available to the public, both of which *Clery* mandates. Additionally, they found the *Clery Act* seemed to increase students' positive perceptions of campus police officers. Further, less than 10 percent of the participants in the study believed that officials on their campus were intentionally hiding crime. Almost three-quarters of the police indicated that crime had remained relatively constant and the Act had little or no impact on decreasing campus crime. In addition, a large majority noted that publication of crime statistics or other information mandated by the *Clery Act* did not change student behavior. Janosik and Gregory concluded that although *Clery* had improved campus crime reporting, such reporting has not created any positive change in students' behavior. They noted that a more positive impact would come from more attention paid to policy improvement and educational programs.

In the second study in this series, Gregory and Janosik (2003) studied the perceptions of campus judicial officers concerning the effectiveness of the *Clery Act*. They first described seven purposes for the *Clery Act,* including:

- improving campus crime reporting by forcing colleges and universities to report campus crime data in a more consistent manner;
- allowing prospective students and their parents to make informed decisions about the relative safety of institutions to which they are considering applying for admission;
- improving campus safety programs;
- improving campus police policies and procedures;
- raising student awareness and thus changing their safety-related behaviors;
- eliminating the perceived hiding of campus crime by institutional officials, and reducing campus crime. (p. 764)

Gregory and Janosik (2003) surveyed 156 (36.7% response rate) members of the Association for Student Judicial Affairs (ASJA) on *Clery*. Findings from the study included respondents indicating increased opportunities for interaction between campus police and student conduct officers because of the *Act*. They also found respondents largely felt that their campuses and the communities in which they were located were safe or very safe; that *Clery* had little impact on campus safety levels; that mandated crime reports had little impact on changing student safety-related behaviors; and that campus officials were not intentionally hiding crime on campus. Student conduct officers at community and other two-year colleges were less aware of the *Clery Act* than were colleagues from four-year institutions (Gregory & Janosik, 2003). Gregory and Janosik (2003) argued that Congress passed *Clery* with the best intentions but that postsecondary institutions have realized few of its avowed purposes. They suggested that a change of focus in *Clery* from reporting crime statistics to emphasizing crime prevention programs and rewarding excellence in such programs would be a better approach.

Janosik (2004) conducted a third study in the series, which involved conducting a survey of 435 parents attending a summer orientation program at a single four-year institution. He found that only 25 percent of parents were aware of the *Act* and about the same percentage reported reading the institution's crime summary. Interestingly, parents' level of awareness was very similar to what studies have shown concerning student awareness (see Janosik, 2001; Janosik & Gehring, 2003). Surprisingly, parents who had experienced crime in their immediate family and those who had already sent children to college were no more aware of *Clery* than other respondent groups and were no more likely to ask about campus safety than were other groups of parents.

Janosik (2004) also found campus crime information played almost no role in college choice decisions. Although most parents reported talking with their sons and daughters about campus safety, they did not report using the information contained in the federally mandated reports in these conversations. Further, a majority of parents identified passive media campaigns as the strategy most likely to change student behavior. Students and a wide variety of college administrators, including campus law enforcement officials, also hold this view (see Janosik & Gehring, 2003; Janosik & Gregory, 2003a, 2006; Gregory & Janosik, 2003). Finally, it is important to note that this group of parents held very positive views about the institution, the administrators with whom they spoke, and those responsible for campus safety. This dynamic may decrease parental "interest" in the issue until an incident occurs.

Janosik and Plummer (2005), in a fourth study in the series, examined perceptions of victim advocates concerning *Clery*. In this study, 147 advocates

(43% response rate) expressed concerns about the reporting requirements of *Clery*. They did not believe students read the mandated reports or changed their crime prevention behavior. Respondents also did not believe *Clery* reduced crime. However, they did express the view that *Clery* may have improved the quality of crime reporting and the consistency of those reports. Advocates also believed that passive ad campaigns and campus programming that focuses on timely reporting of crime activity were more likely to influence students' safety-related behavior. Finally, for some victim advocates, the *Act* provided opportunities to increase communication with other campus officials, resulting in closer working relationships and enhanced services for assault victims and their families. Although campus advocates are often contrasted with campus law enforcement and judicial affairs colleagues, this study indicated that members of all three groups shared similar perceptions about the impact and value of *Clery* on student behavior and campus practices (Janosik & Plummer, 2005, p. 129).

Finally, Gregory and Janosik (2006) studied perceptions of chief housing officers regarding the effectiveness of the *Clery Act* and on issues of campus safety. The study explored six research questions regarding (a) college choice by students, (b) awareness of the *Act* by students and housing administrators, (c) potential changes in perceptions or behavior by students, (d) the safety of campus, (e) perceived reductions of campus crime resulting from the *Act,* and (f) the hiding of crime by administrators.

The authors sent a survey to the 832 individuals identified by ACUHO–I as being chief Residence Life and/or Housing officers. Three hundred thirty-three responses (40% response rate) were received. Among the study's important findings was respondents' relative lack of awareness of campus crime information on their campus, a level much higher than that found by other studies in the series. Additionally, a small percentage of respondents perceived that their institutions might not be providing crime data to applicants for admission and current students. While this situation may simply be reflecting lack of awareness, it is disturbing that senior housing officials did not know the level of compliance with *Clery* mandates. On a positive note, respondents did indicate that students read signs, posters, and other items related to campus safety, and that they attended campus safety programs in large numbers. In addition, housing officers largely also felt their campuses were safe and institutional officials were not hiding crime (Gregory & Janosik, 2006).

RESEARCH REPORTS. In a report funded by the U. S. Department of Justice, Karjane, Fisher, and Cullen (2002) reported results of a national study of campus sexual assault that included data collected from 2,438 institutions. Among other results, Karjane et al. (2002) found significant underreporting by victims of acquaintance sexual assault and that only about one-third of respondent institutions "reported crime statistics in a manner that was fully consistent with the *Clery Act*" (p. viii). The researchers also ascertained that approximately 80 percent of the institutions in their sample had submitted security reports but that less than half included statistics on both forcible and nonforcible sex offenses (Karjane et al., 2002). Additionally, Karjane et al. found less than half of the security reports prepared by the schools included procedures for student reporting of sexual assault to on/or off campus police and that appropriate due process procedures for those accused of sexual assaults were used by just over one-third of the respondent institutions. Among their recommendations were that institutions develop formal guidelines to ensure compliance with *Clery.*

Janosik and Gregory (2003b) and Janosik, Gregory, and Strayhorn (2005) examined campus crime at Virginia's public and private, not-for-profit IHE. In an attempt to place campus crime statistics in perspective (as suggested by Seng (1995) and Seng and Koehler (1993)) the researchers compared crime rates on Virginia college campuses using *Clery* statistical reports, with national collegiate crime statistics from the same source, national crime figures in the same categories reported by the FBI, as well as crime in Virginia in general as reported by the Virginia state police. The studies used a conventional comparison metric of "crimes per 100,000 population," which is the FBI standard for national reporting. Doing this allowed one to view campus crime statistics from a common perspective across categories and crime types. In virtually all categories, national and state crime rates were higher than both national-level campus crime rates and rates at Virginia colleges and universities.

What these data showed is that campuses had much lower crime rates than larger society and that rates at Virginia institutions were much lower than rates either in the state as a whole or the nation. The researchers plan to continue publishing these annual reports to establish and examine trend data over time. However, the reports are somewhat slow in development since the ED general compilation of national collegiate data are not issued until the June following the October 1 deadline for receipt of the statistics from colleges and university each year. Because of the time constraints associated with collecting and reporting national data, reports such as those by Gregory, Janosik, and Strayhorn often lag by 18 to 24 months.

Gregory, Janosik, Strayhorn, and Kalagher (2006) compiled similar crime rate comparisons for the southeastern United States. Here, Gregory et al. compared crime rates of the sixteen states in the region covered by the Southern Association of College Student Affairs (SACSA) as well as the District of Columbia. Crime rates in all of the SACSA states were similar to the pattern found for the Commonwealth of Virginia: state crime rates were generally lower than national rates and the state collegiate crime rates were lower in almost all categories than the national collegiate rates, state rates, and national rates. Thus, campuses in each state had much lower crime rates than the surrounding society, and southeastern campuses were largely safer than were collegiate campuses more generally. The District of Columbia was somewhat of an anathema in this study because of its urban nature and small size. Here, some of the campus figures were as large as those in the surrounding community were and larger than the overall national collegiate and national crime rates.

PROCEEDINGS. The views of senior student affairs officers (SSAOs) have also been assessed (Janosik & Gregory, 2006). These professionals share the belief that students rarely read the mandated reports and do not use the information to make college choice decisions. They also believe that this type of information does little to change student safety-related behavior. Not surprisingly, SSAOs believe that their staff members are candid and forthright when discussing campus safety issues with others.

In these proceedings, Janosik and Gregory (2006) provided a comparison of the findings of several of the above-mentioned studies, as well as a more recent unpublished survey of registrars and admissions officers conducted by Janosik and Baucom (n.d.) to show common perceptions about *Clery*. Table 3.1 below, describes these comparative findings.

A review of this table shows that virtually all of the administrative groups studied knew about *Clery*, but just over one-quarter of students surveyed in multiple studies had such awareness. Of the three groups asked if members believed students read the summary of the *Act* in admissions materials, 12 percent or less of the housing and senior student affairs officers agreed and less that one-quarter of students indicated that they read the summary. No more that 15 percent of members of any of the seven groups questioned answered in the affirmative when asked whether crime statistics influenced admissions decisions. Similarly small numbers within each of the groups indicated that crime statistics were responsible for changes in students' safety related behaviors.

The studies asked six questions regarding passive ad campaigns related to campus safety (e.g., signs, posters, programs, timely warnings, etc.), and whether these programs would change students' safety-related behaviors. While the percentages of positive responses varied from group to group, majorities in six of the seven groups believed that students read such materials. Smaller numbers within each group believed that these campaigns would change student behaviors, but the numbers were generally larger than numbers of respondents who believed the crime statistics would have any impact. Senior student affairs officers, housing officers, and victim advocates were the most positive in this regard.

The final two questions asked to five and four of the groups respectively,

Table 3.1
ANALYSIS OF *CLERY ACT* LITERATURE

Item	NASPA N=327	ACUHO-I N=335	ASJA N=422	IACLEA N=371	AACRO N=630	Advocates N=344	Students N=866
Know about the *Clery Act*	98%	99%	99%	100%	92%	93%	27%
Think students know about the *Act*	–	55%	51%	40%	59%	–	27%
Think students read the summary	10%	12%	-	–	–	–	24%
Think students read the annual report	15%	3%	24%	25%	13%	2%	27%
Think the reports influence college choice decisions	10%	7%	4%	10%	15%	6%	8%
Think the reports influence behavior	18%	14%	7%	10%	22%	12%	–
Think students will read passive ad campaigns	73%	75%	52%	47%	92%	75%	60%
Think passive ads will change how students protect property	65%	46%	29%	36%	40%	46%	37%
Think passive ads will change how students protect them- selves	71%	45%	36%	30%	37%	47%	25%
Think that passive ads will change how students move around campus	56%	45%	36%	30%	37%	47%	25%

continued

Table 3.1–*Continued*
ANALYSIS OF *CLERY ACT* LITERATURE

Item	NASPA N=327	ACUHO-I N=335	ASJA N=422	IACLEA N=371	AACRO N=630	Advocates N=344	Students N=866
Think that passive ads will increase confidence in campus police	24%	20%	47%	53%	34%	25%	25%
Think that passive ads will increase crime reporting	10%	9%	40%	34%	49%	44%	51%
Think that college administrators are hiding campus crime	3%	16%	4%	9%	–	16%	–
Think that college administrators are candid about campus safety issues	99%	91%	86%	–	–	66%	–

addressed perceptions about whether institutional officials were intentionally hiding campus crime and/or were candid about campus safety issues. Very small percentages of each population indicated that officials were hiding crime and large majorities indicated that they believed campus officials were being candid about safety issues.

Discussion and Conclusion

Despite the presence of various versions of the *Clery Act* since 1990, there has been little formal study regarding the legislation's impact. The studies presented above comprise the large majority of available research and reveal common themes and conclusions we discuss below.

First, while the *Clery Act* is an important piece of legislation, many postsecondary institutions and their staff have perceived it as confusing and ill-focused. Even now, after 16 years, some admissions officers, housing officers, and to a lesser extent campus police officers may not fully understand some of the nuances of the *Act* and "institutions still do not report crime data in a way fully consistent with Federal law" (United States Department of Justice, 2005, p. 4). Even such terms as "campus" and "student" are challenging to define in consistent ways and this contributes to inconsistency in reporting (United States Department of Justice, 2005, p. 7). Such difficulties prompted Karjane et al. (2002) to conclude that college administrators need more guidance on how to comply with *Clery*. The lack of compliance with certain aspects of *Clery* is a theme echoed by several researchers whose studies we reviewed. We agree and applaud the ED (2005) for its recently released resource, *The Handbook for Campus Crime Reporting.* This handbook is a first attempt by the ED to assist postsecondary institutions that must comply with *Clery* and provide guidance on how to comply properly. This resource should of great assistance as college administrators prepare their annual crime reports.

Second, *Clery* does not seem to have had the impact that its sponsors had hoped. Fewer than 27 percent of student and parents know of the *Act* and fewer than 25 percent of students acknowledge reading the mandated crime reports (Janosik & Gehring, 2003; Janosik, 2001). Fewer than 10 percent of parents and students use crime information in *Clery* mandated campus security reports to make college choice decisions (Janosik, 2004). Despite efforts by campus administrators to improve reporting, one has to wonder about the efficacy of such a strategy. Perhaps Fisher et al. (2002) are correct and *Clery* is merely a symbolic effort to make campuses safer.

Third, though many critics indicate that campus crimes are still not being reported accurately and skepticism among "watchdog" groups runs high (see Kerkstra, 2006), there appears to be no evidence that this is intentional or that the accuracy is less than that reported by other agencies responsible for reporting crime. Most of the data seem to indicate that students, parents, and institutional officials believe that college administrators are being candid about campus safety issues and that very few administrators intentionally attempt to hide crime. While a number of the studies cited in this chapter suggest that campus crime is underreported, particularly that related to sexual assault, we would argue that much the same phenomenon is true in society as a whole.

Fourth, the research by Janosik, Gregory, and colleagues involving surveys of postsecondary institutional constituent groups showed members of these groups perceived their campuses to be as safe as, or safer than, the surrounding community and this perception is largely borne out by crime rate statistics. The fact is that for the most part, violent campus crime, like violent crime in the general population in the United States, is declining. The wave of youth crime predicted by criminologists in the 1990s never materialized (Greve, 2006), while studies by Fisher et al. (2002); Janosik and Gregory

(2003b); Janosik, Gregory, and Strayhorn (2005); and Gregory, Janosik, Strayhorn, and Kalagher (2006) all report that campuses are safer than the communities which surround them. Almost none of these researchers, however, attribute this finding to the effect of the *Clery Act.* While certainly administrators have work to do to make campuses safer, particularly in the important areas of sexual assault and hate crimes, as well as theft, assault, and substance abuse, campuses are implementing educational programs, have increased training for key personnel, and installed safety equipment, such as blue light safety phones.

Finally, we believe that the *Clery Act* has had an effect on Student Affairs practice. Clearly, college administrators of all types have had to devote resources to comply with the *Act* and to generate the mandated reports required by the *Act.* This allocation of resources varies widely by school and is difficult to quantify with any precision (Janosik & Gregory, 2003a).

Judicial officers and campus law enforcement officers report an increased consistency in crime reporting. These two groups and counselors report a slight improvement in their working relationships (Gregory & Janosik, 2003; Janosik & Gregory, 2003a). About one-quarter of administrative groups, parents, and students report an increased level of confidence in campus police officers (Gregory & Janosik, 2003; Janosik & Gregory, 2003a) and a majority of students report an increased willingness to report campus crime on their respective campuses (Janosik & Gehring, 2003; Janosik, 2001). These better relationships and increased confidence are likely to result in increased reporting of campus crime.

Beyond requiring college and university administrators to prepare mandatory reports, we believe the *Clery Act* has influenced student affairs and other related campus professional practice only on the margins. Even in this respect, readers should remember that many colleges and universities reported crime statistics using the FBI's uniform crime reporting protocols long before the *Act* was passed. We encourage additional research in the area of campus safety, crime prevention, and improvements in the *Clery Act* to make it even more effective. We believe that this can and will occur.

REFERENCES

Bardsley, M., & Huff, S. (n.d.). Disappeared–Taylor Behl. *Court TV Crime Library.* Retrieved, July 1, 2006 from http://www.crimelibrary.com/criminal_mind/ forensic/taylor_behl_jump_page.html.

Carr, J. L. (2005, February). *American College Health Association campus violence white paper.* Baltimore, MD: American College Health Association.

Carter, S. D., & Bath, C. (2007). The Evolution and components of the Jeanne Clery

Act: Implications for higher education. In B. S. Fisher & J. J. Sloan (Eds.), *Campus crime: Legal, social and policy perspectives* (2nd ed.). Springfield, IL: Charles C Thomas.

Cohen, L. A. (2005). *Admission's literature and compliance with the Jeanne Clery Disclosure of Campus Security Policy and Campus Crime Statistics Act.* Unpublished masters thesis Canisius College, Cleveland, OH.

Doolittle, A. (2005, October 7). Missing VCU student's body found. Washington Times. Retrieved July 1, 2006 from http://washingtontimes.com/metro/2005 1006-103659-7840r.htm.

Epstein, J. (2002). Breaking the code of silence: Bystanders to campus violence and the law of college and university safety. *Stetson Law Review, 32,* 91–124.

From lacrosse to Redick to boat accident, Duke's woes continue (2006, July 1). WRAL.com. Retrieved July 1, 2006 from http://www.wral.com/news/9457739/ detail.html.

Fisher, B. S., Hartman, J. L., Cullen, F. T., & Turner, M. G. (2002). Making campuses safer for students: The Clery Act as a symbolic legal reform. *Stetson Law Review, 32,* 61–89.

Gehring, D. D., & Callaway, R. L. (1997). Compliance with the notice requirement of the Campus Security Act. *College and University, 73,* 13–18.

Greenstein, N. S. (2002). *Timely warnings: Alerting and protecting the campus community.* Unpublished doctoral dissertation. University of California at Los Angeles, Los Angeles, CA. Retrieved January 22, 2006 from http://proquest.umi.com/pqd web?did=764692331&sid=3&Fmt=2&clientId=3505&RQT=309&VName= PQD.

Gregory, D. E., & Janosik, S. M. (2002). The *Clery Act:* How effective is it? Perceptions from the field–The current state of the research and recommendations for improvement. *Stetson Law Review, 32,* 7–59.

Gregory, D. E., & Janosik, S. M. (2003). The effect of the Clery Act on campus judicial practices. *Journal of College Student Development, 44,* 763–778.

Gregory, D. E., & Janosik, S. M. (2006, July). The views of senior residence life and housing administrators on the Clery Act and campus safety. *The Journal of College and University Student Housing, 34,* 50–57.

Gregory, D. E., Janosik, S. M., Strayhorn, T. L., & Kalagher, S. S. (2006). Crime on college and university campuses in the southeastern United States: A more accurate method for examining campus crime statistics. Paper presented at the National Student Personnel Association conference. Washington, DC.

Greve, F. (2006, March 9). Feared juvenile 'super-predators' never materialized. *Wisconsin State Journal,* A1, A7.

Hart, T. C. (2007). The violent victimization of college students: Findings from the National Crime Victimization Survey. In B. S. Fisher & J. J. Sloan (Eds.), *Campus crime: Legal, social and policy perspectives* (2nd ed.). Springfield, IL: Charles C Thomas.

Janosik, S. M. (2001). The impact of the Campus Crime Awareness Act on student behavior. *NASPA Journal, 38,* 348–360.

Janosik, S. M. (2004). Parents' views of the Clery Act and campus safety. *The Journal of College Student Development, 45,* 43–56.

Janosik, S. M., & Gehring, D. D. (2003). *The impact of the Jeanne Clery Act Disclosure of Campus Security Policy and the Campus Crime Statistics Act on student decision-making.* EPI Policy Paper No. 10. Blacksburg, VA: Virginia Tech.

Janosik, S. M., & Gregory, D. E. (2003a). The *Clery Act* and its influence on campus law enforcement practices. *NASPA Journal, 44,* 182–199.

Janosik, S. M., & Gregory, D. E. (2003b). *Crime on Virginia's college and university campuses, Annual report 2002.* EPI Policy Paper Number 14, Blacksburg, VA: Virginia Tech. Retrieved July 1, 2006 from http://filebox.vt.edu/chre/elps/EPI/VACC2002.pdf.

Janosik, S. M., & Gregory, D. E. (2006). Senior student affairs officer's perceptions of campus safety and the impact of the *Clery Act.* A paper presented at the National Student Personnel Association conference. Washington, DC.

Janosik, S. M., Gregory, D. E., & Strayhorn, T. (2005). *Crime on Virginia's college and university campuses, Annual report 2003.* EPI Policy Paper Number 15, Blacksburg, VA: Virginia Tech. Retrieved July 1, 2006 from http://filebox.vt.edu/chre/elps/EPI/VACC2003.pdf.

Janosik, S. M., & Plummer, E. (2005). The *Clery Act* and campus safety: The views of victim advocates. *The College Student Affairs Journal, 25,* 116–130.

Jeanne Clery Disclosure of Campus Security Policy and Campus Crime Statistics Act. 20 U.S.C. § 1092[f] (2000).

Karjane, H. M., Fisher, B. S., & Cullen, F. T. (2002). *Campus sexual assault: How America's institutions of higher education respond.* Washington, DC: National Institute of Justice. Retrieved July 6, 2006 from http://www.ncjrs.gov/pdffiles1/nij/grants/196676.pdf.

Kerr, Jr., S. D. (2001). *Disclosure of campus security policies and crime statistics among colleges and universities in the upper Midwest.* Unpublished doctoral dissertation. University of South Dakota, Vermillion, SD. Retrieved January 22, 2006 from http://proquest.umi.com/pqdweb?Did=726118801&sid=1&Fmt=2&clientId=3505&RQT=309&VName=PQD.

Kerkstra, P. (2006, January 15). On campus, creating an illusion by crime data. *The Philadelphia Inquirer,* pp. B16, B18.

Krug, E. G., Dahlberg, L. L., Mercy, J. A., Zwi, A. B., & Lozano, R. (Eds.) (2002). *World report on violence and health.* Geneva, Switzerland: World Health Organization.

McGuire, J. C. (2002). *Public institutions in higher education policies on the Crime Awareness and Campus Security Act of 1990 and the Federal Education and Right to Privacy Act (Buckley Amendment).* Unpublished doctoral dissertation. Illinois State University, Normal, IL. Retrieved January 22, 2006 from, http:// proquest. umi.com/pqdweb?did=764852751&sid=4&Fmt=2&clientId=3505&RQT=309&VName=PQD.

Parkinson, M. R. (2001). *Crime on campus: The effect of the Jeanne Clery Disclosure of Campus Security Policy and the Campus Crime Statistics Act on prospective students' decisions to attend small private liberal arts colleges in rural areas of the Midwest.* Unpublished master's thesis. Western Illinois University, Macomb, IL.

Seng, M. (1995). The Crime Awareness and Campus Security Act: Some observations, critical comments and suggestions. In B. S. Fisher & J. J. Sloan (Eds.), *Campus crime: Legal, social and policy perspectives.* Springfield, IL: Charles C Thomas.

Seng, M., & Koehler, N. (1993). The Crime Awareness and Campus Security Act: A critical analysis. *Journal of Crime and Justice, 16,* 97–110.

Sloan, J. J., Fisher, B. S., & Cullen, F. T. (1997). Assessing the *Student Right-to-Know and Campus Security Act of 1990:* An analysis of the victim reporting practices of college and university students. *Crime and Delinquency, 43,* 146–168.

Smith, M. C. (1988). *Coping with crime on campus.* New York: American Council on Education: Macmillan.

Smith, M. C. (1989). *Crime and campus police: A handbook for police officers and administrators.* Asheville, NC: College Administration Publications.

Smith, M. C., & Fossey, R. (1995). *Crime on campus: Legal issues and campus administration.* Westport, CT: Greenwood Press.

A timeline of bad press for Duke University (2006, Jul. 01). *The Telegraph* (Macon, GA). Retrieved July 1, 2006 from http://www.maconcom/mld/macon/sports/colleges/mercer/14944546.htm.

United States Department of Education (2005). *The handbook for campus crime reporting.* Washington, D.C.: United States Department of Education.

United States Department of Justice (2005). *Sexual assault on campus: What colleges and universities are doing about it.* Washington, D.C.: U.S. Department of Justice.

Chapter 4

REPORTING SEXUAL ASSAULT AND THE *CLERY ACT:* SITUATING FINDINGS FROM THE NATIONAL CAMPUS SEXUAL ASSAULT POLICY STUDY WITHIN COLLEGE WOMEN'S EXPERIENCES

BONNIE S. FISHER, HEATHER M. KARJANE, FRANCIS T. CULLEN,
KRISTIE R. BLEVINS, SHANNON A. SANTANA, AND LEAH E. DAIGLE

INTRODUCTION

Contrary to the traditional image of college campuses as safe havens for young adults, college and university campuses are social domains in which criminal victimization occurs. In particular, research reveals that female students are exposed to high risks of sexual assault[1] and stalking (see Belknap & Erez, 2007; Fisher & Stewart, 2007; Fisher, Cullen, & Turner, 2000; Fisher, Sloan, Cullen, & Lu, 1998). For a substantial number of women, repeat sexual assault is a grim reality during their college years; these women experience a disproportionate amount of sexual assaults ranging from verbal threats to rape (Daigle, Fisher, & Cullen, 2006). Campus research documenting high levels of college student victimization, coupled with media accounts (including in *The Chronicle of Higher Education*) of heinous campus crimes, have stirred the public and the U.S. Congress to question whether campuses are less ivory towers and more "hot spots" for victimization (see Fisher et al., 1998; Mustaine & Tewksbury, 2007).

During the last 20 years, issues concerning the extent and nature of the sexual assault, including stalking, of college women have attracted much congressional attention. Several movements emerged independently that fueled Congress's initial attention. First, on the heels of the feminist movement, Koss, Gidycz, and Wisniewski's (1987) path-breaking national study established that each year, a sizable proportion of college women are sexually victimized. Second, an increasing number of the precedent-setting court decisions held institutions of higher education (IHEs) civilly liable for "foreseeable" crimes, including cases in which students had been raped (Burling, 2003). Third, college student safety advocates, such as Security On Campus, Inc., successfully documented and publicized campus disciplinary inactions in response to rape cases; campus rape reports being mishandled by school officials; and lax security that led to violent victimizations, most notably a few homicides (see Security On Campus, Inc., 2006).

In response to growing public pressure and lobbying by Security On Campus, Inc. and other interested parties in the early 1990s, Congress passed the *Student Right-to-Know and Campus Security Act* (20 U.S.C. 1092[f]) (see Carter & Bath, 2007; Sloan & Shoemaker, 2007, for state-level campus crime legislation). This legislation required all Title IV eligible IHEs to issue an annual security report in which they publicly disclose (1) crime statistics and (2) the crime prevention and security policies and procedures that are in effect on their campuses. Congress first amended the law in 1992 to require that IHEs afford victims specific rights, and again in 1998 to emphasize reporting obligations regarding sexual assault on campus.[2] The 1998 amendments also renamed the *Act* the *Jeanne Clery Disclosure of Campus Security Policy and Campus Crime Statistics Act* (Pub. L. 101-542) (henceforth known as the *Clery Act*).

The primary goal of the *Clery Act* is to require IHEs to develop and provide student safety prevention and response procedures as well as accurate safety and security information for each Title IV IHE. Proponents of the *Clery Act* believe that such information will furnish students and their parents with the basis to make informed decisions about safety and security risks on the campus the students now or will attend (see Shafer, 2007).

Despite the emergence of concern about sexual victimization among postsecondary students and the passage of the *Clery Act,* little systematic information or research exists concerning Title IV IHE compliance with the requirements to publish campus statistics on reported forcible and nonforcible sex offenses and the content of their institutions' sexual assault policies, protocols, and programs (see Gregory & Janosik, 2007). The current state of knowledge about IHEs compliance with the *Clery Act* is based primarily on single cases brought to the attention of the Department of Education–the federal agency with jurisdiction over the *Clery Act.*

In the late 1990s, Congress mandated a national-level study to examine responses by Title IV IHEs to reports of campus sexual assaults. Under Public Law 105–244, Congress specifically mandated that the ground-breaking research address nine issues. These issues covered a range of efforts mandated by the *Clery Act,* spanning from reporting of sexual offense statistics to sexual assault prevention programs to victim support services; sexual assault reporting and adjudication policies, procedures, and practices; perceived facilitators of and barriers to reporting; and adjudication follow-through in campus judicial and criminal courts. Among the goals was to provide baseline information about how IHEs address the sexual assault-related mandates of the *Clery Act.* This chapter draws on the results from the federally funded national-level Campus Sexual Assault Policy Study. Given the comprehensiveness of the Campus Sexual Assault Policy Study, this chapter presents only the results relating to reporting sexual assault.

The chapter begins with a brief overview of the National Campus Sexual Assault Policy Study (see Karjane, Fisher, & Cullen, 2002; 2005). We then discuss the *Clery Act* and its requirements for IHE's reporting of sex offenses that occur on their campuses. As we show, the statistics compiled under the *Clery Act* are inherently inaccurate because they include only those offenses that victims bring to the attention of law enforcement and campus officials and overlook the fact the vast majority of sexual victimizations are not reported. We then present statistics on the extent to which sexual offenses, namely rape, are underreported.

In the remainder of the chapter, we draw on the findings of the National Campus Sexual Assault Policy Study and related scholarly research in our efforts to explore why sexual victimization incidents are underreported. Specifically, we focus on two key issues: (1) factors affecting individuals' decisions not to report, and (2) the lack of sexual assault response training of students and campus officials as barriers to reporting. We also discuss policies and practices that might increase the reporting of sexual victimization. The chapter ends with a discussion of the challenges facing IHEs in their efforts to understand and encourage the reporting of sexual assault incidents.

The National Campus Sexual Assault Policy Study

In 2000, researchers at the University of Cincinnati, Education Development Center, Inc., and the Police Executive Research Forum undertook the Campus Sexual Assault Policy Study.[3] Along with examining compliance with the crime statistics reporting mandates of the *Clery Act,* the larger study also collected information about prevention, reporting procedures, response policies, and practices and protocols for dealing with incidents of sexual assault on campus aimed toward students (rather than students, staff, and faculty).

The sheer breadth and complexity of the issues included in the congressional mandate demanded a rigorous and multi-method research design with a large representative sample of IHEs and their administrators. The national sample was comprised of 2,438 IHEs in the United States and Puerto Rico, including all Historically Black Colleges and Universities (HBCUs; N=98) and all Native American tribal schools (N=28). All nine categories of schools eligible for Title IV funding were represented in the sample: four-year public, four-year private nonprofit, two- to four-year private for profit, two-year public, two-year private nonprofit, less-than-two-year public and private nonprofit, less-than-two-year private for profit, Native American tribal schools, and HBCUs. The final sample consisted of 1,015 IHEs and 1,001 campus administrators.

To investigate comprehensively the wide array of issues and institutional contexts mandated by Congress, the study collected and analyzed multiple forms of data. The data included: (1) results of a content analysis of published sexual assault policy material from a nationally representative sample of randomly selected IHEs,[4] (2) mail surveys of campus administrators from a nationally representative sample of IHEs,[5] (3) field research at eight IHEs determined to be demonstrating promising practices related to sexual assault prevention and response policies and protocols,[6] and (4) electronic focus groups conducted with campus administrators and advocates[7] (see Karjane et al., 2002, 2005). This chapter presents results drawn from these four sources of information and data.

The *Clery Act* Sex Offenses Reporting Requirements

The *Clery Act* crime classifications include murder; sex offenses; robbery; aggravated assault; burglary; motor vehicle theft; manslaughter; arson; and violations relating to alcohol, drugs, and weapons as defined by the Uniform Crime Reporting program (UCR) of the Federal Bureau of Investigation (see Carter & Bath, 2007). The *Clery Act* further requires institutions to distinguish between forcible and nonforcible sex offenses. Forcible sex offenses, defined as "any sexual act directed against another person, forcibly and/or against that person's will or not forcibly or against the person's will where the victim is incapable of giving consent," include forcible rape, forcible sodomy, sexual assault with an object, and forcible fondling. Nonforcible sex offenses, defined as "unlawful, nonforcible sexual intercourse," include incest and statutory rape. Of the schools that responded to our request for materials, 78 percent sent—as requested—their annual security reports (ASRs). The ASR is important because, under the *Clery Act,* Title IV-eligible institutions are required to report crime statistics, including separate statistics on forcible and nonforcible sex offenses as defined in the UCR. The large percentage of IHEs that sent their ASRs suggests that a large proportion of IHEs are complying with this aspect of the *Clery Act.*

Over eight in ten schools that provided ASRs included three years of crime statistics as mandated by the *Clery Act*. However, there was less compliance with the *Clery Act's* stipulation that IHEs divide sexual offenses into the categories "forcible" and "nonforcible." Only 37 percent of IHEs reported crime statistics in a manner fully consistent with the *Clery Act*. Nearly half (49%) of the four-year public schools and 43 percent of the four-year private nonprofit schools included forcible and nonforcible sexual offenses in their crime statistics. Between 19 percent and 31 percent of the other types of schools did not report separate statistics for forcible and nonforcible sexual offenses.

The *Clery Act* crime statistics mandate–the core idea of the *Clery Act*–relies exclusively on data that are based on official statistics, such as those reported in the Uniform Crime Report. These official statistics represent crimes known to and recorded by law enforcement. For IHEs, official statistics are those compiled by campus law enforcement, security departments, or campus officials, based on the reports by students or others (e.g., employees, visitors) victimized while on campus. The mandated reporting of specific crime statistics raises several important issues concerning the validity of these statistics, in particular sex offenses, as measures of the safety of any campus.

Underreporting Rape: Why Individuals Do Not Report Their Victimization

The Extent of Underreporting Rape

Complicating the effective application of the *Clery Act* is underreporting of sexual assaults by victims to campus officials. This underreporting results in gross underestimates of the "true" amount of on-campus sexual offenses. Indeed, the research literature consistently documents the widespread phenomenon of underreporting of rape and other types of sexual assault (see Fisher, Daigle, Cullen, & Turner, 2003a; 2003b). For example, the Sexual Victimization of College Women Study reported that less than 5 percent of rape victims officially reported the incident to campus and/or law enforcement authorities (see Fisher et al. 2000, 2003a; 2003b).

The Victim-Offender Relationship

Researchers also have consistently documented that female college students are far more likely to report rape by a stranger than by a friend or classmate. However, contrary to cultural myths regarding rape, stranger rape represents only a small fraction of the on-campus rapes of students–men known to the victim perpetrate the vast majority of these offenses (see Belknap & Erez, 2007). To illustrate, the Sexual Victimization of College Women Study reported that rape victims knew their attacker as fellow classmates (36%), friends (34%), boyfriends or former boyfriends (24%), or acquaintances (3%). Underreporting by victims of acquaintance sexual assault is one of the most, if not the most, significant factors in low reporting rates on IHE campuses (Fisher et al., 2000).

Individuals' Reasons for Not Reporting

A substantial majority of these victims do not define their experiences using legal terms. That is, even though the incident is legally a criminal offense, they do not call their victimization a "rape" (see Fisher et al., 2003b). This is particularly true when weapons are absent, alcohol is present, and/or physical injury (e.g., choke marks, bruises) is not apparent–the characteristics that are most often found in nonstranger rapes (Bondurant, 2001). Victims not identifying and naming events that meet legal definitions of rape and sexual assault has serious implications for reporting campus sexual assault since one must conceptualize an event as a crime before she (or he) seeks justice.

Victims of rape may not report the violence for a range of reasons. To illustrate, results from the National College Women Sexual Victimization Study indicated that the most common reasons given for not reporting a completed rape included: (1) not thinking it was serious enough (65%); (2) not wanting others to know (47%); (3) not wanting family to know (44%); (4) not clear a crime had occurred or harm was intended (44%); and (5) lack of proof (42%). College women gave some similar reasons and some different reasons as to why they did not report an attempted rape. These reasons included: (1) not thinking it was serious enough to report (77%), (2) not clear a crime had occurred or that harm was intended (40%), (3) believing that the police would not think the incident was serious enough (34%), (4) not wanting other people to know (32%), (5) not wanting family to know (32%). Noteworthy is that not knowing how to report a rape was cited as a reason for not reporting in 14 percent of the completed rape incidents and in 7 percent of the attempted rape incidents (Fisher et al., 2000; 2003a).

Lack of Sexual Assault Response
Training as a Barrier to Reporting

College Students

Another factor that may contribute to low reporting rates among college students may be the lack of responsiveness of IHEs in handling disclosures and formal complaints of sexual assault. In many cases, those who first hear of the sexual assault–whether they are Resident Assistants (RAs), faculty, staff, or other students–are not adequately trained to respond to students' disclosure and to make appropriate referrals, including recommending medical and mental health services and filing a formal complaint (Bohmer, 1993). Results from the campus administrator survey of the Campus Sexual Assault Policy Study revealed that overall, 42 percent of the schools provided sexual assault reporting training for students, with over half of four-year public and private nonprofit schools (77% and 65%, respectively) and HBCUs (61%) doing so. In about half of the IHEs (51%) who provide training, the training is voluntary. In another 45 percent of the IHEs, this training is mandatory for student RAs. In a small percentage of IHEs (14%), training was mandatory for student security officers. Most often (64%), faculty and staff of the institution provide the sexual assault response training, though it can also involve staff from a community agency (40%) or peer educator or trainer (23%). In IHEs where RAs and student security officers receive mandatory training, this is largely due to institutional rules rather than to state laws (see Karjane et al., 2002, Table 4.1).

What remains unclear from these data, however, is the extent and quality of sexual assault response training given to the average college student–precisely the people most likely to learn about sexual assaults. Again, about 60 percent of the schools provide no training whatsoever to students, and it appears that when training occurs, the IHE directs it most often at RAs and student security officers. Accordingly, it seems institutional lack of training for an average student is an issue that warrants further attention and action by college administrators.

Law Enforcement or Security Officers

When asked about security or law enforcement, almost half the campus administrators (48%) stated that they rely on local law enforcement agencies. Other options chosen by administrators (who could select more than one option) were sworn officers employed by the school (28%) and private security employed by the school (8%). Sworn officers were common at four-year public schools and HBCUs (84% and 75%, respectively), and private security was more common at two- and four-year private nonprofit schools. A majority of the remaining five types of schools relied on local law enforcement agencies (see Karjane et al., 2002, Table 4.2).

In any event, when asked if campus law enforcement/security officers are "required by law or institutional policy to be trained to respond to reports of sexual assault," just over one-third (38%) of all campus administrators answered in the affirmative. The figures were higher for four-year public schools (more than 8 in 10) and HBCUs (more than 7 in 10). About half of the four-year private nonprofit and two-year public schools stated that they required training. The key finding here is that while training is fairly standard at four-year public schools and HBCUs which rely primarily on sworn officers employed by the school, at many other institutions *it is not provided to the very people who are most likely to receive formal complaints.*

Although school administrators indicated that a variety of sources provide this training, IHEs most often rely on the state training academy (39%), which presumably provides training of a general nature to law enforcement personnel who will serve in a variety of social settings. How specific this training is to the reporting of sexual victimization by college students is unknown. Other common sources of training for law enforcement/security personnel–each used by about one in five schools–include the faculty or staff of the institution (23%), the faculty or staff of the law enforcement/security agency (22%), and specialized trainers (19%) (Karjane et al., 2002, Table 4.2).

Faculty and Staff

Another source whom students may confide in about their sexual assault is faculty and staff. The survey of campus administrators also furnished information on the training given to the IHEs' faculty and staff. About half of all schools–including three in ten public four-year schools–provide no training to faculty and staff on "how to respond to disclosures of sexual assault." Training is mandatory in about one in three schools and voluntary in 17% of the schools. When the training is required across all the schools, this is most often due to mandatory institutional policy. Finally, when offered, faculty and staff of the institution provide the training (Karjane et al., 2002, Table 4.3).

Barriers to Reporting Identified from Survey of Campus Administrators

Reporting Options

Reporting options also could influence whether or not students report their sexual assault to campus officials. Analysis of the campus administrator surveys revealed that IHEs utilize a variety of reporting options: confidential, anonymous, third-party, and (anonymous) Internet reporting. A majority (84%) of all school types offer a confidential reporting option. And less than half of the small, nonresidential, nontraditional school types offered an anonymous reporting option and slightly more than half of four-year public and private schools (52%) and HBCUs (51%) did the same. Only a small fraction of schools (4%) offered anonymous Internet reports. This finding is salient because the recognition of an anonymous reporting option was found to be a promising practice as well as a policy that student activists, rape trauma professionals, and victim's advocates believed would facilitate reporting of the crime (see Karjane et al. 2002, Table 4.A and Chapter 8).

Also salient is the finding that third-party reporting by witnesses is recognized at only one in three schools, roughly, and only slightly more than half (53%) of four-year public IHEs offered this option. Given Fisher and her colleagues' (2000; 2003a) finding that most victims disclose their experience to their friends but do not report the crime to campus or local law enforcement authorities, the omission significantly impacts reporting rates of sexual assault.

Institutional Barriers

The National Campus Sexual Assault Policy Study also asked campus administrators about the types of institutional policies that might function to discourage or prevent reporting of sexual assaults on their campuses. Two important factors emerged from their responses. First, more than 80 percent of campus administrators indicated that the requirement that victims who file sexual assault complaints must participate in the adjudication process at least "somewhat" discourages victims from reporting the assaults. This insight is consistent with site visit data as well as with research on female sexual assault victims and their low incidence of reporting these assaults to the police (Fisher et al., 2000, 2003a; National Victims Center, 1992). As previously noted, Fisher and her colleagues' (2000) research suggests that female college students do not want their families and other people to know about the victimization, are not certain they can prove that a victimization occurred, and are not convinced that the incident was "serious enough" to warrant a formal intervention. In this light, victims faced with participating in an adjudication process might not report a sexual assault if they wished to avoid public disclosure, were doubtful about proving they were assaulted, and/or did not believe that a formal hearing was the appropriate way to resolve the victimization.

The question remains, however, over the extent victims are informed of (1) their choices regarding informally and formally reporting their assault to campus and/or local criminal justice authorities and (2) how their confidentiality will be protected, if at all, in each type of action taken. Qualitative data collected in this study strongly suggest that any policy or procedure that compromises or, worse, eliminates the student victim's ability to make her or his own informed choices throughout the reporting and adjudication process not only reduces reporting rates, but may also be counterproductive to the victim's healing process. A second factor worth noting is the presence of a campus drug and/or alcohol policy. Typically, the aggressor and victim know each other and the assault frequently emerges from a social encounter in which one or both are drinking or drugging (see Abbey, Zawacki, Buck, Clinton, & McAuslan, 2004). If student victims know that they are in violation of a policy forbidding the use of drugs or alcohol, this might make them fearful to report a sexual assault.

Intrinsically related to this concern is the issue of victims' acknowledging (or failing to acknowledge) their assault as a crime. Research shows that drugs and/or alcohol are frequently present (and used by both perpetrators and victims) when college women are sexually assaulted (see Abbey et al., 2004; Dowdall, 2007). Victims of rape and attempted rape who were drinking before the assault are far less apt to name their experience "rape" or "sexual assault" than victims who did not drink before the assault (Bondurant, 2001; Schwartz & Leggett, 1999). If victims do not name their experience, they do not have a crime to report. Thus, while an association between drinking and campus sexual assault may involve a school's alcohol and drug policies, the two are analytically distinct.

Barriers to Reporting Identified from Field Research

Qualitative interviews with rape crisis counselors, sexual assault nurse examiners, victim's advocates, deans of students, and students themselves provided further insight into the reporting barriers issue. Again, these and related issues are situated within the context of the existing scholarship.

Developmental Issues

Students attending postsecondary institutions, especially traditional schools, are generally between the ages of 18 and 24. Developmentally, these young adults are testing themselves and their new (partial) independence from their parents. These youth feel like they can take care of themselves, or at least feel they should show their parents that they can. Experiencing a sexual assault may make them feel like they have failed to protect themselves, in the midst of their first autonomous living situation. Reporting the incident makes it more real because doing so documents their "failure," while involvement with high-risk behavior, such as drinking or drug use, further exacerbates this feeling.

Trauma Response Issues

Women who experience events that meet the legal definition of sexual assault frequently do not label their victimization as such, particularly when weapons are absent, alcohol is present, and/or physical injury (e.g., choke marks, bruises) is not apparent–the predominant scenario for nonstranger rape (Bondurant, 2001). While some victims deliberately minimize the importance of the assault as a way of mitigating its impact, most victims cannot avoid a traumatic response to what happened to them (Herman, 1992; Karjane, 2002; Kelly, 1988). Whether acknowledged or not, victims of sexual assault may experience intense feelings of shame and self-blame and high levels of psychological distress (see Belknap & Erez, 2007; Karjane, 2002).

Shame is the emotional response to a perceived or actual threat to social bonds (Scheff & Retzinger, 1991). Tragically, for student victims, the fear they have that people will hold them responsible for their own sexual victimization may be warranted. Widespread tolerance for rape and sexual assault in intimate relationships, both in the general population and among college students, helps a "blame the victim" attitude to flourish (Kershner, 2000; Kopper, 1996; Kormos & Brooks, 1994; Stormo, Lang, & Stritzke, 1997). Institutional authorities may (unintentionally) condone victim blaming (for example, by circulating materials that focus on the victim's responsibility to avoid sexual assault rather than on the perpetrator), and certainly the mass media play a part. Students, both prior and subsequent to being sexually victimized, can internalize these attitudes, further exacerbating their own sense of shame and stigmatization and inhibiting their ability to name their experience—and thus making an informed decision to report the assault more difficult. Researchers have even found higher levels of self-blame among victims of acquaintance rape than among victims of stranger rape (Frazier & Seales, 1997; Katz, 1991). Studies also show that student victims of on campus acquaintance rape are far less likely to report their victimization to campus authorities than are victims of campus stranger rape (see Belknap & Erez, 2007).

Research has shown that the victim's ability to name the experience is dependent on the reactions of those to whom she or he first discloses the assault (Bondurant, 2001; Pitts & Schwartz, 1997; Schwartz & DeKeseredy, 1997). When asked during field research interviews what distinguishes those who report from those who do not report, victim advocates, police officers, and campus officials uniformly asserted that victims who report are encouraged to do so by their friends, who frequently accompany them when they make the report to campus and/or criminal justice authorities.

Finally, having just experienced a profoundly disempowering event, victims of sexual assault need to reassert control over basic aspects of their lives and environments (Herman, 1992; Janoff-Bulman, 1992). One way to regain this control is to avoid a lengthy adjudication process—whether through the campus or the criminal justice system—that threatens to dominate the victim's college experience. Some victims believe that if they keep the assault to themselves, they can focus on their academics and maintain their original reason for attending school. In addition, due to a lack of accurate knowledge about the system, victims fear that they will have no control over the reporting and adjudication process, for example, that their confidentiality will not be honored. Student victims often do not realize that reporting a rape or sexual assault is different from pursuing the case criminally or through campus adjudication boards. This need to regain control is an important part of the healing process for the victim; reporting policies that disempower the victim—such as mandatory reporting requirements that do not include an anonymous reporting option—are widely viewed by sexual assault advocates as detrimental to this healing process.

Socio-political and Social Support Issues

In terms of the politics of interpersonal relations, gender politics play a large role in social support. Self-acknowledgement of the rape politicizes the relationship in ways that make it difficult for many people to comprehend what happened (e.g., "he is my friend," "he cares about me," "he raped me") and to recognize themselves as victims of a crime (Karjane, 2002). Overall, assault victims' peers and professors often know the perpetrators. When the victim acknowledges and names the experience "rape" or "sexual assault," the victim is often, at the same time, naming a friend, boyfriend, or classmate a "criminal"—a "rapist." Historically, this act has different meanings and consequences for a white woman naming a white man a rapist and for a black woman naming a black man a rapist. As the criminal justice system incarcerates black men at highly disproportional rates than white men, black women often have to contend with feelings of betraying their race in ways that white and other ethnic minority women do not have to contend with (Crenshaw, 1991; Neville & Pugh, 1997; Wyatt, 1992).

Furthermore, whether victims of sexual assault see themselves as "victims" or as people who have been victimized but retain the ability to willfully act and protect themselves, the social conventions and institutional contexts within which they must name and claim their experience often construct them as victims. As such, others who know they have been raped perceive them as victims. Given that the social definition of "victim" entails a perception of a person who is weak, pitiful, and often blameworthy, and that these assumptions are taken to reflect a life stance rather than an experience, it is not surprising that people would seek to avoid the label of "rape victim" (Karjane, 2002).

Within IHEs, when allegations of rape and sexual assault occur, rumor often becomes the source of information, and campuses may become polarized. This is particularly true when campus, local, and national media cover the trial. Students fear that "ratting" on another student by filing a report with campus or local criminal justice authorities will result in social isolation or, worse, social ostracism. Based on field research, this fear appears to be especially strong at institutions with strong social cliques, such as campuses dominated by Greek life.

As one administrator described it, the campus works "like a microcosm of society where victims get punished for reporting." There does seem to be slight progress, at least among the schools noted to have promising practices regarding sexual assault response, in changing social attitudes toward non-stranger rape. In previous years, the frequent phrase used to describe–and condone–the criminal act of rape was "boys will be boys." Such a phrase negated the victim's perspective altogether, while it conflated a masculine perspective with a rapist's perspective. In essence, the phrase classified forms of criminal activity as normative in heterosexual relations.

Today, administrators almost uniformly use the phrase "It's a he said, she said situation," which acknowledges a (female) victim's perspective, yet still functions to trivialize the crime. This phrase is used by administrators to mean that evidence–forensic and even circumstantial–is frequently absent in sexual assaults committed by "dates" or acquaintances, thus, the two versions of the events must be weighed against each other to establish truth. While certainly an improvement over "boys will be boys," this phrase implies a false equality to the perspectives, thus trivializing the victim's experience.

In the face of this perceptual shift, it is disturbing that the National Campus Sexual Assault Policy Study reported that once a student files a complaint of a sexual assault, only 26 percent of IHEs had an investigation or fact-finding stage for the gathering of information to determine if there is sufficient evidence to decide whether a sexual misconduct code violation has occurred. Lack of a fact-finding stage to gather evidence before a complaint moves to review during a hearing by the adjudication board or another decision-making entity almost inevitably means that the vast majority of complaints of sexual assault stay at the level of the proverbial "he said, she said." It is highly likely, given the importance victims place on their own credibility, that this institutional barrier negatively influences victim-reporting decisions.

Confidentiality Issues

Given the loss of personal control the victim has just experienced, coupled with the way society perceives and individuals respond to "victims," confidentiality issues–that is, how or whether information regarding the student's victimization will circulate throughout the campus–function as important barriers to reporting and following through with adjudication procedures. As such, the use of mandatory reporting (both on campus and in the community), and establishment of reporting Memorandums of Understanding (MOU) between a school and its local prosecutor's office that preclude the victim's consent, are policies that create barriers to reporting, based on site visits.

In one national survey, 50 percent of women rape victims responded that they would be "a lot" more likely and 16 percent would be "somewhat" more likely to report to the police if there were a law prohibiting the news media from disclosing their names and addresses (National Victims Center, 1992). Similarly, on postsecondary campuses, field research found that any policy or procedure that students (particularly student victims) perceived as a risk to their ability to control information about their victimization functioned as a barrier to reporting.

Criminal Justice Issues

While rape reform efforts in the United States have been somewhat successful in eradicating myths about stranger rape and their institutionalization within the criminal justice system, we have only just begun to acknowledge the far more prevalent problem of rape among acquaintances and intimates. As such, student victims still fear unsympathetic treatment by the police and local prosecutors, which inhibits them from reporting their criminal victimization.

Compounding this fear is the legal quandary of many acquaintance rape cases: lack of evidence to substantiate the crime. If a prosecutor is reticent or, more frequently, refuses outright to bring an acquaintance rape case to trial without sufficient evidence, victims often take that to mean the prosecutor does not believe their story. Furthermore, as one victim advocate from a sheriff's office observed, distrust of law enforcement is especially prevalent within some age and ethnic groups "because they're dealing with a criminal justice system that isn't [just] and a playing field that isn't level."

Student victims of campus sexual assault, especially when someone they know perpetrates the assault, do not report, in part, because they do not believe the criminal justice system will punish the perpetrator. While this perception is somewhat accurate–given the slim likelihood of a perpetrator known to the victim being held accountable by the criminal justice system–IHEs are potentially more likely to punish perpetrators, as campus adjudication boards often operate with a preponderance of evidence standard rather than the legal standard of "beyond a reasonable doubt." This empirical issue deserves more attention.

Finally, treatment and forensic evidence collection by a certified sexual assault nurse examiner, when available, is almost always, because of funding structures, contingent on first filing a police report of the crime. Rape trauma professionals see the lack of choice involved in this policy as a barrier to reporting. The state-of-the-art Rape Treatment Center at the Santa Monica–UCLA Medical Center offers free treatment to all victims, whether or not they file a police report first. The preservation of forensic evidence occurs through a chain of custody established in consultation with the Los

Angeles crime lab and the evidence is stored indefinitely so it will be available if the victim ever wishes to pursue criminal charges. Director Gail Abarbanel says that giving the victim the choice of receiving treatment before filing the report frequently results in the victim filing a police report of the crime—the act of being treated and seeing that there is preservation of evidence of the crime seems to be a turning point.

Policies and Practices That Facilitate Reporting Victimization

Facilitators Identified through Campus Administrators' Survey

The project also asked campus administrators about the types of institutional policies that might function to encourage sexual assault reporting. Two findings emerge from these data. First, administrators believe that policies like providing services to potential victims, strategies to make campus personnel more responsive to reports of sexual assault, confidential reporting by victims, and targeted educational programs (for example, to fraternities and student-athletes) encourage reporting. If they are correct, then IHEs could combine a variety of strategies into a multimodal approach to increase the likelihood of victims reporting their assaults. Confirmation as to whether students in general and victims in particular see these factors as salient to the reporting decision remains. Still, the insights of the administrators, at the very least, suggest strategies that might actually facilitate reporting.

Second, but on a less optimistic note, it appears that a large number of campuses do not have many of these policies in place. The exceptions are four-year public schools and HBCUs, where such policies are relatively common. Of these, the administrators' survey results revealed that only six policies are in place in more than half the campuses: confidential reporting options (84%), new student orientation programs on sexual assault issues (68%), providing faculty and staff with information on who can help victims (67%), campus law enforcement protocols for responding to sexual assaults (52%), campus-wide publicity of high-risk factors and/or past crimes on campus (51%), and a coordinated crisis response across the campus and community to provide victim services (50%). Noteworthy is that only three policies (confidential reporting, new student orientation programs, and providing faculty and staff with information) are in place in two-thirds of these campuses.

Facilitators Identified through Field Research

IHE administrators and rape response professionals perceived additional policies, protocols, and practices as facilitating the reporting of campus rape and sexual assault.

EDUCATION AND SOCIAL SUPPORTS. Conversations with student rape response team members, educators/activists, and victim advocates revealed three main facilitators for reporting: on-campus presentations, information dissemination, and social support. Response team members noted that actively courting invitations for sexual assault-oriented presentations at ethnic and sexual minority group organizations increased reports, especially in the weeks immediately following the presentations. Such presentations can target the particular cultural myths surrounding rape and sexual assault in terms of prevalent community norms. Student educators/activists observed that students get the majority of their information through the World Wide Web, word of mouth, and education programs provided by RAs. Therefore, disseminating information on what constitutes a violation of the school's sexual misconduct policy, describing administrative responses and sanctions, and, in particular, publicizing the knowledge that filing a report is different from pressing charges should increase reporting on campus.

As previously noted, victim advocates state that the primary characteristic that distinguishes victims who report their assaults and access professional services and those who do not is the support they receive from their friends—who often accompany them to make the report. As one victim advocate noted, "Sometimes whole groups of kids come; they come with their posse." Witnesses who see the crime occur—or have a strong sense that a crime is about to occur—can provide social support to the victim, encourage the victim to make a report, or make a third-party report of their own. Experts can also train witnesses in techniques to interrupt the behavior.

AN ANONYMOUS REPORTING OPTION. There was strong agreement among field interviewees that an anonymous reporting option increases reporting of campus sexual assault. A primary strength of this option is that the victim can seek out assistance, information, and support referrals without first having to take the step of identifying her- or himself and formally entering a system the victim does not yet have enough information to effectively negotiate. The anonymous reporting option allows student victims to come forward and talk to a trusted school official without the possibility of losing control of the process (e.g., mandated reporters at schools that do not offer anonymous reporting). This option allows victims to receive support and information on which to base informed decisions about filing a report in their own name, while ASR statistics would also allow documentation of the offense even if the student feels uncomfortable making a report.

A VICTIM-DRIVEN POLICY. An anonymous reporting option is a good example of a victim-driven policy. Sexual assault policies that emphasize criminal justice imperatives (e.g., to report disclosures of the crime against the victim's wishes) or higher education imperatives (e.g., to maintain the school's image as a safe haven) at the expense of the immediate and long-term needs of the rape victim are highly problematic. Policies that respect the victim's need (and ability) to make his or her own decision at each and every juncture in the process of seeking information, support, treatment, and, possibly, justice within the campus and/or the criminal justice system have been found to facilitate students coming forth and reporting the crime. As such, students and student victims ideally should receive explicit information about what to expect in each step of the process of seeking help from school authorities. Publicizing information on how the different components of the school's sexual assault and reporting policies relate, are contingent on, or are separate from one another was also found to increase reporting. For example, providing students with information that explains that reporting an assault to campus authorities is different from going forward with an adjudication board hearing or campus and criminal prosecution within the justice system.

Based on these findings, the challenge is two-fold. First, institutions should undertake systematic evaluations to see which policies—whether alone or in combination—increase the very low rate of reporting sexual assaults that now exists. Second, institutions should publish effective policies and combinations of strategies to campus administrators across the nation. One option would be to develop a model sexual assault reporting document that outlines the best strategies—based on empirical evidence—for fostering the reporting of sexual victimizations.

Conclusion

The impetus for student-victim-oriented congressional legislation throughout the 1990s, such as the *Clery Act,* was to ensure that IHEs employ strategies to prevent and respond to reports of sexual assault on campus in a proactive manner and to provide current and prospective students and their parents with an accurate idea of the level of violence on campuses. Both national studies and smaller-scale research have consistently found that one in five female students suffer rape and/or rape attempts during their college years, most frequently at the hands of their peers. As such, prevention, reporting, and response policies should be built on definitions of sexual assault that make it clear that people known to the victim most frequently commit this crime.

A key issue confronted by postsecondary institutions is that the vast majority of students who experience sexual assaults—on and off campus—do not report them to campus or law enforcement officials. The reasons for not reporting victimizations, as discussed in this chapter, are complex and unlikely to be fully overcome (Fisher et al., 2003a). The college community is affected by this underreporting in at least two significant ways.

First, victims of sexual assault are unlikely to secure the counseling and support they need to cope with and heal from this potentially traumatic event in their lives making it more probable that they will engage in "self-blame," self-medication (e.g., disordered eating and excessive drinking), and other self-destructive behaviors. Disclosing their experience to friends also likely affects them, as they may develop their own feelings of anger, fear, and/or helplessness. In this way, one sexual assault can have a ripple effect. Second, and of crucial importance unless sexual assaults are reported, students who sexually assault their classmates will not be subjected to appropriate disciplinary sanctions. Recent research on the "undetected rapist" on college campuses, that is those men who commit rape and are never reported to any authority, suggests that a majority of these unsanctioned rapists will go on to sexually victimize others, or the same person (Lisak & Miller, 2002).

Issues discussed in this chapter concerning the act of reporting a sexual assault raised other pertinent issues that campus administrators as well as campus safety advocates should proactively address (see Shafer, 2007). First, response and reporting policies should be designed to allow victims as much decision-making authority in the process as possible. Victims fear losing control over the reporting and adjudication processes, which is a barrier to their coming forth and making the initial reports. Institutions should design policies to allow victims to make the decision about moving forward, stopping, or slowing down the pace at each juncture of the disclosure, reporting, and adjudication process. Institutions should make explicit to victims information regarding the policy and its different components—and the decisions victims make at each juncture—to inform her or his decisions. The institution should also inform victims of how each juncture in the process affects confidentiality.

Second, adjudication hearings should be fair. Victims of campus crime often seek acknowledgment of and justice for their experience; they seek respect within the campus system. One way to ensure that respect is to provide campus adjudication hearings that are fair to both parties. Operational rules and responsibilities should be explicit, unbiased, communicated to both parties, and adhered to. Current litigation instigated by students found responsible for sexual misconduct often centers on due process rights not being consistently applied.[8] As these suits threaten the validity of the board's determination of responsibility, they also compromise the needs of student sexual assault victims.

Third, response and reporting policies and policy materials should be gender-neutral and refer to the person who has experienced an assault as a "survivor," the term used by many victims of sexual assault in an effort to reclaim their lives. This term connotes the strength of living through and beyond the traumatic experience as opposed to focusing on any implied weakness in not being able to adequately protect oneself. Response policies should provide strategies to empower victims, rather than revictimize them by taking choices away or withholding information.

Fourth, sexual assault protocols and policies should be widely distributed every term, written in lay terms, and explicitly supported by the administration so that all students are aware of their rights and options before they need the system. Distribution of materials should be made every term to ensure that students (and faculty and staff) are reminded of their rights and options.

Addressing the reporting issues discussed in this chapter, as well as implementing and evaluating the recommendations outlined, are two critical steps toward better understanding of campus sexual assault within the context of college students' experiences. Not until institutions and supporters of the *Clery Act* rely on evidence-based understanding to inform campus policies and programs can they take successful steps to ensure campus safety.

Notes

1. Federal reporting requirements define "rape" as a set of crimes that constitute nonconsensual forcible or nonforcible sexual penetration (e.g., unwilling forcible vaginal intercourse). In recent years, rape reform law has moved toward expanding the definition of rape to include various forms of sexual abuse and degrees of severity (e.g., forcible nonconsensual oral intercourse; nonforcible, nonconsensual fondling). This expansion has taken place through the codification of multiple forms of sexual abuse in federal and state law. The term "sexual assault" refers to a range of sexually-oriented criminal acts defined federally by the Federal Bureau of Investigation as well as by state statute. Rape is a form of sexual assault.

2. More recently, Congress enacted the *Campus Sex Crime Prevention Act* on October 28, 2000. The study's results do not include changes pertaining to this act because the changes did not go into effect until October 28, 2002.

3. This project was supported by Grant No. 1999–WA–VX–0008 awarded by the National Institute of Justice, Office of Justice Program, U.S. Department of Justice. Points of view in this chapter are those of the authors and do not necessarily represent the official position or policies of the U.S. Department of Justice.

4. The policy materials response rate ranged from 20 percent (two- and four-year private for profit IHEs) to 88 percent (four-year public IHEs) (average response rate, 42%) (see Karjane et al., 2002, Table 2-5).

5. The survey of campus administrators response rate ranged from 29 percent (two- and four-year for profit IHEs) to 54 percent (four-year public IHEs) (average response rate, 41%) (see Karjane et al., 2002, Table 2-6).

6. See Karjane et al., 2002 pages 32–40 for description of the field research, including selection criteria, and names and location of the eight IHEs.

7. The study used various means to recruit focus group participants. Recruitment of health care professionals occurred through the Student Health Services' on-line mailing list operated by the American College Health Association. Selection of

campus law enforcement professionals occurred via a list maintained by the Police Executive Research Forum and via individual e-mail invitations. Finally, the study used "word of mouth" to recruit residence life directors. A notice was also posted on the DISCUSS on-line mailing list, a "members only" forum maintained by the Association for Student Judicial Affairs and the American College Personnel Association.

8. The Campus Sexual Assault Policy Study reported that only 37 percent of IHEs offer procedures for due process for those accused of sexual assault.

REFERENCES

Abbey, A., Zawacki, T., Buck P., Clinton, M., & McAuslan P. (2004). Sexual assault and alcohol consumption: What do we know about their relationship and what types of research are still needed? *Aggression and Violent Behavior, 9*, 271–303.

Belknap, J., & Erez, E. (2007). The sexual harassment, rape, and intimate partner abuse of college women. In B. S. Fisher & J. J. Sloan (Eds.), *Campus crime: Legal, social and policy perspectives* (2nd ed.). Springfield, IL: Charles C Thomas.

Bohmer, C., & Parrot, A. (1993). *Sexual assault on campus: The problem and the solution.* New York: Lexington Books.

Bondurant, B. (2001). University women's acknowledgement of rape: Individual, situational, and social factors. *Violence Against Women, 7*, 294–314.

Burling, P. (2003). *Crime on campus: Analyzing and managing the increasing risk of institutional liability* (2nd ed.). Washington D.C.: National Association of College and University Attorneys.

Carter, S., & Bath, C. (2007). The Evolution and components of the *Jeanne Clery Act:* Implications for higher education. In B. S. Fisher & J. J. Sloan (Eds.), *Campus crime: Legal, social and policy perspectives* (2nd ed.). Springfield, IL: Charles C Thomas.

Crenshaw, K. (1991). Mapping the margins: Intersectionality, identity politics, and violence against women of color. *Stanford Law Review, 43*, 1241–1299.

Daigle, L., Fisher, B., & Cullen, F. (2006) The repeat sexual and violent victimization of college women: Is it a problem? Working paper, University of Cincinnati Division of Criminal Justice. Cincinnati, Ohio.

Dowdall, G. (2007). The role of alcohol abuse in college student victimization. In B. S. Fisher & J. J. Sloan (Eds.), *Campus crime: Legal, social and policy perspectives* (2nd ed.). Springfield, IL: Charles C Thomas.

Fisher, B., Cullen, F., & Turner, M. (2000). *The sexual victimization of college women.* Washington, DC: National Institute of Justice and Bureau of Justice Statistics.

Fisher, B., Daigle, L., Cullen, F., & Turner, M. (2003a). Reporting sexual victimization to the police and others: Results from a national-level study of college women. *Criminal Justice and Behavior, 30*, 6–38.

Fisher, B., Daigle, L., Cullen, F., & Turner, M. (2003b). Acknowledging sexual victimization as rape: Results from a national-level study. *Justice Quarterly, 20*, 401–440.

Fisher, B., Sloan, J., Cullen, F., & Lu, C. (1998). Crime in the ivory tower: The level and sources of student victimization. *Criminology, 36*, 671–710.

Fisher, B., & Stewart, M. (2007). Vulnerabilities and opportunities 101: The extent, nature, and impact of stalking among college students and implications for campus policy and programs. In B. S. Fisher & J. J. Sloan (Eds.), *Campus crime: Legal, social and policy perspectives* (2nd ed.). Springfield, IL: Charles C Thomas.

Frazier, P., & Seales, L. (1997). Acquaintance rape is real rape. In M. D. Schwartz (Ed.), *Researching sexual violence against women: Methodological and personal perspectives* (pp. 54–64). Thousand Oaks, CA: Sage.

Gregory, D., & Janosik, S. (2007). Research on the Clery Act and its impact on higher education administrative practice. In B. S. Fisher & J. J. Sloan (Eds.), *Campus crime: Legal, social and policy perspectives* (2nd ed.). Springfield, IL: Charles C Thomas.

Herman, J. (1992). *Trauma and recovery: The aftermath of violence, from domestic abuse to political terror.* New York: Basic Books.

Janoff-Bulman, R. (1992). *Shattered assumptions: Toward a new psychology of trauma.* New York: The Free Press.

Kahn, A., & Andreoli Mathie, V. (2000). Understanding the unacknowledged rape victim. In C. Travis & J. White (Eds.), *Sexuality, society, and feminism* (pp. 377–403). Washington, DC: American Psychological Association.

Kahn, A., Andreoli Mathie, V., & Torgler, C. (1994). Rape scripts and rape acknowledgment. *Psychology of Women Quarterly, 18*, 53–66.

Karjane, H. (2002). The communication of trauma in media culture: A Poststructural analysis of women's experience of gender-based violence and healing. Doctoral dissertation, University of Massachusetts at Amherst, 2002. *Dissertation Abstracts International, 63*, 3407.

Karjane, H., Fisher, B., & Cullen, F. (2002). Campus sexual assault: How America's institutions of higher education respond. Final Report, NIJ Grant No. 99-WA-VX-0008. Retrieved February 13, 2007, from http://www.ncjrs.org/pdffiles1/nij/grants/196676.pdf.

Karjane, H., Fisher, B., & Cullen, F. (2005). *Sexual assault on campus: What colleges and universities are doing about it.* United States Department of Justice, NIJ Research for Practice Series. Retrieved February 13, 2007, from http://www.ncjrs.gov/pdf files1/nij/205521.pdf.

Katz, B. (1991). The psychological impact of stranger versus nonstranger rape on victims' recovery. In A. Parrot & L. Bechhofer (Eds.), *Acquaintance rape: The hidden crime* (pp. 251–269). New York: John Wiley & Sons.

Kelly, L. (1988). *Surviving sexual violence.* Minneapolis, MN: University of Minnesota Press.

Kershner, R. (2000). Adolescents' beliefs about rape: A preliminary study. *The Prevention Researcher, 7*, 8–9.

Kopper, B. (1996). Gender, gender identity, rape myth acceptance, and time of initial resistance on the perception of acquaintance rape blame and avoidability. *Sex Roles, 34*, 81–93.

Kormos, K. C., & Brooks, C. I. (1994). Acquaintance rape: Attributions of victim blame by college students and prison inmates as a function of relationship status of victim and assailant. *Psychological Reports, 74,* 545–546.

Koss, M., Dinero, T., Seibel, C., & Cox, S. (1988). Stranger and acquaintance rape: Are there differences in the victims' experience? *Psychology of Women Quarterly, 12,* 1–24.

Koss, M., Gidycz, C., & Wisniewski, N. (1987). The scope of rape: Incidence and prevalence of sexual aggression and victimization in a national sample of higher education students. *Journal of Consulting and Clinical Psychology, 55*(2), 162–170.

Lisak, D., & Miller, P. M. (2002). Repeat rape and multiple offending among undetected rapists. *Violence & Victims, 17,* 73–84.

Mustaine E., & Tewksbury, R. (2007). The routine activities and criminal victimization of students: Lifestyle and related factors. In B. S. Fisher & J. J. Sloan (Eds.), *Campus crime: Legal, social and policy perspectives* (2nd ed.). Springfield, IL: Charles C Thomas.

National Victims Center (1992). *Rape in America: A report to the nation.* Crime Victims Research and Treatment Center, Charleston, SC: Medical University of South Carolina.

Neville, H., & Pugh, A. (1997). General and culture-specific factors influencing African American women's reporting patterns and perceived social support following sexual assault. *Violence Against Women, 3,* 361–381.

Pitts, V., & Schwartz, M. (1997). Self-blame in hidden rape cases. In M. Schwartz (Ed.), *Researching sexual violence against women: Methodological and personal perspectives* (pp. 65–70). Thousand Oaks, CA: Sage.

Scheff, T., & Retzinger, S. (1991). *Emotions and violence: Shame and rage in destructive conflicts.* Lexington, MA: Lexington Books.

Schwartz, M., & Leggett, M. (1999). Bad dates or emotional trauma? The aftermath of campus sexual assault. *Violence Against Women, 5,* 251–271.

Schwartz, M., & DeKeseredy, W. (1997). *Sexual assault on the college campus: The role of the male peer model.* Thousand Oaks, CA: Sage.

Security On Campus, Inc., (2006). "Security on Campus, Inc." Retrieved February 13, 2007, from http://www.securityoncampus.org.

Shafer, L. (2007). Women, gender & safety on campus: Reporting is not enough. In B. S. Fisher & J. J. Sloan (Eds.), *Campus crime: Legal, social and policy perspectives* (2nd ed.). Springfield, IL: Charles C Thomas.

Sloan III, J., & Shoemaker, J. (2007). State level Clery Act initiatives: A critical review of symbolic policies at work. In B. S. Fisher & J. J. Sloan (Eds.), *Campus crime: Legal, social and policy perspectives* (2nd ed.). Springfield, IL: Charles C Thomas.

Stormo, K., Lang, A., & Stritzke, W. (1997). Attributions about acquaintance rape: The role of alcohol and individual differences. *Journal of Applied Social Psychology, 27,* 279–305.

Wyatt, G. (1992). The sociocultural context of African American and White American women's rape. *Journal of Social Issues, 48,* 77–91.

Chapter 5

WOMEN, GENDER, AND SAFETY ON CAMPUS: REPORTING IS NOT ENOUGH

LINDA K. SHAFER

In 1990, Congress passed the *Student Right-to-Know and Campus Security Act* (20 U.S.C. 1092[f]) that required institutions of higher education (IHEs) that receive funding under Title IV of the Higher Education Act of 1965 to annually report crime statistics to the U.S. Department of Education (ED), including rape and other forms of sexual assault. Henceforth the *Clery Act,* it covers alleged crimes in seven categories, including sexual offenses. Passed in the wake of the sexual assault and murder of Jeanne Clery in her dorm room at the hands of a fellow student, it holds special significance for women on campuses (United States Government Accounting Office, 1997b). Together, the chapters in this section of the book present a comprehensive assessment and analysis of the purpose, results, effect, and, its supporters would argue, the need for legislation like *Clery.*

This chapter takes a slightly different path, however, focusing on what the legislation and its supporters fail to consider in assessing *Clery's* value. For instance, despite the *Act's* existence, college men rape college women at a rate little changed for over 20 years, a fact Congress failed to consider when it amended the *Act.* Further, numerous loopholes in enforcement regulations allow and even encourage IHE underreporting, yet the ED bases its assessments of the *Act* on statistics reported by IHEs. Few prospective or current students use or even read IHEs annual crime statistics, yet one of the *Act's* main goals is to provide that information for students to use in choosing schools.

This chapter also turns attention to Congressional and public nonresponse to independent scholarly research on the extent of how men's continued sexual violence against women on campus hinders the progress the *Clery Act* seeks. It explores the role gender plays in discussing male students' sexual assaults against female students on campus and how that can hobble actions ostensibly designed to protect female students.

Further, this chapter addresses a question that begs attention–why legislators and IHE administrators are unwilling to question the *Act* and why its proponents and the public are content with the *Act's* existence. I suggest that the *Act's* proponents are content with the mere existence of the *Act* because of people's reluctance to speak about men's role in sexual assault and the gendered realities of campus life. Despite the growing number of women undergraduates on college campuses, postsecondary education remains the purview of men and, sadly, unsafe for women. Most college presidents, senior administrators, and tenured faculty are men, and the people most likely to call attention to sexual assault on campus are feminist faculty and in women's studies departments–people whose credibility constantly faces marginalization. Before we can understand the role gender in our society plays in the *Clery Act's* implementation and assessment, however, we have to start with the key events that led up to the *Act*.

Background

Evolution of the Clery Act

Four years after Jeanne Clery's murder at Lehigh University, U.S. Representative William Goodling (R-PA) introduced legislation that became Title II of the *Student Right-to-Know and Campus Security Act*. Signed by the president in 1990, the *Act* went into effect September 1991. Since then, Congress has amended the *Act* three times, and each amendment highlighted the *Act's* focus on sexual assaults on campus. The 1992 amendment (in effect October 1994), required IHEs to develop a set of rights and policies for victims of sexual assault. The 1998 amendment (in effect July 2000), clarified reporting requirements with specific attention to sexual assault and changed the *Act's* name to the *Jeanne Clery Disclosure of Campus Security Policy and Campus Crime Statistics*. The 2000 amendment (in effect October 2002) required that schools provide the location (i.e., a website address) where campus community members can obtain the names of registered sex offenders.

Sexual Assaults on IHE Campuses

Koss, Gidycz, and Wisniewski's (1987) landmark national study of sexual aggression and victimization of college women exposed the extent and frequency of sexual assaults on college campuses. The authors found "53.7 percent of women respondents revealed some form of sexual victimization," "25.1 percent of men revealed involvement in some form of sexual aggression," and "nonconsensual intercourse was obtained through intentional intoxification by 57 percent of men who reported 103 incidents" (Koss et al., 1987, pp. 166–167). The victimization rate did not significantly change across location, type, or size of the school (e.g., urban/rural, private/public, large/small, etc.). Koss et al. found a victimization rate of 38 per 1,000 female students during a six-month period in 1984–1985–a rate "10–15 times greater than rates that are based on the [National Crime Statistics]" (Koss et al., p. 168).

While the Koss et al.'s results and Ms. Cleary's death should have been shocking enough on their own to trigger a response, addressing the problem of men's sexual violence against women on campus may not have come into public view if not supported by other, more public events. So what was different in the late 1980s and the 1990s that the Clery family's advocacy and work would have such an impact? Clery's death and the subsequent act and its amendments occurred during a two-decade period when for the first time congressional and national attention focused on the specter of gender-based violence against women.

Congressional Response

The very real problem of gender-based violence against women was brought to light by a series of highly publicized events. The murders of three film and television celebrities in the 1980s brought stalking and murder by an intimate partner into full albeit brief public view. In August 1980, Dorothy Stratten's estranged husband shot her after she left him for another man. In October 1982, an ex-intimate partner strangled Dominique Dunne and in July 1989, a stalker shot Rebecca Schaeffer in her home.

Koss et al.'s 1987 study further enlarged the space through which interested parties and scholars could pursue the problem of sexual violence against women. Then in 1990, Senator Joseph Biden (D-CT) introduced the *Violence Against Women Act* in each of the 101st through 103rd Congresses.

Perhaps more enduring in public memory, however, are three other events. In 1990, the year before the *Clery Act* took effect, the nation joined the Senate Judiciary Committee as it listened to Professor Anita Hill's allegations of sexual harassment by then Supreme Court nominee Judge Clarence Thomas during his confirmation hearings. In September 1992, the sexual assault of 14 female naval officers and 12 female civilians at the hands of military personnel during the annual U.S. Navy aviators' Tailhook Association in Las Vegas stunned the nation. In June of 1994, a shocked nation began to follow what would become the trial of well-known celebrity and athlete

charged with murdering his wife, Nicole Brown Simpson, and her friend
Ronald Goldman. Three months later Congress passed and the president
signed the *Violence Against Women Act.* Given these events, it is not surprising
that Clery's parents were able to successfully not only bring, but also sustain,
national and congressional attention to violence against women on college
campuses.

Perhaps one of the unique aspects of the *Clery Act* is that it took something
once kept private and pushed it into the open. It intended that IHEs would
face and discuss college women's sexual assault by college men. However,
does the *Clery Act* work—does it meet its intent? The passing of legislation can
often be symbolic; whether any legislation works as intended and to what
extent it does work has generally been left to scholars to uncover (Flonden
& Weiner, 1978). Thus to assess the *Act's* success, it is important to compare
the scholarly research with the ED's conclusions.

Evaluating the Act's Effect

In 1990, Congress gave oversight authority of the new act to the ED. The
Clery Act did not require ED to evaluate routinely the impact and effect of the
policy beyond collecting and reporting campus crime statistics nor even to
evaluate the accuracy of the reported statistics (U.S. GAO, 1997a).
Nonetheless, the *Act* required the Secretary of Education to report to
Congress in 1995 on campus crime statistics. Basing its report on a survey of
colleges' reported crime statistics for 1992 through 1994, the ED informed
Congress of a low rate of forcible sexual offenses on campuses: In 1994,
fewer than 9 percent of all reporting institutions reported forcible sex offenses; for 1992–1994, the rate of sexual assault on campus per year was around
.09 per 1,000 students (NCES, 1997, pp. 12, 15). A few years later and again
drawing from the data provided by colleges and universities, the ED
informed Congress "our nation's college campuses are safe." It reported that
the risk of sexual assault among college women was 14.8 per 100,000 students (or .0148%)–and boasted that it was "substantially below the overall
rate for sex offenses nationally where the rate for rapes alone 1999 [*sic*]
exceeded 32.7 per 100,000 persons" (United States Department of
Education, 2001a, p. 7).

Yet these statements are misleading. "Students" and "persons" means all
females *and* males, and slightly over half of all IHE students are female. As
women report the vast majority of rapes, this suggests a *much* higher risk for
female students than reported by the ED. In its 2004 report, the Federal
Bureau of Investigation revealed a rape rate of 32.2 "per 100,000 inhabitants" but also recalculated its figure using only the female population. The
revised figure was 63.46 per 100,000 (FBI, 2004, p. 27).

Whether and how the IHEs comply is another important matter to consider. The threat of sanction for noncompliance with the *Clery Act* requirements is weak. In 1997, for instance, the ED found violations by 63 colleges but levied no sanctions. Congress has made "no systemic attempts to mandate or track compliance" (Karjane, Fisher, & Cullen 2002, p. 8), nor does Congress or the ED require regular evaluative reporting of *Act*. Neither addresses independent evaluations, even those funded by the federal government. If Congress does not require independent evaluations, much of policy evaluation is left to nongovernmental actors, including interest groups but generally those with a scholarly interest in the policy subject or area. Since 1990, federal grants have funded several independent studies related to the *Clery Act*–the results of which cast doubt on the ED's conclusions (see Fisher & Cullen, 2000; Fisher, Cullen, & Turner, 2000; Karjane et al., 2002).

Risk of Rape Is More–Not Less–for College Women

At great odds with the ED's assessment of campus safety as reported to Congress, independent scholarly research reveals that women on campus face a substantial risk of rape. The National College Women Sexual Victimization survey (NCWSV), funded by the National Institute of Justice, allowed researchers to compare the risk of rape on colleges 20 years after the landmark 1987 study (Fisher et al., 2000). The NCWSV data reveal that 35.3 per 1,000 female students surveyed were victims of attempted and/or completed rapes in a 6.91-month period. This translates into a figure of 4.9 percent of college women per annum who were victims of attempted and/or completed rapes–far higher than the ED's calculation of .0148 percent. Further, one study found that the victimization rate and sexual assault of college women compared to their same age population not in college was three and nine times higher, respectively (Fisher, Sloan, Cullen, & Lu, 1998, p. 63).

It has long been well established that rape is grossly underreported to formal authorities. According to the U.S. Department of Justice, between 1992 and 2000, only 36 percent of rapes, 34 percent of attempted rapes, and 26 percent of sexual assaults were reported to police (U.S. DOJ, 2002). But whether on- or off-campus, most college rape victims will tell a friend or someone they trust, most often "a friend, not a family member or college official" (Fisher et al., 2000, p. 23; see also Tjaden & Thoennes, 2000). Yet while most IHEs "have made substantial strides in the direction of developing explicit sexual assault policies, . . . few campuses provide sexual assault response and/or sensitivity training to those most likely to first hear of sexual assaults on their campus: friends and fellow students, campus law enforcement/security officers, and faculty members" (Karjane et al., 2002, pp. viii, ix).

Recent scholarship then, suggests that colleges have not made significant progress toward effectively addressing sexual assault on campus (Fisher, Hartman, Cullen, & Turner, 2002; Karjane et al., 2002; Fisher & Cullen, 2000; Fisher et al., 2000; Ullman, Karabatsos, & Koss, 1999; Fisher et al., 1998). It is thus questionable that the *Clery Act* has been effective.

Admittedly, addressing sexual assault on campus was only one of its goals. Another goal was that the *Clery Act* would compel schools to provide annual crime data statistics to parents and students who would then use the data in deciding which schools to attend. The Clery family's experience was the basis for this goal, and the goal makes several assumptions not based on empirical evidence. It assumes, for instance, that parents, students, and prospective students factor in the types and extent of campus crimes when making choices about colleges. More crucially perhaps, it assumes that all prospective students and their families both ask for and receive schools' annual crime statistics—and that they read the information (see Janasik & Gehring, 2001).

The ED agrees with the *Act's* proponents that campus crime statistics will aid families and students make informed decisions about college choice. In 1998, then Assistant Secretary for Office of Postsecondary Education of ED, David Longanecker, said that the ED's "goal is to administer the *Campus Security Act* in a fashion that assists these schools in providing a safe environment . . . and to make sure that they are well informed about security at the particular institution that they attend or that they are seeking to attend" (U.S. Senate Hearing, 1998). Two years later, then Assistant Secretary A. Lee Fritschler described the purpose of ED's data collection: "to give prospective and current students information to help them make decisions about their potential or continued enrollment in a postsecondary institution" (Fritschler, 2000). In 2001, Secretary of Education Rod Paige claimed: "The security and safety on and around our college campuses is one of several factors they will consider . . . Now, the American people are empowered with the information they need to make informed decisions about campus safety (United States Department of Education, 2001b).

Ideally, of course, students and their parents factor in an array of information *including* crime statistics when making college choices. Janosik's (2001) study as to whether the reported data mandated by the *Clery Act* affected students' choices about school, however, suggests that Assistant Secretaries Langanecker and Fritschler, and Secretary Paige may have been naively optimistic. Of the 1,465 students Janosik surveyed, 71 percent of students indicated they did not know about the *Act*, 21 percent indicated they read the summary, and only 4 percent indicated it influenced their enrollment decision. In fact, the "majority of students remain unaware of the *Act* and do not use the information contained in the summary or annual report"

(Janosik & Gehring, 2001, p. 17). (It should be noted that neither Janosik (2001) nor Janosik and Gehring (2001) addressed whether *students' parents* were familiar with the *Act* and/or IHE crime statistics or whether the crime statistics affected their choice of school for their children.) As Janosik and Gehring's reports focus only on whether–and if so how–the reporting requirements of *Clery* affect students' college choices but did not question the statistics submitted yearly to the ED, they agree with the ED that "the incidents of crime on college campuses, in most cases, are much lower than the nation as a whole" (Janosik & Gehring, 2001, p. 19).

If the vast majority of students (and/or parents) (1) are unaware of the *Act* or the IHE crime statistics, or (2) are aware of the *Act* or the IHE crime statistics but do not factor in crime rates when choosing colleges, then colleges are struggling under the requirements of an unfunded mandate that fails to meet its goals. Further, relying on yearly crime summaries reported by IHEs ignores the fact that college men continue to rape college women at a rate little changed over the last two decades, and that both victims and college campuses underreport rape.

Underreporting While Complying

There is a wide disparity between the ED's conclusions on sexual assault rates and safety of IHE campuses in its reports to Congress and the research of independent scholars. That the crime statistics reported by the IHEs are, at best, low-ball figures is clear. The ED's most recent data reveal that the approximately 6,000 IHEs receiving Title IV funds reported a total of 3,704 incidents of forcible sexual assault and 93 incidents of nonforcible sexual assault in 2003. According to the U.S. Census Bureau (2003), of the 30,518,000 students enrolled in IHEs in 2003, 15,956,000 were female. This calculates to a reported sexual assault rate of .0237 percent, compared to the independently attained rate of 4.9 percent (Fisher et al., 2000), and the ED's rate of .0148 percent or .0296 percent if the ED based its calculations on just the female student population (United States Department of Education, 2001; United States Department of Education, ND). This is not to suggest that the ED doctors its reports; rather, it bases its reports on the crime statistics reported to it by IHEs in compliance with the *Act*.

Karjane, Fisher, and Cullen (2002, pp. 8, viii) found that schools had varying levels of compliance with the requirements of the *Clery Act*. For instance, though the *Act* requires all schools to send their annual crime report upon request, 40 percent did not, and 63.5 percent of the schools failed to report crimes in accord with the *Clery Act* requirements. Over one-quarter of schools failed to meet another crucial requirement of the *Act:* they did not publish their sexual assault policies. There are other discrepancies in IHEs' compli-

ance with the *Clery Act.* For instance, the ED description of "campus security authority"–designated persons on college campuses with responsibility to
report–goes beyond the campus security authorities and includes an "official
of an institution who has significant responsibility for student and campus
activities, including, but not limited to, student housing, student discipline,
and campus judicial proceedings" (34 CFR §668.46(a)(1)). It exempts only
campus professionals (e.g., faculty members and campus physicians) and
pastoral counselors when acting as such (i.e., not as an advisor to a student
group), and includes deans of students, athletic directors, team coaches, and
faculty advisors to student groups. In fact, "campus security authorities" may
also include students (e.g., monitoring dormitory access).

As IHEs vary widely as to their administrative positions, there is a lot of
space for noncompliance. The regulations offer further space for either
expanding or limiting reporting options when they state that a campus security authority may be "[a]ny individual or organization specified in an institution's statement of campus security policy as an individual or organization
to which students and employees should report criminal offenses" (34 CFR
§668.46(a)(3)). While IHEs' annual security reports filed with the ED must
contain statements of compliance–that is, what each school *does* do to comply–schools do not have to report what they *could* do but do not do. Thus,
schools' failure to leave out a wide array of potential reporting options and
research studies suggest IHEs' reluctance to be proactive.

If all schools were to implement a wide array of reporting options (e.g., all
authorities in residence life, all faculty, all deans, all dormitory residential
advisors, anonymous, Internet, and third-party), schools would have a much
clearer picture of the extent of sexual assault on campus. Yet not all colleges
have established institutional procedures facilitating easy reporting of sexual
assaults. While 84.3 percent of the colleges offer confidential reporting
options, only 45.8 percent offer anonymous reporting, 3.7 percent offer
anonymous Internet reporting, and 34.6 percent allow third-party reporting.
Thus, colleges continue to have sexual assault policies and practices that
either prevent or discourage victims from reporting their rapes (Karjane et
al., 2002). Nor are all "campus security authorities," as defined by the ED,
trained to receive reports of rape. Yet unless *all* schools aggressively address
male students' role in rape culture on campus, any lone school that does so
and reports higher crime statistics runs the risk of looking, by comparison,
like "Rape U."

This dilemma raises the question as to whether the public, parents,
Congress, and IHE faculty either *want* to know the true extent of sexual
assault and campus and/or would be *willing* to address the problem at its
core. Johnson (1980, p. 137) suggests that "[a] feminist interpretation does not
attribute violence to the aberrant behavior of a lunatic fringe of normal male

society; rather, it locates the etiology of sexual violence in the everyday fabric of relations between men and women in patriarchal society" (see also Johnson, 1997). If this is the case and violence against women is woven into the fabric of our society, those addressing men's role in that violence often find themselves thought of as being at the "fringe" of polite society.

Discussing the gendered nature of relations in a patriarchal society makes most people–except feminists and feminist scholars–decidedly uncomfortable. This may help explain why the ED, college administrators, IHEs, the *Act's* proponents, and Congress seem to find it is less problematic to ignore the extent and nature of sexual assault by men against women on IHE campuses, relying only on the crime statistics reported to the ED by IHEs. The next section discusses the limits of the attempts made by IHEs and advocacy groups to address sexual assault when they hesitate to turn the spotlight from the female student rape survivors to the male student rapists.

Discussion

Despite the existence of the *Clery Act,* the "massive problem of young men's sexual violence toward their coeducational peers" continues–virtually unchanged over the last 20 years (Karjane et al., 2002, p. vi). The *Act* fails to spotlight young college men's sexually predatory treatment of young college women and enables IHEs to avoid confronting the realities of sexual assault on their campuses.

Security on Campus, Inc., the advocacy group established by Jeanne Clery's parents, serves as a watchdog group and continually reminds Congress that crime on college campuses is a serious problem. While there is no arguing with that position, pursuing greater enforcement of the *Clery Act* to address and resolve the problem of crime on campus is not enough. Mandating IHEs to anticipate, address, and prevent crime on campus, for instance, creates an administrative and financial burden on college campuses to comply. This is particularly critical at a time when colleges and universities across the nation are scrambling for funding, affordable tuition, contributions, and endowments. It is also doubtful that crime on campuses–outside of sexual assault–is a serious problem. In fact, Fisher and Cullen (2000, p. 22) note, "with the exception of rape, violence is a rare event."

Further, the *Act* assumes that colleges have both the resources and the knowledge to address campus crimes. This is especially problematic regarding sexual assault. The vast majority of senior-level college administrators and senior- and tenured faculty are male and do not necessarily have any particular experience, interest in, or knowledge about rape in general or, in particular, on campus. Thus, it is much easier to shift the burden of safety onto the prospective victims. For example, a popular tactic of IHEs is to offer sessions for incoming first-year college women about how to "stay safe" on campus by behavior modification (e.g., women should go to parties as a group of several other college women, stay together, not eat anything, and not drink anything from an opened source, etc.). Some IHEs specifically warn incoming female students about the high risk of sexual assault during the "Red Zone"—the period between the beginning of Fall semester and Thanksgiving break. These methods are much simpler to implement than addressing male students' sexual violence or sexually predatory behavior towards female students. These methods, however, put the burden of safety on women and set the stage for women to blame themselves or be blamed for crimes against their persons (e.g., if a woman accepts a cup of punch from someone and it turns out to contain a date rape drug, the woman erred in accepting the punch in the first place).

Another popular approach colleges have employed is to gather young male homosocial bonding groups—fraternities and athletic teams—to talk about the relationship between men and sexual violence. While this can be very effective if done by a skilled, trained, and educated facilitator, it can also fall on its face. On January 23, 2003 at Allegheny College, I attended what the school advertised as a presentation and discussion about men and violence titled "Babes, Booze & Brawls." The speaker was Luoluo Hong, an educational consultant, administrator at the University of Wisconsin, and "activist, educator, motivator, comedian, survivor" (Campuspeak, 2006). Speaking to an audience almost exclusively of young male college students, Hong began with a lengthy, emotional, and sad account of her experience as a victim of date rape as a college student. She transitioned to the second half of her presentation with a segue that included several comments that seemed to be designed to be reassuring to her young male audience—about how she liked men and, particularly, liked her "men masculine," all accompanied by a lot of body shaking and wiggling.

In the second part of her presentation, Hong advanced a male victim's discourse—a dangerous avenue to pursue with defensive and discomfited young male college students forced to confront their role in a rape culture—and blamed women for men's violence against them. She said, for example, that "women help reproduce masculinity because [women] expect men to be that way." She said she *used* to think that rape was about (men's) power and not sex until "a man told me that that wasn't right, that women have the power." The audience roared with laughter when she pretended to be a man back-slapping his "little wife." She mugged, hopped up and down, and joked with the male students as she told them they (men) are more likely than are women to be the victims of violence, and that society should focus on them (men). There was no virtually discussion; she both asked and answered her questions. Later that night as I wrote up the voluminous notes I took during her presentation, I could well imagine her audience members on their way back to their dorms and fraternities angry over women forcing them (men) to be violent.

While certainly not all trainings focused on educating men about their role in a rape culture are so off base, the above example serves to show how talking about rape on campus with the group most likely to perpetrate rape–male students–is difficult for many people. A well-trained professor, administrator, or counselor–female or male–should be able to talk to young men about men's role in rape without feeling the need to either apologize or soften their words with comedy and prancing footwork. Rape and sexual violence are no joking matters, yet audiences are generally more comfortable with speakers who "soften" the ugliness of rape by men, of rape cultures, and of sexual predation of women by using humor or sex. I cannot think of any other crime that people feel a need to "soften" by this method. Allan Johnson (1997, pp. 104–105) notes:

> People of color, for example, generally lack a sense of humor around the subject of white racism and how it affects their lives, and yet whites rarely chide blacks for being angry and humorless ("Come on, lighten up; where's your sense of humor about racism?"). For women, however, getting angry is socially unacceptable, even when the anger is over violence, discrimination, misogyny, and other forms of oppression.

Further, when they do speak about rape, most people–including IHE administrators, professors, bureaucrats, and legislators–speak in passive voices. College administrators and faculty talk of how many women *were* raped instead of talking about how many college men *raped* college women. Rape victims become statistics that officials count; men who rape do not. The passive voice highlights rape victims and their friends while protecting rapists and their friends. While we may talk about rape *victims* on campus, we do not talk about *rapists* on campus–especially, it seems, when they are our students, sons, and classmates. People are much more comfortable hearing "35 out of every 1,000 college women will be sexually assaulted per year" instead of "every year college men will sexually assault 35 out of every 1,000 college women." By using the former language, rapists are ephemeral, disembodied, and faceless; they are, in essence, sexless. This language sets the ground for sexual assault being a sort of rite of passage for campus life; the victim is simply one of many each year. This does not create an environment either conducive to addressing men's role in a rape culture, or supportive of women who report rapes (Johnson 1980, p. 146). Use of the latter phrasing–"every year college men will sexually assault 35 out of every 1,000 college women"–clearly suggests both sexual aggression and responsibility for the sexual assaults lie with male students known to others in the campus community.

While the work of advocacy organizations such as Security on Campus, Inc. is important, it fails to address what is at the core of men's sexual violence against women: the gendered nature of power promoted and sustained by patriarchy. This triggers other questions: Are we as a society willing to address the existence of a patriarchal system that advantages the male sex and empowers men? Are men willing to give up gender power? Exploring these questions thoroughly is far beyond the confines of this chapter. However, I suggest that there is scant evidence on IHE campuses that most male faculty, students and administrators are willing to even talk about gender power.

Few male students, for example, are comfortable exploring the gendered nature of power by taking courses from women's studies departments or courses with "Gender &" or "Women &" in the titles. Many male students consciously avoid taking classes by known female professors who are feminists or, when they find themselves in a class taught by a feminist with whom they do not agree, demonize or attempt to marginalize the professor as an angry man-hater or lesbian. Sadly, male faculty and administrators on campus do not seem much more willing to talk about gender power than are their young students. My own experiences in academia capture this. I do not think my experiences are rare; however, members of postsecondary institutions, outside of small groups of feminist faculty, rarely address these issues.

For instance, the senior members of my department once reprimanded me for "showing pugnacious disrespect for the institution" after I spoke at a faculty meeting a week earlier to urge Residence Life to not reclassify rape as "other forms of sexual harassment" in its new student handbook. I was the only faculty member in a room of about 200 faculty and administrators who addressed this. I also experienced, as did many of my feminist colleagues, constant marginalization and attempts to delegitimate my work by male colleagues, both overtly and covertly. By way of example, during the question and answer session following my presentation to an audience of professors (mostly male), on the *Violence Against Women Act,* also called VAWA, a tenured male professor in the front row suggested that VAWA's 2000 reauthorization would have received more media attention had it a better acronym and suggested VULVA. The room fell silent; and neither my department chair nor the dean—both of whom were present—spoke to me of it. At professional conferences in my areas of political science and public policy, few (if any) males attend panels and roundtables that focus on gender and politics or policy, though males far outnumber females in my field.

Granted, female scholars are responsible for the bulk of the scholarship on gender theory and gender power, yet gender is not a woman's issue, nor is it something biologically created. People "do" gender—they live and act it in certain ways; society also genders men's lives. Men's unwillingness to seriously address the gendered nature of power in our culture does not bode well for either women's equality (generally) or for effectively addressing and preventing rape on campuses.

Conclusion

The *Clery Act,* while laudable for its intent and goals, has neither effectively addressed the problem of male students' assault on female students on campuses of IHEs nor effectively encouraged IHEs to investigate and deal with the real extent of sexual assault on their campuses. Requiring reporting while leaving numerous loopholes for IHEs to support underreporting does not resolve the problem that all IHEs face—that is, their male students' sexual violence toward female students and the apparent willingness of faculty and administrators to accept it. Further, the open book reporting policy may encourage IHEs to facilitate what is, in effect, underreporting. In addition, there is no evidence that students, prospective students, or their parents use the information from the crime statistic reports mandated by the *Clery Act* in their decision making process in choosing schools.

In 2003, Congress appropriated $750,000 to write a handbook about complying with the *Clery Act* (United States Department of Education, 2005). Yet compliance with the *Act* as written and enforced will not stop or even slow male students from raping females on college campuses. It will not guarantee accurate reporting of the rate at which men rape women on college campuses, nor will it guarantee IHEs treat rape survivors fairly. It will also not guarantee that men who rape women on campus will face punishment appropriate for their crimes. Until senior faculty and administrators at IHEs, the public, federal agencies (such as the ED and the U.S. Department of Justice), Congress, and scholars are willing to speak directly about a campus culture that shields male students who rape female students; to explore why they do not question the methods of collecting campus crime statistics but are satisfied with underreporting; or consider how gender affects how we live, speak, and act, campuses will remain unsafe for women.

REFERENCES

CAMPUSPEAK. (2006). Retrieved September 25, 2006, from http://www.campuspeak.com/speakers/hong/.

Code of Federal Regulations, Title 34, Volume 3, Chapter VI, §668.46(a)(3) (rev'd 7/1/05), Washington, DC: United States Government Printing Office.

Code of Federal Regulations, Title 34, Volume 3, Chapter VI, §668.46(a)(4) (rev'd

7/1/05), Washington, DC: United States Government Printing Office.

Federal Bureau of Investigation. (2004). *Crime in the United States 2004.* Washington, DC: United States Department of Justice.

Fisher, B. S., & Cullen, F. T. (2000). *The extent and nature of violent victimization among college women.* Washington, DC: United States Department of Justice.

Fisher, B. S., Cullen, F. T., & Turner, M. G. (2000). *The sexual victimization of college women.* (NCJ 182369). Washington, DC: United States Department of Justice.

Fisher, B. S., Hartman, J., Cullen, F. T., & Turner, M. G. (2002). Making campuses safer for students: The *Clery Act* as a symbolic legal reform. *Stetson Law Review, XXXII*(1), 61–89.

Fisher, B. S., Sloan, J. J., Cullen, F. T., & Lu, C. (1998). Crime in the ivory tower: The level and sources of student victimization. *Criminology, 35*(3), 671–710.

Flonden, R. E., & Weiner S. S. (1978). Rationality to ritual: The multiple roles of evaluation in governmental processes. *Policy Sciences, 9,* 9–18.

Fritschler, A. L. (2000). Assistant Secretary, Office of Postsecondary Education, United States Department of Education, letter dated July 26.

Janosik, S. M. (2001). The impact of the Campus Crime Awareness Act of 1998 on student decision-making. *NASPA Journal, 38*(3), Spring.

Janosik, S. M., & Gehring, D. D. (2001). *The impact of the Jeanne Clery Disclosure of Campus Crime Security Policy and Campus Crime Statistics Act on college student behavior.* (Educational Policy Institute of Virginia Tech, Policy Paper, No. 10). Blacksburg, VA: Virginia Tech University.

Johnson, A. G. (1997). *The gender knot: Unraveling our patriarchal legacy.* Philadelphia: Temple University Press.

Johnson, A. G. (1980). On the prevalence of rape in the United States. Signs: *Journal of Women in Culture and Society, 6,* 136–146.

Karjane, H. M., Fisher, B. S., & Cullen, F. T. (2002). *Campus sexual assault: How America's institutions of higher education respond.* Newton, MA: Educational Development Center.

Koss, M. P., Gidycz, C. A., & Wisniewski, N. (1987). The scope of rape: Incidence and prevalence of sexual aggression and victimization in a national sample of higher education students. *Journal of Counseling and Clinical Psychology, 55*(2), 162–70.

National Center for Education Statistics. (1997). *Statistical analysis report: Campus crime and security at postsecondary education institutions.* Washington DC: United States Department of Education.

34 CFR 668.46(a))1): This refers to Title 34, Code of Federal Regulations, vol. 3 (revd 7/1/02), section 668.46(a)(1), Washington, DC: U.S. Government Printing Office.   (See http://a257.g.akamaitech.net/7/257/2422/14mar20010800/edocket.access.gpo.gov/cfr_2002/julqtr/34.

Tjaden, P., & Thoennes, N. (2000). *Full report of the prevalence, incidence, and consequences of violence against qomen* (NCJ 183781). Washington, DC: National Institute of Justice

Ullman, S. E., Karabatsos, G., & Koss, M. P. (1999). Alcohol and sexual assault in a national sample of college women. *Journal of Interpersonal Violence, 14*(6), June, 603–625.

United States Census Bureau. (2003). Enrollment of the population 15 years old and over, by school type, attendance status, control. Table 9. *Current Population Survey,* 23 October.

United States Department of Education, Office of Postsecondary Education. (2005). *The handbook for campus crime reporting.* Washington, DC.

United States Department of Education, Office of Postsecondary Education (N.D.). Retrieved December 4, 2005 from http://www.ed.gov/admins/lead/safety/campus.html#data Criminal Offenses, Forcible Sex Offenses. Retrieved December 4, 2005 from http://www.ed.gov/admins/lead/safety/crime/criminal offenses/edlite-forcesex.html); Nonforcible Sex Offenses. Retrieved December 4, 2005 from http://www.ed.gov/admins/lead/safety/crime/criminaloffenses/edlite-nonforcesex.html.

United States Department of Education, Office of Postsecondary Education. (2001a). *The incidence of crime on the campuses of United States postsecondary education institutions: A report to Congress.* Washington, DC: U.S. Department of Education.

United States Department of Education. (2001b). Secretary Paige releases latest campus crime data for postsecondary institutions, November 19, 2002. Retrieved September 17, 2006 from http://www.ed.gov/PressReleases/11-2001/11192001a.html.

United States Department of Justice, Office of Justice Programs, Bureau of Justice Statistics. (2002). Rape and Sexual Assault: Reporting to Police and Medical Attention, 1992–2000 (.NCJ 194530). Washington, DC: U.S. Department of Justice.

United States General Accounting Office. (1997a). *Campus crime: Difficulties meeting federal reporting requirements,* GAO HEHS–97–52 (March).

United States General Accounting Office. (1997b). Letter from Health, Education and Human Services Division (B–276054) to the Honorable James M. Jeffords, Chairman, Committee on Labor & Human Resources, United States Senate (March).

United States Senate Hearing. (1998). *Hearing before a Subcommittee of the Committee on Appropriations.* United States Senate, 105th Congress, Second Session, 607. March 5. Washington, DC: United States Government Printing Office.

Chapter 6

STATE-LEVEL *CLERY ACT* INITIATIVES: SYMBOLIC POLITICS OR SUBSTANTIVE POLICY?

JOHN J. SLOAN, III AND JESSICA SHOEMAKER

Those who would treat politics and morality
apart will never understand the one or the other
—Rousseau

INTRODUCTION

In 1990, Congress passed the *Student Right-to-Know and Campus Security Act* (20 U.S.C. 1092[f]), now known as the *Jeanne Clery Disclosure of Campus Security Policy and Campus Crime Statistics Act.*[1] The legislation requires postsecondary institutions participating in federal financial programs to annually report to the U.S. Department of Education (ED) and make available for public inspection a comprehensive campus security report, annual statistics covering multiple prior years for crimes and drug/alcohol-related offenses known to campus police, and other information. Included in the legislation is a provision allowing the ED to levy fines and other sanctions on institutions for noncompliance. By passing this legislation, Congress appeared to send a clear signal that the federal government was both concerned about, and willing to address, campus crime/security issues by requiring colleges and universities to "come clean" with their crime statistics and security policies, and sanctioning institutions for failing to comply.

With Congress taking such a step, one might assume state legislatures would follow and pass their own legislation, if for no other reason than to show constituents they, too, were concerned about campus crime. There are numerous examples of states passing what, in effect, is legislation working in parallel with federal law (e.g., in the areas of welfare reform, immigration, and illegal drug possession). In some cases, state laws are stricter than are their federal counterparts, impose sanctions on offenders that are more serious, or create an entire new class of offenses. In the case of campus crime and security information, Griffaton (1995, p. 67) has argued:

> While the passage of the federal *Crime Awareness and Campus Security Act* ensures minimum disclosure and security standards for most institutions of higher education, *states remain in the best position to require their public and private colleges to adopt specific policies and procedures* (emphasis added).

Griffaton (1995) then argued that states could then insure that all current and prospective students have access to campus crime and security facts by withholding state-level aid or accreditation of not only public colleges and universities, but private schools as well. In other cases, state statutes do little more than "echo the sentiments" of the federal legislation and become examples of symbolic politics (see Edelman, 1964, 1971, 1988). Here, legislators use the issue to notify targeted constituents that they are concerned, in the hope of rallying political capital.

Thus, in some instances, legislators pass state laws in parallel with federal statutes that have a substantive effect, while in others, the legislation involves little more than symbolic politics. The question we explore in this chapter is whether state-level *Clery* legislation falls into the former or the latter category.

As discussed more fully below, as of late June 2006, 19 states have what we classify as *Clery*-style legislation.[2] As also discussed below, these statutes evidence wide variation in their provisions. For example, some states' campus crime legislation focuses only on policies relating to on-campus sexual assaults occurring at public, postsecondary institutions. Other statutes focus on institutional compiling of, and public access to, security reports. Still others simply indicate that schools should report their crime statistics to the state agency responsible for compiling statistics received from state, county, and local police agencies participating in the FBI's annual Uniform Crime Reports program.[3] Since the passage of the original version of *Clery* in 1990, just over one-third of the states have passed "campus crime" legislation, but almost none of this legislation mirrors *Clery* and some of the legislation is so narrow it barely fits the label.

We begin this chapter by briefly discussing the major provisions of *Clery*. Following this, we discuss the methods we used to identify state-level *Clery* statutes. Next, we examine the extent state-level legislation possesses certain key *Clery* provisions, including whether it prescribes penalties for institutional noncompliance. We end the chapter by presenting evidence showing that state-level *Clery* legislation constitutes symbolic public policy, rather then genuine efforts by the states to address crime and security issues at postsecondary institutions.

The *Clery Act:* A Brief Overview

Following the brutal rape and murder of their daughter as she slept in her dorm room at Lehigh University in 1986, Jeanne Clery's parents used this tragedy as impetus for a grass-roots movement to try to prevent other students from experiencing the same fate. They spearheaded a tireless campaign lobbying first the Pennsylvania legislature, and later Congress, to pass legislation that required colleges and universities to "come clean" with their crime statistics and security policies. Their efforts culminated first with Pennsylvania passing "campus crime" legislation and later Congress passing the *Student Right-to-Know and Campus Security Act of 1990* (20 U.S.C. 1092[f]) (henceforth the *Clery Act*). Subsequent amendments, including one in 1998, resulted in renaming the legislation the *Jeanne Clery Disclosure of Campus Security Policy and Campus Crime Statistics Act.*

Considered part of the *Higher Education Act of 1965* (PL89–329, 79 STAT 1219), the *Clery Act* requires that colleges and universities participating in federal student aid programs disclose both timely and annual information about campus crime and security policies, including those relating to on-campus sexual assault, and the power/authority of campus police/security. The ED, the agency charged with enforcing *Clery* and to which citizens are supposed to file complaints of alleged violations, can levy civil fines on violators of up to $27,500 or take other enforcement action including suspending federal aid to the school.[4]

Key Clery Provisions[5]

ANNUAL REPORT. One key *Clery* provision is that postsecondary institutions must publish, by October 1 each year, an "annual report" containing the following information: three years' worth of campus crime statistics and security policy statements relating to sexual assault (assuring basic victims' rights); a description of the power/authority of campus police; and the location where students should go to report crimes. The report is supposed to be automatically available to all current students and employees, while prospective students and employees can obtain copies as well. The school is supposed to provide the report and all statistical information to the ED.

CRIME STATISTICS. A second *Clery* provision is that each school must also disclose crime statistics for the campus, unobstructed public areas immediately adjacent to or running through the campus, and certain noncampus facilities including Greek housing and remote classrooms. The school must gather the statistics from campus police/security, local police, and student judicial affairs directors. Institutions are supposed to compile data for seven categories and sub-categories of crime including homicide (broken down into the sub-categories murder and nonnegligent manslaughter, and negligent manslaughter); sex offenses (broken down by forcible sex offenses (including rape), and nonforcible sex offenses); robbery; aggravated assault; burglary; motor vehicle theft; and arson. Schools are also required to report three types of incidents if they resulted in either an arrest or a disciplinary referral: liquor law violations, drug law violations, and illegal weapons possession.

TIMELY INFORMATION AND CRIME LOGS. *Clery* also requires schools to provide "timely warnings" to the campus community about crimes "in progress," and make available to it a daily log of crimes known to campus police/security. The "timely warning" requirement is triggered when the school considers a crime to pose an ongoing "threat to students and employees." Timely warnings are limited to the crimes also contained in the annual report.

Logs, on the other hand, are records of all incidents reported to campus police or security and include all crimes, not just those contained in the annual report, such as theft; state crime definitions may be used for classification purposes.[6] Schools that maintain a police or security department are required to disclose in the log any reported crime occurring within the patrol jurisdiction of the campus police/campus security department. The log must include the nature, date, time, and general location of each crime as well as its disposition, if known, and be publicly available and accessible by students and employees, and the public, including parents or the local press. Logs remain open for 60 days and subsequent to that time, must then be available within two business days of a request.

CAMPUS POLICE/SECURITY. An additional key *Clery* provision is that postsecondary institutions with campus police or security departments must disseminate the power and authority of these agencies. This includes their arrest power, limits of their jurisdiction, and other information about their operational and administrative operations.

SEXUAL ASSAULT INFORMATION AND POLICIES. *Clery* also requires institutions to publish a statement of policy concerning the institution's campus sexual assault prevention programs and procedures followed once a sex offense has occurred. The institution is also supposed to list its policies concerning on-campus disciplinary action in cases of alleged sexual assault, including a clear statement that the accuser and accused are entitled to the same opportunities to have others present during a disciplinary proceeding and have the board inform both parties of the outcome of the disciplinary proceeding.

SANCTIONS FOR INSTITUTIONAL NONCOMPLIANCE. Finally, one of the most important provisions of *Clery* is the stipulation that the federal government may impose sanctions on institutions failing to comply with *Clery's* provisions. Congress granted the ED the power to investigate allegations of noncompliance and to impose civil penalties involving fines of up to $27,500 for institutions found violating one or more of *Clery's* provisions. Additional sanctions are possible, including loss of federal financial aid funds. Implicit in the provision is the prospect of public censure due to adverse publicity arising from institutional noncompliance. No college or university wants to endure negative press for failing to provide required information to current or prospective members of the campus community. Thus, Congress gave "teeth" to the legislation by allowing the ED to impose sanctions for institutional noncompliance.

In summary, *Clery's* drafters apparently intended it to force campus officials to be more forthcoming with their crime statistics and security policies, make this information available to the public, and quickly disseminate information of a serious "crime in progress" to the campus community. Theoretically, current and prospective students and their parents, current and prospective employees, and the media would use this information to assess a particular campus's level of safety and insure that schools implemented reasonable security policies. In combination, the crime statistics and security policies were supposed to result in a reduction of on-campus victimization by raising the awareness of students, faculty members, and staff.

At the state level, supporters of *Clery*-style legislation might argue that such legislation would create further pressure on campus authorities to report their crime data and security policies. States could also impose their own sanctions on institutions that fail to comply. Critics, on the other hand, might argue: (1) there is no need for state-level legislation when the federal *Clery Act* applies to all postsecondary institutions (public and private) participating in federal student aid programs and (2) state-level campus crime legislation, like its federal counterpart, is an example of "symbolic policy" (Edelman, 1964). Symbolic policy involves the drafting and passage of legislation designed to placate constituents with concerns about an issue (e.g., campus crime), without substantively affecting institutional or individual behavior—in this case, actually forcing schools to make campuses safer. In effect, forcing schools to report their crime statistics and security policies is hardly the same as requiring them to *actually develop and implement* programs and policies that *effectively* reduce crime and enhance security on campus. This chapter sheds light on these issues by exploring state-level *Clery* legislation.

We now discuss how we identified, and then analyzed the content of, state-level "campus crime" legislation.

Identifying and Analyzing State-Level *Clery*-Style Legislation

To examine the extent and nature of state-level *Clery* legislation, during the period July 20th–23rd of 2006 we conducted a computerized search of the *LexisNexis*™ "state codes and regulations" database. We conducted these searches in several steps.

First, to identify state codes and regulations relating to higher education, we used the search terms "postsecondary institutions" and "higher education" to find legislation specifically relating to colleges and universities. Next, we conducted a search within the results, using the terms "campus crime," "campus security," "*Clery Act*," "campus police," and "campus sexual assault" to identify legislation one could reasonably construe as *Clery*-type statutes.

In deciding whether a particular state statute constituted *Clery*-type legislation, we focused on the whether the law contained the key provisions of *Clery* discussed above, including: (1) were institutions required to disseminate an annual report on crime and security issues; (2) were institutions required to report their crime statistics; (3) were institutions required to keep publicly accessible daily crime logs; (4) were institutions required to provide "timely warnings" of crimes occurring on campus; (5) were institutions required to report the power and authority of campus police/security officials; (6) were institutions required to report policies relating to on-campus sexual assaults; and (7) were sanctions included for institutional noncompliance. Using these parameters, our search uncovered 19 states possessing what we consider *Clery*-type legislation and an additional 12 states that passed much narrower legislation that addresses campus police/security authority.

Analyzing State-Level Clery Legislation

Table 6.1 presents results of our search, organized as follows. The first column in the table contains the name of the state with the legislation–either *Clery*-type or enabling legislation addressing the power/authority of campus police officials. The second column identifies the specific statute we analyzed. The next seven columns present key provisions of *Clery* and indicate whether the state's legislation contained that particular provision (Yes/No). The final column of the table presents a count of the number of key *Clery*-type provisions (of the seven listed) the legislation contains. The final row of the table contains the number of states whose statute contained the individual provision listed in the column.

Results

As mentioned, 19 states passed what we characterize as *Clery*-type legislation, including California, Connecticut, Delaware, Florida, Illinois, Iowa,

Kentucky, Louisiana, Massachusetts, Minnesota, New Jersey, New York, Oregon, Pennsylvania, Tennessee, Virginia, Washington, West Virginia, and Wisconsin. Twelve other states, Alabama, Georgia, Indiana, Kansas, Maryland, Montana, North Carolina, Ohio, Oklahoma, Rhode Island, South Carolina, and Texas, passed narrower legislation that enables postsecondary institutions to create campus police or security departments, and which outlines the power/authority of campus police/security officers and thus does not constitute true *Clery*-style legislation.

KEY PROVISIONS. The first aspect of our analysis was determining the extent the provisions of the state statutes mirror those found in *Clery*. As shown in Table 6.1, California and Pennsylvania come closest to containing all the key requirements of *Clery*: California's legislation contains six of the seven "key" provisions, and Pennsylvania's has five of seven.[7] Among the remaining states, Tennessee's legislation contains four provisions, seven states' legislation contains at least three provisions, and four states' legislation contains two provisions. Seventeen states–the previously identified 12 states whose legislation only addressed the power/authority of campus police and five others–have legislation containing only one key provision of *Clery*. Thus, of the 31 states that seemingly passed *Clery*-type legislation, only three (California, Pennsylvania, and Tennessee) contain most of the key provisions of *Clery* and 12 states have legislation that only addresses the power/authority of campus police/security officers.

BREADTH OF CLERY PROVISIONS. Having identified how many of the key provisions states' legislation possessed, we next examined which states' legislation contained specific key provisions of *Clery*. As shown in the table, the most commonly occurring *Clery* provision was that relating to institutions having to describe the power/authority of the campus police/security, where 68 percent of the states we examined (N=21) had such a provision in their statutes. Recall, however, that legislation in 12 of these states simply enabled postsecondary institutions to create campus police/security forces and defined the power and authority of their officers. None of this legislation, however, indicated that postsecondary institutions were to *provide* the information to consumers, students, staff, etc. This means that in only nine states was there a provision for disseminating to the public, information on the power and authority of campus police/campus security.

The next most commonly occurring provision in the states' legislation actually involved two provisions: dissemination of an annual security report and annually reporting campus crime statistics. Here, we found that 39 percent (N=12 each) of the states' *Clery* legislation contained both provisions. Following closely was the provision requiring institutions to publicly report policies addressing sexual assaults occurring on campus; we found that 35 percent of the states (N=11) had such a provision in their legislation.

Table 6.1
KEY REQUIREMENTS OF STATE-LEVEL CLERY LAWS

State	*Statute*	*Dissemination of Annual Security Report*	*Institutions Annually Report Campus Crime Statistics*	*Institutions Compile Daily Crime Log*	*Institutions Provide "Timely Warning" Regarding "Crimes in Progress"*	*Institutions Describe Power/ Authority of Campus Police or Security Personnel*	*Institutions Publish Policy on Handling of On-Campus Sexual Assault Cases*	*Penalty for Non-Compliance*	*Total # of Clery Requirements in Legislation*
Alabama[a]	Code of Ala. §16–22–2	No	No	No	No	Yes	No	N/A	1/7
California[b]	Cal Ed Code §67382 §67385.7	Yes	Yes	Yes	Yes	Yes	Yes	None	6/7
Connecticut	Conn. Gen. Stat. §10a-55a	Yes	Yes	No	No	No	Yes	None	3/7
Delaware	14 Del. C. §9003 & §9004	Yes	Yes	No	No	No	Yes	None	3/7
Florida	Fla. Stat. §1006.67	Yes	Yes	No	No	No	No	None	2/7
Georgia[a]	OCGA §20–3–72	No	No	No	No	Yes	No	N/A	1/7
Illinois[c]	PA 88–629; 110 ILCS	No	No	No	No	No	Yes	None	1/7

continued

Table 6.1—*Continued*
KEY REQUIREMENTS OF STATE-LEVEL CLERY LAWS

State	Statute	Dissemination of Annual Security Report	Institutions Annually Report Campus Crime Statistics	Institutions Compile Daily Crime Log	Institutions Provide "Timely Warning" Regarding "Crimes in Progress"	Institutions Describe Power/Authority of Campus Police or Security Personnel	Institutions Publish Policy on Handling of On-Campus Sexual Assault Cases	Penalty for Non-Compliance	Total # of Clery Requirements in Legislation
Indiana[a]	Ind. Code Ann. 20–12–3.5–2	No	No	No	No	Yes	No	N/A	1/7
Iowa	Iowa Code §262.9	Yes	No	No	No	No	Yes	None	2/7
Kansas[a]	KSA 22–2401a; 72–8222	No	No	No	No	Yes	No	None	1/7
Kentucky	KRS §164.9481	No	Yes	Yes	Yes	No	No	None	3/7
Louisiana	La. R.S. 17:3351	Yes	Yes	No	No	Yes	No	None	3/7
Maryland[a]	Md. Educ. Code Ann. §13–601	No	No	No	No	Yes	No	N/A	1/7

continued

Table 6.1—*Continued*
KEY REQUIREMENTS OF STATE-LEVEL CLERY LAWS

State	*Statute*	*Dissemination of Annual Security Report*	*Institutions Annually Report Campus Crime Statistics*	*Institutions Compile Daily Crime Log*	*Institutions Provide "Timely Warning" Regarding "Crimes in Progress"*	*Institutions Describe Power/Authority of Campus Police or Security Personnel*	*Institutions Publish Policy on Handling of On-Campus Sexual Assault Cases*	*Penalty for Non-Compliance*	*Total # of Clery Requirements in Legislation*
Massachusetts	ALM GL Ch. 6 §168C	Yes	Yes	No	No	Yes	No	None	3/7
Minnesota	Minn. Stat. §135A.15	No	No	No	No	No	Yes[d]	None	1/7
Montana[a]	Mont. Code Anno. §20–25–321	No	No	No	No	Yes	No	N/A	1/7
New Jersey	N.J. Stat. §18A:6–4.2 §18A:6 1E–2	No	No	No	No	Yes	Yes	None	2/7
New York	NY CLS Educ. §6433	Yes	Yes	No	No	No	Yes	None	3/7
North Carolina[a]	N.C. Gen. Stat. §74G–6 §74G–2	No	No	No	No	Yes	No	N/A	1/7

continued

Table 6.1–*Continued*
KEY REQUIREMENTS OF STATE-LEVEL CLERY LAWS

State	*Statute*	*Dissemination of Annual Security Report*	*Institutions Annually Report Campus Crime Statistics*	*Institutions Compile Daily Crime Log*	*Institutions Provide "Timely Warning" Regarding "Crimes in Progress"*	*Institutions Describe Power/Authority of Campus Police or Security Personnel*	*Institutions Publish Policy on Handling of On-Campus Sexual Assault Cases*	*Penalty for Non-Compliance*	*Total # of Clery Requirements in Legislation*
Ohio[a]	ORC Ann. 1713.50	No	No	No	No	Yes	No	N/A	1/7
Oklahoma[a]	74 Okla. St. §360.18	No	No	No	No	Yes	No	N/A	1/7
Oregon	ORS §352.385	No	No	No	No	Yes	No	N/A	1/7
Rhode Island[a]	R.I. Gen. Laws §16–52–2	No	No	No	No	Yes	No	N/A	1/7
South Carolina[a]	S.C. Code Ann. §59–116–30	No	No	No	No	Yes	No	N/A	1/7
Tennessee	Tenn. Code Ann. §49–7–129	Yes	Yes	No	No	Yes	Yes	None	4/7

continued

Table 6.1–*Continued*
KEY REQUIREMENTS OF STATE-LEVEL CLERY LAWS

State	*Statute*	*Dissemination of Annual Security Report*	*Institutions Annually Report Campus Crime Statistics*	*Institutions Compile Daily Crime Log*	*Institutions Provide "Timely Warning" Regarding "Crimes in Progress"*	*Institutions Describe Power/Authority of Campus Police or Security Personnel*	*Institutions Publish Policy on Handling of On-Campus Sexual Assault Cases*	*Penalty for Non-Compliance*	*Total # of Clery Requirements in Legislation*
Texas[a]	Tex. Educ. Code §51.203	No	No	No	No	Yes	No	N/A	1/7
Virginia	Va. Code Ann § 9.1–102	No	No	No	No	Yes	No	N/A	1/7
Washington	Rev. Code Wash. (ARCW) §28B.10.569	Yes	Yes	No	No	Yes	No	None	3/7
West Virginia	W. Va. Code §18B–4–5a	No	Yes	No	No	No	No	None	1/7
Wisconsin	Wis. Stat. §36.11	Yes	No	No	No	Yes	Yes	None	2/7

continued

Table 6.1–*Continued*
KEY REQUIREMENTS OF STATE-LEVEL CLERY LAWS

State	Statute	Dissemination of Annual Security Report	Institutions Annually Report Campus Crime Statistics	Institutions Compile Daily Crime Log	Institutions Provide "Timely Warning" Regarding "Crimes in Progress"	Institutions Describe Power/Authority of Campus Police or Security Personnel	Institutions Publish Policy on Handling of On-Campus Sexual Assault Cases	Penalty for Non-Compliance	Total # of Clery Requirements in Legislation
Number of states possessing this provision		12/31 (39%)	12/31 (39%)	3/31 (9.7%)	3/31 (9.7%)	21/31 (68%)	11/31 (35.5%)	0/31 (0%)	

N/A = not applicable

a. This legislation is limited to enabling postsecondary institutions to create such entities and detailing their power and authority. In two states, Ohio and Nevada, the enabling legislation authorizes private, nonprofit colleges and universities to create campus police departments and details the power and authority of these officers.

b. The statue(s) also has/have specific requirements concerning institutional responses to allegations of sexual assaults occurring on campus.

c. The Illinois statutes only address the limits of information about a suspect that officials can legally release (and to whom) upon the suspect's on-campus arrest.

d. The statute also requires that postsecondary institutions implement an "anti-hazing" policy.

We found that very few states' legislation contained either the provision that institutions should keep daily "crime logs" and make these available to the public, and/or the provision involving institutions sending a "timely warning" to the campus community if a serious crime has just occurred or is in progress. Finally, we found that none of the states' legislation contained a provision for sanctioning institutions for failing to follow legislative dictates. While the legislation occasionally directed institutions to submit their statistical or other information to a specific state-level agency, such as the attorney general's office, even when the legislation listed *mandatory requirements* (regardless of breadth) for institutions to follow, *we could find not a single instance where the legislation listed any possible sanction(s) for institutional noncompliance.* Thus, among the key provisions of *Clery*, crime logs, "timely warnings," and sanctions for noncompliance were the least commonly occurring provisions found in states' legislation.

Discussion

The patterns emerging from our analyses lead us to conclude state-level *Clery* initiatives are examples of "symbolic public policy" (Edelman 1964, 1971, 1988), where legislators drafted, supported, and then passed *Clery*-style initiatives to promote personal and public policy goals, to protect themselves electorally, and to (theoretically) "represent their constituents" (see also Bell & Scott, 2006). In effect, when legislators drafted the *Clery*-style statutes, they used certain language in the provisions. This language helped target certain constituent groups and to gain their support for not only the legislation but for those legislators who drafted and supported it. U.S. presidents have also used symbolic language in directives that have little substantive impact, but which constituents greet with much political support (Oliver, 2001; Marion, 1994; Stolz, 1992). According to Oliver (2001, p. 1) in symbolic politics ". . . [T]he words themselves 'become the action,'" and thus in both the legislative and executive arenas "symbols derive their meaning not from content, but from the values people attach to them" (Oliver, 2001, p. 3). We believe the evidence presented below strongly suggests state-level *Clery* statutes fit into this framework.

First, among the 50 states and the District of Columbia, 31 of them (61%) have legislation relating to campus crime, campus security, or campus police. On the surface, this may seem impressive and would be indicative of a clear majority of states apparently concerned about campus related crime and security issues. However, on closer analysis of these states' statutes, 12 of the 31 states passed simple enabling legislation allowing postsecondary institutions to create campus police/campus security departments and detail their power/authority. This means that only 19 states (37%) have actually passed legislation that one might describe as *Clery*-based. However, among these states, only three of their statutes contain most of the major provisions found in *Clery*. The remaining states' statutes fall short of providing the kind of coverage designed by the drafters of *Clery* by containing only one or two of the key provisions found in *Clery*.

That so few states would pass comprehensive versions of *Clery* speaks volumes. Were "campus crime" a legislatively significant issue, states would either have (1) pre-empted Congress and passed their own legislation (Pennsylvania actually did this, but was the only state that did, as far as we know), or (2) quickly followed on the heels of *Clery* and passed their own laws to increase political pressure on schools to "come clean." Neither occurred, which could indicate state legislatures have not felt pressed to pass their own versions of *Clery.* The states thus missed an opportunity to "get the jump" on federal legislation by: (1) passing their own statutes first; (2) bolstering existing law (such as what California did regarding campus sexual assault policies); or (3) creating additional more stringent provisions (such as requiring institutions to report additional offenses not required by *Clery,* such as larceny-theft and simple assault, which research consistently shows as the most common offenses occurring on campus) (e.g., Fisher, Sloan, Cullen, & Lu, 1998). Instead, most state legislators did nothing or, at best, drafted and passed quasi *Clery*-type statutes to gain political support by showing they "cared" about campus crime and security issues.

Second, beyond the limited number of states passing *Clery*-type legislation, the provisions contained in the legislation that *has* passed hardly mirror those found in *Clery.* Only three states—California, Pennsylvania, and Tennessee—have legislation containing a majority of *Clery's* key provisions. Among them, California's provisions come closest to *Clery* and actually exceed *Clery's* provisions concerning policies on sexual assaults occurring on campus (at least for community colleges and institutions in the California State System). Of the remaining 16 states, most have provisions that mirror only one or two of those found in *Clery,* primarily in the area of disseminating campus security reports and reporting annual campus crime figures. Apparently, the "public reporting" aspects of *Clery* struck something of a chord with at least some state legislatures. Interestingly, however, almost none of the states' statutes include either a "timely warning" or "campus crime log" provision, both of which would likely create significant burdens for postsecondary institutions. Instead, one could argue that the provisions that are included in the legislation allow postsecondary institutions to "kill two birds with one stone"—by fulfilling the requirements of *Clery,* they also fulfill the requirements of the state statutes. Thus, even when states *did* pass *Clery*-type legislation, more often than not its scope has been far narrower than that of its federal counterpart. One could also argue that limiting the scope of state-level provisions represents the legislature symbolically "doing something" about campus crime without really placing any burden on colleges and universities beyond those already imposed by *Clery.* In effect, the provisions allow postsecondary institutions to address both state and federal requirements simultaneously.

A third finding relates to the large number of states who either passed enabling legislation to create campus police agencies or included a provision in their *Clery* legislation to publicly disseminate the power/authority of campus police/security officers. While beyond the scope of the current discussion, it would be interesting to examine when states passed these statutes. Sloan (1992), Peak (1995), and Bromley (2007) have each argued that the campus turmoil of the 1960s and early 1970s led to the creation of "modern" police agencies on college campuses. Their primary mandate was to secure the physical plant, prevent and respond to disorders, and officers received broad-based powers to do so (none of these authors, however, examined the extent the newly formed International Association of Campus Law Enforcement Administrators (IACLEA) became involved in lobbying for such legislation). Regardless, one could certainly argue that legislatures taking these steps were less concerned with preventing the type of attack that ultimately took Jeanne Clery's life and more concerned with keeping order and "the peace" on campus. Assuming these statutes are some 30 years old, their passage had little relationship to public pressure to "do something" about the crime/security issues brought to light by the Clerys' ongoing lobbying efforts that began during the late 1980s and continue today. The legislation had already existed long before Ms. Clery's brutal rape and murder.

Our final but perhaps most important finding is that none of the provisions found in state-level *Clery* legislation include any mention of institutional sanctions for non-compliance.[8] This fact, perhaps more than any other, provides strong evidence that state-level *Clery* legislation is symbolic at best.[9] If state legislatures were serious about creating additional pressure on postsecondary institutions to publicly disseminate their crime and security information; create policies to better address campus sexual assault; and do more to keep the campus community informed of serious crimes via "timely warnings," those same legislatures would surely have provided either civil or criminal (or both) sanctions for institutional noncompliance.

Based on our analyses of state-level *Clery*-type legislation, we agree with scholars who suggest that in both the legislative and the executive arenas, symbolic politics represents a reasonable explanation for "loud support" followed by little chance of substantive impact (see Fisher et al., 2002 for elaboration). When state legislators (or members of Congress) support legislation allegedly designed to address key crime and security-related issues affecting postsecondary institutions, yet the legislation largely omits most (if not all) key provisions of *Clery*, generally does not require postsecondary institutions to expend any effort beyond that needed to comply with *Clery*, and contains no provision for sanctions for institutional noncompliance, one can hardly expect such legislation to have much impact.

Conclusion

Since 1990 when Congress passed the *Student Right-to-Know and Campus Security Act of 1990*, now referred to as the *Clery Act*, an apparently large number of states passed their own legislation designed to address crime and security issues at postsecondary institutions. However, when we closely scrutinized these statutes, we found most of this legislation, at best, could be considered "symbolic politics" at work rather than substantive legislative efforts to pressure postsecondary institutions to "come clean" with their crime data and security policies. Importantly, even among the handful of states that apparently tried to either mirror *Clery* or even enhance some or all of its provisions, because the legislation makes no provision for sanctioning offending institutions, one could reasonably assume a less than stellar level of compliance (although this is an empirical question that future research could address).

In the state-level policy arena, legislation allegedly addressing concerns over crime and related issues on postsecondary institutions seemingly reflect efforts by legislators to generate support for their political futures rather than policies that pressure colleges and universities to "come clean" with their crime and security information. Perhaps the future holds a day when state legislatures will develop substantive policies to address campus crime. Until then, symbolic politics better describes state-level efforts to address campus crime.

Notes

1. See Carter & Bath (2007) for a complete review and analysis of the *Clery Act.*
2. Twelve states have legislation that enumerates the power and authority of campus police/campus security officers at public (and in two instances, private, nonprofit) postsecondary institutions. Generally, the legislation empowers officers as "sworn peace officers" of the state with the same authority as municipal officers, but limits that authority to property owned by the institution or property within a short distance from the campus.
3. The FBI developed the UCR program in the 1930s and has administered it ever since. Each year, the Bureau solicits data from thousands of state, county, and municipal law enforcement agencies including crimes known to, and arrests made by, the agencies representing jurisdictions in which over 95 percent of the U.S. population lives. The FBI then analyzes and compiles this information into an annual report, *Crime in the United States.* The report contains such information as trend analysis of crimes known to police and arrests over time; comparisons of crime levels across jurisdictions (based on standardized rates per unit population); characteristics (e.g., age, race, and gender) of persons arrested; and information on law enforcement agencies operating in the U.S. The report is available from most public libraries or downloaded from the following website: http://www. fbi.gov/ ucr/ucr.htm#cius.
4. To date, however, the ED has sanctioned only a few postsecondary institutions for failing to comply with the statute's provisions. (See Sloan, Fisher, & Cullen (1997), Karjane, Fisher & Cullen (2002), and Fisher, Karjane, Cullen, Blevins, Santana, & Daigle (2007) for analysis of postsecondary institutional compliance with *Clery* legislation.)

5. We took information for this section from material found at the Security on Campus, Inc. website, retrieved July 20, 2006 from http://www.securityoncam pus.org.

6. This is a key problem with the logs. Because state-by-state definitions of crimes vary (a situation remedied by the UCR reporting program that provides "standardized definitions" of offenses which makes interstate comparisons of crime rates possible), it becomes next to impossible to compare the logs of schools in one state with those in another. A classic example would be for burglary (one of the offenses for which *Clery* includes in its crime reporting provision), where some states (e.g., Maryland) still use the common law definition of burglary while others (e.g., California and Arkansas) have modified this definition. At common law, burglary involved four elements. First, the behavior had to occur at night. Second, the place where the act occurred must be a "mansion house" (a church was included as a "house"). Third, there must be both a breaking and an entering. The fourth and final requirement was that the offender intended to commit a felony while inside the "mansion house," usually theft. To illustrate how things have changed, California defines burglary as:

> . . . entering any house, room, apartment, tenement, shop, warehouse, store, mill, barn, stable, outhouse, or other building, tent, vessel, as defined in Section 21 of the Harbors and Navigation Code, floating home, as defined in subdivision (d) of Section 18075.55 of the Health and Safety Code, railroad car, locked or sealed cargo container, whether or not mounted on a vehicle, trailer coach, as defined in Section 635 of the Vehicle Code, any house car, as defined in Section 362 of the Vehicle Code, when the doors are thereof, with intent to commit grand or petit larceny or any felony (Cal Pen Code 459).

Arkansas, on the other hand has a much simpler definition: "a person commits residential burglary if he enters or remains unlawfully in a residential occupiable structure of another person with the purpose of committing therein any offense punishable by imprisonment" (A.C.A. 5–39–201). Thus, a student contemplating attending a university in California cannot compare that school's burglary rates with those found at schools in Arkansas because the definitions for the offense of burglary disseminated via campus crime reports differ. Retrieved August 11, 2006 from http://www.iejs.com/Law/Criminal_ Law/Burglary.htm.

7. California's legislation has additional stipulations concerning institutional responsibility to disseminate information on sexual assault victimization and the prevention of such incidents. Interestingly, while the legislation *mandates* all postsecondary institutions in the California State System and all community colleges follow its requirements, the legislation "requests of" or "suggests that" the Regents of the University of California system follow its dictates, but does not mandate they do so. Thus, even the most comprehensive piece of state level legislation contains a significant loophole concerning institutional noncompliance: institutions in the University of California System are not required to follow the legislation's dictates.

8. One could make a convincing argument that *Clery* is also symbolic policy. *Clery's*

provision of a maximum civil penalty of $27,500 for noncompliance, combined with the fact the ED has sanctioned so few schools for noncompliance does little to foster a belief that through *Clery,* Congress sought to genuinely pressure postsecondary institutions to do more to address campus crime and security issues. Fisher, Hartman, Cullen, and Turner (2002) make exactly that argument.

9. To be fair, some states (e.g., California) have provisions in their codes of civil procedure that allow individuals to bring civil actions against postsecondary institutions for failing to provide the requestor with campus crime information. Other states (e.g., Pennsylvania and Delaware) permit the state's Attorney General to bring an action against schools for noncompliance. Still other states (e.g., Tennessee and Wisconsin) have legislation allowing for the imposing of criminal sanctions on administrators who fail to comply with a school's general obligation to follow state law. The point is that these enforcement/compliance provisions appear in legislation that is *outside the Clery statute and in more general higher education statutes.*

REFERENCES

Bell, L. C., & Scott, K. (2006). Policy statements or symbolic politics? Explaining congressional court limiting attempts. *Judicature, 89,* 196–201.

Bromley, M. L. (2007). The evolution of campus policing: Different models for different eras. In B. S. Fisher & J. J. Sloan (Eds.), *Campus crime: Legal, social and policy perspectives* (2nd ed.). Springfield, IL: Charles C Thomas.

Carter, S. D., & Bath, C. (2007). The evolution and components of the *Jeanne Clery Act:* Implications for higher education. In B. S. Fisher & J. J. Sloan (Eds.), *Campus crime: Legal, social and policy perspectives* (2nd ed.). Springfield, IL: Charles C Thomas.

Edelman, M. (1964). *The symbolic uses of politics.* Urbana, IL: University of Illinois Press.

Edelman, M. (1977). *Political language: Words that succeed and policies that fail.* Chicago: Academic Press.

Edelman, M. (1988). *Constructing the political spectacle.* Chicago: University of Chicago Press.

Fisher, B. S., Hartman, J. L., Cullen, F. T., & Turner, M. G. (2002). Making campuses safer for students: The Clery Act as symbolic legal reform. *Stetson Law Review, 31,* 61–91.

Fisher, B. S., Karjane, H. M., Cullen, F. T., Blevins, K. R., Santana, S. A., & Daigle, L. E. (2007). Reporting sexual assault and the Clery Act: Situating findings from the National Campus Sexual Assault Policy Study within college women's experiences. In B. S. Fisher & J. J. Sloan (Eds.), *Campus crime: Legal, social and policy perspectives* (2nd ed.). Springfield, IL: Charles C Thomas.

Fisher, B. S., & Sloan, J. J. (1993). University response to the *Campus Security Act of 1990:* Evaluating programs designed to reduce campus crime. *Journal of Security Administration, 16,* 67–81.

Fisher, B. S., Sloan, J. J., Cullen, F., & Lu, C. (1998). Crime in the 'Ivory Tower': The level and sources of student victimization. *Criminology, 33,* 671–711.

Griffaton, M. C. (1995). State-level initiatives and campus crime. In B. S. Fisher & J. J. Sloan (Eds.), *Campus crime: Legal, social and policy perspectives* (pp. 53–73). Springfield, IL: Charles C Thomas.

Karjane, H. M., Fisher, B. S., & Cullen, F. T. (2002). *Campus sexual assault: How America's institutions of higher education respond.* Final Report, National Institute of Justice Grant No. 99–WA–VX–0008. Retrieved July 6, 2006 from http://www.ncjrs.org/pdffiles1/nij/grants/196676.pdf.

Marion, N. E. (1994). Symbolism and federal crime control legislation, 1960–1990. *Journal of Crime & Justice, 17,* 69–91

Oliver, W. M. (2001). Executive orders, symbolic politics, criminal justice policy, and the American presidency. *American Journal of Criminal Justice, 26,* 1–20.

Peak, K. J. (1995). The professionalization of campus law enforcement: Comparing campus and municipal law enforcement agencies. In B. S. Fisher & J. J. Sloan (Eds.), *Campus crime: Legal, social and policy perspectives* (pp. 228–245). Springfield, IL: Charles C Thomas.

Sloan, J. J. (1992). The modern campus police: An analysis of their origins, structure, and function. *American Journal of Police, 16,* 85–103.

Sloan, J. J., Fisher B. S., & Cullen, F. T. (1997). Assessing the *Student Right-to-Know and Campus Security Act of 1990:* An analysis of the victim reporting practices of college and university students. *Crime and Delinquency, 43,* 168–185.

Stolz, B. A. (1992). Congress and the war on drugs: An exercise in symbolic politics. *Journal of Crime and Justice, 15,* 119–136.

Part II:

THE SOCIAL CONTEXT OF CAMPUS CRIME

Part II

THE SOCIAL CONTEXT OF CAMPUS CRIME

INTRODUCTION

During the last decade, social scientists from a variety of disciplines and perspectives have studied the social context of campus crime. Some of their studies addressed definition and measurement issues plaguing the field and helped answer basic questions about the *extent* of criminal victimization among students by providing much-improved estimates of student victimization rates. Other studies have focused on the *nature* of student victimization. These theoretically driven studies used rigorous methods to test hypotheses and model the causal dynamics of *why* students are victims for the dual purposes of further understanding student victimization experiences and identifying associated risk factors. Still other studies, using rapidly advancing crime mapping technology, have examined the spatial distribution of crime on campus and the clustering of crime in specific physical locations. Together, these efforts have produced a sizable body of campus crime research that has contributed a fuller understanding of the nature and extent of student victimization, but which also suggest policy changes postsecondary institutions can take to address on-campus crime and safety. Part II of the book explores these issues.

In Chapter 7, "The Violent Victimization of College Students: Findings from the National Crime Victimization Survey," Timothy Hart uses data from the National Crime Victimization Survey, an annual national-level victimization survey of several thousand adults, to answer several questions asked by victimization researchers concerning the extent and nature of violent victimizations suffered by college students. By comparing victimization patterns of students and nonstudents, Hart shows significant differences between the groups. He also profiles other aspects of college student victimization. Answers to basic questions about the extent and nature of violent victimization of college students are clearly important, particularly since the

Clery Act focuses on institutional reporting of such offenses.

Elizabeth Mustaine and Richard Tewskbury, in Chapter, 8 provide a comprehensive overview of the current state of theoretically based victimization research of college students. As the title of their chapter, "The Routine Activities and Criminal Victimization of Students: Lifestyle and Related Factors," implies, they frame their discussion of past research findings in the social context of campus crime, by focusing on how potential offenders, suitable targets, and guardianship (or lack thereof) efforts impact on college students' victimization risk. Their summary of how students' lifestyles and "routine activities" heightens or reduces victimization risk provides postsecondary administrators with ideas for crime prevention strategies such as including self-protection and alcohol and drug use/abuse education into new student orientation. Mustaine and Tewksbury suggest that postsecondary schools consider ways to increase students' use of currently available programs and services and "thereby effectively lower their [students'] risks."

In Chapter 9, George Dowdall explores "The Role of Alcohol Abuse in College Student Victimization," by discussing the important but complex relationship between alcohol use/abuse and college student victimization. Drawing largely from results obtained by the *College Alcohol Study* conducted by Harvard University's School of Public Health, Dowdall describes the extent of students' drinking behavior, including levels of binge drinking, over the past decade and into the present. He also discusses both precollege and college-level factors that shape college drinking patterns and presents empirical evidence suggesting alcohol is associated with a wide range of problematic outcomes, including interpersonal violence. Well aware of the necessary conditions to establish causality, Dowdall presents a balanced assessment of whether a causal link exists between alcohol use/abuse and violence, and then closes the chapter by discussing what research shows about preventing college student abuse of alcohol.

Chapter 10, "The Acquaintance and Date Rape, Sexual Harassment, and Intimate Partner Abuse of College Women," by Joanne Belknap and Edna Erez, synthesizes more than three decades worth of published victimization research that focuses on college women. Taking a feminist perspective, Belknap and Erez describe what research has uncovered about the incidence and characteristics of aggression against college women and institutional and attitudinal factors related to aggression against women on campus. Although they conclude that, ". . . great headway has been made in raising awareness about various kinds of victimizations of women on college campuses," they also outline actions that campus administrators can take to acknowledge and address the reality of sexual victimization on college and university campuses.

In the first edition of the book, we did not include a chapter about college student stalking because very few published studies of college stalking victimization or perpetration existed. That gap is now filled by Chapter 11, "Vulnerabilities and Opportunities 101: The Extent, Nature, and Impact of Stalking Among College Students and Implications for Campus Policy and Programs," by Bonnie Fisher and Megan Stewart. To understand the extent and nature of stalking among college students, Fisher and Stewart discuss how both the sociodemographic characteristics of the student body, their lifestyles and routine activities, and campus characteristics meld to make students vulnerable stalking targets while simultaneously providing perpetrators with ample stalking opportunities. Drawing from findings of studies of campus stalking victims and perpetrators, Fisher and Stewart discuss a range of pertinent issues that provide the reader a detailed picture of who is stalked, for how long they are typically stalked, and why they are stalked, and tactics stalkers use to pursue targets. Because a sizable proportion of students have experienced a stalking victimization, they also highlight coping strategies students report using to stop the stalking and the emotional and psychological toll stalking takes on targets. They conclude their chapter by presenting evidence-based policy and program suggestions for campus administrators to adopt in an effort to prevent stalking behavior.

Chapter 12 concludes Part II. Written by Matthew Robinson and Sunghoon Roh, "Crime on Campus: Spatial Aspects of Campus Crime at a Regional Comprehensive University" examines a place-specific approach to understanding the spatial distribution of student victimization and crime prevention efforts arising from such an approach. Robinson and Roh used campus police calls-for-service data for different types of crime and drug and alcohol violations and plotted the campus location of these offences during the 2004–2005 academic year at Appalachian State University. Their explanation for the patterns of "hot spots" on campus provide campus administrators and police with results that should inform place-based or situational crime prevention strategies administrators may wish to implement.

These six chapters address a range of issues that are pertinent to understanding the social context of campus crime. Each chapter provides results from published social scientific research studies to describe the extent of student victimization experiences and explain known correlates or predictors of student victimization. Chapter authors show that many questions concerning the social context of student victimization have been addressed over the past decade and their answers have crime prevention policy, program, and service implications. Most important, each chapter lays the foundation for *future* theoretically and empirically driven research on the social context of campus crime.

Chapter 7

THE VIOLENT VICTIMIZATION OF COLLEGE STUDENTS: FINDINGS FROM THE NATIONAL CRIME VICTIMIZATION SURVEY

INTRODUCTION

Research examining the extent and nature of campus crime, its impact on students, and the response to it by college administrators and security officials has improved our understanding of this important social issue. A growing body of research suggests that on-campus victimization of college students is a rare occurrence, consisting mostly of nonviolent incidents such as personal theft and other property crimes (Bromley, 1992, 1995a; Fisher, Sloan, Cullen, & Lu, 1998; Sellers & Bromley, 1996; Sigler & Koehler, 1993; Sloan, 1992, 1994). In spite of relatively low campus crime rates, however, college students often express high levels of fear about becoming crime victims (Fisher, 1995; McCreedy & Dennis, 1996; Meijer, 1995). Responding to these fears, campus administrators and security officials have addressed environmental design and contextual factors believed to reduce campus crime and fear, such as improving exterior lighting, enhancing residence hall security, and developing educational "crime prevention programs" (Bromley, 1994; 1995b; Fisher & Nasar, 1992; Fisher & Sloan, 1993).

Although studies of the predictors of campus crime rates and college student victimization are enlightening, many relied upon a convenient sample at a single campus, used a limited number of schools, or provided anecdotal evidence (e.g., Gross, Winslett, Roberts, & Gohm, 2006; Henson & Stone, 1999; Nicholson, Maney, Blair, Wamboldt, Mahoney, & Yaun, 1998; Robinson & Mullen, 2001). Indeed, few national-level studies of college student victimization exist (Barberet, Fisher, & Taylor, 2004; Fisher & Cullen, 1999; Fisher,

Cullen, & Turner, 2000; Fisher et al., 1998). As a result, our understanding of college student victimization—especially incident-level characteristics of violent victimization—is limited (see Fisher et al., 2000). Improving our awareness of college student victimization is vital to the development of effective prevention policies and programs, especially situational crime prevention efforts. Furthermore, understanding the social and physical characteristics of these incidents enables campus administrators and security officials to tailor prevention and response efforts to specific situations and places. Data gathered by the National Crime Victimization Survey (NVCS), an annual national-level victimization survey conducted by the U.S. Department of Justice's Bureau of Justice Statistics, is well suited for this task.

This chapter uses NCVS data collected from 1995 through 2004 to provide estimates of the extent and nature of nonfatal violent victimizations experienced by college students. Specifically, the chapter compares levels of violence experienced among college students and similarly aged nonstudents; presents incident characteristics such as where (on or off campus) and when (during the day or at night) college students are likely victimized; and details college student victim characteristics such as gender, race, and Hispanic origin. The chapter also examines offender characteristics, including victim-offender relationship, whether the victim perceived the offender was under the influence of drugs and/or alcohol during the incident, and whether the offender was armed during the crime. Collectively, the findings presented provide a new and informative perspective on the social context of violent crime involving students. Discussion now turns to an overview of the National Crime Victimization Survey (NCVS).

The National Crime Victimization Survey

The NCVS is a national-level victimization survey that has collected information on the characteristics of crime incidents, crime victims, and victimization trends since the early 1970s. The NCVS uses a stratified, multistage, cluster sample that includes a rotating panel design. For selected households, the NCVS conducts interviews with respondents once every six months for a period of three years. Household members eligible for interview are individuals age 12 or older residing in the sampled household at the time of the survey. Respondent interviews are conducted both in person and over the telephone.

As part of an initial screening interview, the NCVS collects demographic information such as age, gender, race, and Hispanic origin for each eligible household member. The screening interview also determines whether an eligible household respondent was victimized sometime during the six-month reference period. For each violent crime, property crime, or property theft identified during the screening process, detailed incident-level information is also collected. Some of the incident-level characteristics of an identified victimization include when and where the crime occurred, whether a weapon was used, whether the victim was injured, and whether the crime was reported to the police. During the most recent series of NCVS surveys for which annual data is available, more than 84,000 households and nearly 150,000 individuals age 12 or older were interviewed; the response rates were 91 percent of eligible households and 84 percent of eligible individuals (Catalano, 2006).

This chapter presents findings from a subset of NCVS data collected during the period 1995 through 2004. With the exception of explicit comparisons involving students and nonstudents, all other data presented are limited to college students defined as a respondent who self-identified himself or herself as between the ages of 18 and 24 and enrolled in a college or university at least part-time at some point during the six months prior to the most recent NCVS interview.

Although violent, property, and personal theft victimization is identified by the survey, only nonfatal *violent* victimizations are included at present. Violent victimizations include threatened, attempted, or completed rape or sexual assault, robbery, aggravated assault, and simple assault. The NCVS defines rape as forced sexual intercourse that includes both psychological coercion as well as physical force, including heterosexual and homosexual rape as well as rape committed against both males and females. Attempted rape includes verbal threats of rape. Sexual assault is separate from rape or attempted rape and consists of incidents involving attacks or attempted attacks generally associated with unwanted sexual contact between victim and offender. Sexual assaults may or may not involve force and include such behavior as grabbing or fondling; they also include verbal threats.

Robbery constitutes property or cash taken directly from a person by use or threat of force, with or without a weapon, and with or without injury. Aggravated assault is defined as an actual or attempted attack with a weapon, regardless of whether injury resulted, or an attack or attempted attack without a weapon when serious injury results. Finally, simple assault involves an attack without a weapon resulting in either minor injury such as a bruise, cut, scrape or scratch, or no injury.

Violent Victimization of College Students

Violent Victimization Rates of Students and Nonstudents

Using NCVS data to estimate rates of violent victimization adds to the social scientific understanding of the nature and extent of campus crime, and provides the basis for other comparisons, such as comparing violence between students and nonstudents and changes in levels of violence among each group over time. Here, the chapter presents such comparisons.

Past research suggests college students, compared to others of similar ages, are at increased risk of being victimized (e.g., Fisher & Cullen, 1999; Fisher et al., 2000; Fisher et al., 1998). NCVS data can assess these claims by comparing rates of violent victimization of students with those of nonstudents. Table 7.1 reports average annual rates of violent victimization experienced by both college students and nonstudents between 1995 and 2004. Table 7.1 shows that students experienced annual rates of violent victimization below levels presented in previous studies (e.g., Fisher et al., 1998) and that the rates are significantly lower than victimization rates for nonstudents.

From 1995 through 2004, college students experienced overall nonfatal violence at a lower rate than similarly aged nonstudents: 56.4 victimizations

Table 7.1
NONFATAL VIOLENT VICTIMIZATION OF
COLLEGE STUDENTS AND NONSTUDENTS, 1995–2004

Victims age 18–24	Violent crime	Rape/ sexual assault	Robbery	Aggreavated assault	Simple assault	Serious violent crime[a]
College students						
Average annual rate	56.4[b]	3.7	5.1[c]	12.9	34.6	21.8[c]
Percent change, '95–'04	-53.0[d]	-40.0	-5.2	0.6	-73.5[df]	-7.6
Nonstudents						
Average annual rate	70.4	3.7	8.4	16.2	42.0	28.3
Percent change '95–'04	-54.2[d]	-33.3	-67.4[de]	-61.0[de]	-50.7[d]	-59.9[de]

Note: On average, from 1995 through 2004, the estimated student population was 8,223,690. For nonstudents, the estimated population during that period was 18,066,600.

a. Serious violent crime includes rape/sexual assault, robbery, and aggravated assault.

b. The difference between the college students' rate and nonstudents' rate is at the 95%-significance level.

c. The difference between the college students' rate and nonstudents' rate is at the 90%-significance level.

d. The difference from 1995 to 2004 is at the 95%-significance level.

e. The difference between the decline in rates among college students and nonstudents from 1995 to 2004 is at the 95%-significance level.

f. The difference between the decline in rates among the college students and nonstudents from 1995 to 2004 is at the 90%-significance level.

per 1,000 students versus 70.4 victimizations per 1,000 nonstudents, respectively. This includes students experiencing fewer robbery victimizations than did nonstudents (a rate of 5.1 per 1,000 students versus 8.4 per 1,000 nonstudents) and fewer serious (rape, sexual assault, robbery, and aggravated assault) violent victimizations as well (21.8 per 1,000 students versus 28.3 per 1,000 nonstudents).

Further, not only were there differences in levels of violent victimizations experienced by students and nonstudents, violence against both groups declined significantly during the 1995–2004 period, attributed mainly to a decline in rates of simple assault because simple assault accounts for more of the overall total than any other offense.

Although declines in the violence experienced by both students and non-students occurred between 1995 and 2004, the level of decline for specific violent crimes varied. For example, between 1995 and 2004, nonstudents experienced a greater decline in the rates of robbery victimization (67%), aggravated assault (61%), and serious violent crime (60%) than did students (5% for robbery, 1% for aggravated assault, and 8% for serious violent crime). In contrast, students had a larger decline in rates of simple assault (73%) than did nonstudents (51%).

In summary, Table 7.1 shows that, based on NCVS data, levels of violent victimization among college students is lower than levels described by previous studies. Further, college students' levels of violence are significantly lower nonstudents' levels. Additionally, NSVS data indicate that during the period 1995–2004, with the exception of simple assault, the rate of decline in violent victimization among nonstudents was greater than the rate of decline in violent victimization among students.

Although this information is informative and provides a general understanding of the extent of violent victimization of college students, examining event-specific characteristics associated with violent crimes among college students is prudent. The following section examines these characteristics.

Incident-Level Characteristics

NCVS data provide greater insight into the issue of campus crime because these data include information about the characteristics of incidents. Such information is unavailable in the crime statistics collected and reported by colleges and universities in accordance with the *Jeanne Clery Disclosure of Campus Security Policy and Campus Crime Statistics Act of 2000* (Pub. L. 101--542), since such statistics include only those offenses reported to campus police, campus security, other campus officials, or local law enforcement.

This section presents analyses of violent victimization incidents involving college students that occurred during the period 1995–2004. In doing so, the section addresses such issues as where (on- or off-campus) and the time of day these victimizations occurred; the extent students suffered injuries during these incidents; whether students reported their victimization to authorities; and whether victims took advantage of services available to them.

LOCATION OF INCIDENTS. A perennial question among campus crime researchers is this: Are college students more likely to experience victimization while they are on or off the campus? Figure 7.1 presents trends in rates of on-campus and off-campus violence experienced by college students between 1995 and 2004 and shows that most violent victimizations occurred off campus. In 2004, for example, the rate of *off-campus* victimization among college students (38.9 per 1,000 students) was nearly 20 times the rate of *on-campus* victimization (2.3 per 1,000 students). While this finding reveals that the *magnitude* of difference in levels of on- and off-campus violent victimization of college students is much greater than previously demonstrated (e.g., Fisher et al., 1998), it is consistent with previous research indicating that violence against college students is *more likely* to occur away from campus (Fisher et al., 1998; Sellers & Bromley, 1996; Sigler & Koehler, 1993).

NCVS findings also reveal an interesting pattern with respect to declines in on- and off-campus violence. Specifically, from 1995 through 2004, while there was a significant decline in rates of off-campus violence against college

Rate of violent crime per 1,000 students age 18-24

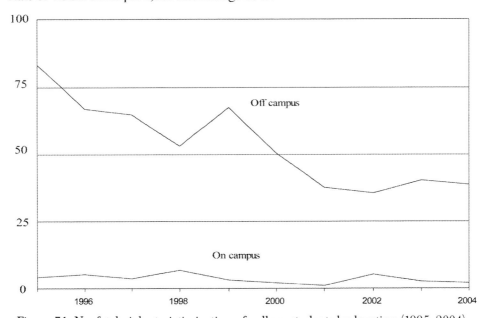

Figure 7.1. Nonfatal violent victimization of college students by location (1995–2004).

students, such a significant decline in on-campus violence did not occur. Thus, NCVS data not only demonstrate that the relative risk of violent victimization among college students is far greater off campus than on, but that similar trends in on-campus and off-campus victimization rates have not occurred the past several years.

TIME OF INCIDENTS. In addition to producing information on *where* college student victimization occurs, NCVS data also provide insight into *when* college students experience these victimizations. That is, NCVS data can answer the question: When are college student most likely to become victims of violent crime?

Table 7.2 presents incident-level information on college student violence occurring both on campus and off campus by when the incident occurred. Results show students experienced about 2.5 times more violence at night–between the hours of 6 p.m. and 6 a.m.–than during the day (6 a.m. to 6 p.m.). However, a different pattern emerges for violence occurring on campus when one considers location *in conjunction* with time. On-campus incidents involving violence are more likely to take place during the day (58%) than at night (37%), while incidents of off-campus violence occur more frequently at night (72%) than during the day (26%).

This pattern is likely the result of two factors: opportunity and behavior. That is to say, most of the on-campus violence that college students experience occurs during the day simply because that is where students spend most of their time. Although students traditionally are on campus during the day engaging in behavior that tends not to be associated with violent victimization (i.e., going to class, studying at the library, or hanging out at the student union), the opportunity for such victimization is greater, given the number of students on campus. Recall that *most* violence against students occurs off campus and an estimated two-thirds of all college student violence occurs there between the hours of 6 p.m. and 6 a.m. During the evening and away from school, college students are more likely to engage in behavior that can lead to increased risk of violent victimization (e.g., partying, drinking, and "blowing off steam").

INJURIES INCURRED BY STUDENT VICTIMS. Incident-level data can also address the question "To what extent does injury result when students are violently victimized?" Results shown in Table 7.2 indicate that about one-in-four violent crimes committed against college students result in an injury and are consistent with prior research suggesting that college student victims of violence infrequently sustain injuries (Baum & Klaus, 2005; Hart, 2003).

Because approximately 14 of every 15 violent incidents involving college students occur off campus, the extent violence resulting in injury occurs while *on campus* can be overshadowed if not examined separately. Indeed, when one examines location of the incident, a different pattern emerges.

Table 7.2 shows that the amount of off-campus violence resulting in injury (26%) is greater than the amount of on-campus violence that results in injury (20%). These findings suggest that not only are college students safer from violence when they are on campus, the violence they experience while on campus is less severe.

INCIDENTS REPORTED TO POLICE. One can also use NCVS data to assess the extent college students report their violent victimizations to police. Research shows that among the general population, only about one-half of all violent crime is reported to the police (see Catalano, 2006; Hart & Rennison, 2003). As discussed below, although patterns of reporting for college students vary from those observed in the general population, students do provide similar reasons for why they do not report their violent victimizations (Hart & Rennison, 2003).

Findings presented in Table 7.2 show that students report about two-fifths of all violent victimizations experienced to police. Stated differently, the police are *unaware* of most of the violence sustained by college students. Although an estimated 37 percent of *off-campus* violence among college stu-

Table 7.2
NONFATAL VIOLENT VICTIIZATION OF COLLEGE STUDENTS
BY LOCATION AND INCIDENT CHARACTERISTICS, 1995–2004

Incident characteristics	Average annual number		Percent of all violence	
	on campus	*off campus*	*on campus*	*off campus*
Time of incident				
Day (6 a.m.–6 p.m.)	17,600	110,270	57.7	25.6
Night (6 p.m.–6 a.m.)	11,200	309,880	36.6	72.0
Don't know	1,740 [a]	9,270	5.7 [a]	2.2
Injuries				
No	24,780	318,190	80.2	73.5
Yes	6,110	114,610	19.8	26.5
Reported to the police				
No	21,140	263,150	68.4	60.8
Yes	8,970	161,450	29.0	37.3
Don't know	780 [a]	7,660	2.5 [a]	1.8
Victims' assistance				
No	28,980	408,060	93.8	94.3
Yes	1,900 [a]	21,720	6.2 [a]	5.0
Don't know	0	1,350 [a]	0.0	0.3 [a]

Note: Detail may not add to 100% due to rounding or missing data.
a. Based on 10 or fewer sample cases.

dents is reported to the police, on-campus violent crime is reported to police less often (29%). These findings indicate that while college students are far less likely to experience violence on our nation's campuses, when it does occur, it is less likely to be reported to police. Why might this be the case?

Table 7.3 presents reasons given by students concerning why they did not report their violent victimizations to police, and shows the most common reason given was because students considered the victimization a "private or personal matter" (29%). Moreover, while 19 percent of on-campus violence is not reported to police because it is reported to another official, fewer incidents of off-campus violence are not reported to police for the same reason (6%). Conversely, a greater percentage of off-campus victimization is not reported to police because the violence reportedly resulted in a "small loss or no loss at all" (26% versus 14%, respectively). From 1995 through 2004, about 9 percent of off-campus violence against college students was not reported to police because reporting the crime was "inconvenient," while about 4 percent of on-campus violence was not reported for this reason." Fear of reprisal was cited about 3 percent of the time for off-campus violence; however, none of the students who experienced on-campus violence indicated fear of reprisal was the reason for not reporting the incident to police.

VICTIMS' USE OF ASSISTANCE AGENCIES OR ORGANIZATIONS. Recently, colleges and universities have either developed or expanded victim assistance programs, with most providing group presentations on awareness and

Table 7.3
NONFATAL VIOLENT VICTIMIZATION OF COLLEGE
STUDENTS BY LOCATION AND REASONS FOR NOT
REPORTING VIOLENCE TO POLICE, 1995–2004

	Percent of reasons	
Reasons for not reporting	*on campus*	*off campus*
Private or personal matter	28.6	25.4
Reported to another official	18.8	5.9
Small/no loss	13.6	25.6
Inconvenient	8.5	3.7
Lack of proof	7.8	4.5
Not important to police	5.9	3.8
Not clear a crime occurred	3.1	4.7
Protect offender	1.5	3.8
Police inefficient	1.3	1.3
Fear of reprisal	0.0	3.2
Other	10.7	18.1

Note: Detail may not add to 100% due to rounding or missing data.

prevention, or publishing crime-safety bulletins or announcements (Bromley & Fisher, 2002; Karjane, Fisher, & Cullen, 2005). Moreover, although recent findings by Karjane et al., (2005) show that mental health crisis counseling is the most widely available victims' service for students experiencing a sexual assault, little is known about the extent to which student victims utilize organizations or agencies designed to help crime victims.

Findings presented in Table 7.2 reveal that overall only about 5 percent of all student victims seek assistance after suffering a violent victimization, and the pattern holds regardless of whether an incident occurred on campus or off campus. That is, college students victimized on campus are no more likely to seek help from victim assistance agencies or organizations (6%) than are students who are victimized off campus (5%).

In summary, analysis of incident-specific characteristics associated with college student victimization reveals patterns associated with (1) when campus violence occurs, (2) the extent to which campus violence results in injury, (3) the extent to which violence is reported to police, and (4) whether college student victims reportedly seek assistance from organizations or agencies designed to aid victims of violence. Findings show that most violence against college students occurs off campus at night, is not likely to result in injurious harm, is not likely to be reported to the police, and is not likely to result in the victim seeking assistance from organizations or agencies designed to help them. In addition to answering important questions about the event-specific characteristics of college student victimization, NCVS data can also provide insight into questions pertaining to crime-victim characteristics.

Characteristics of College Student Victims of Violence

NCVS data provide detailed information about crime victims, unlike official statistics gathered and produced by colleges and universities. Student victim characteristics, such as gender, race, and ethnic origin, are examined below to identify whether individual-level characteristics of college students are linked to increased risk of violent victimization such as those identified in the general population (e.g., Sampson & Lauritsen, 1994).

Gender

The most recent results from the NCVS show that males in the general population age 12 or older experience overall violent crime, robbery, and assault at higher rates than females (see Catalano, 2006). A similar pattern emerges among students victimized on college campuses.

Table 7.4 provides demographic information on student victims and reveals that between 1994 and 2005, both male and female college students experienced higher levels of overall violence, serious violence, and simple assault while off campus. As shown in the table, the overall rates of off-campus violence, as well as rates of serious violence and simple assault were significantly higher among males (67.7, 40.2, and 27.5 per 1,000 students, respectively) than among females (38.6, 24.2, and 14.4 per 1,000 students, respectively). On-campus victimization levels also showed that male students experienced higher overall levels of violence (5.8 per per 1,000 students) and serious violence (1.3 per 1,000 students) than did female students (1.9 per 1,000 students and 0.8 per 1,000 students, respectively). The on-campus rate of simple assault among male students (4.4 per 1,000 students) was not significantly different than was the rate for female students (1.1 per 1,000 students).

Race and Ethnicity

Results presented in Table 7.4 also demonstrate that, between 1994 and 2005, regardless of race or ethnic origin, college students were at greater risk of experiencing any violent victimization, serious violence, and simple assault while off campus. For example, among white students, the rate for overall violence (55.0 per 1,000 students) while off campus was about 12 times the rate of on campus violence (4.4. per 1,000 students). The rate of off-campus victimization of African American students (54.7 per 1,000 students) was about 25 times the rate of on-campus violence (2.7 per 1,000 students). Likewise, Hispanic students experienced off-campus violence at a rate estimated at about 25 times the rate of on-campus violence (50.4 versus 2.1 per 1,000 students).

Although these data show that regardless of race, college students were at increased risk for violent victimization while off campus, NCVS data also indicated differences exist in rates of violent victimization across racial/ethic groups by location. For example, overall violence rates for white students while on campus were higher than were rates for Hispanic students (4.4 versus 2.1 per 1,000 students), while rates of off-campus violence for the two groups were statistically similar (55.0 versus 50.4 per 1,000 students, respectively). Hispanic college students were, however, more likely than students who were niether white nor African American to experience violent crime off campus (50.4 versus 30.9 per 1,000 students), yet when victimization rates associated with these two groups are examined for violent crime that occurs *on campus,* differences are no longer measurable (2.1 versus 2.2 per 1,000 students). Finally, while away from campus, white students were victims of simple assault at rates significantly greater than African American students (35.6 versus 22.6 per 1,000 students); yet when only on-campus incidents are considered, there is no measurable difference in the rates of simple assaults between the two groups (3.1 versus 2.3 per 1,000 students).

Table 7.4

NONFATAL VIOLENT VICTIMIZATION OF COLLEGE STUDENTS
BY LOCATION AND DEMOGRAPHIC INFORMATION, 1995–2004

Victims of violence	*Population*		*Violent crime*	*Rape/ sexual assault*	*Robbery*	*Aggravated assault*	*Simple assault*	*Serious violent crime*
		Average annual rates per 1,000 students age 18–24						
College students	8,223,690		56.4	3.7	5.1	12.9	34.6	21.8
On campus								
Gender								
Male	3,960,350		5.8	0.0ᵃ	0.3ᵃ	1.0	4.4	1.3
Female	4,263,340		1.9	0.3ᵃ	0.1ᵃ	0.3ᵃ	1.1	0.8
Race/ethnicityᵇ								
White	5,767,480		4.4	0.2ᵃ	0.3ᵃ	0.8	3.1	1.3
Black	950,090		2.7ᵃ	0.0ᵃ	0.0ᵃ	0.4ᵃ	2.3ᵃ	0.4ᵃ
Other	626,480		2.2ᵃ	0.0ᵃ	0.5ᵃ	0.0ᵃ	1.7ᵃ	0.5ᵃ
Hispanic, any race	879,640		2.1	0.0ᵃ	0.0ᵃ	0.8ᵃ	1.3ᵃ	0.8ᵃ
Off campus								
Gender								
Male	3,960,350		67.7	1.2	7.2	19.1	40.2	27.5
Female	4,263,340		38.6	5.7	2.8	5.9	24.2	14.4
Race/ethnicityᵇ								
White	5,767,480		55.0	3.5	4.2	11.7	35.6	19.4
Black	950,090		54.7	3.6ᵃ	10.9	17.5	22.6	32.0
Other	626,480		30.9	1.5ᵃ	5.3ᵃ	9.5	14.6	16.3
Hispanic, any race	879,640		50.4	4.7	3.0ᵃ	12.6	30.1	20.4

a. Based on 10 or fewer sample cases.
b. All racial categories do not include Hispanics. "Other" category includes Asians, Native Hawaiians, Pacific Islanders, Alaska Natives, and American Indians combined.

The above analyses of the demographic characteristics college student victims of violence identified several important patterns. For example, significant differences in levels of violence experienced by college students exist by gender as well as by race and Hispanic origin. Furthermore, when viewed in light of event-specific information such as where violence against college students occurs (i.e., on campus or off campus), a broader understanding of the link between increased risk of violent victimization and individual-level characteristics of college students is developed.

Attention now turns to the characteristics of offenders who commit violence against college students. As with event- and victim-characteristics, NCVS-based information pertaining to the characteristics of offenders expands our understanding of student victimization experiences involving violence, including the extent the offenders were known to victims, were perceived as under the influence of drugs or alcohol, and whether offenders presented/used weapons.

Offender Characteristics

In addition to gathering information on the characteristics of incidents and victims, NCVS data also include information on offenders. For each incident identified during an interview, the interviewer then asks a respondent to recall the characteristics of the person or persons who victimized them. For example, the interviewer asks victims whether the offender was someone they knew and whether the victim perceived that the offender was under the influence of drugs or alcohol, and whether the offender had a weapon. Similar to event- and victim-specific information, offender-based information aids in developing a more robust understanding of the nature and extent of violent victimization of college students.

Victim-Offender Relationship

Do strangers or persons known to victims perpetrate most of the violence against college students? Table 7.5 presents information on the extent to which victims knew their offenders or if the offenders were strangers. Significantly, NCVS data reveal that most offenders (51%) perpetrating on-campus violence against students were strangers. Non-strangers (38%) constituted a much smaller percentage of off-campus violent offenders.

Perceived Drug/Alcohol Use by the Offender

The NCVS interview also asks victims if they believe the offender was under the influence of either drugs or alcohol at the time of the incident. Respondents' answers to this question can help social scientists further

Table 7.5
NONFATAL VIOLENT VICTIIZATION OF COLLEGE STUDENTS
BY LOCATION AND OFFENDER CHARACTERISTICS, 1995–2004

Offender characteristics	Average annual number		Percent of all violence	
	on campus	*off campus*	*on campus*	*off campus*
Relationship to victim				
Known[c]	12,510	162,480	40.5	37.9
Stranger	15,830	253,060	51.2	59.1
Don't know	2,550 [a]	12,700	8.3 [a]	3.0
Perceived alcohol/drug use[b]				
Using	8,270	180,400	26.8	41.7
Not using	13,930	84,270	45.1	19.5
Don't know	8,410	163,580	27.2	37.8
Presence of weapon				
No	20,820	281,980	67.4	65.2
Yes	7,150	118,180	23.2	27.3
Don't know	2,920 [a]	32,640	9.4 [a]	7.5

Note: Detail may not add to 100% due to rounding or missing data.

a. Based on 10 or fewer sample cases.

b. Alcohol/drug use based on whether the victim believed the offender(s) was under the influence at the time of the incident.

c. A spouse, ex-spouse, boyfriend, girlfriend, parent, child, other relative, or a victim's friend or acquaintance.

understand the extent drugs and alcohol use plays a role in the violent victimization of students.

Findings presented in Table 7.5 indicate that, according to victims of on-campus violence, 45 percent of offenders in these incidents were perceived as not under the influence of drugs or alcohol, while the pattern is reversed for off-campus incidents. Here, NCVS data indicated that victims said more off-campus incidents were committed by an offender whom the victim believed under the influence of drugs or alcohol (42%) than by an offender whom the victim believed was not (19%).

Use of Weapon by the Offender

Finally, findings from past research suggest a growing number of students carry weapons on college campuses (e.g., Summers & Hoffman, 1998). As weapon carrying among students increases, so does the risk the person using the weapon to perpetrate a crime. However, NCVS data show that between

1995 and 2004, most violence experienced by college student did not involve the use of a weapon. Specifically, results in Table 7.5 show that an estimated 67 percent of nonfatal violence experienced by college students on campus and about 65 percent of college student victimization occurring off campus did *not* involve a weapon. In short, regardless of whether college students were victimized on campus or off, most of the time, weapons were not involved.

Analyses of NCVS data reveal a number of interesting patterns associated with violent offenders and crimes committed against college students. For example, most violent crimes experienced by college students are not committed by a spouse, boyfriend, girlfriend, parent, child, other relative, or by the victim's friend or acquaintance. In short, strangers commit the majority of violence against college students. Furthermore, the likelihood that a college student experiences violence by an offender who is under the influence of alcohol or drugs is largely dependent on whether the incident occurs on campus or off campus. Finally, regardless of whether incidents occur on campus or off, most of the violence against college students does not involve an armed offender. As with the event-specific information and victim-level characteristics associated with violent crime, information obtained during NCVS about violent offenders provides important details about the violent victimization of college students that help us better understand this important social issue.

Conclusion

Self-report victimization data produced from the NCVS offer several noteworthy results relating to the extent and nature of violence experienced by college students. First, college students experience violent crime at rates lower than do nonstudents of similar age. Second, while the rate of violent victimization among college students declined significantly over the past decade, the magnitude of this decline was comparable for both students and nonstudents alike. Third, violence against college students most often occurred off campus. Indeed, on-campus violence among students was a rare event, occurring about 17 times less often than off-campus crime. Fourth, college students tended not to report their victimizations to police–regardless of whether it occurred on or off campus. The data revealed that victims of on-campus violence were more likely to report the incident to another campus official than to police. Fifth, most victims did not seek help from organizations designed to provide them with assistance or services. Sixth, male students and white, non-Hispanic students were more likely than female students and non-Hispanic students of color, respectively, to experience campus violence. Finally, victims indicated that most violence on college campuses did *not* involve a weapon or injury to the victim. Victims also perceived that offenders perpetrating these incidents were not under the influence of drugs or alcohol at the time of the incident.

Patterns and trends identified above provide useful insight into violence against college students and suggest ways that campus administrators and security officials can improve responses to college student violence. For example, NCVS data revealed that college students victimized by violence rarely seek support from organizations designed to help them. Apparently, an institution establishing victim assistance programs is not an adequate response to violent student victimization. University officials must constantly remind students—especially victims of violence—that assistance programs are not just available, but should be utilized.

In some instances, current findings challenge past research in ways that offer new guidance to the research community. Prior studies suggest that college women are at increased risk for sexual victimization on college campuses (Belknap & Erez, 2007; Brantingham & Brantingham, 1999; Fisher et al., 2000), and reveal certain lifestyle factors that play a role in female students' increased risk of campus crime such as sexual victimization (e.g., Fisher et al., 1998; Mustaine & Tewksbury, 2002; Schwartz & Pitts, 1995). NCVS data indicate, however, that neither the average annual rate of rape/sexual assault nor the decline in the rate of rape/sexual assault experienced by college students is measurably different from that of similarly aged nonstudents. Although estimates of sexual victimization of college students produced from current analyses are seemingly at odds with past research, differences could be due to the methodological approaches to the way studies operationalize and measure victimization (Fisher & Cullen, 2000; Rand & Rennison, 2004a, 2004b).

Analyses of NCVS data add to the scientific dialog associated with the violent victimization of college students. Using NCVS data to analyze patterns and trends over time relating to violence involving college students broadens our overall understanding of the nature and extent of campus crime and college student victimization beyond that which can be gleaned from official statistics such as those made available by postsecondary institutions in compliance with the *Jeanne Clery Disclosure of Campus Security Policy and Campus Crime Statistics Act of 2000* (Pub. L. 101–542). NCVS data can thus serve as an additional source of information that campus policy makers can consult when making decisions about the design and implementation of campus security policies and victim assistance programs.

REFERENCES

Baum, K., & Klaus, P. (2005). *Violent victimization of college students, 1995-2002* (NCJ 20636). Washington, DC: Bureau of Justice Statistics, United States Government

Printing Office.

Barberet, R., Fisher, B. S., & Taylor, H. (2004). *University student safety in East Midlands.* London: Home Office.

Belknap, J., & Erez, E. (2007). The sexual harassment, rape, and intimate partner abuse of college women. In B. S. Fisher & J. J. Sloan (Eds.), *Campus crime: Legal, social, and policy perspectives* (2nd ed.). Springfield, IL: Charles C Thomas.

Brantingham, P. L., & Brantingham, P. J. (1999). A theoretical model of crime hot spot generation. *Studies on Crime and Crime Prevention, 8,* 7–26.

Bromley, M. L. (1992). Campus and community crime rate comparisons: A statewide study. *Journal of Security Administration, 15,* 49–64.

Bromley, M. L. (1994). Correlates of campus crime: A nationwide exploratory study of large universities. *Journal of Security Administration, 17,* 37–52.

Bromley, M. L. (1995a). Comparing campus and city crime rates: A descriptive study. *American Journal of Police, 14,* 131–148.

Bromley, M.L. (1995b). Factors associated with college crimes: Implications for campus police. *Journal of Police and Criminal Psychology, 10,* 13–19.

Bromley, M. L., & Fisher, B. S. (2002). Campus policing and victim services. In L. Moriarty (Ed.), *Policing and victims.* Upper Saddle River, NJ: Prentice-Hall.

Catalano, S. M. (2006). *Criminal victimization, 2005* (NCJ 214644). Washington, DC. Bureau of Justice Statistics, United States Government Printing Office.

Fisher, B. S. (1995). Crime and fear on campus. *Annals of the American Academy of Political and Social Science, 53,* 85–101.

Fisher, B. S., & Cullen, F. T. (1999). *The extent and nature of violence against college women: Results from a national-level Study: Final report* (NCJ 179977). Washington, D.C.: Bureau of Justice Statistics.

Fisher, B. S., & Cullen, F. T. (2000). Measuring the sexual victimization of women: Evolution, current controversies, future research. In D. Duffee (Ed.), *Criminal justice 2000: Vol. 4. Measurement and analysis of crime and justice.* Washington, DC: National Institute of Justice, United States Government Printing Office.

Fisher, B. S., Cullen, F. T., & Turner, M. G. (2000). *Sexual victimization of college women* (NCJ 182369). Washington, DC: National Institute of Justice, United States Government Printing Office.

Fisher, B. S., & Nasar, J. L. (1992). Students' fear of crime and its relation to physical features of the campus. *Journal of Security Administration, 15,* 65–75.

Fisher, B. S., & Sloan, J. J. (1993). University response to the *Campus Security Act of 1990:* Evaluating programs designed to reduce campus crime. *Journal of Security Administration, 16,* 67–80.

Fisher, B. S., Sloan, J. J., Cullen, F. T., & Lu, C. (1998). Crime in the ivory tower: The level and sources of student victimization. *Criminology, 36,* 671–710.

Gross, A. M., Winslett, A., Roberts, M., & Gohm, C. L. (2006). Examination of sexual violence against college women. *Violence against women, 12,* 288–300.

Hart, T. C. (2003). *Violent victimization of college students* (NCJ 196143). Washington, DC: Bureau of Justice Statistics, United States Government Printing Office.

Hart, T. C., & Rennison, C. M. (2003). *Reporting crime to the police, 1992–2001* (NCJ 195710). Washington, DC: Bureau of Justice Statistics, United States Government

Printing Office.

Henson, V. A., & Stone, W. E. (1999). Campus crime: A victimization study. *Journal of Criminal Justice, 27,* 295–307.

Karjane, H., Fisher, B. S., & Cullen, F. T. (2005). *Sexual assault on campus: What colleges and universities are doing about it* (NCJ 205521). Washington, DC: National Institute of Justice, United States Government Printing Office.

McCreedy, K. R., & Dennis, B. G. (1996). Sex-related offenses and fear of crime on campus. *Journal of Contemporary Criminal Justice, 12,* 69–80.

Meijer, J. (1995). Surveying campus crime: What can be done to reduce crime and fear? *Campus Law Enforcement Journal, 25,* 4, 6, 15.

Mustaine, E. E., & Tewksbury, R. (2002). Sexual assault of college women: A feminist interpretation of a routine activities analysis. *Criminal Justice Review, 27,* 89–123.

Nicholson, M. E., Maney, D. W., Blair, K., Wamboldt, P. M., Mahoney, B. S., & Yaun, J. (1998). Trends in alcohol-related campus violence: Implications for prevention. *Journal of Alcohol and Drug Education, 43,* 34–52.

Rand, M. R., & Rennison, C. M. (2004a). How much violence against women is there? In B. S. Fisher (Ed.), *Violence against women and family violence: Developments in research, practice, and policy.* Washington, DC: United States Government Printing Office.

Rand, M. R., & Rennison, C. M. (2004b). Bigger is not necessarily better: An analysis of violence against women estimates from the National Crime Victimization Survey and the National Violence Against Women Survey. *Journal of Quantitative Criminology, 21,* 267–291.

Robinson, M. B., & Mullen, K. L. (2001). Crime on campus: A survey of space users. *Crime Prevention and Community Safety: An International Journal, 3,* 33–46.

Sampson, R. J., & Lauritsen, J. L. (1994). Violent victimization and offending: Individual-, situational-, and community-level risk factors. In A. J. Reiss & J. A. Roth (Eds), *Understanding and preventing violence: Social influences on violence, vol. 3.* Washington, DC: National Research Council.

Schwartz, M. D., & Pitts, V. L. (1995). Exploring a feminist routine activities approach to explaining sexual assault. *Justice Quarterly, 12,* 9–31.

Sellers, C. S., & Bromley, M. L. (1996). Violent behavior in college student dating relationships: Implications for campus service providers. *Journal of Contemporary Criminal Justice, 12,* 2–27.

Sigler, R. T., & Koehler, N. (1993). Victimization and crime on campus. *International Review of Victimology, 2,* 331–343.

Sloan, J. J. (1992). Campus crime and campus communities: An analysis of crimes known to campus police and security. *Journal of Security Administration, 15,* 31–47.

Sloan, J. J. (1994). Correlates of campus crime: An analysis of reported crimes on college and university campuses. *Journal of Criminal Justice, 22,* 51–61.

Summers, R. W., & Hoffman, A. M. (1998). Weapon carrying on campus. In A. M. Hoffman, J. H. Schuh, & R. H. Fenske (Eds.), *Violence on campus: Defining the problems, strategies for action.* Fredrick, MD: Aspen.

Chapter 8

THE ROUTINE ACTIVITIES AND CRIMINAL VICTIMIZATION OF STUDENTS: LIFESTYLE AND RELATED FACTORS

ELIZABETH EHRHARDT MUSTAINE AND RICHARD TEWKSBURY

INTRODUCTION

The last few decades have seen significant advances in understanding college students' victimization experiences. Studies exploring student victimization on campus have included discussions of the dynamics of criminal incidents, the participation and interaction of students in these criminal incidents as victims and offenders, and the role guardianship can play in the thwarting (or not) of criminal events in progress or the warding off (or not) of criminal attempts before they begin. Routine activities theory has been the driving perspective in much of this research, utilizing two central propositions–that daily routine activities, or lifestyles, create criminal opportunities by increasing (or decreasing) the frequency of contact between individuals who are potential offenders and those who are potential victimization targets. Second, the suitability of a target along with its level of guardianship determines victim selection. Routine activities theory–originally proposed by Cohen and Felson (1979)–incorporates both structural aspects of the environment as well as issues of physical environments and free will (e.g., choice) in explaining criminal victimization (Meithe & Meier, 1990). Research inspired by routine activities theory has consistently shown that criminal victimization risks are not randomly distributed in society but are related to the lifestyles and routine activities of victims and offenders, particularly those lifestyles and routines that increase the likelihood of victims and offenders coming together in the same space and time outside the purview of effective and willing guardians.

147

Theoretically, college students have above average risks for criminal victimization because they tend to have daily routines that put them into situations and locations where there are a large number of potential offenders (Maxfield, 1987). Additionally, college students have routines whereby at these more dangerous or risky locations they are more vulnerable as targets due to a lack of capable guardianship, or an inability to recognize the danger(s) involved in their circumstances. For example, college students are more likely to frequent bars or other public places to drink alcohol; they attend parties where alcohol and drugs may be present; and while they may start their evenings out in groups, these groups do not necessarily stay together throughout the course of the night. Further, many students live in off-campus apartments which are typically full of transient students largely unknown to each other and who cannot effectively guard each other's persons or property since they do not know who should be present or not. For these reasons, routine activities theory is well suited to serve as a framework for explaining the criminal victimization patterns of college students.

In the remainder of the chapter, we discuss and highlight common conclusions of routine activities scholars regarding how potential offenders, suitable targets, and lack of guardianship efforts affect the victimization risks of college students. We first discuss potential offenders, their characteristics, proximity to college student potential victims, and daily activities of those who may be motivated to take advantage of presented criminal opportunities. We follow this by discussing how the lifestyles of college students heighten (or reduce) their chances for criminal victimization. Here, we highlight the types of activities, interaction contexts, and college student lifestyles that place them in close proximity to potential offenders, as well as those routines that decrease their self-protective behaviors or result in a failure to utilize effective guardianship practices. We then discuss specific self-protective behaviors and guardianship practices that may be effective in reducing college students' chances for criminal victimization. Finally, we conclude the chapter by summarizing common conclusions from routine activities researchers and consider how they are policy relevant for university administrators and other personnel concerned with reducing the victimization experiences of students.

Potential Offenders

Co-Presence with Potential Offenders

Central to routine activities theory is the idea that victimization is contingent upon the presence of potential offenders. Suitable targets can and only will become victims when others seeking opportunities to offend encounter them in situations and settings that lack capable guardianship. Therefore, one's presence in certain settings, at certain times, and presenting oneself to others in certain ways are critical issues for predicting victimization, especially when potential offenders are present.

The persons that one spends time with are important for understanding students' exposure to potential offenders. This may be especially important for college students, as the most common perpetrators of crimes against students are other students (Fisher & Sloan, 1995; Siegel & Raymond, 1992). For example, students on campuses with a greater proportion of minority students experience generally increased rates of officially reported campus crime (Sloan, 1992; 1994). Students who spend more of their weekdays and weekends alone have decreased risks of violent victimization, as one might expect (Mustaine & Tewksbury, 2000); however, those who spend more time with strangers (as opposed to friends, family, and acquaintances) also have decreased risks of experiencing an assault. Yet, for some offenses, such as stalking, married women or those cohabitating (and presumably spending more time with their domestic partners), have lower odds of being stalked (Fisher et al., 2002).

Where and with whom students spend their social time are also important for determining proximity to potential offenders, and hence the chances of being a victim. Perhaps best established in the literature regarding campus locations is evidence that fraternity houses may be especially risky for victimization. Women who spend more time in fraternity houses have significantly increased risks for sexual assault (Stombler, 1994) and fraternity members are overrepresented among college campus sexual assault perpetrators (Frintner & Rubinson, 1993; Martin & Hummer, 1989; Copenhaver & Grauerholz, 1991). To elaborate, fully 24 percent of sorority women report having experienced an attempted and 17 percent report a completed sexual assault (Copenhaver & Grauerholtz, 1991), with many of these victimizations occurring in fraternity houses. These facts contribute to the beliefs of some that fraternities maintain and perpetuate a rape culture among college men (Martin & Hummer, 1989; Sanday, 1990; Tyler, Hoyt, & Whitbeck, 1998). Evidence, then, suggests that these increased risks are due to women being in close proximity to fraternity men who have higher levels of acceptance for rape myths (Schaeffer & Nelson, 1993).

Proximity to potential offenders may also be a function of time. As stated above, students who spend time away from home, especially in the evening, are at a generally increased risk of victimization. Sexual assaults of female college students may be especially likely in the evenings or late at night, as the majority of unwanted sexual experiences for women occur at or after parties (Barberet, Fisher, & Taylor, 2004; Ward, Chapman, Cohn, White, & Williams, 1991). Also related is time of day, where afternoons are the most risky time for theft victimization (see Barberet et al., 2004; Seng, 1996).

The most influential of predictors related to proximity to potential offenders are the activities in which one's friends, acquaintances, and associates participate. When spending more time on campus "partying," victimization risks increase (Fisher, Sloan, Cullen, & Lu, 1998). Further, the younger are the people with whom one drinks alcohol, the higher are the chances of victimization (Mustaine & Tewksbury, 1998c). Similarly, students who are present when others are using drugs experience increased vandalism victimization risks (Tewksbury & Mustaine, 2000).

Students who engage in behaviors that victimize others (typically in a group setting) are themselves more likely to be victimized (Tewksbury & Mustaine, 2000). The simple act of intending to engage in a variety of risk-taking behaviors may increase one's risk for sexual assault (Combs-Lane & Smith, 2002). Similarly, research shows increased risks of victimization arise from participating in a physical fight (Tewksbury & Mustaine, 2000). Risk of theft victimization increases for students who are aggressive and threaten others–whether with a weapon or not (Mustaine & Tewksbury, 1998a). Research shows that students who live in all-male dorms have higher risk of theft victimization, especially when residing in small dorms (Fisher et al., 1998).

Other locations in which one spends time and the type of persons with whom one spends time are important predictors of college student victimization. Mustaine and Tewksbury (1998c) have shown that the number of evenings students spend away from home for leisure purposes, and the later one returns home from leisure activities are strong predictors of violent crime victimization for students. When victimized, college students are more likely to be engaged in leisure activities than noncollege students who were more likely to be doing something other than leisure (Baum & Klaus, 2005). Additionally, at least for violent victimizations, most of the victimization happens off campus (Barberet et al., 2004; Sigler & Koehler, 1993; Baum & Klaus, 2005). Fully 72 percent of the violent victimization of students happens away from campus (Baum & Klaus, 2005). It is not only leisure activities, however, that take students into public domains. So too do many students leave home for purposes of studying. As the amount of time that students spend away from their homes to study increases, so too do their risks of property crime (Mustaine & Tewksbury, 1998a).

Another form of immersion with potential offenders occurs when students engage in recreational activities. Simple endeavors such as going to a shopping mall frequently, eating out frequently, and going to the gym or playing organized sports (for men) have all be shown to be related to violent crime victimization risks (Mustaine & Tewksbury, 1998c). Also, regularly spending time in bars can increase risks for sexual assault (Mustaine & Tewksbury, 1998b; Tewksbury & Mustaine, 2001), "uncomfortable" sexual advances (Schwartz &

Pitts, 1995), and stalking (Mustaine & Tewksbury, 1999). Similarly, simply "hanging out" and doing nothing in particular is related to increased sexual assault risks for women (Mustaine & Tewksbury, 2002). Women who have friends who get women drunk for the purpose of gaining sexual access are also more likely to be sexually victimized (Schwartz & Pitts, 1995).

All of these activities are presumed to increase the risks of victimization not because of anything inherent in the activities, but rather because of the types of persons with which such activities brings one in contact. Conversely, research shows that other common forms of recreational activities predict reduced levels of victimization risks, presumably because these activities are less likely to immerse students with potential offenders. Such activities include going to the movies (Mustaine & Tewksbury, 2002), playing basketball or tennis in a public setting (Mustaine & Tewksbury, 1998a), attending community festivals/events (Mustaine & Tewksbury, 2000), and attending church services (Mynatt & Allgeier, 1990).

Finally, the role of athletic activities and their relationship to victimization risks can be seen in the experiences of college athletes. Simply being a college athlete can increase risks for both physical assault (Bausell, Bausell, & Siegel, 1991) and sexual victimization, for both females (Mustaine & Tewksbury, 2002) and males (Tewksbury & Mustaine, 2001). Here, the possible relationship may be that, as with fraternity men, male college athletes may support rape myths (Benedict, 1997; Benedict & Klein, 1997). Property crime likelihood is higher for members of university athletic teams–athletes have higher rates of theft victimization (Fisher et al., 1998). Again, risks are considered to be greater not because of anything about athletic activities themselves, but because of the types of persons with whom athletic activities may bring one in contact.

Being with and near others who may be motivated to offend is critically important to understanding the victimization risks of college students. Being away from one's "safe zone" of home and out-and-about with others–especially while engaging in leisure activities and/or committing criminal offenses–are especially important predictors of victimization risks. The types of locations where college students are likely to encounter and be exposed to potential offenders are many, but those most dangerous are those away from where students actually live. While both on- and off-campus locations increase or decrease risks of victimization (depending on type of activities in which students engage), recreational settings appear the most risky.

Similarities between Offenders and Victims

In addition to the locations where individuals spend their time, routine activities scholars also argue that it is important to assess the general characteristics of potential offenders and victims. Typically, researchers employ demographic characteristics as proxy indicators of lifestyle. The thinking here is based on the idea that a number of demographic variables (e.g., lifestyles) are shared by persons found in similar locations; or, said different-ly, lifestyle variables are theoretically linked to characteristics based on the patterns people with these similarities establish. For example, research shows that nonwhites, younger students, and students of lower socioeconomic class-es more likely suffer victimizations because of their similarity to offenders (and the connection that criminal offenders victimize those who are similar to themselves). Similarly, studies of victimization show that students with cer-tain demographic characteristics have specific lifestyles. For example, mar-ried persons have lower risks for victimization than students who are single because married people do not go out as often for leisure activities (Laub, 1990).

While research occasionally finds demographic characteristics are signifi-cant indicators of heightened (or reduced) victimization risks, more recent routine activities theory scholars have found that their effects are attenuated when other, more specific indicators of lifestyle are examined concurrently (see Mustaine & Tewksbury, 1997). The literature, however, does regularly show two such factors influence the victimization risks of college students, after controlling for the effects of lifestyle: students from lower socioeco-nomic backgrounds have a higher risk for larceny victimization and employed students have a higher risk for property victimization (Mustaine & Tewksbury, 1998a; Tewksbury & Mustaine, 2000).

In short, lifestyles that are similar to those of "typical" criminal offenders are also those associated with increased victimization risk. Because many set-tings are largely (although not universally) homogenous in regards to the characteristics of persons in the setting, it is only logical that potential offend-ers are going to have the most frequent and easy access to individuals with whom they share lifestyles and characteristics.

Suitable Targets

A second element in the examination of the lifestyle and related risks for college student victimization is the presence of suitable targets. Routine activ-ities theory generally acknowledges that suitable targets could be either per-sons or property that prospective offenders view as easily victimized or valu-able. In this way, persons or property could either be acceptably vulnerable or worth the risk of being caught. It is also possible that persons and prop-erty could be suitable simply because of the opportunity each presents to a potential offender.

Although its creators originally proposed routine activities theory as a macro-level theory (Cohen & Felson, 1979), more recent scholars working with the theory have moved to examinations of suitable targets on the micro-sociological level. In this way, the focus has moved away from looking at patterns and trends across social institutions and instead looks at specific lifestyle behaviors or statuses that make someone (or some thing) more likely to be targeted for victimization. This also means that routine activities theory suggests that victimization is most likely for people (and things) who are less able to mount effective resistance; are more desirable or valuable; are found more often in circumstances that inhibit self-protective concerns or help-seeking behaviors; are in circumstances that are risky, dangerous, or otherwise crime prone; and/or are frequently in exposed circumstances with those who are potential offenders.

Research assessing college students and their behaviors and statuses that are associated with higher risks for criminal victimization (due to increased suitability as a target) looks at both risky behaviors found to be associated with victimization in the general populace and behaviors specifically found among college students. Such scholars find a number of lifestyles or other risky factors to be important sources.

Location of College Student Residences

One aspect of college students' lifestyles that is often unique to their circumstances is the location of college student residences. For example, students who live in all-male dorms have been shown to have higher theft risks, especially when residing in small dorms (Fisher et al., 1998). Typically, college students live in either dorms on campus, or off-campus apartments, often in more transient or less-well physically maintained neighborhoods. Some research has also shown that most violence happens in students' residences (Fisher et al., 1998). Students who spend many nights on campus per week have increased victimization risks, especially for crimes of theft (Fisher et al., 1998). For the crime of stalking, research shows that college women are most likely stalked, whether on campus, off campus, or both, at their residence (Fisher et al., 2002).

Theoretically, the living situation of the on-campus dorm should protect students from criminal victimization because students in dorms know each other, they know who lives in their dorm and who does not, and most on-campus dorms have resident assistants, who are older and more experienced students, who reside on each floor and function to help, advise, and offer a certain amount of protection for students.

Conversely, living in an apartment or complex in a more socially disorganized neighborhood is more likely to be associated with increased criminal victimization because of the anonymous nature of apartment living (Zito,

1974). Students in apartments often move from year to year, change room-mates, spend a great deal of time away from their residence, and as a result, may be leaving their residence and possessions unguarded (Robinson, 1997). These neighborhoods are also less able to utilize effective crime prevention efforts because residents do not know each other or who should be hanging around the complex and who should not (Zito, 1974; Robinson, 1997). As such, routine activities theory would posit that students living in dorms on campus should experience an insulated effect with crime, while students living off campus would encounter more crime and criminal victimization.

A final theoretical relationship between location or residence and criminal victimization risks is whether students live near other community structures or conditions that are crime-prone locations (e.g., places that are not well guarded, places where unsupervised youth hang out, etc.). As discussed below, research on these relationships between residential location and criminal victimization risks has some contrary findings but more often than not supports these assertions.

Regarding on-campus or off-campus residential location, research has found that women who live on campus have lower risks for stalking victimization (Mustaine & Tewksbury, 1999). However, female students who live on campus have increased risks for sexual victimization (Fisher et al., 2000). It is interesting and important to point out that research examining this relationship with data other than self-reports of victimization provide contradictory findings. For instance, Sloan (1992) reported that when a greater proportion of students lived on campus, the crime rates reported in the Uniform Crime Reports (e.g., those offenses reported to law enforcement agencies) increased. However, others have found that based on self-reports of victimization, when there are more students who live on campus, the on-campus theft rate decreases (Fisher et al., 1998).

Among certain college students, living in the dorm does not insulate them from criminal behavior. Research has found that victimization risks increase when students are in authority positions or possess items desirable to steal. Palmer (1993) has shown that dormitory resident assistants are the most likely targets of violence, vandalism, and verbal harassment in dormitories. Further, students who spend large sums of money on nonessential items are more likely than are other students to be theft victims (Fisher et al., 1998).

Proximity to crime-prone locations is also related to criminal victimization risks, thus supporting routine activities theory assertions. To elaborate, living near a park produces higher risks for victimization in general (Mustaine & Tewksbury, 1998c), as well as for vandalism specifically (Tewksbury & Mustaine, 2000). Not surprisingly, when students perceive their neighborhood as having too much crime and/or being too noisy, their risks for victimization in general, as well as theft in particular, are increased (Mustaine &

Tewksbury, 1998a; Tewksbury & Mustaine, 2000). Further, students who perceive their neighborhoods as having disruptive neighbors have higher assault victimization risks (Mustaine & Tewksbury, 2000). Interestingly, using a macro perspective, Grossman and Markowitz (1999) found that communities with lower priced beer had higher rates of sexual victimization.

Relatedly, with whom one resides is an important aspect of victimization risk. To specify, female college students living with their parents have lower rates of sexual victimization than do women not living with parents (Buddie & Testa, 2005); women living alone have higher risks of being victims of stalkers than women who do not live alone (Fisher et al., 2002).

In sum, college students who live in settings characterized by transience and low levels of social cohesion (and hence, higher levels of social disorganization) are at increased risks for victimization. The effects on victimization are not from only the actual residence of students, but also from the structures (and hence people and activities) that are in the immediate vicinity of the student's residence. Additionally, students' activities may also be important for understanding their risks of victimization.

The Role of Alcohol

Student lifestyles that research frequently finds associated with criminal victimization are those in which students frequently use alcohol. Important measures for explaining why some college students have higher risks of criminal victimization than are other college students also include frequency of alcohol consumed, quantities consumed while drinking, and locations where alcohol is consumed.

Initially, researchers showed that simply the use of alcohol is a predictor of sexual victimization for women (Combs-Lane & Smith, 2002; Schwartz & Pitts, 1995). Nevertheless, more recently, routine activities theory scholars have examined the specifics of alcohol consumption; for example, assessments of the amount of drinking in which students engage, rather than simply whether or not they drink alcohol. The number of times a college student drinks alcohol in a particular period relates strongly not only to that individual's risks for criminal victimization in general, but violent victimization in particular (Harford, Wechsler, & Muthen, 2003; Mohler-Kuo, Dowdall, Koss, & Wechsler, 2004; Wechsler, Davenport, Dowdall, Moeykems, & Castillo, 1994). Theoretically, when a person drinks alcohol, it dulls his/her responses and she/he is less able to identify potentially dangerous situations and resist victimization attempts after they begin. To specify, research has found that students who consume alcohol a greater number of days per week experience higher risks for victimization (Mustaine & Tewksbury, 1998c) and specifically, violent victimization (Mustaine & Tewksbury, 1998b). Additionally, students who are victims of violence multiple times use significantly more alcohol and drugs than students who are victimized only once (or never) (Bausell et al., 1991). Not surprisingly, female students who have a higher frequency of alcohol consumption, both in conjunction with sexual activities and in general, have higher sexual assault victimization risks (Schwartz & Pitts, 1995; Testa & Durmen, 1999).

Not only is the frequent use of alcohol important in specifying students' risks for victimization, but also the quantity of alcohol the student consumes when drinking. Routine activities theory suggests that persons who are drunk, specifically those who are drunk in dangerous places are particularly vulnerable to criminal attack. Intoxicated students are hampered from being aware of the goings on around them, taking any necessary evasive action, or putting up effective resistance efforts. Research tends to validate this theoretical assertion. For example, students who got drunk frequently during the week had increased assault victimization risks (Mustaine & Tewksbury, 2000), and college females who had been drunk in public recently had increased risks for violent victimization (Fisher et al., 2000; Mustaine & Tewksbury, 1998b, 1999; Parks & Miller, 1997; Schwartz & Pitts, 1995; Tanioka, 1986; Testa & Durmen, 1999; Testa & Livingston, 2000; Tewksbury & Mustaine, 2001; Ullman, Karabatsos, & Koss, 1999). More specifically, Mustaine and Tewksbury (1998c) found that the number of days a student was intoxicated was associated with higher risks for victimization.

Others have also found a similar relationship between the frequent consumption of large quantities of alcohol and higher victimization risks. Higher weekly consumption of alcohol was related to higher sexual assault victimization risks for females (Testa & Durmen, 1999). Women who drank, consumed greater quantities of alcohol, and/or got drunk in public places had increased risks for sexual assault than women who did not engage in these behaviors (Fisher et al., 2000; Parks & Miller, 1997; Schwartz & Pitts, 1995; Tanioka, 1986; Testa & Livingston, 2000; Ullman, Karabatsos, & Koss, 1999; Tewksbury & Mustaine, 2001). Researchers have also found this relationship present at a more macro level, as students who attend schools with high rates of binge drinking are more likely to be victims of violence or sexual violence than students at schools with lower rates of binge drinking (Wechsler et al., 1994). Unfortunately, this relationship between alcohol use and sexual assault victimization of college women should not be surprising; however, as in one study, one in four male undergrads admitted to purposely getting a woman drunk in order to have sex with her (Tyler et al., 1998).

Some researchers have also considered location of alcohol consumption and its association with victimization risks. Specifically, female students who, when they drink alcohol, drink at home have increased risks for stalking victimization (Mustaine & Tewksbury, 2002), although the authors did note that drinking alcohol at home could be a response to stalking victimization rather than a source. Additionally, just because a student drinks at home does not mean that the student is immune from victimization risks. Indeed, fully 81 percent of violent acts in residence halls are alcohol related (Rickgarn, 1989). However, drinking in public settings may be the most risky. College student women who go to bars have higher risks for sexual assault, and amongst those in bars, women with the highest risks are those who are younger, have a history of victimization, and spend a greater amount of time in bars (Parks & Zettes-Zanatta, 1999). Even though scholars have used a variety of measures to capture the use, extent, frequency, and location of alcohol consumption among college students, clearly there is a strong and consistent relationship between their alcohol consumption and higher student victimization risks.

The research regarding college students' alcohol consumption and victimization risks is clear: students who drink have increased risks. The more one drinks, the higher the risk. The more one drinks away from one's home, and the more one drinks away from home among others who may either have a "reason" to see one get intoxicated or that the individual does not know well, the greater are the risks of victimization. Alcohol, while perhaps the most common intoxicating substance used by college students, is not the only such substance; so too may illicit drug use be related to victimization risks.

The Role of Drug Use

Related to alcohol use is illegal drug use. This lifestyle has a similar relationship to increased risks for criminal victimization as alcohol, in that it typically lowers one's ability to recognize dangerous or risky situations, or to respond appropriately, effectively, or timely enough to threats or attempts to victimize one. Drug use, however, also has the element of illegality, and as such, can be used as an assessment of a student's proximity to potential offenders. In this way, people who use, buy, or sell drugs, are already in the proximity of offenders (not those who are still potential offenders), and may suffer victimization as a result. To specify, students who use recreational drugs are more likely to suffer criminal victimizations than are students who do not (Fisher et al., 1998; Fisher & Wilkes, 2003; Tewksbury & Mustaine, 1998b). Additionally, even smoking tobacco increases risks for violent crime victimization in general (Tanioka, 1986). College students who use marijuana have higher risks for larceny victimization (Mustaine & Tewksbury, 1998a) and sexual assault (Tewksbury & Mustaine, 2001), as well as for any type of personal victimization whenever they are participating in "leisure activities" (Mustaine & Tewksbury, 1998b).

Beyond an examination of the risks for victimization due to simple illegal drug use, researchers have also examined students who are involved with illegal drugs in other ways. For example, female college students who have bought drugs recently have higher risks for violent victimization (Mustaine & Tewksbury, 1998b), stalking victimization (Mustaine & Tewksbury, 1999), and sexual assault (Mustaine & Tewksbury, 2002). Relatedly, men who grow marijuana are more likely to be victims of violence (Mustaine & Tewksbury, 1998b).

Similar to alcohol, one's location of drug use is also an important predictor of victimization risks for college students. One's risk for sexual assault victimization increases when a greater proportion of one's drug use occurs either at parties or in other public settings (Mustaine & Tewksbury, 2002; Tewksbury & Mustaine, 2001).

In sum, scholars have examined various aspects of illegal drug use with regard to a variety of types of criminal victimization, and consistently have shown a strong relationship between higher or more serious drug use and higher rates of victimization. As is the case with alcohol, drug use may bring one into contact with motivated offenders and is likely to reduce one's ability (and perceived ability) to protect one from victimization. Thus, alcohol and drug use clearly increases the risk of victimization.

Membership in Student Clubs and Organizations

Other lifestyle behaviors that are specific to college students and are related to their risks for criminal victimization include membership in a variety of student organizations. Theoretically, membership in student organizations could have the effect of spending more time with others who may be criminally inclined or simply having student be absent from home more frequently (and therefore leaving their homes unguarded). Or, such memberships and participation could serve as safe, organized activities that would lessen one's exposure to criminally motivated others. Previous research tends to support the assertion that membership in clubs, organizations, or Greek social groups has the effect of increasing one's exposure to potential offenders. For example, researchers have found that students who are members of a larger number of groups, clubs, or organizations have increased risks for theft (Mustaine & Tewksbury, 1998a). Further, women who are members of a larger number of groups, clubs, or organizations also have increased risks for sexual assault in particular (Mustaine & Tewksbury, 2002).

Greek social organizations, in particular, are seen as dangerous and risky groups to which one may belong. Previous research has found that similar to the situation for collegiate athletes (Benedict, 1997; Benedict & Klein, 1997 to mention a few), fraternities are places where men have attitudes that promote the use of forced sex against women who frequent their houses, either at parties or for other purposes. To elaborate, Siegel and Raymond (1992) concluded that membership in a fraternity or sorority was important in constructing an at-risk model for college students. Specifically, sorority women are more likely than are nonsorority women to have experienced forced sexual intercourse (Kalof, 1993; Tyler et al., 1998; Johnson & Sigler, 1996). Further, in terms of theft victimization, fraternity and sorority members were more likely to have their purses or wallets stolen (Sigler & Koehler, 1993), but less likely to be victims of theft in general (Fisher et al., 1998). Finally, when using a macro-perspective, Sloan (1992, 1994) found that colleges and universities with a greater number of national Greek organizations had higher rates of officially reported crimes on campus.

Exposure to large numbers of other persons through organization and club membership is also exposure to increasing numbers of potential offenders. As such, students who are involved in more organizations and organized activities have a greater likelihood of being victimized. Interpersonal and close relationships, however, may have a different effect on risks.

Relationships and Sexual Activity

Another lifestyle highly studied among college students is sexual activity and relationship statuses. Theoretically, routine activities theory would suggest that students who are in relationships may be more likely to be victims of intimate partner crimes (e.g., sexual assault, stalking, physical abuse) but would be less likely to be victims of theft or other property crimes because they may not go out as frequently for leisure as single, unpartnered college students. Specifically, regarding crimes for which women are the most likely victims, routine activities theory predicts that sexually active women would more likely be victims of sexual assault, given their closer exposure to others who may be willing to use criminal means to gain access to sex.

Previous research tends to bear out these theoretical assertions. Specifically, sexually active women are more likely to be sexually assaulted (Johnson & Sigler, 1996; Mynatt & Allgeier, 1990; Fisher et al., 2002). Similarly, women who have had a greater number of casual sexual encounters and partners are more likely to be sexual assault victims (Testa & Durmen, 1999). Number of sexual partners is also related to risks for victimization, as Johnson and Sigler found that women with a greater number of sexual partners in the previous year were more likely to be sexually assaulted (1996, see also Koss & Dinero, 1989). If one examines dating violence in particular, these relationships persist. Dating violence is more likely in relationships with greater degrees of intimacy and commitment (Sellers & Bromley, 1996).

Dating, with or without sexual intimacy, is a lifestyle that is related to college students' (particularly women) risks for victimization. For example, college women who are dating, especially those who have been dating someone for less than a year, have higher odds of being stalked (Fisher et al., 2002). Additionally, female college students who had a greater number of dating partners, who dated more often, and/or had more sexual experience, were more likely to be victims of sexual assault than other women (Abbey, Ross, McDuffie, & McAuslan, 1996; Combs-Lane & Smith, 2002).

Finally, college students (particularly females) who have a prior sexual victimization also have increased odds of another sexual victimization (Fisher et al., 2000; Stets & Pirog-Good, 1989; Gidycz, Coble, Latham, & Layman, 1993). Relatedly, college men who report having used sexually coercive strategies with female partners are also more likely to be sexually victimized (Russell & Oswald, 2002).

Although not a great deal is known about the effects of relationships and sexual activities on the victimization risks of men, it is clear that women who date more often and who are sexually active (especially with multiple partners) have significantly higher risks of victimization than other college women. These risks are especially keen for risk of sexual assault.

Guardianship

The third of the routine activities concepts necessary for a criminal event (e.g., victimization) to occur is that a setting and meeting between a potential offender and suitable target must occur in the absence of a capable guardian. This means that the potential target is neither equipped nor capable of avoiding or fending off a victimization attempt, and that no outside guardian is present to intervene or deter a criminal event. Unfortunately, few studies have assessed the efficacy of guardianship, including how it affects victimization. This applies not only to research on the victimization of college students, but in fact to all forms of victimization, for all types of persons and property.

Generally, college students do not employ guardianship tools or activities in their daily routines (Barberet et al., 2004; Fisher et al., 1997; Sloan, Fisher, & Wilkins, 1995; Tewksbury & Mustaine, 2003). Especially for crimes of theft, students routinely fail to engage in simple guardianship, which could reduce their risks for theft (Fisher et al., 1997; Sloan et al., 1995).

While some college students do utilize measures of self-protection (Tewksbury & Mustaine, 2003), students who spend more time with strangers are also seemingly more trusting, and show lower rates of guardianship utilization (Tewksbury & Mustaine, 2003). Some students do actively seek to protect themselves from victimization. For example, Miller, Hemenway, and Wechsler (2002) report that 4.3 percent of a national sample of students report owning and carrying a gun. Those most likely to do so are those who have previously been threatened by someone else with a gun. Conversely, students who live near police stations, those who are in social settings with strangers on weekends, and those who use "hard drugs" are all more likely than are their counterparts to engage in self-protective activities (Tewksbury & Mustaine, 2003). Additionally, college students whose main form of transportation in the evening is to walk are more likely than are other students to employ at least one means of attempting to protect themselves (Tewksbury & Mustaine, 2003).

Data regarding the presence of formal agents of guardianship (e.g., law enforcement on campuses) is not clear on the deterrent effect of such a presence. However, Sloan (1992) found that as the ratio of students to full-time police on campus increases, so too does the official crime rate. Campuses that have higher levels of police enforcement also report higher crime rates (Fox & Hellman, 1985). However, this may be an issue of enforcement activities being a reaction to crime on campus. Another view on this is that if potential offenders believe they will not be caught, their likelihood to offend (including to sexually assault) increases (Schwartz & Pitts, 1995). Nevertheless, overall, the research suggests that formal guardianship agents/efforts may not significantly affect victimization risks.

The types of effective self-protective behaviors that college students engage in to lower their risks of victimization—at least for property crimes—includes installing extra locks on doors and window, and having a dog in the residence (Mustaine & Tewksbury, 1998a). Other activities such as simply asking another person to keep a watch on one's property (Fisher et al., 1998) or attending a crime prevention educational workshop (Fisher et al., 1998) can also effectively reduce college students' victimization risks.

The research on the effects of guardianship activities on college students' victimization risks is not especially well developed to date. However, what is known is that many students do take steps to attempt to protect themselves and their property, but the efficacy of such efforts are largely unknown. Formal agents of guardianship, while common and sometimes highly visible on college campuses, also may or may not be effective. The issue of guardianship in routine activities theory is by far the least developed of the three central concepts, and one that clearly calls for more research.

Conclusion

In sum, it is safe to say that students' daily activities and lifestyles relate to their risk for criminal victimization. Their lifestyles encompass many types of behaviors, locations, and associations, and while some of these behaviors are common among the general population, some are unique to college students. Research has found that college students who engage in activities that bring them in close proximity to potential offenders have higher risks for many types of criminal victimization. Further, college students who engage in behaviors that make them more vulnerable or desirable have higher odds for victimization. Additionally, since most students do not use even the most simple of items or strategies for guardianship, their risks for victimization are increased. Finally, the lifestyles of college students frequently encompass all of the above relationships: they engage in behavior that lessens their abilities to recognize or resist danger, while going to events or gatherings that are likely to have many potential offenders in attendance, while at the same time, neglecting to utilize self-protection. In all, this makes college students, in general, and many in particular, experience high risks for criminal victimization.

These findings have policy implications for university administrators, law enforcement personnel, and victim advocates, among others (e.g., Greek affairs directors, residence hall directors, student success coordinators). Obvious suggestions are to increase student programming and services related to self-protection and reduction of alcohol and drug use. However, most universities have plenty of programs and services to offer students already. Further, as noted by Barberet et al. (2004), only a small proportion of students are aware of such programming and services, and of those who are aware (in most cases, less than one-half), only a small proportion utilize such benefits (often less than one-third).

So, the most important question may be how to convince students that they are, in fact, vulnerable to crime, and worse, that they have an above average risk of being a crime victim. If students believe that they have a heightened risk for being victims, they may utilize the already present programs and services and thereby effectively lower their risks.

REFERENCES

Abbey, A., Ross, L. T., McDuffie, D., & McAuslan, P. (1996). Alcohol and dating risk factors for sexual assault among college women. *Psychology of Women Quarterly, 20,* 147–169.

Barberet, R, Fisher, B. S., & Taylor, H. (2004). *University student safety in the East Midlands.* London: Home Office.

Baum, K., & Klaus, P. (2005). *Violent victimization of college students: 1995–2002.* Washington, DC: Bureau of Justice Statistics.

Bausell, R. B., Bausell, C. R., & Siegel, D. G. (1991). *The links among alcohol, drugs and crime on American college campuses: A national follow-up study.* Towson, MD: Towson State University.

Benedict, J. (1997). *Public heroes, private felons: Athletes and crimes against women.*

Boston: Northeastern University Press.

Benedict, J., & Klein, A. (1997). Arrest and conviction rates for athletes accused of sexual assault. *Sociology of Sport, 14,* 86–94.

Buddie, A. M., & Testa, M. (2005). Rates and predictors of sexual aggression among students and nonstudents. *Journal of Interpersonal Violence, 20,* 713–724.

Cohen, L. E., & Felson, M. (1979). Social changes and crime rate trends: A routine activities approach. *American Sociological Review, 44,* 588–608.

Combs-Lane, A. M., & Smith, D. W. (2002). Risk of sexual victimization in college women: The role of behavioral intentions and risk-taking behaviors. *Journal of Interpersonal Violence, 17,* 165–183.

Copenhaver, S., & Grauerholtz, E. (1991). Sexual victimization among sorority women: Exploring the link between sexual violence and institutional practices. *Sex Roles, 24,* 31–41.

Fisher, B. S., Cullen, F. T., & Turner, M. G. (2002). Being pursued: Stalking victimization in a national study of college women. *Criminology and Public Policy, 1,* 257–308.

Fisher, B. S., Cullen, F. T., & Turner, M. G. (2000). *The sexual victimization of college women.* Washington, DC: United States Bureau of Justice Statistics.

Fisher, B. S., & Sloan, J. J. (Eds.) (1995). *Campus crime: Legal, social and policy perspectives.* Springfield, IL: Charles C Thomas.

Fisher, B. S., Sloan, J. J., Cullen, F. T., & Lu, C. (1998). Crime in the ivory tower: The level and sources of student victimization. *Criminology, 36,* 671–710.

Fisher, B. S., Sloan, J. J., Cullen, F. T., & Lu, C. (1997). The on campus victimization patterns of students: Implications for crime prevention by students and postsecondary institutions. In S. P. Lab (Ed.) *Crime prevention at a crossroads.* Cincinnati, OH: Anderson.

Fisher, B. S., & Wilkes, A. R. P. (2003). A tale of two ivory towers: A comparative analysis of victimization rates and risks between university students in the United States and England. *British Journal of Criminology, 43,* 526–545.

Fox, J. A., & Hellman, D. A. (1985). Location and other correlates of campus crime. *Journal of Criminal Justice, 13,* 429–444.

Frintner, M. P., & Rubinson, L. (1993). Acquaintance rape: The influence of alcohol, fraternity membership, and sports team membership. *Journal of Sex Education and Therapy, 19,* 272–284.

Gidycz, C. A., Coble, C. N., Latham, L., & Layman, M. J. (1993). Sexual assault experience in adulthood and prior victimization experience: A prospective analysis. *Psychology of Women Quarterly, 17,* 151–168.

Grossman, M., & Markowitz, S. (1999). *Alcohol regulation and violence on college campuses.* Cambridge, MA: National Bureau of Economic Research.

Harford, T. C., Wechsler, H., & Muthen, B. O. (2003). Alcohol-related aggression and drinking at off-campus parties and bars: A national study of current drinkers in college. *Journal of Studies on Alcohol, 64,* 704–711.

Johnson, I. M., & Sigler, R. T. (1996). Forced sexual intercourse on campus: Crime or offensive behavior? *Journal of Contemporary Criminal Justice, 12,* 54–68.

Kalof, L. (1993). Rape supportive attitudes and sexual victimization experiences of sorority and nonsorority women. *Sex Roles, 29,* 767–780.

Koss, M. P., & Dinero, T. E. (1989). Discriminant analysis of risk factors for sexual victimization among a national sample of college women. *Journal of Consulting and Clinical Psychology, 57,* 242–250.

Laub, J. H. (1990). Patterns of criminal victimization in the United States. In A. J. Lurigio, W. G. Skogan, & R. C. Davis (Eds.), *Victims of crime: Problems, policies, and programs.* Newberry Park, CA: Sage.

Martin, P. Y., & Hummer, R. A. (1989). Fraternities and rape on campus. *Gender & Society, 3,* 457–473.

Maxfield, M. G. (1987). Household composition, routine activity, and victimization: A comparative analysis. *Journal of Quantitative Criminology, 3,* 301–320.

Meithe, T. D., & Meier, R. F. (1990). Opportunity, choice, and criminal victimization: A test of a theoretical model. *Journal of Research in Crime and Delinquency, 27*(3), 243–266.

Miller, M., Hemenway, D., & Wechsler, H. (2002). Guns and gun threats at college. *Journal of American College Health, 51,* 57–65.

Mohler-Kuo, M., Dowdall, G. W., Koss, M. P., & Wechsler, H. (2004). Correlates of rape while intoxicated in a national sample of college women. *Journal of Studies on Alcohol, 65,* 37–45.

Mustaine, E. E., & Tewksbury, R. (1997). Obstacles in the assessment of routine activities theory. *Social Pathology, 3,* 177–194.

Mustaine, E. E., & Tewksbury, R. (1998a). Predicting risks of larceny theft victimization: A routine activity analysis using refined lifestyle measures. *Criminology, 36,* 829–857.

Mustaine, E. E., & Tewksbury, R. (1998b). Specifying the role of alcohol in predatory victimization. *Deviant Behavior, 19,* 173–199.

Mustaine, E. E., & Tewksbury, R. (1998c). Victimization risks at leisure: A gender-specific analysis. *Violence and Victims, 13,* 231–249.

Mustaine, E. E., & Tewksbury, R. (1999). A routine activity theory explanation of women's stalking victimizations. *Violence Against Women, 5,* 43–62.

Mustaine, E. E., & Tewksbury, R. (2000). Comparing the lifestyles of victims, offenders and victim-offenders: A routine activity theory assessment of similarities and differences for criminal incident participants. *Sociological Focus, 33,* 339–362.

Mustaine, E. E., & Tewksbury, R. (2002). Sexual assault of college women: A feminist interpretation of a routine activities analysis. *Criminal Justice Review, 27,* 89–123.

Mynatt, C. R., & Allgeier, E. R. (1990). Risk factors, self-attributions, and adjustment problems among victims of sexual coercion. *Journal of Applied Social Psychology, 20,* 130–153.

Palmer, C. J. (1993). *Violent crimes and other forms of victimization in residence halls.* Ashville, NC: College Administration Publications.

Parks, K. A., & Miller, B. A. (1997). Bar victimization of women. *Psychology of Women Quarterly, 21,* 509–526.

Parks, K. A., & Zettes-Zanatta, L. M. (1999). Women's bar-related victimization: Refining and testing a conceptual model. *Aggressive Behavior, 25,* 349–364.

Rickgarn, R. L. (1989). Violence in the residence halls: Campus domestic violence. In J. M. Sherrill & D. G. Siegel (Eds.), *Responding to violence on campus.* San Francisco: Jossey-Bass.

Robinson, M. B. (1997). Environmental characteristics associated with residential burglaries of student apartment complexes. *Environment and Behavior, 29,* 657–675.

Russell, B. L., & Oswald, D. L. (2002). Sexual coercion and victimization of college men: The role of love styles. *Journal of Interpersonal Violence, 17,* 273–285.

Sanday, P. R. (1990). *Fraternity gang rape: Sex, brotherhood, and privilege on campus.* New York: University Press.

Schaeffer, A., & Nelson, E. (1993). Rape supportive attitudes: Effects of on campus residence and education. *Journal of College Student Development, 34,* 175–179.

Schwartz, M. D., & Pitts, V. L. (1995). Exploring a feminist routine activities approach to explaining sexual assault. *Justice Quarterly, 12,* 9–31.

Sellers, C. S., & Bromley, M. L. (1996). Violent behavior in college student dating relationships: Implications for campus service providers. *Journal of Contemporary Criminal Justice, 12,* 1–27.

Seng, M. J. (1996). Theft on campus: An analysis of larceny-theft at an urban university. *Journal of Crime and Justice, 19,* 33–44.

Siegel, D. G., & Raymond, C. H. (1992). An ecological approach to violent crime on campus. *Journal of Security Administration, 15,* 19–27.

Sigler, R. T., & Koehler, N. (1993). Victimization and crime on campus. *International Review of Victimology, 2,* 331–343.

Sloan, J. J. (1994). The correlates of campus crime: An analysis of reported crimes on college and university campuses. *Journal of Criminal Justice, 22,* 51–61.

Sloan, J. J. (1992). Campus crime and campus communities: An analysis of crimes known to campus police and security. *Journal of Security Administration, 15,* 31–46.

Sloan, J. J., Fisher, B. S., & Wilkins, D. L. (1995). *Crime, fear of crime, and related issues on the U.A.B. campus: Final report.* Birmingham, AL: University of Alabama at Birmingham, Office of the V.P. for Administration.

Stets, J. E., & Pirog-Good, M. A. (1989). Patterns of physical and sexual abuse for men and women in dating relationships: A descriptive analysis. *Journal of Family Violence, 4,* 63–77.

Stombler, M. (1994). 'Buddies' or 'Slutties': The collective sexual reputation of fraternity little sisters. *Gender & Society, 8,* 297–323.

Tanioka, I. (1986). Evidence links smoking to violent crime victimization. *Sociology and Social Research, 71,* 58.

Testa, M., & Durmen, K. H. (1999). The differential correlates of sexual coercion and rape. *Journal of Interpersonal Violence, 14,* 548–561.

Testa, M., & Livingston, J. A. (2000). Alcohol and sexual aggression: Reciprocal relationships over time in a sample of high-risk women. *Journal of Interpersonal Violence, 15,* 413–427.

Tewksbury, R., & Mustaine, E. E. (2003). College students' lifestyles and self-protective behaviors: Further considerations of the guardianship concept in routine activity theory. *Criminal Justice and Behavior, 30,* 302–327.

Tewksbury, R., & Mustaine, E. E. (2001). Lifestyle factors associated with the sexual assault of men: A routine activity theory analysis. *Journal of Men's Studies, 9,* 153–182.

Tewksbury, R., & Mustaine, E. E. (2000). Routine activities and vandalism: A theoretical and empirical study. *Journal of Crime and Justice, 23,* 81–110.

Tyler, K. A., Hoyt, D. R., & Whitbeck, L. B. (1998). Coercive sexual strategies. *Violence and Victims, 13,* 47–61.

Ullman, S. E., Karabatsos, G., & Koss, M. P. (1999). Alcohol and sexual assault in a national sample of college women. *Journal of Interpersonal Violence, 14,* 603–625.

Ward, S. K., Chapman, K., Cohn, E., White, S., & Williams, K. (1991). Acquaintance rape and the college social scene. *Family Relations, 40,* 65–71.

Wechsler, H., Davenport, A., Dowdall, G., Moeykems, B., & Castillo, S. (1994). Health and behavioral consequences of binge drinking in college: A national survey of students at 140 campuses. *Journal of the American Medical Association, 272,* 1672–1677.

Zito, J. M. (1974). Anonymity and neighboring in an urban high-rise complex. *Urban Life and Culture, 3,* 243–263.

Chapter 9

THE ROLE OF ALCOHOL ABUSE IN COLLEGE STUDENT VICTIMIZATION[1]

GEORGE W. DOWDALL

Alcohol plays a very important but complex role in campus crime. Many of the college crime incidents reported to the police are alcohol related, and many, if not most, of the serious crimes on college campuses involve alcohol. Students who abuse alcohol are more likely to be victims of crime than nonusers or nonbinging users. That many college students abuse alcohol is well known, but its impact on other aspects of college life is more controversial. The role that alcohol plays in campus crime, particularly victimization, deserves reexamination. Is student use of alcohol the engine that drives most of campus crime or is it merely one of a number of factors, and perhaps a minor one at that, that play very limited roles? Should colleges and universities focus on preventing alcohol abuse as a way for them to prevent campus crime?

This chapter describes the nature and extent of alcohol use and alcohol-related crime among college students. A beginning section discusses alcohol and campus crime, noting that most violations reported by campus police involve alcohol and that alcohol violations have increased over the past 12 years, a time when crime in the broader society was falling. The chapter discusses the extent of college drinking in detail, including the nature of binge drinking, followed by a section that examines the factors that shape college drinking. We then examine the consequences of college drinking by looking at the kinds of alcohol-related problems associated with it, among the most serious of which is rape. The following section explores whether alcohol is a cause of violence, given the very powerful correlation between alcohol and violence. The chapter then turns to an examination of what research shows about preventing college alcohol abuse. A conclusion offers a summary of

167

the chapter and some implications for those trying to understand or contain campus crime. We begin by exploring the relationship between alcohol and campus crime.

Alcohol and Campus Crime

A series of sensational student deaths and rapes, including most recently allegations against Duke University Lacrosse team members, has made urgent the task of examining the relationship between alcohol and campus crime. In this section, we explore that relationship, given that alcohol-related incidents have become the most common kind of crime activity on American college campuses.

Like other Americans, the more than 14 million college students are at risk of crime victimization, ranging from larceny to violent events such as rape (Fisher & Sloan, 1995). During the period 1995–2002, rates of violent victimization of Americans ages 18 to 24 fell for both college students (a decrease of 54%) and for nonstudents (a decrease of 45%), part of a broad decline in violent crime experienced for most Americans during these years (Baum & Klaus, 2005; Hart, 2003). The same data show that college students ages 18–24 experience lower rates of violent crime such as robbery, aggravated assault, and simple assault (except for rape/assault) than do nonstudents; the glaring exception is rape, experienced by both students and nonstudents at the same rate.

For college students, studying or living on a college campus brings a unique set of both risk and protective factors (Fisher & Sloan, 1995). Arguably highest among the risks is the greater use of alcohol and other drugs than among noncollege youth in the broader society. National Crime Victimization Survey (NCVS) data on violent victimizations of college students show that roughly 40 percent of offenders were perceived to be using alcohol or drugs, whether the crime was any violence (41%), rape/sexual assault (40%), aggravated assault (44%), or simple assault (42%). Only robbery (25%) had lower rates of perceived drug and alcohol use by the perpetrator (Baum & Klaus, 2005; Hart, 2003). Observers widely suspect substance use plays an important role in crime, especially violence, in the broader society and that it is involved in much, if not most, campus crime. The most extensive study of college student victimization found that recreational drug use and a lifestyle with high levels of partying were the main predictors of a college student being the victim of a violent crime (Fisher, Sloan, Cullen, & Lu, 1998).

Alcohol and drug use is a particularly strategic issue for those concerned with college crime prevention for two reasons. First, drugs are illegal for all students and alcohol for most undergraduates, so substance use is of immediate importance to campus police and other college administrative personnel; they place alcohol and drug use high if not on the top of the list of problems they must deal with. Second, researchers believe substance use increases the overall risk of criminal victimization on campus, as it does in the broader society, and that it raises the risk of some forms of criminal victimization, suggesting that campus police and security play a crucial role in restricting access to alcohol and other drugs (AOD). Published reports of such phenomena as "date rape" present widely different and even contradictory pictures of whether college students are at very low or very high risk of victimization, and the role of alcohol and other drug use in victimization of all forms is even more unclear.

Crimes associated with alcohol and drug use are arguably the most prevalent crimes on college campuses today. Since alcohol is overwhelmingly the substance of choice on college campuses, we will focus our attention on alcohol use and abuse. On college campuses, as in the broader society, heavy episodic or binge drinking poses a danger of serious safety, health, and other consequences for both the alcohol abuser and others in the immediate environment. As such, it poses a major challenge to the criminal justice system and college and university administrators, with one estimate that alcohol is involved in two-thirds of college student suicides, in 90 percent of campus rapes, and 95 percent of violent crime on campus (CASA, 1994). Alcohol contributes to the leading causes of accidental death, such as motor vehicle crashes and falls. Alcohol abuse contributes to almost half of motor vehicle fatalities, the most important cause of death among young Americans (Robert Wood Johnson Foundation, 2001). On college campuses, alcohol-related crime involves underage drinking, driving under the influence, public intoxication, and a variety of criminal acts ranging from theft to violence (Engs & Hanson, 1994; Perkins, 2002).

Hoover (2005) reports on the latest data about campus crime gathered as part of the requirements of the *Clery Act* by the U.S. Department of Education (ED) (2005).[2] Alcohol arrests have increased at American colleges for 12 years running; liquor law violations rose from 108,846 reported in 1999 to 161, 974 in 2003.[3] These figures may reflect both rising amounts of alcohol-related crime and increased attention to alcohol issues by college security officials. In any case, the numbers of alcohol arrests are far more numerous than other kinds of reported crime. For the period 2001 to 2003, the ED's data on campus crimes listed 84 murders and/or manslaughters, 7,941 forcible/nonforcible sex offenses, 566 hate crimes, and 514,568 liquor law arrests and/or cases involving disciplinary proceedings (Security on Campus, Inc. 2006).

In summary, alcohol and college crime are powerfully connected. There is little doubt that alcohol plays some kind of role in much of the crime and even violence on college campuses, and that alcohol use is a major risk factor for college student victimization. We now turn to a closer look at alcohol consumption by college students. In the next section, we examine the extent and nature of alcohol consumption among college students.

The Extent of Drinking Among College Students

In this section, we assess the extent of drinking among American college students with particular attention paid to the amount of binge or heavy episodic drinking. Over the past decade or so, several published studies of college drinking include four large-scale national surveys produced by the Harvard School of Public Health College Alcohol Study (CAS) (see Wechsler & Wuetrich, 2002 for a summary of the study). CAS results have been very consistent with other large-scale efforts, but the CAS uses superior scientific sampling techniques to produce a representative national sample of colleges and students, and so we will mostly refer to its findings here. For its original survey, the CAS chose 195 four-year colleges and universities using probability proportionate to size sampling; 140 colleges participated in the study. Because CAS promised confidentiality to each participating institution, it is not possible to describe the sample's characteristics in detail except to say the sample is representative of American colleges and universities with full-time, four-year students. Each college provided the researchers with a random sample of full-time students, with roughly 60 percent completing a very detailed 20-page questionnaire about their alcohol and drug use as well as behaviors and values. The CAS conducted surveys of large samples of roughly 15,000 to 17,000 students in 1993, 1995, 1997, and 2001.

Almost all college students drink occasionally, but roughly two out of every five four-year full-time college students are binge drinkers (Wechsler, Davenport, Dowdall, Moeykens, & Castillo, 1994). Binge drinking has been operationalized in these studies by the "5/4" definition: male binge drinkers consume five or more drinks in a row in the two weeks prior to completing the questionnaire, while female bingers consume four or more drinks in a row in the same time period (Dowdall & Wechsler 2002; Wechsler, Dowdall, Davenport, & Rimm 1995). Note that the "5/4" definition includes the phrase "or more," since many bingers do not just stop at the cutoff. Table 9.1 presents data from the four CAS surveys about college drinking, with little evidence of much change over the years. Roughly one in five college students meets the definition of "frequent binge drinking" by binging at least three times in the two-week period.

Any discussion of college drinking should, of course, highlight the fact that most college students do not binge drink. But this is hardly cause for celebration, since Table 9.1 shows that a substantial minority do binge; even

Table 9.1
SELF-REPORTED DRINKING BEHAVIOR OF
AMERICAN COLLEGE STUDENTS (1993–2001)

Type of behavior	Year			
	1993 (%)	1997 (%)	1999 (%)	2001 (%)
Abstained	16.4	19.6	19.8	19.3
Drank in past year	83.6	30.8	79.8	80.7
Binge drinking	43.9	43.2	44.5	44.4
Frequent binge drinking	19.7	21.0	22.6	22.8
Drank on 10 or more occasions in the past 30 days	18.1	21.1	23.1	22.6
Was drunk 3+ times in the past month	23.4	29.0	30.2	29.4
Drink to get drunk	39.9	53.5	47.7	48.2

Source: Pastore and Maguire, 2003 (http://www.albany.edu/sourcebook/ accessed 3/3/06).

more troubling, one out of five college students is a frequent binge drinker, and almost a third of all college students were drunk three or more times in the past month. Almost half of all students drink to get drunk. Many of the undergraduates at U.S. colleges are under the minimum drinking age, guaranteeing that many episodes of drinking by college students violate various state laws (Wechsler, Kuo, Lee, & Dowdall, 2000).

Most college students drink only occasionally throughout the year, but four in ten binge drink, and roughly one in five frequently binge drinks. Considerable evidence exists about the amount and form of college drinking, and the risks and consequences of that drinking. The next section reviews the evidence about college drinking by exploring the factors that shape college drinking, including how much colleges vary in rates of binging.

Factors That Shape College Student Drinking

What are the causes of college drinking? While no definitive answer exists, we know an increasing amount about the factors that shape drinking behavior.[4] Figure 9.1 suggests some of the most important issues, grouped into those that precede college and those that occur during college (Dowdall &

Wechsler, 2002; Wechsler & Wuetrich, 2002).

Of those factors preceding college, considerable current research has pursued genetic issues, with one recent study suggesting that college students who binge may have different genetic components than those who do not (Herman, Philbeck, Vasilopoulos, & Depetrillo, 2003). Parental drinking, as well as such factors as religion, race, and social class, all play some role in college drinking. Public policy shapes college drinking, including the minimum legal drinking age of 21 and its enforcement, and students who live in states with effective alcohol control policies or who attend schools with few alcohol outlets nearby drink less than their peers (Dowdall, 2006; Nelson, Naimi, Brewer, & Wechsler, 2005). Although alcohol may play a more significant role in crimes of violence than illegal drugs, public policy stretching back almost a century makes alcohol a legal substance for those over 21 (Parker & Rebhun, 1995; Wagenaar & Toomey, 2002). The overall alcohol environment shapes the level of drinking in a community, with the cost of alcohol, its promotion through advertising and marketing, and its availability all playing a role (Dowdall, 2006). Finally, subcultures of drug and alcohol use within high schools or neighborhoods exert some influence as well.

Figure 9.1 includes college factors that shape college drinking. For the individual student, researchers have identified age of drinking onset as an important factor in alcohol abuse and dependence; the earlier the onset, the higher the risk of later problems with alcohol (National Institute on Alcohol Abuse and Alcoholism, 2000). Other personal factors include gender (with men still drinking more than women), high school binging, current drug or alcohol use, and attaching little importance to religion in college all raising the likelihood of college binge drinking (Wechsler, Dowdall, Davenport, & Castillo, 1995). Other factors are components of the college environment. Students who misperceive the amount of drinking on a campus may drink more than those who accurately perceive the norms. Students who are part of the social worlds of athletics or fraternities and sororities drink more, while students who think religion should be an important part of their college lives or who regularly perform community service drink less. The alcohol environment on and off campus plays an important role, with the cost, availability, and promotion of alcohol products shaping how much drinking takes place.

Figure 9.1 hardly exhausts the factors that shape college drinking, but it does support the important argument that what may seem like a purely individual choice–to drink, or to binge drink–is shaped by many factors including some that are part of a larger context. Research about college drinking and interventions to change college drinking need to take into account this broader view by "widening the lens and sharpening the focus" on all of these precollege and college factors, not merely the traits of the individual student

	Before College		College	
	Family Factors: • Genetics • Parental drinking behavior • Social class • Race or ethnicity • Religion		Individual Factors: • Age of drinking onset • High school drinking • Drug or tobacco use • Gender • Race	
	Public Policy: • National laws • State laws • Enforcement of minimum drinking age • Local community ordinances		College Environment: • Peer norms • Residential system • Greek life • Athletics • Community service • Religious involvement	
	Alcohol Environment: • Price of alcohol • Advertising • Marketing practices • Outlet density • Hours of sale		Alcohol Environment On Campus: • Dry or wet campus • Availability • Price • Alcohol policy	
	Social/Institutional Structures: • Neighborhood • Middle and high school • Church, synagogue, mosque • Subcultures		Alcohol Environment Off Campus: • Retail price • Outlet density and proximity • Advertising • Marketing	

Source: Adapted from Dowdall and Wechsler (2002).

Figure 9.1. Factors shaping college students' drinking.

(Dowdall & Wechsler, 2002).

Binge drinking varies greatly from college to college. Figure 9.2 presents the percent binge drinking among students at the 140 colleges in the original study, but a very similar pattern has marked each of the four CAS surveys. At one college, almost no students binge, while more than 70 percent do so at the top campus. About one-third of the schools had more than 50 percent of their students defined as binge drinkers. Figure 9.2 helps make the important point that there is no single pattern of binge drinking that describes college students in general, with each campus having its unique configuration.

Many factors, ranging from personal traits and values to campus characteristics and public policy, shape college drinking. Moreover, colleges vary greatly in how much binge drinking occurs among their students, with some having virtually no binge drinkers and others having a significant majority of

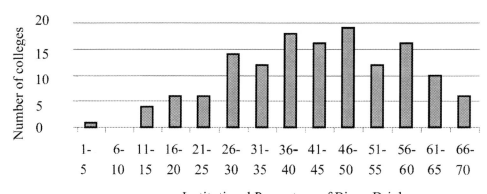

Figure 9.2. Distribution of colleges by percent of binge drinkers. Source: Adapted from Wechsler, Davenport, Dowdall, Moeykems, and Castillo, 1994.

binge drinkers. Having described patterns of drinking among college students, we now turn to the crucial question of what are the health and behavioral consequences of college drinking.

Consequences of College Student Drinking

Many adults view binge drinking as a harmless rite of passage, but the CAS and other studies point to a darker reality. Recently, the National Institute on Alcohol Abuse and Alcoholism's (NIAAA) Task Force on College Drinking (2002a) commissioned extensive new studies of the issue.[5] The NIAAA Task Force Report (2002a; Hingson, Heeren, Winter, & Wechsler, 2005) summarized the outcomes associated with college drinking:

- Deaths: 1,400 die each year from alcohol-related unintentional injuries
- Injuries: 500,000 unintentionally injured under the influence of alcohol
- Unsafe sex: 400,000 have unprotected sex; more than 100,000 have sex without consent
- Academic problems: 25% report negative academic consequences
- Health problems/suicide attempts: more than 150,000 report an alcohol-related health problem; 1.5% attempt suicide
- Alcohol abuse and dependence: 31% met the criteria for a diagnosis of alcohol abuse and 6% for diagnosis of alcohol dependence in the past 12 months

For present purposes, of particular importance are the numbers associated with crime perpetration and victimization:

- Assaults: 600,000 assaulted by another student who has been drinking
- Sexual abuse: 70,000 victims of sexual assault or date rape

- Drunk driving: 2.1 million drove under the influence of alcohol
- Vandalism: 11% report damaging property while under the influence
- Property damage: 50% of administrators at schools with high binge levels report "moderate" or "major" alcohol-related damage
- Police involvement: 110,000 students arrested for a alcohol-related violations

Research has linked crime victimization on college campuses to alcohol consumption. Table 9.2 presents CAS data on alcohol-related problems, including ties between alcohol abuse and campus crime victimization. A significant minority of American college students report very troubling alcohol-related problems; almost one-third drive after drinking. One in ten report damaging property and the same proportion are hurt or injured because of their own drinking. Over 6 percent say that they have gotten into trouble

Table 9.2
ALCOHOL-RELATED PROBLEMS AMONG
COLLEGE STUDENTS (1993–2001)

Nature of Problem	*1993* %	*1997* %	*1999* %	*2001* %
Missed a class	26.9	31.1	29.9	29.5
Got behind in school work	20.5	24.1	24.1	21.6
Did something you regret	32.1	37.0	36.1	35.0
Forgot where you were or what you did	24.7	27.4	27.1	26.8
Argued with friends	19.6	24.0	22.5	22.9
Engaged in unplanned sexual activities	19.2	23.3	21.6	21.3
Did not use protection when you had sex	9.8	11.2	10.3	10.4
Damaged property	9.3	11.7	10.8	10.7
Got into trouble with campus or local police	4.6	6.4	5.8	6.5
Got hurt or injured	9.3	12.0	12.4	12.8
Required medical treatment for an overdose	0.5	0.6	0.6	0.8
Drove after drinking alcohol	26.6	29.5	28.8	29.0
Had five or more different alcohol-related problems	16.6	20.8	19.9	20.3

Source: Pastore and Maguire, 2003 (http://www.albany.edu/sourcebook).

with campus or local police because of their drinking. Each one of these outcomes is very strongly associated with the level of alcohol consumption, with those who are frequent binge drinkers much more likely to report victimization than are infrequent binge drinkers; nonbinge drinkers are least likely to report being crime victims.

Another large survey of college students sheds additional light on the question of alcohol-related victimization. Unlike the Harvard CAS data cited earlier, data collected by the Core Institute at Southern Illinois University are not based on a representative sample of colleges and universities, but only those institutions who chose to participate in the survey.[6] Frequently the survey is not given to a representative sample of students at each school but is distributed in classes whose instructors choose to do so. Nonetheless, the Core data are collected at a large number of institutions across the country with an impressive number of student participants. In 2004, for example, the Core surveys had 68,000 undergraduate respondents at 133 colleges and universities. Table 9.3 presents Core survey data for 2002 showing that many students experienced threats of physical violence (9.6%), ethnic or racial harassment (5.7%), actual physical violence (4.7%), forced sexual touching or fondling (5.0%), or theft involving force or threat of force (1.9%). Many students reported that they had consumed alcohol or drugs before the incident. Except for ethnic or racial harassment, prior alcohol use by the victim powerfully links to risk of victimization. To be sure, no one but the perpetrator of a crime is responsible for that crime, and these data should not be used to

Table 9.3
STUDENTS SELF-REPORTING CRIMINAL VICTIMIZATION
AND SUBSTANCE USE PRIOR TO VICTIMIZATION, 2002

Type of victimization	*Reported being a victim (%)*	*Consumed drugs or alcohol prior to victimization (%)*
Threat of physical violence	9.6	34.2
Ethnic or racial harassment	5.7	13.5
Actual physical violence	4.7	67.3
Forced sexual touching or fondling	5.0	74.0
Theft involving force or threat of force	1.9	47.9

Source: Pastore and Maguire, 2003 (http://www.albany.edu/sourcebook, accessed 2/4/07).

"blame the victim." Nevertheless, the data clearly suggest how alcohol use is associated with a higher likelihood of victimization as well as other consequences (Perkins, 2002).

Alcohol is associated with a wide range of problematic outcomes among college students. More than 1,700 students die each year because of drinking. Hundreds of thousands of other students are affected either because of their own drinking or because of the secondhand effects of others' drinking. The next section examines one of the most serious consequences of alcohol abuse, rape and sexual assault among college women.

Alcohol Use/Abuse and Rape Among College Women

Arguably one of the most serious forms of alcohol-related crime on campus is rape, so this section presents data on the extent of rape, including rape when a woman is too drunk to give consent to sex, termed "intoxicated rape" (Mohler-Kuo, Dowdall, Koss, & Wechlser, 2004). Research has implicated rape as an outcome of alcohol consumption in many settings (Abbey, 2002; Bachar & Koss, 2001). The number of reports of rape on college campuses is clearly the small tip of a large iceberg. For a number of reasons, women rape victims do not usually report their victimizations to the campus or community police (Koss, Gidycz, & Wisniewski, 1987).

A Department of Justice-sponsored study (Fisher et al., 2000) estimated that the chances of a woman experiencing a rape during her undergraduate studies were between one in four and one in five. Koss and colleagues (1987) found that more than 15 percent of college women had experienced a completed rape, and another 12 percent an attempted rape, since age 14. Abbey (2002, 1991) reviewed research reporting similar prevalence rates, and noted that alcohol-related sexual assault was a common problem, with alcohol associated with more than half of college sexual assaults on women. After reviewing the alcohol-sexual assault research, Abbey argued that alcohol increased the likelihood of sexual assault through several related pathways. She concluded ". . . beliefs about alcohol, deficits in higher order cognitive processing and motor impairments induced by alcohol and peer group norms that encourage heavy drinking and forced sex" (Abbey, 2002:125).

Using data from the 1997, 1999, and 2001 CAS surveys of students who were attending 119 colleges, Mohler-Kuo, Dowdall, Koss, and Wechsler (2004) assessed the correlates of rape while intoxicated among a large national cross-section of over 25,000 women students at four-year colleges. Questions that conformed to the legal definition of rape in many states were included to indicte rape while forced ("Since the beginning of the school year, have you ever had sexual intercourse against your wishes because someone used force?"); rape while threatened ("Apart from question 1, since

Table 9.4
PREVALENCE OF RAPE SINCE THE BEGINNING OF THE SCHOOL YEAR

	Year			
Type of rape	*All years (%) (N=23,980)*	*1997 (%) (N=8,567)*	*1999 (%) (N=8,425)*	*2001 (%) (N=6,988)*
Any type	4.7	5.1	4.5	4.3
While intoxicated	3.4	3.6	3.4	3.2
Forced	1.9	2.1	1.8	1.7
Threatened	0.4	0.5	0.3	0.3

Source: Mohler-Kuo, Dowdall, Koss, and Wechsler (2004).

the beginning of the school year, have you had sexual intercourse against your wishes because someone threatened to harm you?"); and rape while intoxicated ("Apart from questions 1 and 2, since the beginning of the school year, have you had sexual intercourse when you were so intoxicated that you were unable to consent?"). The CAS surveys' possible responses ("0 times, 1 time, 2 times, 3 or more times") were dichotomized into "yes" or "no."

Table 9.4 presents the prevalence of these types of rape based on asking women during the spring semester whether they had sex without consent "since the beginning of the school year," a period on average of about seven months. Roughly one in 20 college women have been raped in that short time period, with 72 percent of those raped experiencing rape while intoxicated, the most frequent form of rape. Except for rape by threat, there were no significant differences across the three surveys.

Women who went to colleges with medium and high binge-drinking rates had more than a 1.5 fold increased chance of being raped while intoxicated than those from institutions with lower binge drinking rates. Other factors that raised the risk of rape included being under the age of 21, being white, residing in sorority houses, using illicit drugs, and having binge drank in college. These findings have important implications for prevention programs:

College prevention programs must give increased attention to educating male students that one of the first questions they must ask themselves before initiating sex with a woman is whether she is capable of giving consent. . . . College men must be educated for their own protection that intoxication is a stop sign for sex. College women need to be warned not only about the vulnerability created by heavy drinking, but also about the extra dangers imposed in situations where many other people are drinking heavily. The person who commits rape is, of course, responsible in both the legal and the moral sense, and we must view rape from that perspective. For purposes of prevention, however, identifying the factors that place women at increased vulnerability to rape is also important. (Mohler-Kuo et al., 2004, p. 43)

Alcohol is clearly present in many of the crimes of violence among college students, and in more than seven of ten rapes that occur among college women. The powerful correlation of alcohol abuse and rape victimization is one of the most robust findings about the consequences of college drinking. However, does its presence indicate that it is a cause of violence? The next section examines this controversial question.

Is Alcohol a Cause of College Student Violence?

The data presented so far make a strong case for a powerful correlation between alcohol and crime among individual college students and among campuses. However, is there a *causal* link between alcohol and crime? The question is not merely of academic concern. If the two are causally linked, then there would be strong evidence supporting the thesis that preventing crime on campus depends in part on somehow lowering the rate of alcohol abuse. If no causal link exists, reigning in binge drinking might have no effect on crime rates.

The question of whether alcohol is a cause of violence provokes considerable controversy, at least in part because it may inadvertently shift attention away from the issue of the criminal responsibility of the perpetrator. It is also controversial because of the difficulty of establishing causality in the social sciences. Some observers (e.g., Abbey, 1991, 2002) claim alcohol and drug use and criminal events are closely, even causally, linked, while others argue that there is almost no relationship or "less than meets the eye" (e.g., Collins, 1989; Giancola, 2002; Martin, 1992, 1993).

A researcher need provide three pieces of evidence to prove causality. First, time order (temporal priority) needs to be established: changes in alcohol use must precede changes in crime. Second, the researcher must demonstrate that alcohol and crime co-occur. Finally, the researcher must eliminate other possible causal factors: in other words, the researcher has to remove the possibility that some third factor brings about both alcohol use and crime.

While the data presented earlier make a powerful case for correlation, no research has yet proved definitively a causal link between alcohol use and crime on college campuses or among college students. However, the fact that research has found this same correlation among noncollege populations strengthens the case for the causal link at the college level (Fagan, 1993; Greenfield, 1998). Abbey (2002, 1991) provides a helpful discussion of how alcohol might be associated with sexual assault among college students. Establishing time order would help understand this relationship. For example, instead of alcohol consumption causing sexual assault, the reverse could be true: men consumed alcohol before perpetrating assault to provide an excuse for their criminal behavior. Finally, eliminating rival causal hypotheses would increase confidence in the alcohol-rape connection. For example, some third factor such as peer group norms that promote heavy drinking and the perpetration of sexual assault might explain the correlation and therefore negate a possible causal link. Research cannot yet present a definitive answer to these questions, given methodological limitations in the studies of sexual assault reviewed by Abbey (2002). For similar reasons, considerable controversy exists in the broader scientific literature about whether a causal link exists between alcohol use/abuse and violence (National Institute on Alcohol Abuse and Alcoholism, 2000).

If alcohol plays a causal role in much if not most of the violence among college students, then preventing alcohol abuse becomes part of the way to lower crime among students. Put another way, without dealing with the high rates of alcohol abuse among college students, can institutions make progress campus crime? How can colleges reduce rates of alcohol abuse and thus lower the risk of crime? The next section examines what research shows about preventing college student abuse of alcohol.

Preventing Binge Drinking and Alcohol-Related Crime

Studying the link between college alcohol use and campus crime is important in its own right, but the hope is that researchers can use that knowledge to figure out ways of reducing the amount of college crime.

This section examines how to prevent college alcohol abuse. A reasonable working assumption is that high rates of alcohol abuse among college students relate to substantial amounts of college crime. Put another way, it will be difficult to make much progress against certain kinds of college crime– particularly violence against women and vandalism on campus–unless something is first done to lower the rates of alcohol abuse. Research shows that purely educational efforts against both violence and alcohol abuse fail (Bachar & Koss, 2001; National Institute on Alcohol Abuse and Alcoholism, 2002a, 2002b). What researchers need is a fresh line of thought that explores linking them. On a more theoretical level, Abbey (1991, 2002) has presented some important ideas about how alcohol and sexual violence might be connected. On a practical level, Langford (2005, 2006) offers suggestions about how administrators and activists can attack the roots of much campus crime, in part, by reducing abusive drinking.

A particularly important set of findings from the NIAAA task force report concern what works, or shows promise of working, in lowering the risk of college drinking. The NIAAA report divides strategies into four tiers, based on how much evidence supports their efficacy, according to a review by a panel of experts of published studies about prevention. The following discussion highlights the main findings from the NIAAA (2002a).[7]

Tier 1 comprises strategies with evidence of effectiveness among college students who are problem, at-risk, or alcohol-dependent drinkers. This tier includes several strategies:

- Combining cognitive-behavioral skills training with norms clarification and motivational enhancement interventions.
- Offering brief motivational enhancement interventions.
- Challenging alcohol expectancies.

One of the best known of these programs is called BASICS (Brief Alcohol Screening and Intervention for College Students):

BASICS is administered in the form of two individual sessions in which students are provided feedback about their drinking behavior and given the opportunity to negotiate a plan for change based on the principles of motivational interviewing. High-risk drinkers who participated in the BASICS program significantly reduced both drinking problems and alcohol consumption rates, compared to control group participants, at both the 2-year follow-up . . . and 4-year outcome assessment periods. BASICS has also been found to be clinically significant in an analysis of individual student drinking changes over time. . . . (National Institute on Alcohol Abuse and Alcoholism, 2002a:17)

Tier 2 strategies consist of those for which there is evidence of success with general populations and that could be applied to college environments. This tier includes strategies such as:

- Increased enforcement of minimum legal drinking age laws.
- Implementation, increased publicity, and enforcement of other laws to reduce alcohol-impaired driving.
- Restrictions on alcohol retail outlet density.
- Increased price and excise taxes on alcoholic beverages.
- Responsible beverage service policies in social and commercial settings.
- The formation of a campus and community coalition involving all major stakeholders.

These strategies seek to change the broader environment, with many affecting not only college students, but also underage persons who are not in college.

A primary example of a Tier 2 strategy is the increased enforcement of the minimum legal drinking age (MLDA) laws. An examination of 241 empirical analyses of the MLDA published between 1960 and 2000 shows powerful evidence of an inverse relationship between the MLDA and both alcohol consumption and traffic crashes (Wagenaar & Toomey, 2002). The MLDA is effective in spite of minimal enforcement–public policies of this type have an impact on problematic drinking and alcohol-related problems among college students (Dowdall, 2006).

Tier 3 strategies include those showing evidence of logical and theoretical promise but which require comprehensive evaluations to establish their effectiveness. Among these strategies are:

- Campus-based policies and practices that appear to be capable of reducing high-risk alcohol use, including eliminating keg parties, banning alcohol on campus, and expanding alcohol-free events.
- Increased enforcement at campus-based events that promote excessive drinking
- Increased publicity about and enforcement of underage drinking laws on campus and eliminating "mixed messages."
- Conducting marketing campaigns to correct student misperception about alcohol use.

Among the strategies listed in this tier are attempts to change the social norms about drinking that students perceive to be prevalent on a campus, usually via a marketing campaign that contrasts actual drinking behavior with perceived drinking behavior. Proponents of this approach claim to have had success in lowering drinking, but evidence published so far remains below the level necessary to label the approach a proven, as opposed to a promising, strategy.

Tier 4 lists strategies shown to be ineffective when used alone include:

- Informational, knowledge-based, or values clarification interventions about alcohol and the problems related to its excessive use, when used alone.
- Providing blood alcohol content feedback to students.

Purely informational programs assume that students lack the knowledge of the effects of alcohol, and that providing them with more information will change their behavior; by contrast, moving toward broader changes in the environment does change behavior (DeJong & Langford, 2002). Yet purely informational programs remain perhaps the most popular response to college drinking problems.

The NIAAA Task Force report provides support for moving from purely educational interventions (with limited or no evidence of effectiveness), to environmental strategies that have been proved effective (DeJong & Langford, 2002). Since publication of the NIAAA Report (2002a & b; Goldman, Boyd, & Faden, 2002), new research has demonstrated that comprehensive environmental interventions (like the American Medical Association's "A Matter of Degree" or AMOD Program) can be effective in lowering the health and behavioral consequences of excessive college drinking (Weitzman, Nelson, Lee, & Wechsler, 2004). Comparison of those campuses that implemented the AMOD environmental interventions most fully showed small but statistically significant decreases in alcohol consumption and in alcohol-related harms, including criminal victimization, when compared with those institutions that had not properly implemented the AMOD program. Additional recent research shows that "the state sets the rate," that public policies and effective enforcement play an important role in lowering the rate of binge drinking; whether such policies change alcohol-related crime remains to be tested (Nelson, Naimi, Brewer, & Wechsler, 2005; see also: Dowdall, 2006).

This section has summarized the NIAAA Task Force Report's findings about the effectiveness of different college prevention strategies. A critical issue concerns the validity of the general assumption that broad environmental management strategies (that might include combinations of Tiers 1 through 3) will probably have the best effects on college populations (DeJong & Langford, 2002).[8] A mixture of countermeasures will probably work better than one single prevention approach.

Conclusion

There is a powerful link between alcohol use/abuse and crime. Data consistently show that individual college students who report binge drinking are much more likely to be either the victims or the perpetrators of crime. Campuses with high rates of binge drinking also experience relatively higher rates of criminal victimization. At a time when societal-wide rates of crime have fallen significantly, campus alcohol-related crimes such as rape appear stable, probably reflecting the largely unchanged rate of alcohol abuse among college students.

Changing the culture of alcohol use on college campuses will be neither easy nor simple, and commitment to change should be realistic and assume the necessity of long-term efforts. But there is a glimmer of hope. By better understanding the alcohol-crime connection, we can begin to field interventions that will lower both the rates of binge drinking and the rates of crime. Some crime on campus has little to do with binge drinking, so one should not cast alcohol abuse reduction in the role of panacea. Nonetheless, environmental interventions offer evidence of successfully reducing both alcohol abuse and its primary and secondary consequences, including college student victimization (Langford, 2006). College administrators who specialize in addressing crime, sexual assault, or alcohol abuse should forge partnerships to address more effectively the alcohol-crime connection.

Notes

1. I wish to thank the following people for help or suggestions: Antonia Abbey, Catherine Bath, Kathleen Bogle, Fred Donodeo, Bonnie Fisher, Mary Koss, Linda Langford, Stephanie Menninger, John Sloan, and Henry Wechsler. Any errors are entirely mine.
2. The Department of Education website, http://www.ope.ed.gov/security/index. asp, presents data on reported campus crime and alcohol and drug violations at thousands of college campuses across the country.
3. It is difficult to compare *Clery Act* data over time because of changes in definitions and requirements. *Clery Act* alcohol violations do not include public drunkenness, underage drinking, or driving under the influence, and thus represent only some of the alcohol-related crime. The data on liquor law violations were taken from http://www.securityoncampus. org/crimestats/index htm, retrieved 6/01/06.
4. For a recent review of natural and social science research about alcohol use and abuse, see: National Institute on Alcohol Abuse and Alcoholism (2000). For comprehensive reviews of the literature about college student drinking, see Goldman, Boyd, and Faden (2002).
5. Readers interested in an extensive discussion should go to its website, www.collegedrinking prevention.gov, which contains its final report, a special supplement of *Journal of Studies on Alcohol,* and a series of reports about the question.
6. For a full discussion of the Core Survey and its basic findings, see http://www. siu.edu/departments/coreinst/public_html/.
7. Detailed discussion of how the findings were generated and the content of each of the strategies can be found in the expert panel report (NIAAA 2002b[0]).
8. Readers interested in more detailed examination of the alcohol-crime link on college campuses might want to explore websites of the Higher Education Center (www.edc.org/hec) and Security on Campus (http://www.securityoncampus. org/).

REFERENCES

Abbey, A. (1991). Acquaintance rape and alcohol consumption on college campuses: How are they linked? *Journal of American College Health, 39,* 165–169.

Abbey, A. (2002). Alcohol-related sexual assault: A common problem among college students. *Journal of Studies on Alcohol, Supplement No. 14,* 118–128.

Bachar, K., & Koss, M. P. (2001). From prevalence to prevention: Closing the gap between what we know about rape and what we do. In C. M. Renzetti, J. L.

Edelson, & R. K. Bergen (Eds.), *Sourcebook of violence against women.* Thousand Oaks, CA: Sage.

Baum, K., & Klaus, P. 2005. Violent victimization of college students: 1995–2002. Washington, DC: United States Department of Justice, Office of Justice Programs.

CASA Commission on Substance Abuse at Colleges and Universities. (1994). *Rethinking rites of passage: Substance abuse on America's campuses.* New York: Columbia University.

Collins, J. (1989). Alcohol and interpersonal violence: Less than meets the eye. In N. A. Weiner & M. E. Wolfgang (Eds.). *Pathways to criminal violence* (pp. 49–67). Newbury Park, CA: Sage.

DeJong, W., & Langford, L. M. (2002). A typology for campus-based alcohol prevention: Moving toward environmental management strategies. *Journal of Studies on Alcohol, Supplement No. 14,* 140–147.

Dowdall, G. W. (2006). How public alcohol policy shapes prevention. In R. J. Chapman (Ed.) *When they drink: Practitioner views and lessons learned on preventing high-risk collegiate drinking.* Glassboro, NJ: Rowan University.

Dowdall, G. W., & Wechsler, H. (2002). Studying college alcohol use: Widening the lens, sharpening the focus. *Journal of Studies on Alcohol, Supplement No. 14,* 14–22.

Engs, R. C., & Hanson, D. J. (1994). Boozing and brawling on campus: A national study of violent problems associated with drinking over the past decade. *Journal of Criminal Justice, 22,* 171–180.

Fagan, J. (1993). Interactions among drugs, alcohol, and violence. *Health Affairs, 12,* 65–79.

Fisher, B. S., & Sloan III, J. J. (1995). *Campus crime: Legal, social, and policy perspectives.* Springfield, IL: Charles C Thomas.

Fisher, B. S., Cullen, F. T., & Turner, M. G. (2000). *The sexual victimization of college women.* (NCJ 182369). Washington, DC: National Institute of Justice.

Fisher, B. S., Sloan, J. J., Cullen, F. T., & Lu, C. (1998). Crime in the ivory tower: The level and sources of student victimization. *Criminology, 36,* 671–710.

Giancola, P. R. (2002). Alcohol-related aggression during the college years: Theories, risk factors and policy implications. *Journal of Studies on Alcohol, Supplement No. 14,* 129–139.

Goldman, M. S., Boyd, G. M., & Faden, V. (2002). College drinking, what it is, and what to do about it: A review of the state of the science. *Journal of Studies on Alcohol, Supplement No. 14,* 23–37.

Greenfield, L. A. (1998). *Alcohol and crime: An analysis of national data on the prevalence of alcohol involvement in crime.* Washington, DC: United States Department of Justice.

Hart, T. C. (2003). *Violent victimization of college students.* Washington, DC: United States Department of Justice.

Herman, A. I., Philbeck, J. W., Vasilopoulos, N. L., & Depetrillo, P. B. (2003). Serotonin transporter promoter polymorphism and differences in alcohol consumption behaviour in a college student population. *Alcohol & Alcoholism, 38,* 446–449.

Hingson, R., Heeren, T., Winter, M., & Wechsler, H. (2005). Magnitude of alcohol-related mortality and morbidity among U.S. college students ages 18–24: Changes from 1998 to 2001. *Annual Review of Public Health, 26,* 259–279.

Hoover, E. (2005, June). For the 12th straight year, arrests for alcohol rise on college campuses. *The Chronicle of Higher Education, 51,* June 24.

Koss, M. P., Gidycz, C. A., & Wisniewski, N. (1987). The scope of rape. *Journal of Consulting and Clinical Psychology, 55,* 162–170.

Langford, L. (2005). *Preventing violence and promoting safety in higher education settings: Overview of a comprehensive approach.* Newton, MA: The Higher Education Center for Alcohol and Other Drug Abuse and Violence Prevention.

Langford, L. (2006). The role of alcohol and other drugs in campus violence prevention. *Catalyst, 7,* 206.

Martin, S. (Ed.) (1993). *Alcohol and interpersonal violence: Fostering multidisciplinary perspectives.* Rockville, MD: National Institute on Alcohol Abuse and Alcoholism.

Martin, S. (1992). The epidemiology of alcohol-related interpersonal violence. *Alcohol Health & Research World, 16,* 230–237.

Mohler-Kuo, M., Dowdall, G. W., Koss, M. P., & Wechsler, H. (2004). Correlates of rape while intoxicated in a national sample of college women. *Journal of Studies on Alcohol, 65,* 37–45.

National Institute on Alcohol Abuse and Alcoholism (2002a). *A call to action: Changing the culture of drinking at U.S. colleges.* Rockville, MD: author.

National Institute on Alcohol Abuse and Alcoholism (2002b). *Task force on college drinking: Final report of the panel on prevention and treatment–How to reduce high-risk college drinking.* Rockville, MD: author.

National Institute on Alcohol Abuse and Alcoholism (2000). *10th special report to the U.S. congress on alcohol and health.* Rockville, MD: author.

Nelson, T. F., Naimi, T. S., Brewer, R. D., & Wechsler, H. (2005). The state sets the rate: The relationship among state-specific college binge drinking, state binge drinking rates, and selected state alcohol control policies. *American Journal of Public Health, 95,* 441–446.

Pastore, A. L., & Maguire, K. (Eds.) 2003. *Sourcebook of criminal justice statistics* [Online]. Accessed March 30, 2006 from, http://www.albany.edu/sourcebook.

Parker, R. N., & Rebhun, L. (1995). *Alcohol and homicide.* Albany, NY: State University of New York Press.

Perkins, H. W. (2002). Surveying the damage: A review of research on consequences of alcohol misuse in college populations. *Journal of Studies on Alcohol, Supplement No. 14,* 91–100.

Robert Wood Johnson Foundation (2001). *Substance abuse: The nation's number one health problem.* Princeton, NJ: Robert Wood Johnson Foundation.

Security on Campus, Inc. (2006). *Campus Watch, 12,* 7.

United States Department of Education, Office of Postsecondary Education (2005). *The handbook for campus crime reporting.* Washington, DC: United States Department of Education.

Wagenaar, A. C., & Toomey, T. L. (2002). Effects of minimum drinking age laws: Review and analyses of the literature from 1960 to 2000. *Journal of Studies on Alcohol, Supplement No. 14,* 206–225.

Wechsler, H., & Wuetrich, B. (2002). *Dying to drink: Confronting binge drinking on college campuses.* Emmaus, PA: Rodale.

Wechsler, H., Dowdall, G., Davenport, A., & Rimm, E. (1995). A gender-specific measure of binge drinking among college students. *American Journal of Public Health, 85,* 982–985.

Wechsler, H., Dowdall, G., Davenport, A., & Castillo, S. (1995). Correlates of college student binge drinking. *American Journal of Public Health, 85,* 921–926.

Wechsler, H., Davenport, A., Dowdall, G., Moeykens, B., & Castillo, S. (1994). Health and behavioral consequences of binge drinking in college: A national survey of students at 140 colleges. *JAMA, 272,* 1672–1677.

Wechsler, H., Kuo, M., Lee, H., & Dowdall, G. W. (2000). Environmental correlates of underage alcohol use and related problems of college students. *American Journal of Preventive Medicine, 19,* 24–29.

Weitzman, E. R., Nelson, T. F., Lee, H., & Wechsler, H. (2004). Reducing drinking and related harms in college: Evaluation of the A Matter of Degree Program. *American Journal of Preventive Medicine, 27,* 187–196.

Chapter 10

VIOLENCE AGAINST WOMEN ON COLLEGE CAMPUSES: RAPE, INTIMATE PARTNER ABUSE, AND SEXUAL HARASSMENT

JOANNE BELKNAP AND EDNA EREZ

INTRODUCTION

Until the 1980s, most people assumed that college campuses were a safe environment for women. The little concern that existed for women's safety on campus was limited to stranger rapes, though these assaults are relatively rare compared to women's victimizations by men they know (Aizenman & Kelly, 1988; Lott, Reilly, & Howard, 1982; Reilly, Lott, Caldwell, & DeLuca, 1992; Roark, 1987; Warshaw, 1988).

Although intimate partner abuse (domestic violence), stranger rape, and sexual harassment were recognized as social problems at the beginning of the 1970s, it was not until the late 1970s and early 1980s that intimate partner abuse in dating relationships, acquaintance rapes (including "date rapes"), and the sexual harassment of college students began to receive attention (e.g., Aizenman & Kelly, 1988; Belknap & Erez, 1997; Koss, Gidycz, & Wisniewski, 1987; Makepeace, 1981; Project on the Status and Education of Women, 1978; Warshaw, 1988).

Victimizations of college women include various expressions of coercive sexuality in the social and institutional aspects of campus life: physical and sexual abuse in dating relationships, in student parties, and unethical sexual advances by professors and staff (Leidig, 1992). This chapter explores these phenomena. It presents the definitions and characteristics of aggression against college women, and addresses explanations for the frequency and persistence of these violations. It then reviews the dynamics of intimate partner abuse, acquaintance rape, and sexual harassment and their consequences for offenders and victims. Finally, the chapter discusses policy recommendations to deter and better respond to aggression against college women.

Defining the Concepts

Sexual harassment, rape, and intimate partner abuse are distinctively feminist issues. First, the victims of these offenses are predominantly women and the offenders are predominantly men. Furthermore, when females use physical aggression in intimate and dating relationships, it is rarely sexual; it is usually in self-defense (to fight back against male-initiated aggression); and the violence is generally far less extreme, injurious, and fear-inducing than the violence men direct against women (Belknap & Melton, 2005; Das Dasgupta, 2001; Lane & Gwartney-Gibbs, 1985; Makepeace, 1983, 1986; Molidor & Tolman, 1998; O'Keefe & Treister, 1998). Stated alternatively, when women are "violent" in dating and martial relationships, it is typically to resist abuse initiated by their male dates or partners. Thus, the perspective guiding our analysis of women's sexual victimization on campus reflects the reality of the phenomenon, namely, that men commit the overwhelming majority of rapes, intimate partner abuses, and sexual harassments against women.

Historical Context and Concept Development

The phrases "sexual harassment" and "battered woman" did not exist until the 1970s, while the term "date rape" was not coined until the early 1980s. Although not named until the second wave of the women's movement, such behavior has been prevalent for centuries. For example, what we currently call acquaintance and date rape occurred with alarming frequency in England during the eighteenth and nineteenth centuries (Clark, 1987). Similarly, research from the 1950s (e.g., Kanin, 1957) reported the same rate of unwanted sexual contact (including rapes) on dates as research from the 1980s and 1990s. Early sexual harassment research in the 1970s focused on its occurrence in the workplace and only later was it extended to academic settings (Project on the Status and Education of Women, 1978). The lack of labels for violence and violations against women has resulted in their prolonged invisibility (Belknap, 2007). Persistent beliefs that sexual harassment is just "good fun" added to the behavior going unnoticed, as did the notion that sexual assault by one's date is not "real rape" but merely miscommunication or women changing their mind after the fact.

Since the 1970s, feminist activism on behalf of women helped reverse the invisibility of these phenomena, and revealed misconceptions about men's aggression toward women. Once social scientists and activists identified and labeled the behavior, they helped institute education programs and policies to deter and respond to these violations. However, one of the problems in identifying and responding to perpetrators of violence against women has been the ambiguity of definitions used for aggression and harassment including those used for intimate partner abuse or domestic abuse, sexual assaults, rape, and sexual harassment (see Fitzgerald, 1990; Rivera & Regoli, 1987). Are date rapes a form of acquaintance rape? Are rapes occurring during college parties rape? Research, for instance, has documented that college women are most at risk of unwanted sexual contact (including rape) perpetrated by male acquaintances or friends, followed by boyfriends, and strangers (e.g., Banyard, Plante, Cohn, Moorhead, Ward, & Walsh, 2005; Ward, Chapman, White, & Williams, 1991). Additionally, research shows that many rapes and other types of sexual abuse that college women experience occur during fraternity, dormitory, house, and apartment parties, and not necessarily on a date (Banyard et al., 2005; Black, Belknap, & Ginsberg, 2005; Boswell & Spade, 1998; Ehrhart & Sandler, 1985; Gwartney-Gibbs & Stockard, 1989; Martin & Hummer, 1989; Sanday, 1990; Schwartz & Nogrady, 1996; Ward et al., 1991; Warshaw, 1988).

For the purposes of this chapter, it is useful to make distinctions between sexual harassment, rape, and intimate partner abuse, at the same time that it is vital to understand the overlap among them. A professor's or a boss's sexual harassment of a student or employee can include inappropriate touching and sexual inquiries and comments, but it can also include a violent rape. A boyfriend, date, or husband can slap or hit a woman, but *he* can also rape her. Thus, while we make the distinctions between these types of abuses, it is important to remember that they are not always distinct.

Brandenburg (1982) defined *sexual harassment* as "any attempt to coerce an unwilling person into a sexual relationship, or to subject a person to unwanted sexual attention, or to punish a refusal to comply." These behaviors range from "leering" and telling offensive sexual jokes or making offensive sexual comments or inquiries, to violently forcing sex. Most commonly, both socially and legally, sexual harassment comprises inappropriate sexual behaviors that occur at work (a violation of Title VII of the *Civil Rights Act*) or in an educational context (a violation of the Title IX of the *Civil Rights Act*) (see Belknap & Erez, 1997). It is useful to recognize that sexual harassment definitions in more recent years recognize that such behavior can be perpetrated not just by those with power over the victim (e.g., a professor or boss), but can also be perpetrated by peers (e.g., coworkers or "fellow" students).

This chapter refers to *rape* as nonconsensual oral, anal, or vaginal penetration or nonconsensual oral sex performed on another's genitals. Although this is typically thought of as "forceful" (see Estrich, 1987), it is important to remember that such sexual violations are often more "exploitative" and "coercive" than "forceful" (see Russell, 1984). For example, Estrich (1987) reports that the general public views "real rape" in terms of strangers jumping out of alleys and bushes and forcing penile-vaginal intercourse. While that is most certainly rape, so is having sex with someone too intoxicated from alcohol and/or debilitated by drugs (be they prescription, illegal recreational, or "date rape" drugs) to be able to consent to sexual activity. Research (McGregor, Lipowska, Shah, Du Mont, & De Siato, 2003) has identified a significant increase in recent years of what they labeled DFSA, or "drug facilitated sexual assaults." So-called "date rape drugs" such as hydroxy (commonly referred to as "roofies") and gamma hydroxyl-butyrate ("GHB") are often slipped into women's drinks by sexual predators (often known to the women, or men they meet at bars or parties) with the precise goal of causing unconsciousness and loss of memory so that they can be sexually abused (McGregor et al., 2003). While these sexual acts (rapes) are not always per se violent, they are most certainly *violating, unethical, and illegal.*

The final victimization of college women covered in this chapter is that of *intimate partner abuse:* the physical, sexual, and/or emotional/psychological abuse committed by a current or former date, lover, boy/girlfriend, or spouse (see Belknap & Potter, 2006). While the public often minimize emotional/ psychological abuse of partners, it can devastate victims. Examples of this type of abuse would include a boyfriend who physically assaults his girlfriend, but threatens to harm himself if she breaks up with him or flirts with another man; a male student who does not physically assault his girlfriend, but calls her "ugly," "stupid," "fat," and so on, when he is alone with her or around others.

Notably, sexual harassment can also be physical and verbal/emotional/psychological. For example, a professor could grab a student's breast during his office hours (physical abuse), shove her against a wall and force a kiss (physical abuse), promise to give her an A if she performs a sexual act (psychological abuse), or threaten to fail her if she will *not* perform a sexual act (psychological abuse). All of these examples legally constitute sexual harassment and are violations of Title IX of the *Civil Rights Act.* Similarly, a boyfriend can push his girlfriend out of a moving car (physical violence), punch her in the face and knock out a tooth (physical violence), steal her keys and lock her out of her own apartment to "punish" her for his belief that she flirted with someone else (psychological abuse), threaten to kill himself if she breaks up with him (psychological abuse), or drive in a threatening way while she is a passenger in order to scare her (psychological abuse).

The Continuum of Sexual Victimization

To understand behaviors constituting sexual victimizations (including sexual harassment), it is useful to present these victimizations as occurring along a continuum from coercion to force, as seen in Figure 10.1.

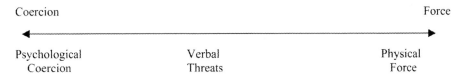

Figure 10.1. The continuum of sexual victimization.

It is important for readers to understand and distinguish ***force*** from ***coercion*** (as well physical abuse from psychological/emotional abuse) when explaining the dynamics of the victimization of college women. Examples of ***coercion*** include a professor telling a student he will not pass her in the course if she docs not perform a sexual favor for him, or a man who tells his date that he will not drive her home unless she has sex with him. Other forms of coercion include sexually victimizing someone in an altered state from alcohol or drug use. ***Force,*** on the other hand, includes physically pushing a woman down or using a weapon and the perpetrator actually making the victim have sex with him. Clearly, this is physical as well as sexual violence. Between coercion and force lay behaviors like ***verbal threats*** of violence, for example, "If you don't comply and have sex with me, then I will physically force you to do so."

To assess the various forms of coercion and force in sexual victimizations, researchers have devised distinct categories of behaviors that one can position on the continuum of coercion to force. Figure 10.2 presents examples of researchers' categorizations of sexually victimizing behaviors and identifies where those behaviors fit on the coercion to force continuum.

Koss et al. (1987) developed four categories of male dating behavior: (1) ***sexually nonaggressive*** males participated only in mutually desired, noncoercive, and nonabusive sex; (2) ***sexually coercive*** males used extreme verbal pressure such as false promises and threats to end the relationship if the woman would not have sexual intercourse; (3) ***sexually abusive*** males obtained sexual contact or attempted intercourse (where penetration did not occur) through force or threat of force; and (4) males used the threat of harm or actual force to obtain oral, anal, or vaginal intercourse. DeKeseredy and Kelly (1993) developed a similar continuum of behavior (see Figure 10.2); other research on college students also supports such a continuum in the levels of sexual aggression in date rapes (Banyard et al., 2005; Gross, Winslett, Roberts, & Gohm, 2006; Koss & Oros, 1982; Rivera & Regoli, 1987; Ward et al., 1991).

Researchers have undertaken similar efforts to describe the continuum of sexual harassment, again ranging from coercion to force. Figure 10.3 presents two representative examples of such work. Adams and Abarbanel

Koss et al. (1987):

Coercion   Force

sexually   sexually   sexually   sexually
non-aggressive   coercive   abusive   assaultive

DeKeseredy & Kelly (1993):

Coercion   Force

unwanted   sexual   attempted   completed

Figure 10.2. Research examples of different continuums of date rape.

(1988), for example, suggest that categories of sexual harassment in an educational context (e.g., perpetrated by professors or instructors at students) could include: (1) *undue attention,* like being too eager to please or help; (2) *body language,* including leering or standing too close; (3) *verbal sexual advances,* like expressions of sexual attraction; (4) *invitation for dates;* (5) *physical advances,* including kissing, touching, and fondling breasts; and (6) s*exual bribery,* involving pressure to sexually comply to receive a good grade (see also Benson & Thomson, 1982), which capture the range from coercion to force.

Fitzgerald, Weitzman, Gold, and Ormerod (1988) suggest a similar continuum exists for sexual harassment, which comprises the categories of: (1) *gender harassment,* including general sexist remarks and behavior; (2) *seductive behavior,* like sanction-free sexual advances; (3) *sexual bribery,* soliciting sex by promise of reward; (4) *sexual coercion,* coercing sex through threat of punishment, and finally; (5) outright *sexual assault.* In one study, female college seniors reported experiencing harassing behaviors perpetrated by their instructors ranging from "vague to blatant," from invitations to dinner, to invitations to a weekend at a mountain resort. Many students reported instructors would not accept "no" for an answer and would call repeatedly after being firmly rejected (Benson & Thomson, 1982).

The varying degrees of coercion in sexual harassment make it difficult to define, both legally and personally (Paludi, Grossman, Scott, Kindermann, Matula, Oswald, Dovan, & Mulcahy, 1990). While categories along the continuum involving force and punishment for failure to comply are severe, victims of harassment find less extreme categories of behavior very confusing and extremely disturbing. It is thus necessary to understand that coercion—as much as force—is a serious violation of a person's self-determination. Further, understanding the continuum of sexually exploitive behaviors

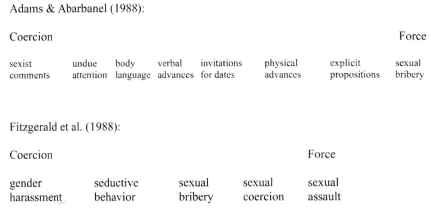

Figure 10.3. Research examples of continuums in sexual harassment.

acknowledges that sexual aggression, even by men known to victims, can involve both coercive violations as well as extreme violence. Viewing violence against women on a continuum facilitates an understanding of the wide spectrum of violations, recognizes the objectification of women underlies these victimizations, and increases appreciation of the impact these offenses have on students' lives (Leidig, 1992).

Finally, it is important to mention the potentially damaging ramifications of consensual sexual relationships between students and faculty members. Research has well documented the occurrence of intimate relationships between faculty members and students on college campuses (see Fitzgerald et al., 1988; Glaser & Thorpe 1986; Skeen & Nielson, 1983), and many universities are currently debating whether there should be policies against these relationships. Proponents of policies prohibiting such relationships argue that a relationship between a faculty member and a student is *always* asymmetric in nature and that students have as much to lose by participating in them as by refusing to do so. Moreover, it is sometimes difficult to determine whether student-faculty relationships are inherently coercive (or whether such is true in specific cases). Women students who experienced consensual sexual relationships with male faculty members reported they later felt the actions of the professor were coercive, and the relationship had resulted in negative consequences for the students (see Glaser & Thorpe, 1986). Because academic opportunities (and work in general) are characterized by vertical stratification and asymmetrical relations between teachers and students and supervisors and subordinates, individuals in positions of power can use their positions to receive sexual compliance from students or subordinates. The interaction of gender and organizational power in an institutional structure increases the likelihood resistance will be minimal or nonexistent.

The Incidence and Characteristics of Aggression Perpetrated Against College Women

Studies of intimate partner abuse have found that about three of every five students in college know someone involved in a violent dating relationship, and about one in five has actually experienced violence in a dating relationship (Bogal-Allbritten & Allbritten, 1985; Cate, Henton, Koval, Christopher, & Lloyd, 1982; Knutson & Mehm, 1986; Makepeace, 1981; Matthews, 1984; Stets & Pirog-Good, 1987). One recent survey study of women at two U.S. universities, however, found that almost half (48%) reported experiencing dating violence (Amar & Gennaro, 2005). Another study comparing battering in intimate relationships as documented in police reports found that physical violence and weapon use was more common in unmarried (boyfriend/girlfriend and ex-marital relationships) than married couples (Erez, 1986). Similarly, studies of college students found that cohabitating couples (unmarried heterosexual couples living together) report more violence and physical injury than heterosexual couples who date but do not live together or are married (Makepeace, 1989; Stets & Straus, 1989).

The most frequent reasons given for intimate partner abuse are jealousy, disagreements over drinking behaviors, and anger over sexual denial (Lane & Gwartney-Gibbs, 1985; Makepeace, 1981, 1986; Matthews, 1984). Thus, sexuality and jealousy are associated with nonsexual physical violence in intimate partner abuse.

It should not be surprising, then, that many relationships in which intimate partner abuse occurs will include sexual violence. For example, a study of unmarried college students found that injury was most common in rapes where the victim and offender were an estranged couple, "suggesting that some men use rape and violence during a rape to punish the victim for some grievance" (Felson & Krohn, 1990). Other research confirmed that acquaintance rapes could be quite violent. In fact, one study on acquaintance rapes found that the better known the acquaintance, the more likely (1) the victim suffers injuries and (2) attempts at rape will be completed (Belknap, 1989).

In the U.S., date rape is largely invisible because such rapes have not been viewed as "real rape" (Estrich, 1987). Self-report victimization studies of women suggest that between 8 percent and 15 percent of women experienced *forced* intercourse, mostly as college students (Amick & Calhoun, 1987; Berger, 1986; DeKeseredy & Kelly, 1993; Gross et al., 2006; Korman & Leslie, 1982; Koss et al., 1987; Koss & Oros, 1982; Lane & Gwartney-Gibbs, 1985; Lott et al., 1982; Muehlenhard & Linton, 1987; Reilly et al., 1992; Rivera & Regoli, 1987; Ward et al., 1991; Warshaw, 1988). Rates of self-reported coerced intercourse are much higher (Miller & Marshall, 1987). The *National College Women Sexual Victimization Study* (NCWSV) (see Fisher,

Cullen, & Turner, 2000) estimated that 2.8 percent of their national sample of college women had experienced either a completed rape (1.7 percent) or an attempted rape incident (1.1 percent). These percentages translate to a victimization rate of 27.7 rapes per 1,000 female students. Of those incidents, 12.8 percent of completed rapes, 35.0 percent of attempted rapes, and 22.9 percent of threatened rapes took place on a date. One study found that, using the same survey in 1988 and in 2000, unwanted sexual contact of women decreased, but rates of unwanted intercourse remained the same (Banyard et al., 2005).

One recent study found that over one-quarter (27%) of college women reported an unwanted sexual experience that ranged from kissing and petting to oral, anal, or vaginal intercourse, with African American women reporting a higher rate (36%) than white women (26%) (Gross et al., 2006). One-third of these sexually victimized women reported multiple forced sexual experiences (Gross et al., 2006) and one-fifth (19%) of this sample of college women reported experiencing forced anal, oral, or vaginal intercourse. Notably, in this study, the most frequently reported victim-offender-relationship was boyfriend (41% of the rapes), followed by friends (29%), and acquaintances (21%), emphasizing that college women are most at risk of rape by known and sometimes well-trusted males.

Notably, the research on self-reported sexual assaults by college males, while confirming the frequency of date rape, generally suggests that such victimizations are less common than women report (DeKeseredy & Kelly, 1999; Miller & Marshall, 1987; Ward et al., 1991). This might be due to few men committing rapes against many women and/or because male offenders are less likely than are female victims to report a behavior as rape or force. Regarding self-reported male behavior, one study found that over half of college men "thought it was somewhat justifiable to force kissing with tongue contact; [and] over a fifth thought it was somewhat justifiable to touch the woman's genitals against her wishes" (Muehlenhard & Linton, 1987).

Sexual harassment is also prevalent on college campuses. As noted previously, the behavior most commonly researched is harassment perpetrated by male faculty members or instructors against female students. Studies of sexual harassment among college women estimate that between 30 and 35 percent of all female students (graduate and undergraduate) experience sexual harassment by at least one faculty member over the course of their education (Benson & Thomson, 1982; Dziech & Weiner, 1984; McKinney, Olson, & Satterfield, 1988), and over one half (56%) when peers (other students), staff, and administrators were included (Huerta, Cortina, Pang, Torges, & Magley, 2006). When definitions of sexual harassment include sexist remarks and other forms of "gender harassment," the incidence in undergraduate populations nears 70 percent (Lott et al., 1982) or even 92 percent when peers are included as potential sexual harassers (Huerta et al., 2006). Studies have also found little variation across departments in sexual harassment victimizations occurring in academic settings (Benson & Thomson, 1982; Fitzgerald et al., 1988). College women students report that sexual harassment often interferes with their education, makes them uncomfortable, threatens their self-confidence and commitment to academic pursuits, and causes them to wonder about their true classroom abilities (Benson & Thomson, 1982; McKinney et al., 1988). Victims may be reluctant to go to a professor's office to receive academic guidance or request a letter of recommendation, and victims find themselves in a situation where they must adopt strategies to minimize interactions with the potential for further harassment (Benson & Thomson, 1982; Dziech & Weiner, 1984). Sexual harassment thus not only impedes victims' opportunities, but also can deter fellow women students from pursuing additional classes with the harasser. Indeed, students report they avoid working with, or taking classes from, faculty members with a reputation for making sexual advances at students (McKinney et al., 1988). "Sexual harassment may be particularly stressful during college years when young women are at a critical stage of their personal and professional development" (Huerta et al., 2006).

Finally, it is important to note that the research on campus sexual harassment has routinely omitted the students' race in analyses of this problem, and thus failed to account for the role and dynamic of race in exploring harassment. It is likely that women of color are sexually harassed more often than are their white counterparts because of the interaction of racism and sexism (DeFour, 1990). For example, attitudes that African-American women are "sexually free," Asian women are "docile and submissive," Hispanic women are "hot-blooded," and so on, greatly impact women of color's vulnerability to sexual harassment (DeFour, 1990). The research on date rape and intimate partner abuse has also failed to account adequately for race. Future research needs to elucidate the effect of the student's race on the risk of victimization and the university and criminal legal system responses to her allegations.

Factors Related to Sexual Aggression Against Women on Campus

The Climate

About one-third of college males have reported that they would rape women under some circumstances if they knew that they would not get caught (Check & Malamuth, 1985; Malamuth, 1981; Reilly et al., 1992; Tieger, 1981). Additionally, compared to women, men view sexually related behavior on the job and at school as more natural, less serious, and something to be expected (Lott et al., 1982).

Campus fraternity practices and values, in particular, are conducive to coercive and violent sex and aggression against women as they overemphasize a macho conception of men and masculinity, and a narrow and stereotyped conception of women and femininity. Fraternities use activities associated with these conceptions to commodify women, such as using them for "bait" to attract new members or to "take care of the guys," and provide sexual access to them as a presumed "benefit" of fraternity membership. Excessive alcohol use, competitiveness between fraternities, and normative support for secrecy within fraternities further facilitates coercive sex and the treatment of rape as an intrafraternity sport or contest. Women thus become the prey in the intrafraternity rivalry games (Black et al., 2005; Martin & Hummer, 1989).

Two studies found that the risk of rape relates to the culture of a particular fraternity on a given campus (Black et al., 2005; Martin & Hummer, 1989). More specifically, rape is unheard of in some fraternities, happens occasionally in others, and there is a high-risk of rape in still others. This explains why some people who hear or read about fraternity rapes claim they do not believe it because the fraternity with which they have been associated is not one where rape occurs.

One study comparing African American and white fraternities found that nonsexual male-on-male physical aggression was far more common at in African American than in white fraternities, but sexual violence against women was almost unheard of in the African American fraternities but very common in some white fraternities (Black et al., 2005). Black et al. (2005) speculated that structural differences related to race and class between white and African American fraternities explained the differences. White fraternities typically had their own "houses" where there was no security overseeing parties. On the other hand, the African American fraternities did not have their own houses, so they had to reserve various halls to hold parties and dances, had to pay security officers to oversee the party, and were not allowed to consume alcohol or drugs. Thus, the black fraternity members who wanted to get "high" would arrive at the party already having consumed drugs and/or alcohol, whereas at the white fraternities, members would typically consume increasing amounts of alcohol and drugs as the night wore on. The white fraternities also had private rooms to take women where they could be raped (Black et al., 2005).

Reports also note that date or fraternity rapists, sexual harassers, or men who physically abuse their girlfriends are rarely sanctioned (DeKeseredy et al., 1993; Lopez, 1992; Sanday, 1990; Warshaw, 1988). This failure to sanction violators is partly due to victims' unwillingness to report the incident, but also to university authorities' and the criminal justice system's reluctance to take action against such offenders. Men may trivialize these victimizations and joke about them as the "sporting parts" of men's lives (Leidig, 1992).

One answer, then, as to why some men rape, abuse, and sexually harass women on campus is because they can. Recent research confirms that men who abuse women rarely receive negative consequences and their male peers seldom shun them (Gamache, 1991; Martin & Hummer, 1989; Siegel & Raymond, 1992). In fact, some research has found that men who participate in intimate partner abuse and date rape often receive peer support from their male friends, who may even encourage the abuse (DeKeseredy, 1988; Gwartney-Gibbs & Stockard, 1989; Martin & Hummer, 1989). Other studies find that although couples in physically abusive relationships most frequently attach anger and confusion as the reason for the abuse, some one-quarter believe abuse signifies "love" by the abuser (Cate et al., 1982; Matthews, 1984).

Gender Differences and Stereotypes

As expected, men in general, and particularly men who report being abusive, are more likely than are women to believe rape myths and support sexual aggression (Gilmartin-Zena, 1988; Malamuth, 1989; Muehlenhard & Linton, 1987; Reilly et al., 1992; Warshaw, 1988; Wilson, Raison, & Britton, 1983). However, there is significant evidence that many women also express hostility towards rape and sexual harassment victims and blame them for their experiences (Gowan, 2000). One study found that college men are more likely to blame women for their sexual victimizations if the women consented to a certain level of sexual activity, and then wanted to stop (Yescavage, 1999). One recent self-report study of college men found that men who participated in aggressive high school sports were more likely than were counterparts not in these sports to report psychological, physical, and sexual aggression against their dating partners, and causing injuries to their dates. Former aggressive high school athletes were also more likely to adhere to rape myths and were more homophobic than are nonathletes (Forbes, Adams-Curtis, Pakalka, & White, 2006).

Male Entitlement

Male entitlement is a common theme throughout the analysis of the causes of intimate partner abuse, date rape, and sexual harassment. Whether it is the professor who believes he has the right to date or harass his students, the fraternity member who believes all women who attend parties are "fair game," or the boyfriend who "justifies" hitting his girlfriend because she talked with another man, perceptions of male entitlement are common in the victimization of women. Perhaps nowhere is this more evident than women students physically and sexually victimized by male athletes (Bohmer & Parrot, 1993; Eskenazi, 1990; Warshaw, 1988; Yescavage, 1999). Athletes often view these victims as "groupies" who got what they "asked for" and women who changed their minds after the "consensual" sex are "gold diggers" trying to make money off athletes. Yescavage's (1999) study of the self-reported behaviors of college men viewed male entitlement as a significant risk factor for these men victimizing women. These men held patriarchal views that women are the property of men, and thus women have no right to deny men sex, can be treated as men want, and sometimes deserve to be "taught a lesson" when they are too independent.

Altered States: The Effect of Alcohol and Drugs

Research on date rape and fraternity gang rape finds strong links between alcohol/drug consumption and unwanted sexual experiences, including intimate partner abuse (Abbey, Zawacki, Buck, Clinton, & McAuslan 2001; Bogal-Allbritten & Allbritten, 1985; Fisher, Cullen, & Turner, 2000; Lott et al., 1982; Martin & Hummer; 1989; Muehlenhard & Linton, 1987; Pritchard, 1988; Testa, Vanzile-Tamsen, & Livingston, 2004; Ward et al., 1991; Warshaw, 1988). Moreover, there is considerable evidence that these rapists often *plan* before the date or party how to debilitate their victims through drugs and alcohol (Ehrhart & Sandler, 1985; Kanin, 1985; Martin & Hummer, 1989; Sanday, 1990) and that many college men self-report alcohol-related sexual coercion and hold "many rape-supportive attitudes and beliefs" (Carr & VanDeusen, 2004). A potential victim placed in an altered state increases her inability to resist the attacker, particularly if she is unconsciousness. Additionally, while the public and criminal justice decision makers view the rapist as *less* responsible for raping if he was drunk, they view the rape *victim* as *more* responsible for being raped if she was drunk (Bromley & Territo, 1990; Ehrhart & Sandler, 1985; Lundberg-Love & Geffner, 1989; Warshaw, 1988).

The Dynamics and the Consequences of Victimization

Given that women are blamed for their sexual and intimate partner victimizations (see Estrich, 1987; Warshaw, 1988; Yescavage, 1999), it is hardly surprising that many victims internalize that blame and fail to define themselves as victims (Fisher et al., 2000; Koss, 1990; Rabinowitz, 1990). First, there is a cultural stigma attached to being a victim of these crimes. Victims often trivialize their experiences to protect their senses of vulnerability and integrity (Koss, 1990). Second, along with society, victims often blame themselves for their own battering, rape, or sexual harassment victimization (Berger, Searles, Salem, & Pierce, 1986; Koss, 1990). They often feel ashamed of their victimizations, particularly if they were attracted to their dates or professors before being raped, battered, or sexually harassed. A long period usually passes before a victim acknowledges her victimization. One exception to this generalization involves women who resist and respond immediately: "Often the woman who speaks out is a person with a strong sense of integrity who can no longer ignore injustice" (Koss, 1990).

Not surprisingly, college women who report dating violence have significantly higher levels of depression, anxiety, hostility, and other mental health dysfunction than do their nonabused counterparts (Amar & Gennaro, 2004). Unfortunately, fewer than 3 percent of those experiencing college dating violence visited a mental health professional (Amar & Gennaro, 2004). Similarly, college women reporting sexual harassment evidence increased levels of psychological distress, lower academic satisfaction, greater physical illness, and higher rates of eating disorders than do college women who have not experienced sexual harassment (Huerta et al., 2006). When higher status individuals, such as faculty, staff, and administrators, perpetrated the sexual harassment, academic satisfaction among victims was lower than among nonvictims. However, sexual harassment was equally detrimental to the victims' mental health, regardless of the status of the perpetrator (e.g., student, faculty, staff, or administrator) (Huerta et al., 2006).

Women often do not report sexual harassment, date rape, or intimate partner abuse to formal authorities (e.g., university personnel or the police) and often not even to informal support persons (e.g., friends, family, and counselors) (Belknap, 1989; Benson et al., 1992; DeKeseredy & Kelly, 1993; Fisher et al., 2000; Miller & Marshall, 1987; Pirog-Good & Stets, 1989; Ward et al., 1991). Many victims fear the authorities will not take them seriously (Berger et al., 1986; U.S. Merit Systems Protection Board, 1981), believe the authorities will hold them responsible for the victimization, or doubt the authorities will take any corrective action (Brandenburg, 1982). At least some of these fears are realistic–offenders frequently go unpunished, whereas victims are negatively sanctioned in the media, on the campus, or at the work site (Sanday, 1990; U.S. Merit Systems Protection Board, 1981). In fact, many victims of date and fraternity rapes, and sexual harassment, drop out of school while their offenders continue at the university (Sanday, 1990; Warshaw, 1988).

Policy Implications and Conclusion

In the last decade, activists have made great headway in raising awareness about the various kinds of victimizations of women on college campuses. Yet there is still denial about the magnitude of the problem, and considerable ignorance of the harm these actions inflict on victims. Furthermore, students, faculty, and staff are often unsure about resources available for the victims, as well as the policies and procedures regarding acquaintance victimizations (Metha & Nigg, 1982; Sullivan & Bybee, 1987). For too long, focus has been preventing stranger rape, for example, by improving campus lighting and providing extra security locks, which ignores the far more common victimizations involving acquaintances (Miller & Marshall, 1987; Steenbarger & Zimmer, 1992).

To deter and prevent violence against and violations of college women, certain steps need to be taken. The first and most important action that college or university administration can take is to acknowledge that sexual harassment, date rape, and intimate partner abuse are realities on campuses (Benson et al., 1992; Roark, 1989). The second step is prevention. Enforcing policies and laws regarding acquaintance victimizations often results in accepting one person's word (and credibility) against another's, making prevention particularly important. Institutions can best serve prevention by promoting education and awareness of the dynamics of sexual harassment, date rape, and intimate partner abuse to students, faculty members, and staff (Amick & Calhoun, 1987; Benson et al., 1992; Bohmer & Parrot, 1993; Leidig, 1992; Roark, 1989; Steenbarger & Zimmer, 1992; Ward et al., 1991; Warshaw, 1988). Awareness may prevent potential offenders from committing these offenses and keep potential victims from experiencing them. Moreover, such knowledge will help those in the academic community to better understand, and thus respond appropriately to victims who approach them.

Third, it is important that institutions make clear policy statements about sexual harassment, date rape, and intimate partner abuse. These policy statements should identify: (1) definitions of sexual harassment, date rape, and intimate partner abuse; (2) who is responsible for handling charges regarding victimizations on campus, both formally (e.g., the police or a grievance board) and informally (e.g., mediation through a counselor or ombudsman's office); and (3) the consequences for offenders of violating the policies (Benson et al., 1992; Bohmer & Parrot, 1993; Brandenburg, 1982; Metha & Nigg, 1982; Virginia State Council on Higher Education, 1992).

Fourth, the grievance boards or administrators in charge of processing the charges should ensure that institutions take action quickly, efficiently, confidentially, and as carefully as possible. Key to this is providing a safe place on campus and "safe people" where and to whom victims report their experiences (Grauerholz, Gottfried, Stohl, & Gabin, 1999).

Fifth, the university needs to disseminate the policies so everyone in the academic community (students, faculty members, and staff) has access to them (Amar & Gennaro, 2004; Bohmer & Parrot, 1993; Benson et al., 1992;

Brandenburg, 1982; Metha & Nigg, 1982). Use of handbooks, postings to university websites, on including policy statements in semester course schedules are examples of how these policies can be communicated.

Sixth, there needs to be an ongoing evaluation of the effectiveness of the policies to ensure that those responsible for enforcement take these violations seriously (Bohmer & Parrot, 1993; Brandenburg, 1982; Metha & Nigg, 1982). Surveys of victims, workers involved with delivering victim services, and counselors could be used to collect data on the extent policies and procedures are followed and on satisfaction with them.

Seventh, there must be on-campus victim advocate services available to respond to the short- and long-term emotional, medical, and logistical needs associated with filing complaints by victims/survivors (Amar & Gennaro, 2004; Benson et al., 1992; Bohmer & Parrot, 1993; Leidig, 1992; Roark, 1989).

Eighth, it is useful to remember that violence against women is not simply a "woman's problem"–most men have women who are close to them in life (e.g., mothers, sisters, girlfriends, friends, etc.) *and* men are usually the perpetrators (Scully, 1990). Given that men are the ones who commit most of the abuse of women, men can be key in stopping male-perpetrated abuse and violence of women. DeKeseredy, Schwartz, and Alvi (2000) point out that "pro-feminist men can begin to tilt the balance against male aggression. This can include shaming or working with bullies or those who are abusive, protesting pornography, and involving oneself with education programs and/or support groups."

Ninth, campus policies and strategies to combat abuse and victimization of women must take into account racial and ethnic differences among women (Koikari & Hippensteele, 2000). Treating such sexual victimizations as a "white woman's issue" or as race/ethnicity-neutral poses the threat of splintering those groups which are advocating for equality and better treatment on campus.

Finally, student victims need to know that they may take a sexual harassment grievance directly to the Office of Civil Rights in the U.S. Department of Education or press charges in a private lawsuit against offenders perpetrating sexual harassment, date rape, and intimate partner abuse, regardless of whether a grievance procedure exists on their campus (Brandenburg, 1982). Such an option should convince university administrators that if they fail to adequately work toward prevention and inadequately respond once victimizations occur, victims can appeal to the legal system and move the issue outside the academic community.

The *Higher Education Amendment Act of 1992* is not only landmark in recognizing campus sexual victimization, but it is well thought out and provides funding for its stated goals of developing rape education/awareness, disciplinary boards, victim counseling and medical services, and dissemination of legal information and assistance to victims. Such federal recognition of one of the victimizations that college women frequently encounter is an important step in legitimizing the seriousness of campus rapes. We hope that similar state-level legislation will help combat sexual harassment and intimate partner abuse on college campuses.

REFERENCES

Abbey, A., Zawacki, T., Buck, P. O., Clinton A. M., & McAuslan, P. (2001). *Alcohol and sexual assault. Alcohol Research and Health, 25,* 43–51.

Adams, A., & Abarbanel, G. (1988). *Sexual assault on campus: What colleges can do.* Santa Monica, CA: Rape Treatment Center.

Aizenman, M., & Kelly, G. (1988). Incidence of violence and acquaintance rape in dating relationships among college men and women. *Journal of College Student Development, 29,* 305–311.

Amar, A. F., & Gennaro, S. (2004). Dating violence in college women: Associated physical injury, healthcare usage, and mental health symptoms. *Nursing Research, 54,* 235–242.

Amick, A. E., & Calhoun, K. S. (1987). Resistance to sexual aggression. *Archives of Sexual Behavior, 16,* 153–163.

Banyard, V. L., Plante, E. G., Cohn, E. S., Moorhead, C., Ward, S., & Walsh, W. (2005). Revisiting unwanted sexual experiences on campus. *Violence Against Women, 11,* 426–446.

Belknap, J. (2007). *The invisible woman: Gender, crime, and justice* (3rd ed.). Belmont, CA: Wadsworth.

Belknap, J., & Erez, E. (1997). Redefining sexual harassment: Confronting sexism in the 21st century. *Justice Professional, 10,* 143–159.

Belknap, J., & Melton, H. (2005, March). Are heterosexual men also victims of intimate partner abuse? Retrieved from http://www.vawnet.org/DomesticViolence/Research/ VAWnetDocs/AR_MaleVictims.pdf on September 6, 2006.

Belknap, J., & Potter, H. (2006). Intimate partner abuse. In C. Renzetti, L. Goodstein, & S. Miller (Eds.), *Women, crime, and criminal justice* (2nd ed.). Los Angeles: Roxbury.

Benson, D., Charleton, C., & Goodhart, F. (1992). Acquaintance rape on campus. *Journal of American College Health, 40,* 157–65.

Benson, D. J., & Thomson, G. E. (1982). Sexual harassment on a university campus: The confluence of authority relations, sexual interest, and gender stratification. *Social Problems, 29,* 236–251.

Berger, R. J., Searles, P., Salem, R. G., & Pierce, B. A. (1986) Sexual assault in a college community. *Sociological Focus, 19,* 1–26.

Black, T., Belknap J., & Ginsburg J. (2005). Racism, sexism and aggression: A study of black and white fraternities. In T. Brown, G. Parks, & C. Phillips (Eds.), *African*

American fraternities and sororities: The legacy and the vision. Lexington, KY: The University Press of Kentucky.

Bogal-Allbritten, R., & Allbritten, W. L. (1985). The hidden victims: Courtship violence among college students. *Journal of College Student Personnel, 26,* 201–204.

Bohmer, C., & Parrot, A. (1993). *Sexual assault on campus.* New York: Lexington.

Boswell, A. A., & Spade, J. D. (1996). Fraternities and collegiate rape culture: Why are some fraternities more dangerous places for women? *Gender & Society, 10,* 133–147.

Brandenburg, J. B. (1982). Sexual harassment in the university: Guidelines for establishing a grievance procedure. *Signs, 8,* 320–336.

Bromley, M. L., & Territo, L. (1990). *College prevention and personal safety awareness.* Springfield, IL: Charles C Thomas.

Carr, J. L., & VanDeusen, K. M. (2004). Risk factors for male sexual aggression on college campuses. *Journal of Family Violence, 19,* 279–289.

Cate, R. M., Henton, J. M., Koval, J., Christopher, F. S., & Lloyd, S. (1982). Premarital abuse: A social psychological perspective. *Journal of Family Issues, 3,* 79–90.

Check, J., & Malamuth, N. (1985). An empirical assessment of some feminist hypotheses about rape. *International Journal of Women's Studies, 8,* 414–423.

Clark, A. (1987). *Women's silence, men's violence: Sexual assault in England, 1770-1845.* London: Pandora Press.

Das Dasgupta, S. (2001). Towards an understanding of women's use of non-lethal violence in intimate heterosexual relationships. Retrieved January 20, 2005 from, http://www. vawnet.org/DomesticViolence/Research/VAWnetDocs/AR_womviol.php.

DeFour, D. C. (1990). The interface of racism and sexism on college campuses. In M. A. Paludi (Ed.), *Ivory power: Sexual harassment on campus.* Albany, NY: State University of New York Press.

DeKeseredy, W. S. (1988). *Woman abuse in dating relationships: The role of male peer support.* Toronto: Canadian Scholars Press.

DeKeseredy, W. S., & Kelly, K. (1993). The incidence and prevalence of woman abuse in Canadian university and college dating relationships. *Canadian Journal of Sociology, 18,* 137–159.

DeKeseredy, W. S., Schwartz, M. D., & Alvi, S. (2000). The role of pro-feminist men in dealing with woman abuse on the Canadian college campus. *Violence Against Women, 6,* 918–935.

Dziech, B. W., & Weiner, L. (1984). *The lecherous professor: Sexual harassment on campus.* Boston: Beacon Press.

Ehrhart, J. K., & Sandler, B. R. (1985). Campus gang rape: Party games? In Project on the Status of Education and Women (Eds.), *Sexual harassment: Hidden issue.* Washington, DC: National Association of Colleges.

Erez, E. (1986). Intimacy, violence, and the police. Human Relations, 39, 265–281.

Eskenazi, G. (1990). The male athlete and sexual assault. *The New York Times,* June 30, p. 27.

Estrich, S. (1987). *Real rape.* Cambridge, MA: Harvard University Press.

Felson, R. B., & Krohn, M. (1990). Motives for rape. *Journal of Research in Crime & Delinquency, 27,* 222–242.

Fisher, B. S., Cullen, F. T., & Turner, M. G. (2000, December). *The sexual victimization of college women* (NCJ 182369). Washington DC: National Institute of Justice.

Fitzgerald, L. F. (1990). Sexual harassment: The definition and measurement of a construct. In M. A. Paludi (Ed.), *Ivory power: Sexual harassment on campus.* Albany, NY: State University of New York Press.

Fitzgerald, L. F., Weitzman, L. M., Gold, Y., Ormerod, M. (1988). Academic harassment. *Psychology of Women Quarterly, 12,* 329–340.

Forbes, G. B., Adams-Curtis, L. E., Pakalka, A. H., & White, K. B. (2006). Dating aggression, sexual coercion, and aggression-supporting attitudes among college men as a function of participation in aggressive high school sports. *Violence Against Women, 12,* 441–455.

Gamache, D. (1991). Domination and control: The social context of dating violence. In B. Levy (Ed.), *Dating violence: Young women in danger.* Seattle, WA: Seal.

Gilmartin-Zena, P. (1988). Gender differences in students' attitudes toward rape. *Sociological Focus, 21,* 279–292.

Glaser, R. D., & Thorpe, J. S. (1986). Unethical intimacy. A survey of sexual contact and advances between psychology educators and female graduate students. *American Psychology, 41,* 43–51.

Gowan, G. (2000). Women's hostility toward women and rape and sexual harassment myths. *Violence Against Women, 6,* 238–246.

Grauerholz, L., Gottfried, H., Stohl, C., & Gabin, N. (1999). There's safety in numbers: Creating a campus advisers' network to help complainants of sexual harassment and complaint receivers. *Violence Against Women, 5,* 950–977.

Gross, A. M., Winslett, A., Roberts, M., & Gohm, C. L. (2006). An examination of sexual violence against college women. *Violence Against Women, 12,* 288–300.

Gwartney-Gibbs, P., & Stockard, J. (1989). Courtship aggression and mixed-sex peer groups. In M. Pirog-Good and J. E. Stets (Eds.), *Violence in dating relationships.* New York: Praeger.

Huerta, M., Cortina, L. M., Pang, J. S., Torges, C. M., & Magley, V. J. (2006). Sex and power in the academy: Modeling sexual harassment in the lives of college women. *Personality and Social Psychology Bulletin, 32,* 616–628.

Kanin, E. J. (1957). Male aggression in dating courtship relations. *American Journal of Sociology, 63,* 197–204.

Kanin, E. J. (1985). Date rapists: Differential sexual socialization and relative deprivation. *Archives of Sexual Behavior, 14,* 219–31.

Knutson, J. F., & Mehm J. G. (1986). Transgenerational patterns of coercion in families and intimate relationships. In G. Russell (Ed.), *Violence in intimate relationships.* New York: PMA Publishing Corporation.

Koikari, M., & Hippensteele, S.K. (2000). Negotiating feminist survival: Gender, race, and power in academe. *Violence Against Women, 6,* 1269–1296.

Korman, S. K., & Leslie, G. R. (1982). The relationship of feminist ideology and date expense sharing to perceptions of sexual aggression in dating. *Journal of Sex Research, 18,* 114–129.

Koss, M. P. (1990). Changed lives: The psychological impact of sexual harassment. In M. A. Paludi (Ed.), *Ivory power: Sex and gender harassment in the academy.* Albany, NY: State University of New York Press.

Koss, M. P., & Oros, C. J. (1982). Sexual experiences survey: A research instrument investigating sexual aggression and victimization. *Journal of Consulting and Clinical Psychology, 50,* 455–457.

Koss, M. P., Gidycz, C. A., & Wisniewski, N. (1987). The scope of rape: Incidence and prevalence of sexual aggression and victimization in a national sample of higher education students. *Journal of Consulting and Clinical Psychology, 55,* 162–170.

Lane, K. E., & Gwartney-Gibbs, P. A. (1985). Violence in the context of dating and sex. *Journal of Family Issues, 6,* 45–59.

Leidig, M. W. (1992). The continuum of violence against women: Psychological and physical consequences. *Journal of American College Health, 40,* 149–55.

Livingston, J. A., & Testa, M. (2000). Qualitative analysis of women's perceived vulnerability to sexual aggression in a hypothetical dating context. *Journal of Social and Personal Relationships, 17,* 729–741.

Lopez, P. (1992). He said . . . she said . . . An overview of date rape from commission through prosecution through verdict. *Journal of Criminal Justice, 13,* 275–302.

Lott, B., Reilly, M. E., & Howard, D. R. (1982). Sexual assault and harassment: A campus community case study. *Signs, 8,* 296–319.

Lundberg-Love, P., & Geffner, R. (1989). Date rape: Prevalence, risk factors, and a proposed model. In M. A. Pirog-Good & J. E. Stets (Eds.), *Violence and dating relationships: Emerging social issues.* New York: Praeger.

Makepeace, J. M. (1981). Courtship Violence among college students. *Family Relations, 30,* 97–102.

Makepeace, J. M. (1983). Life events, stress and courtship violence. *Family Relations, 32,* 101–109.

Makepeace, J. M. (1986). Gender differences in courtship violence victimization. *Family Relations, 35,* 383–388.

Makepeace, J. (1989). Dating, living together and courtship violence. In M. A. Pirog-Good & J. E. Stets (Eds.), *Violence in dating relationships.* New York: Praeger.

Malamuth, N. (1981). Rape proclivity among males. *Journal of Social Issues, 37,* 138–157.

Martin, P. Y., & Hummer, R. A. (1989). Fraternities and rape on campus. *Gender & Society, 3,* 457–73.

Matthews, W. J. (1984). Violence in college couples. *College Student Journal, 18,* 150–158.

McGregor, M. J., Lipowska, M., Shah, S. Du Mont, J., & De Siato, C. (2003). An exploratory analysis of suspected drug-facilitated sexual assault seen in a hospital emergency department. *Women & Health, 37,* 71–80.

McKinney, K., Olson, C., & Satterfield, A. (1988). Graduate students' experiences with and responses to sexual harassment. *Journal of Interpersonal Violence, 3,* 319–325.

Metha, A., & Nigg, J. (1982). Sexual harassment: Implications of a study at Arizona State University. *Women's Studies Quarterly, 10,* 24–26.

Miller, B., & Marshall, J. C. (1987). Coercive sex on the university campus. *Journal of College Student Personnel, 28,* 38–47.

Molidor, C., & Tolman, R. (1998). Gender and contextual factors in adolescent dating violence. *Violence Against Women, 4,* 180–194.

Muehlenhard, C. L., & Linton, M. A. (1987). Date rape and sexual aggression in dating situations: Incidence and risk factors. *Journal of Counseling Psychology, 34,* 186–196.

O'Keefe, M., & Treister, L. (1998). Victims of dating violence among high school students: Are predictors different for males and females? *Violence Against Women, 4,* 195–223.

Paludi, M. A., Grossman, M., Scott, C. A., Kindermann, J., Matula, S., Oswald, J., Dovan, J., & Mulcahy, D. (1990). Myths and realities: Sexual harassment on campus. In M. A. Paludi (Ed.) *Ivory power: Sexual harassment on campus.* Albany, NY: State University of New York Press.

Pritchard, C. (1988). *Avoiding rape on and off campus.* Wenonah, NJ: State College.

Project on the Status and Education of Women (1978). *Sexual harassment: A hidden issue.* Association of American Colleges, Washington, DC.

Rabinowitz, V. C. (1990). Coping with sexual harassment. In M. A. Paludi (Ed.), *Ivory power: Sexual harassment on campus.* Albany, NY: State University of New York Press.

Reilly, M. E., Lott, B., Caldwell, D., & DeLuca, L. (1992). Tolerance for sexual harassment related to self-reported sexual victimization. *Gender & Society, 6,* 122–138.

Rivera, G. F., Jr., & Regoli, R. M. (1987). Sexual victimization experiences of sorority women. *Sociology and Social Research, 72,* 39–42.

Roark, M. L. (1987). Preventing violence on college campuses. *Journal of Counseling and Development, 65,* 367–370.

Russell, D. E. H. (1984). *Sexual exploitation: Rape, child sexual abuse, and workplace harassment.* Beverly Hills, CA: Sage.

Sanday, P. R. (1990). *Fraternity gang rape: Sex, brotherhood, and privilege on campus.* New York: New York University Press.

Schwartz, M. D., & Nogrady, C. A. (1996). Fraternity membership, rape myths, and sexual aggression on a college campus. *Violence Against Women, 2,* 163–179.

Scully, D. (1990). Understanding sexual violence. Boston: Unwin Hyman.

Siegel, D. G., & Raymond, C. H. (1992). An ecological approach to violent crime on campus. *Journal of Security Administration, 15,* 21.

Skeen, R., & Nielson, J. M. (1983). Student-faculty sexual relationships: An empirical test of two explanatory models. *Qualitative Sociology, 6,* 99–117.

Steenbarger, B. N., & Zimmer, C. G. (1992). Violence on campus. *Journal of American College Health, 40,* 147-148.

Stets, J. E., & Pirog-Good, M.A. (1987). Violence in dating relationships. *Social Psychology Quarterly, 50,* 237–246.

Stets, J. E., & Straus, M. A. (1989). The marriage license as a hitting license. In M. A. Pirog-Good and J. E. Stets (Eds.), *Violence in dating relationships.* New York: Praeger.

Sullivan, C. M., & Bybee, D. (1987). Female students and sexual harassment. *Journal of the National Association for Women Deans, Administrators, and Counselors, 50,* 11–16.

Testa, M., Vanzile-Tamsen, C., & Livingston, J. A. (2004). The role of victim and perpetrator intoxication on sexual assault outcomes. *Journal of Studies on Alcohol, 65,* 320–329.

Tieger, T. (1981). Self-rated likelihood of raping and the social perception of rape. *Journal of Research in Personality, 15,* 147–158

United States Merit Systems Protection Board. (1981). *Sexual harassment in the federal workplace: Is it a problem?* Office of Merit Systems Review and Studies. Washington DC: United States Government Printing Office.

Virginia State Council of Higher Education. (1992). *Sexual assault on Virginia's campuses.* (Senate Document No. 17). Richmond, VA: Commonwealth of Virginia.

Ward, S. K., Chapman, K., White, S., & Williams, K. (1991). Acquaintance rape and the college social scene. *Family Relations, 40,* 65–71.

Warshaw, R. (1988). *I never called it rape.* New York: Sarah Lazin Books.

Wilson, K., Raison, R., & Britton, G. M. (1983). Cultural aspects of male sex aggression. *Deviant Behavior, 4,* 241–255.

Yescavage, K. (1999). Teaching women a lesson: sexually aggressive and sexually non-aggressive men's perceptions of acquaintance and date rape. *Violence Against Women, 5,* 796–812.

Chapter 11

VULNERABILITIES AND OPPORTUNITIES 101: THE EXTENT, NATURE, AND IMPACT OF STALKING AMONG COLLEGE STUDENTS AND IMPLICATIONS FOR CAMPUS POLICY AND PROGRAMS

BONNIE S. FISHER AND MEGAN STEWART

Every breath you take
Every move you make
Every bond you break
Every step you take

I'll be watching you

Every single day
Every word you say
Every game you play
Every night you stay

I'll be watching you

Oh can't you see
You belong to me
How my poor heart aches with every step you take
　　　　　　　–The Police, "Every Breath You Take"

INTRODUCTION

These lyrics are not from a love song, as many individuals believe. Quite the contrary, these lyrics are about a man stalking his ex-girlfriend (Stingetc.com, 2006). Unfortunately, being stalked–repeatedly pursued in a manner that causes a reasonable person fear for his or her safety–is much more than just lyrics to this popular song. In the United States, stalking is a criminal act in all 50 states, the District of Columbia, and at the federal level (see Fisher, Cullen, & Turner, 2002).

Stalking is also a grim reality for a large proportion of women and men (Cupach & Spitzberg, 2004; Davis & Frieze, 2000). To illustrate, the National Violence Against Women Survey (NVAWS)–the only national-level study of stalking among the general population ever completed–estimates that between 8 percent and 12 percent of women and 2 percent and 4 percent of men in the United States have been stalked at some point in their lives, while 1 percent to 6 percent of women and 0.4 percent to 1.5 percent of men are stalked annually.[1] To provide some perspective, these respective annual stalking estimates for women and men exceeded those of annual rape estimates (Tjaden & Thoennes, 1998).

There is overwhelming evidence that stalking is common among young adults, especially those between 18–29 years old and that women are primary targets of stalkers (Tjaden & Thoennes, 1998). Furthermore, stalkers are most likely to be a male, known to the victim, typically some type of intimate partner–such as a current or former spouse or boyfriend, or a date–or an acquaintance (Tjaden & Thoennes, 1998). While stalking victims adopt various coping strategies, research consistently shows that stalking victims suffer both psychological and physical effects, which may include death (although such is extremely rare, contrary to media reports and sensationalization) (see Cupach & Spitzberg, 2004; Davis, Frieze, & Maiuro, 2002; Ravensberg & Miller, 2003).

This chapter provides an overview of the stalking research that has focused on the experiences of college students in the United States.[2] We begin the chapter by describing the sociodemographic characteristics, lifestyle, and routine activities of college students that make them vulnerable to stalking while simultaneously providing opportunities to stalk others. We also highlight the characteristics of campuses that provide many opportunities for stalking. Second, we review studies of college students that have examined the extent and nature of stalking victimization and perpetration. Third, we highlight what researchers know about the "pursuit behaviors" stalkers use; the frequency and duration of stalking; and its role in dating and intimate relationships. We also present results that provide insights into the known characteristics of stalking victims and stalkers. Fourth, we summarize the strategies student victims have used to cope with their stalking victimization, including the personal, reporting, and legal strategies students have used to stop the stalker. Fifth, we examine the emotional and psychological toll stalking has on its targets. Finally, we conclude the chapter by providing effective evidence-based policy and program information that campus administrators may find useful for addressing stalking victimization and perpetration on their respective campuses.

Opportunities for Stalking and the Vulnerabilities of Being Stalked Among College Students

Two sizable bodies of interdisciplinary research suggest certain individuals are more vulnerable to criminal victimization and more likely to commit deviant or criminal acts. Research consistently shows that particular demographic characteristics, as well as lifestyle and routine activities among the public, significantly predict who is at a high risk of experiencing predatory victimization and which are common among predatory offenders in the general population (Cohen, Kluegel, & Land, 1981; Hindelang, Gottfredson, & Garofalo, 1978; Lauritsen, Sampson, & Laub, 1991; Meithe & Meier, 1994). Importantly, college students' demographics, their lifestyles, and routine activities are similar to those that research reports as creating vulnerabilities for stalking victimization and opportunities to stalk. Below, we discuss these characteristics.

College Student Sociodemographic Characteristics and Stalking

Over the past decade, researchers developed a better understanding of the demographic characteristics of both stalking victims and stalkers. For example, both the NVAWS (Tjaden & Thoennes, 1998) and Hall (1998) found over one-half of stalking victims were between the ages of 18 and 29. While Tjaden and Thoennes (1998, p. 5) refer to stalking as "a gender-neutral crime" and research shows both females and males are stalked, with females at a much greater risk. Tjaden and Thoennes (1998) reported, for example, that 78 percent of stalking victims were female while Cupach and Spitzberg (2004) calculated national estimates of stalking perpetration prevalence across eight studies and found, on average, nearly 15 percent of males and almost 9 percent of females reported they had stalked another person.

The college population possesses key characteristics that research suggests makes those in the general population vulnerable to being stalked (young and female) or being a stalking perpetrator (young and male). Of the full-time students enrolled at postsecondary institutions in 2004, 77.4 percent were under age 25 (National Center for Education Statistics, 2005), while 57.2

percent of all students enrolled at postsecondary institutions in 2004 were female. Finally, the chance of becoming a stalking target or of stalking someone may be enhanced by consumption of alcohol (including binge drinking) and by experimentation with illegal drugs that often occurs among a substantial portion of college students at parties and social events (Dowdall, 2007).

Thus, the sheer number of young, unmarried women and men who routinely converge in classes and in social settings during their time at college provides a sizeable pool of both potential stalking victims and perpetrators. However, an additional element in stalking involves access, which, as discussed below, colleges and universities readily provide.

The Campus Setting

A necessary element of criminal stalking is that the pursuit must be a repeated course of behavior. Therefore, a stalker must have access–physical or electronic–to the target, as well as the time to engage in repeated pursuit behavior.

From the stalker's perspective, access to campus and its facilities, including dormitories and parking areas, is relatively easy, especially if he or she is also a student. The ease of access onto a college campus is evident in its park-like setting with seemingly no physical boundaries other than a public thoroughfare or a sizable body of water (e.g., lake, ocean) that is contiguous. Campuses typically are "open" 24 hours, seven days a week, 365 days of the year to house, educate, employ, and entertain not only students, faculty, and staff, but also daily visitors.

This eclectic campus population easily flows legitimately from building to building or dorm to dorm during all hours of the day or night. Routine locking of many buildings during the school year, especially when classes are scheduled, is uncommon. Even buildings such as dormitories, whose users or residents are supposed to secure the doors, can jimmy them to remain open and go unnoticed. On-campus parking garages and lots are also relatively easy to access. Because of the daily fluidity of the campus population, many parking areas have unrestricted admission and any patron can park and pay a fee, or freely walk in parking areas unnoticed by an attendant or closed circuit TV.

Students' academic, employment, and social schedules make them easy to communicate with and easily found. First, their classes occur usually occur in the same classroom, at the same day and time over a 10- or 15-week term. Though students' specific classes change from term to term, their schedules are relatively predictable during the course of an academic year. Predictable class schedules coupled with ease of access to classroom buildings and the larger campus provide an endless number of opportunities for watching someone, waiting for someone outside or inside a building, and for leaving written notes or objects.

Second, many students live in university-owned or affiliated housing and park their vehicles on campus in assigned areas. One can easily find students' campus and email addresses, and telephone numbers, in printed or electronic directories available from the school. For would-be stalkers, obtaining this information is as easy as going to a schools' main website, searching an electronic directory for a specific person, and waiting a few seconds for the results to appear on the screen. Many schools assign all their students name-based email accounts, so it is not too difficult to figure out a student's email address even without a web-based directory. Finding where a student parks his or her car on campus is just as easy, as most schools have designated student-parking areas. Stalkers can use this contact and location information to approach the victim by following him/her to class, waiting outside a classroom or their car, communicating via email or postal service, sending gifts, or damaging the target's property.

Third, students spend much time on campus—a physical space easily monitored by a stalker. For example, a large proportion of students work in the library, as a parking attendant, or lab assistant for their work-study requirements. Students' routine work schedules thus make them easy prey for a stalker once he or she knows the victim's place of employment. Students also frequently participate in regularly scheduled recreational activities on campus that provide another setting for stalking.

Thus, combined with important sociodemographic characteristics of students that research links to stalking perpetration and victimization (young and unmarried), the campus itself and the time students spend there provide ready opportunities for stalking perpetration. We explore the final link in the necessary conditions for stalking—students' lifestyles and routine activities—in the next section.

Students' Lifestyle and Routine Activities

The lifestyles and routine activities that are characteristic of "average" college students may provide opportunities for stalking victimization and perpetration. First, stalking not only involves having access to the victim, but also having the time during the day or night to engage in pursuit behaviors. While at college, students have fairly unrestricted access to campus facilities around the clock, seven days a week during the academic term. Couple this ease of access with the large amounts of relatively flexible and unsupervised time that most students have, and what arises are ample opportunities to stalk another student.

Second, researchers have shown that stalking happens throughout the dating continuum from the absence of a relationship (but wanting one to develop), to during the relationship, to after the relationship ends (Williams & Frieze, 2005). Stalking research has established that in well over a majority of incidents, some type of prior relationship–spouse/former spouse, intimate partner (including current/former cohabiting partner, date girl/boyfriend), or acquaintance–existed between the victim and pursuer (see Davis & Frieze, 2000). In fact, the most likely perpetrator of female stalking victims is a current or former intimate partner (through marriage, cohabitation, or dating), whereas men are most likely to stalked by a stranger or an acquaintance (Tjaden & Thoennes, 1998).

Third, college students widely use technology–the Internet and cell phones–that provides opportunities for a would-be stalker to easily and repeatedly access them day and night. A recent poll of Generation 2001 conducted by Harris Interactive (2001) reported that 100 percent of the sampled college students use the Internet, compared to only two-thirds of the general population. The students' Internet usage averaged from 6 to 11 hours a week, with 9 out of 10 of them sending and receiving emails on a daily or frequent basis. Furthermore, the annual *360 Youth College Explorer Study* sponsored by Harris Interactive (2004) revealed that 82 percent of college women and 74 percent of men own cell phones and equally likely to use Instant Messaging daily (43% of women compared to 42% of men), with 60 percent of students with cell phones sending and receiving text messages on their phones. Market researchers are not the only interested parties to recognize the potential opportunities created by a large proportion of college students frequently using such technology. Stalkers may also take advantage of new technologies to easily and quickly monitor their prey's phone calls or computer use, track their prey using hidden cameras or global positioning systems, or pursue their prey via email or cell phones (Spitzberg & Hoobler, 2002).

Fourth, the college years provide many opportunities for routinely encountering a variety of individuals, including other students and their friends, professors, staff, and visitors. Making acquaintances, developing friendships, initiating and maintaining dating relationships, and experiencing sexual intimacy are popular social activities for most college-aged populations, especially undergraduates who are typically single. Each of these experiences, however, may also be a stalking opportunity waiting to happen. Furthermore, Spitzberg and Rhea (1999) claimed that relational mobility (which also suggests relationship termination) might be highest during the college years. In their study of a single campus using a convenience sample of students enrolled in a basic communication course at a large public university in Texas, Spitzberg and Rhea (1999) reported that students had dated an average of five persons since high school. Other studies show a large proportion of stalking occurs among college students within the context of dating and relationship continuums (see Cupach & Spitzberg, 2004).

In sum, characteristics ranging from youthfulness and lifestyles to the campus setting provide many opportunities for a stalker to pursue easily and repeatedly his/her prey. Combined with students' knowledge of, and willingness to use, technology such as cell phones, instant messaging, the Internet, etc., one can easily understand that for a substantial proportion of students, being a stalking victim or stalking someone is a reality. We now review research that has examined the extent and nature of stalking within the college student population.

Stalking Victimization and Perpetration Among College Students

The Extent of Stalking Victimization

Estimates of the proportion of college students who have ever been or are currently being stalked are based on one national-level study of a large representative sample of 4,000 college women at 233 two- and four-year postsecondary institutions, the National College Women Sexual Victimization (NCWSV) study (Fisher, Cullen, & Turner, 2000; 2002) and numerous single-campus studies using nonprobability, primarily convenience, samples of students (e.g., Cupach & Spitzberg, 2004; Fisher, 2001; Ravensberg & Miller, 2003). Results from these studies show that compared to lifetime stalking estimates compiled by the NVAWS, college students are at a higher risk of experiencing stalking than are members of the general population. Lifetime prevalence estimates of stalking for female college students range from 12.2 percent (LeBlanc, Levesque, Richardson, & Ladislav, 2001) to 30.7 percent (Fremouw, Westrup, & Pennypacker, 1997), with an average across those studies plus those conducted by Bjerregaard (2000), Del Ben and Fremouw (2002), Westrup, Fremouw, Thompson, and Lewis (1999) of 22.1 percent. Lifetime prevalence stalking victimization estimates for males range from 1.7 percent (LeBlanc et al., 2001), to 10.9 percent (Bjerregaard, 2000), to 16.7 percent (Fremouw et al., 1996), with an average estimate across the three studies of 9.8 percent.

The NCWSV research (Fisher et al., 2000; 2002) found that about 13 percent of college women experienced a stalking victimization during the academic school year. Noteworthy is that similar to the NVAWS results (Tjaden & Thoennes, 1998), the NCWSV study reported that a much larger proportion of college women experience a stalking victimization during an academic term (13%) than experience a rape (3%). Mustaine and Tewksbury

(1999), using a convenience sample female college students enrolled at nine schools, found 11 percent of the women in their sample reported they experienced a stalking victimization over a six-month period (roughly the equivalent of two academic semesters).

Three studies focused on stalking behaviors after the break-up of a heterosexual dating or marital relationship. From this limited research, it appears that college students, like those in the general population, are not immune from experiencing stalking after a relationship ends. Estimates range from between 9 percent and 34 percent of college women who had recently ended a romantic relationship reporting their former romantic partner had stalked them (Coleman, 1997; Logan, Leukefeld, & Walker, 2002; Roberts, 2002). What is still unknown among college students is whether the stalking began *before* the relationship ended and why some stalking behaviors cease.

Characteristics of Stalking Victims

Overwhelmingly, studies of stalking among college students indicate that demographic characteristics do not differentiate victims from nonvictims (Bjerregaard, 2000; Coleman, 1997; Mustaine & Tewksbury, 1999; Roberts, 2002). This lack of demographic differentiation among stalking victims and nonvictims is most likely due to the fact that college students are a relatively homogeneous group, especially with respect to age (18–25 years old) and marital status (single or never married). However, the NCWSV (Fisher et al., 2000) did identify distinguishing characteristics among females significantly related to being a stalking victim. Compared to Caucasians and non-Hispanic or non-Latina college students, Native Americans and Alaska Natives were significantly more likely to be victims, while Asians or Pacific Islanders were significantly less likely to be stalking victims. Fisher et al. (2000) also found that stalking victims were more likely to come from families of higher socioeconomic status and that undergraduate students were more likely to be stalked than graduate students. Fisher and her colleagues (2000) speculated this is because undergraduate students place themselves in a wider diversity of social situations that increase their exposure to the types of people who prey on young adults, especially women.

Research has also shown that the lifestyles and routine activities of college women are significant risk factors for stalking victimization. Mustaine and Tewksbury (1999) found females who: (1) frequently go to the mall for shopping, (2) live off campus, (3) are employed, and (4) who participate in some drinking and drug use behaviors increased their risk of experiencing a stalking victimization. From a lifestyle perspective, they suggested that frequently going to the mall exposes females to more perpetrators or that stalking victims may go to the mall because it is a public place offering a potentially safer atmosphere than home. Employment, they argued, increases exposure to potential perpetrators, and living off campus decreased the guardianship provided by living on campus.

Fisher et al.'s NCWSV (2000, 2002) reported results comparable to those reported by Mustaine and Tewksbury (1999). Fisher et al. (2000) found that living alone, dating or being in the early stages of a relationship, having a propensity to be in places with alcohol, and having experienced a prior victimization were significant predictors of female stalking victimization. It is certainly plausible that individuals living alone are more suitable targets for stalking then are those living with others. Those who date or in the early stages of a romantic relationship were more likely to be victims of stalking than others, possibly because they were being stalked by former partners as previous research has shown. Finally, similar to Mustaine and Tewksbury's (1999) findings, Fisher et al.'s NCWSV results support the finding that those who frequent places with alcohol present may be more vulnerable and have greater exposure to stalking perpetrators.

Most recently, Fox (2006), using a convenience sample of 1,490 undergraduates enrolled at the University of Florida, reported that three factors significantly influenced having ever been stalked. Students who experienced child abuse, had low self-control, and engaged in sexual risk-taking behaviors increased the odds of ever being a stalking victim.

Characteristics of Stalkers

A handful of studies mostly using small convenience samples of students have estimated the extent of stalking perpetration among members of the college student population. Among the first such studies, Fremouw et al. (1997) reported that a very small proportion of students at West Virginia University—2 percent of males and 0 percent of the females—had stalked someone in their lifetime. Lewis et al. (2001) reported slightly higher proportions of students—just over 4 percent of males and 5 percent of females—had met their behavioral criteria for having stalked someone within the last 18 months and while a student at West Virginia University. Asked if they had ever been a stalker, nearly 3 percent of LeBlanc et al.'s (2001) sample of undergraduates at Worcester Polytechnic Institute admitted to ever doing so. None of the females in their sample reported that they had stalked anyone. Most recently, Fox (2006) reported that nearly 7 percent of students reported perpetrating stalking behaviors in their lifetime. A majority of the 100 students identified as stalking perpetrators were female (58%).

Research has shown that stalkers have identifying sociodemographic characteristics. In their summary of published studies of stalkers, Westrup and Fremouw (1998) concluded that a majority of stalkers are (1) single and never had been married, and (2) better educated, and (3) have a higher IQ than comparable nonstalking criminal populations.

Lewis et al. (2001) found that male stalkers, when compared to nonstalker controls, had considerably less developed problem-solving skills and cognitive flexibility. They also found that stalkers (both male and female) reported increased difficulty with dependency, trust, abandonment, and security issues. Several studies have also found that stalkers lack social skills or are socially incompetent (e.g., Meloy, 1996; Mullen, Pathé, Purcell, & Stuart, 1999). Logan et al. (2000) found differences between male and female stalking perpetrators. For men, stalking perpetration was associated with heavy drinking and the use of alcohol or drugs during sex. For women, stalking perpetration was significantly associated only with the use of alcohol and drugs during sex (Logan et al., 2000). Fox's (2006) multivariate analysis of undergraduate men and women showed that having experienced child abuse and consuming alcohol often increased the odds of stalking perpetration.

Research also suggests individuals known on some level by the victim perpetrate most stalking incidents. In the NCWSV study, for example, Fisher et al. (2002) found that 80.3 percent of stalking victims reported they either knew or had seen their stalker before (53% of victims reported they knew the stalker "well") and that only 17.7 percent of the victims identified the stalker as a complete stranger. Similarly, in a sample of students enrolled at a large southeastern public university, Bjerregaard (2000) found that most victims had a former relationship with their stalker (e.g., partner, acquaintance, or friend). To elaborate, 38.5 percent of females and 40.7 percent of males reported an ex-boyfriend/girlfriend had stalked them, while only 18 percent of females and 11.1 percent of males reported a stranger had stalked them. Fremouw et al. (1997) found over 80 percent of male *and* female victims reported they knew their stalker. Thus, someone known to the victim apparently perpetrates the large majority of stalking incidents, most commonly a former romantic partner or someone the victim knows very well.

A small number of studies have also looked at perpetrators of stalking and found a wide array of characteristics differentiating stalkers from nonstalkers. Roberts (2002) examined characteristics of those who stalked former partners. He found that relative to nonstalkers, such individuals were more likely to: (1) frequently use alcohol and nonprescription drugs, (2) have mental health problems, (3) have criminal convictions, (4) have a history of violence, (5) have difficulty forming relationships, (6) frequently react with inappropriate emotion, (7) be jealous of relationships with others, and (8) be suspicious of relationship with others. Del Ben and Fremouw (2002) reported female victims' perceived differences between male stalkers and nonstalkers. Specifically, they found victims rated stalkers as controlling, hostile, and jealous while in the relationship, and tended to have an insecure attachment style. Victims in the "serious relationship" group also reported that they experienced a greater number of stalking behaviors than those females who were in the "casual relationship" group.

Results from these studies suggest that stalking perpetrators commonly have mental health problems, social-skill deficits and emotional problems, histories of violence, insecure attachments, and substance abuse issues. A majority of victims also report that former partners who stalk also had problems in relationships, usually involving reacting inappropriately with feelings of anger, jealousy, and suspiciousness.

The Nature of Stalking Behavior Among College Students

State and federal antistalking laws define a variety of repeat pursuit behaviors as illegal. Researchers have examined not only these illegal behaviors but also those behaviors not specifically defined as illegal but used to pursue someone (Cupach & Spitzberg, 2004). Below, we discuss the pursuit behaviors stalking perpetrators commonly use to prey on their targets.

Types of Stalking Behaviors

Overall, research suggests the two most common types of stalking behaviors involve *approaching* (e.g., some form of contact via mail, face-to-face, email) and *surveillance* (e.g., spying on or watching from afar). For example, Fisher et al. (2000, 2002) reported that 77.7 percent of female victims indicated their stalkers telephoned them, 47.9 percent said their stalkers waited for them either outside or inside a specific location, 44 percent reported their stalkers watched from afar, 42 percent reported their stalker followed them, 30.7 percent received letters, and 24.7 percent received emails. In studies comparing stalking behaviors experienced by female and male students, the most common type of behavior students experienced was the stalker calling them on the telephone (Logan et al., 2000). Bjerregaard (2000) found that 76.2 percent of female victims said their stalker had telephoned them, 74.6 percent reported that their stalker had attempted face-to-face contact, and 27.9 percent received mail. Over 82 percent of victims reported the stalker successfully contacted them. For male victims, 72.4 percent said the stalker telephoned them, 69 percent reported that their stalker attempted face-to-face contact, and 24.1 percent received letters. Over 84 percent of victims reported the stalker had successfully contacted them. Interestingly, the average number of telephone calls made to female victims was 43.7, whereas for male victims the average number of calls was, 89.2–more than double the average for females.

Stalkers commonly used surveillance behaviors, especially after the termination of a romantic relationship. A substantial proportion of students reported the stalker would unexpectedly show up at places. For example, in Logan et al.'s (2000) study, 62.5 percent of the females stalked by their former partner were called at home while nearly 21 percent of the former partners stalked these women by driving by the victim's house. For male victims stalked by a former partner, 54.5 percent were called at home by their stalker and 36.4 percent of the stalkers came to the victim's house. A similar percent of stalkers came to the victim's work or school.

Duration and Frequency of Stalking

Stalking victims have indicated that the duration and frequency that the stalker pursues them does not involve a trivial amount of time. Fisher et al. (2000) reported that for college women, the median duration of the stalking behavior was 60 days, while the average (skewed by outliers) was 147 days. Roberts (2002) reported a much higher average amount of time female undergraduates were stalked: 19.5 months (approximately 585 days). This is also a much higher estimate than Bjerregaard (2000) reported. She found that men reported being stalked, on average, 182 days. Female students reported being stalked, on average, many days less (83.4) than the male students.

Stalking in Dating and in the Cycle of Intimate Partner Violence

The occurrence of abusive and aggressive behavior during an intimate or dating relationship appears related to the occurrence of stalking after the relationship ends. Davis, Frieze, and Maiuro (2002, p. 482) pointed out that "Kurt (1995) reminds us that stalking is part of the constellations of behaviors associated with domestic violence."

Results from Logan et al.'s (2000) study of stalking among college students after a difficult breakup are supportive of Kurt's claim that stalking is another stage in an abusive relationship (see Cupach & Spitzberg, 2004; Davis & Frieze, 2000). Logan and her colleagues reported that student victims of stalking after a breakup experienced significantly more physical and psychological victimization during the relationship than those who reported no stalking after the breakup. They also reported differences among females and males. Stalking was significantly associated with physical and psychological abuse for women victims. For male victims, stalking was associated with psychological abuse. Given their results, Logan et al. (2000) concluded, "stalking is a continuation of intimate partner violence toward a partner after the relationship ends" (p. 102).

Studies also show that length of the relationship is significantly related to stalking by former partners. Roberts (2002) found that the duration of the former relationship for stalking victims was significantly longer than for harassed students and nonharassed students. Stalking victims, on average, were in the former relationship for 34.7 months compared to harassed victims who averaged 21.5 months and nonharassed victims who averaged 20.7 months.

Coping Strategies Used to Stop Stalking Behaviors

The duration and frequency of stalking and its unpredictable timing and uncertain potential to become troubling and problematic for the victims raises the issue of how victims reacted to and cope with their experience. A large proportion of students respond to being stalked. Bjerrregaard (2000) found that 77.9 percent of females and 55.2 percent of males specifically requested the person stop the behavior. Fisher et al. (2002) found that 72.5 percent of female victims reporting taking some action due to a stalking incident.

Students use a variety of strategies, many in conjunction with each other, in an attempt to cope with, and eventually stop the stalking (Cupach and Spitzberg, 1998). Fremouw et al. (1997) examined coping behaviors for both male and female stalking victims assessed by mean ratings, and found that students most frequently chose to change their social environment or ignore their stalker. Female victims commonly (1) ignored/hung up on their stalker, (2) confronted their stalker, (3) changed their schedule, and/or (4) carried a weapon (repellent spray). Male victims responded with similar strategies. They commonly (1) confronted their stalker, and/or (2) ignored/hung up on their stalker. Unlike females, males were more likely to reconcile with their stalker. In Bjerrregaard's (2000) study, the most common action females took was to change their phone number (22.1%) or to change their residence (22.1%). She also found that female victims were more fearful than the male victims and more likely to call the police, but this fear was substantiated by findings that showed females were more likely to be threatened and/or harmed, as compared to males.

Fisher and her colleagues (2000, 2002) reported that the most common types of action taken among their sample of college women included: (1) avoiding or trying to avoid the stalker (43.2%), (2) confronting the stalker (16.3%), (3) not acknowledging messages or email (8.8%), (4) becoming less trustful or more cynical of others (5.6%), (5) installing caller ID (4.9%), (6) improving the security system of their residence (4.1%), and (7) traveling with a companion (3.9%). A large percentage of victims (21.8%), adopted an unspecified form of action.

Although stalking is illegal, most students do not report their experience to the police or initiate the court's authority for relief. To illustrate, similar to the results from other national-level victimization surveys, many college student victims of stalking do report stalking incidents to either the campus or local police. Westrup et al. (1999) found that only 41.7 percent of the stalking victims reported the incident to the police. Among college women, Fisher et al. (2002) found that over 83.1 percent of the stalking incidents were reported to neither the local police nor campus police. These women cited numerous reasons for not reporting that included not thinking the incident was serious enough (72%), not knowing that the incident was a crime or that there was intent to harm (44.6%) , and believing that the police would think the incident was serious enough (33.6%).

College women were also not likely to use the courts to address the stalker's pursuit behaviors. Fisher et al. (2002) reported that in less than 4 percent of the stalking incidents did a respondent seek a restraining order from the court. In only 1.9 percent of incidents did women file criminal charges against perpetrators, while they filed civil charges in a little over 1% of the incidents. Supportive of these results, Fremouw et al. (1997) found that very few students resorted to legal interventions–either reporting to the police or having a restraint/warrant issued against the stalker. Bjerregaard (2000) reported that female victims are more likely than are male victims to go to court regarding their stalking incident. Nine percent of females went to court while none of the males did so.

No published study, to our knowledge, has evaluated the *effectiveness* of coping strategies used by students to stop their stalker's behaviors. We need such a study because, as we discuss later, institutions of higher education (IHEs) have not adequately responded to students either who are the victims of stalking or who stalk other students.

The Psychological Toll Suffered by Stalking Victims

Clinical and self-report studies of stalking victims have concluded that stalking causes an array negative of psychological and emotional problems (see Hall, 1998; Pathé & Mullen, 1997). Well documented is the pervasiveness of fear, anger, and stress at not being able to control one's privacy (Davis & Frieze, 2000). Not surprisingly, studies of college students have come to the same dismal conclusion: stalking has serious psychological and emotional consequences for student victims.

Westrup et al. (1999), for example, found that female victims suffered significant negative psychological effects due to stalking. Stalking victims reported more psychological symptoms compared to harassed or control groups of students. Victims of stalking also reported significantly higher levels of Posttraumatic Stress Disorder symptoms relative to the harassed and control groups. Bjerregaard (2000) found that female victims were more likely to seek counseling than males. Female victims are more likely than males to go to court regarding their stalking incident, with 9 percent of females and none of the males going to court. Although close to 6 percent of the women in Fisher et al.'s study (2002) became less trustful or more cynical of others, only 2.9 percent of the stalking victims sought psychological counseling. This is significantly less than the 30 percent of stalked women in the NVAWS who sought counseling (and the 20% of stalked men who did) (Tjaden & Thoennes, 1998).

Implications for Campus Policy and Programs

Recognizing Stalking as a Crime

Stalking is a pressing issue–a crime defined by laws that have been upheld by the courts–that warrants recognition by campus administrators so that appropriate policies, educational programs, and services can be designed to address stalking victims and perpetrators. At this point, however, there is little evidence suggesting that college administrators recognize the seriousness of stalking victimization or perpetration among students or the need to respond systematically.

This is somewhat ironic since over the last two decades campus administrators have begun addressing sexual victimizations of college students, in part because schools have been held civilly liable for these victimizations (see Burling, 2003). Also influential was the passage of *The Jeanne Clery Disclosure of Campus Security Policy and Campus Crime Statistics* that requires Title IX schools to publish an annual security report which include their crime statistics, such as forcible and nonforcible sex offenses and to establish a sexual assault policy that describes many aspects of prevention (e.g., educational programs) and responses (e.g., procedures when a sexual assault happens, sanctions for offenders) to campus sexual assault (Carter & Bath, 2007).

Despite recent gains, results from a national-level study of the content of sexual assault polices of IHEs suggest that stalking has largely fallen outside the formal concerns of campus officials. Karjane, Fisher, and Cullen (2001) reported that only 1.5 percent of all schools surveyed mentioned having a stalking policy in their sexual assault policies and an equally small 1.5 percent reported having a separate stalking policy. Four-year private schools were most likely to have a stalking policy (3.6%), while four-year public schools were most likely to have a separate policy (3.7%). Notably, 97 percent of four-year schools have not addressed stalking in mandated sexual assault materials that are distributed annually to students. One explanation could be that since the *Clery Act* does not require reporting of stalking statistics, campus administrators feel they are under no legislative mandate to address stalking.

Beyond the issue of publicly reporting stalking statistics is the matter of campus administrators recognizing the extent stalking victimization and perpetration happens to their students both on and off campus. Documenting the extent of stalking through the ease of a web-based victimization and perpetration survey can result in administrators more fully understanding the extent and nature of stalking among students. Such a survey can inform campus administrators about not only the characteristics of victims and stalkers and the negative toll these experiences have on students, but also which campus characteristics create opportunities for stalking to occur. With evidence-based information, administrators can be judicious in their approaches to addressing the extent and nature of stalking among their students.

Content of Stalking Awareness and Education Policies and Programs

Assuming that the first step in effective public policy is recognizing that a substantial proportion of students are stalking targets and perpetrators, the next steps are getting these issues on the active policy agenda. This second step includes the development of strategies for stalking awareness and education and mental health services. Here, administrators should exercise caution so they do not simply implement generic "crime prevention programs" or provide generic "mental health services" for victims in a symbolic effort to "do something about the problem." As the research has shown, stalking presents unique challenges due to its repetitive nature, frequency, and duration and the ample opportunities presented by the physical campus setting and its operations, and students' lifestyle and routines, including high dating mobility.

These challenges, however, provide the opportunity for a comprehensive approach to addressing the needs of students (and faculty and staff, too) who have been stalked or have stalked someone. This comprehensive approach involves the entire campus community—students, as well as academic, housing, judicial or disciplinary affairs, counseling, medical, dining services, athletic, parking and other support staff—that can and should play a part in educating the campus community about the extent and nature of stalking among students, and working together to stop it. For example, residence hall personnel, professors, and campus security could be trained in how to identify stalkers who are looming in a location (e.g., on a dorm floor, outside a classroom, or in a parking area) and effectively intervene.

One way to increase awareness and education among the campus community is to incorporate the topic of "unwanted and repeated" pursuit behaviors into sexual awareness and prevention program and healthy dating programs at not only orientation sessions but also throughout the school year at strategic times (e.g., at the beginning of each academic term, during national sexual awareness week or month). Another means of disseminating information could be through the *Clery Act* mandated annual security report. A crucial element would be to use all educational materials to encourage victims to report stalking to residential hall personnel, campus and law enforcement officials. Informing family, friends, roommates, and coworkers about the stalking and seeking their support can also provide added safety for the target by having additional "eyes and ears" watching and listening. Since the research is quite clear that stalking is psychologically and even physically harmful, targets should be encouraged to seek counseling services and medical-related services. Colleges and universities should tailor these clinical services to the specific needs of both the stalking target and perpetrator (see Ravensberg & Miller, 2003).

Another means to educating the campus community is to develop an antipursuit behavior or antistalking policy, similar to the sexual assault policy required by the *Clery Act,* or a sexual harassment policy. An antistalking policy could be included in the student and faculty code of conduct. Among the purposes of this policy would be to inform the stalking target of safety and procedural issues and the perpetrator to unacceptable behaviors that are subject to disciplinary and legal response. Included in this policy could be the state's legal definition of and penalties for criminal stalking, a description of the types of pursuit behaviors using campus setting examples, formal and legal redresses that victims can take both on and off campus to address (and hopefully stop) the pursuit behaviors, and a description of the school-based disciplinary sanctions (e.g., warning, dismissal). Formal actions include documenting the location and times of the pursuit behaviors, saving all text communications, recoding all telephone messages, saving all gifts, etc., for criminal complaints. Information can also be provided that tells the victim that he/she has an option of filing a formal grievance or complaint against a student or campus employee perpetrator. The anti-stalking policy could also advise students that they can refer criminal stalking cases to local law enforcement and prosecutors. Seeking help for treatment from counseling or medical staff should also be clearly included in such a policy.

Beyond the educational programming or antistalking policy, administrators need to innovatively think about how the campus setting and it operations may facilitate pursuit behaviors. This could range from access policies to buildings (especially residence halls) to rethinking the availability of student contact information on the web or assigning name-based email addresses.

Conclusion

The results from college student stalking studies (and other student victimization studies) suggest students do not exist in an ivory tower that protects them from crime (see Belknap & Erez, 2007; Mustaine & Tewskbury, 2007). Stalking among college students, as we have noted, provides an opportunity for campus administrators to take a proactive approach to addressing stalking among their respective students. From a legal perspective, the courts have held campuses liable for "foreseeable" victimization (Burling, 2003). Given the repeated nature of stalking, the criterion for foreseeability may help to establish legal liability if campuses have not taken any procedural or substantive steps to address stalking and a stalking incident turns into a fatal attack. From an educational perspective, administrators should be concerned that many of their female students are stalking targets and many of their perpetrators are fellow students. Being either a victim of stalking or stalking others should not be included in the rising costs of attending college or, if experienced or initiated, students should not have to be alone without any support from the campus community.

Notes

1. The range in the estimates reflects the degree of fear in the definition of stalking. The lower estimate is when respondents reported that the pursuit behavior made them feel a high level of fear. The upper estimate resulted in them being somewhat or a little frightened.
2. In this chapter, we limit our discussion to only those studies of college students that examined either legally defined or self-defined criminal stalking. We did not include studies that examined "unwanted pursuit behaviors" (e.g., Langhinrichsen-Rohling, Palarea, Cohen & Rohling, 2000) or "obsessive relational intrusion" (e.g., Cupach & Spitzberg, 2004). Researchers have reported that both type of behaviors are prevalent among college students, yet we decided not to include them into our discussion of stalking as it is unknown if they would be legally defined or self-defined as stalking. This exclusionary decision on our part clearly points to the need for an acceptable definition and measurement of repeated pursuit behaviors if researchers are to advance the comparative stalking research (Davis & Frieze, 2000; Fisher, 2001).

REFERENCES

Belknap, J., & Erez, E. (2007). The sexual harassment, rape, and intimate partner abuse of college women. In B. S. Fisher & J. J. Sloan (Eds.), *Campus crime: Legal, social and policy perspectives* (2nd ed.). Springfield, IL: Charles C Thomas.

Bjerregaard, B. (2000). An empirical study of stalking victimization. *Violence and Victims, 15,* 389–405.

Burling, P. (2003). *Crime on campus* (2nd ed.). Retrieved February 13, 2007 from http://www.nacua.org/onlinepubs/crimeoncampus/CrimeonCampus.pdf.

Carter, S. D., & Bath C. (2007). The evolution and components of the Jeanne Clery

Act: Implications for higher education. In B. S. Fisher & J. J. Sloan (Eds.), *Campus crime: Legal, social and policy perspectives* (2nd ed.). Springfield, IL: Charles C Thomas.

Cohen, L., Kluegel, J., & Land, K. (1981). Social inequality and predatory criminal victimization: An exposition and a test of a formal theory. *American Sociological Review, 46,* 505-524.

Coleman, F. (1997). Stalking behavior and the cycle of domestic violence. *Journal of Interpersonal Violence, 12,* 420-432.

Cupach, W. R., & Spitzberg, B. H. (1998). Obsessional relational intrusions and stalking. In B. H. Spitzberg & W. R. Cupach (Eds.), *The dark side of close relationships.* Mahwah, NJ: Erlbaum.

Cupach, W. R., & Spitzberg, B. H. (2004). *The dark side of relationship pursuit: From attraction to obsession and stalking.* Mahwah, N.J: Erlbaum.

Davis, K. E., & Frieze, I. H. (2000). Research on stalking: What do we know and where do we go? *Violence and Victims, 15,* 47--487.

Davis, K. E., Frieze, I. H., & Maiuro, R. (Eds.) (2002). *Stalking: Perspectives on victims and perpetrators.* New York: Springer.

Del Ben, K., & Fremouw, W. (2002). Stalking: Developing an empirical typology to classify stalkers. *Journal of Forensic Sciences, 47,* 152–158.

Dowdall, G. W. (2007). The role of alcohol abuse in college student victimization. In B. S. Fisher & J. J. Sloan (Eds.), *Campus crime: Legal, social and policy perspectives* (2nd ed.). Springfield, IL: Charles C Thomas.

Fox, K. A. (2006). *In pursuit of factors that predict stalking perpetration and victimization among college students.* Unpublished master's thesis, University of Florida, Gainesville, Florida.

Fisher, B. S. (2001). Being pursued and pursuing during the college years: The extent, nature, and impact of stalking on college campuses. In J. A. Davis (Ed.), *Stalking crimes and victim protection: Prevention, intervention, threat assessment, and case management.* Boca Raton, FL: CRC Press LLC.

Fisher, B. S., Cullen, F. T., & Turner, M. G. (2000). *Sexual victimization of college women.* Washington, DC: National Institute of Justice.

Fisher, B. S., Cullen, F. T., & Turner, M. G. (2002). Being pursued: Stalking victimization in a national study of college women. *Criminology and Public Policy, 4,* 257–308.

Fremouw, W. J., Westrup, D., & Pennypacker, J. (1997). Stalking on campus: The prevalence and strategies for coping with stalking. *Journal of Forensic Sciences, 42,* 666–669.

Hall, D. M. (1998). The victims of stalking. In J. R. Meloy (Ed.), *The psychology of stalking: Clinical and forensic perspective.* San Diego, CA: Academic Press.

Harris Interactive (2001). Presenting: The class of 2001. Retrieved June 5, 2006 from http://www.harrisinteractive.com/news/printerfriend/index.asp?NewsID=292.

Harris Interactive (2004). *College women close technology gender gap.* Retrieved June 5, 2006 from http://www.harrisinteractive.com/news/allnewsbydate.asp? NewsID= 773.

Hindelang, M. J., Gottfredson, M. R., & Garofalo, J. (1978). *Victims of personal crime:*

An empirical foundation for a theory of personal victimization. Cambridge, MA: Ballinger.

Karjane, H. M., Fisher, B. S., & Cullen, F. T. (2001). *Campus sexual assault: How America's institutions of higher education respond.* Washington, DC: National Institute of Justice.

Lauritsen, J. L., Sampson, R. J., & Laub, J. H. (1991). The link between offending and victimization among adolescents. *Criminology, 29,* 265–292.

LeBlanc, J. J., Levesque, G. J., Richardson, J. B., & Ladislav, H. B. (2001). Survey of stalking at WPI. *Journal of Forensic Sciences, 46,* 367–369.

Lewis, S. F., Fremouw, W. J., Del Ben, K., & Farr, C. (2001). An investigation of the psychological characteristics of stalkers: Empathy, problem-solving, attachment and borderline personality features. *Journal of Forensic Sciences, 46,* 80–84.

Logan, T. K., Leukefeld, C., & Walker, B. (2000). Stalking as a variant of intimate violence: Implications from a young adult sample. *Violence and Victims, 15,* 91–111.

Meithe, T. D., & Meier, R. F. (1994). *Crime and its social context: Toward an integrated theory of offenders, victims, and situations.* Albany, NY: State University of New York Press.

Meloy, J. R. (1996). Stalking (obsessional following): A review of some preliminary studies. *Aggression and Violent Behavior, 1,* 147–162.

Mullen, P. E., Pathé, M., Purcell, R., & Stuart, G. W. (1999). Study of stalkers. *American Journal of Psychiatry, 156,* 1244–1249.

Mustaine, E. E., & Tewksbury, R. (1999). A routine activity theory explanation for women's stalking victimizations. *Violence Against Women, 5,* 43–62.

Mustaine, E. E., & Tewksbury, R. (2007). The routine activities and criminal victimization of students lifestyle and related factors. In B. S. Fisher & J. J. Sloan. (Eds.), *Campus crime: Legal, social and policy perspectives* (2nd ed.). Springfield, IL: Charles C Thomas.

National Center for Education Statistics (2005). Integrated postsecondary education system, "Fall enrollment survey." Retrieved June 18, 2006 from, http://www.nces.ed.gov.

Pathé, M., & Mullen, P. E. (1997). The impact of stalkers on their victims. British *Journal of Psychiatry, 170,* 12–17.

Ravensberg, V., & Miller, C. (2003). Stalking among young adults: A review of the preliminary research. *Aggression and Violent Behavior, 8,* 455–469.

Roberts, K. A. (2002). Stalking following the breakup of romantic relationships: Characteristics of stalking former partners. *Journal of Forensic Sciences, 47,* 1070–1077.

Spitzberg, B. H., & Hoobler, G. (2002). Cyberstalking and the technologies of interpersonal terrorism. *New Media and Society, 4,* 71–92.

Spitzberg, B. H., & Rhea, J. (1999). Obsessive relational intrusion and sexual coercion victimization. *Journal of Interpersonal Violence, 14,* 3–20.

Sting (1983). Every breath you take [Recorded by The Police]. On *Synchronicity* [CD]. United Kingdom: A&M Records.

Stingetc.com (2006). What is "Every Breath You Take" about? Retrieved February 13, 2007, from http://stingetc.com/police.html.

Tjaden, P., & Thoennes, N. (1998). *Stalking in America: Findings from the National Violence Against Women survey.* Denver, CO: Center for Policy Research.

Westrup, D., & Fremouw, W. J. (1998). Stalking behavior: A literature review and suggested functional analytic assessment technology. *Aggression and Violent Behavior, 3,* 255–274.

Westrup, D., Fremouw, W. J., Thompson, R. N., & Lewis, S. F. (1999). The psychological impact of stalking on female undergraduates. *Journal of Forensic Sciences, 44,* 554–557.

Williams, S. L., & Frieze, I. H. (2005). Courtship behaviors, relationship violence, and breakup persistence in college men and women. *Psychology of Women Quarterly, 29,* 248–257.

Chapter 12

CRIME OF CAMPUS: SPATIAL ASPECTS OF CRIME AT A REGIONAL COMPREHENSIVE UNIVERSITY

MATTHEW B. ROBINSON AND SUNGHOON ROH

INTRODUCTION

If people knew *why* crime occurred, it should be easier to prevent, because we could focus prevention efforts on those factors that correlate with those likely to engage in crime (Bohm, 2000). Similarly, if we knew *where* crime was likely to occur, it should also be easier to prevent because we could focus efforts at those places where crime is most likely to occur (Rengert, Mattson, & Henderson, 2001). While neither approach–focusing on people or places–is necessarily superior to the other, it is fair to conclude that the place-specific approach has led to more effective crime prevention techniques (e.g., Paulsen & Robinson, 2004).

In this chapter, we utilize the place-specific approach by examining police statistics at a university campus in the southeast United States. Our primary goal is to identify the places that host the most crimes, as reflected in campus crime data, in order to determine why some places have many crimes known to the police while others have few or none. Another goal is to suggest place-specific crime prevention strategies for those places that generate the most crime.

Previous studies at the same campus have shown there is very little serious criminal activity; students, faculty, and staff do not feel there is a "crime problem" on the campus; there are low levels of fear and perceived risk of victimization; and the campus is rated as "highly attractive" and "aesthetically pleasing" (see Mullen, Robinson, & Paulsen, 2001; Robinson & Mullen, 2001). While these previous studies have been useful to policy-makers in various ways–including demonstrating the high level of safety on the campus and identifying at least one significant crime problem (i.e., underage alcohol use and illicit drug use)–their main limitation is that they did not directly address the spatial aspects of crime on the campus. That is, the studies did not address *where* crimes most occur and what might explain the spatial variation on campus. Our current study attempts to overcome this weakness.

Literature Review

The literature on campus crime is sparse. A recent search utilizing the database, Criminal Justice Periodicals Index, found 115 articles on campus crime, but almost none of them were published in refereed academic journals, and only a handful were published since 2000. Thus, there has been very little rigorous research on campus crime.

As the chapters in this volume show, campus crime research addresses issues such as criminal victimization on college and university campuses, lifestyles and routine activities and criminal victimization, and potential crime prevention strategies that can be implemented to reduce or eliminate opportunities for criminality on campus (Brantingham & Brantingham, 1994; Brinkley & Laster, 2003; Bromley, 1994; Fisher, Sloan, Cullen, & Lu, 1998; Fox & Hellman, 1985; Henson & Stone, 1999; Johnson & Sigler, 1996; Moriarty & Pelfrey, 1996; O'Kane, Fisher, & Green, 1994; Richards, 1996; Siegel & Raymond, 1992; Sloan, 1992, 1994). Other studies address university obligations involving federal and state laws designed to increase safety on campus and inform the public about crimes on campus (Fisher & Sloan, 1993; Sloan, Fisher, & Cullen, 1997).

These previous studies demonstrate several notable realities about campus crime. First, levels of crime against persons on campus are less than that against the general population off campus. Second, the vast majority of campus crime involves property offenses, while violent crimes are rare. Third, the majority of students feel safe on campus even though perceptions of safety vary depending on student demographics and time/space correlates. Fourth, many victims of crime occurring on campus (especially property crimes) do not report the event to the police, making difficult a correct estimation of campus crime under the FBI's Uniform Crime Reports (UCR) system. Fifth, students' risky lifestyles (e.g., the use of alcohol and illicit drugs) increase their vulnerability to some forms of criminal victimization (Abbey, 2002; Abbey et al., 2001; Fisher et al., 1998; Robinson, 2004; Testa & Livingston, 1999; Wechsler et al., 1995; Wechsler & Wuethrich, 2003).

An additional reality of crime generally (that has not been widely documented on college and university campuses) is that crime tends to cluster in some areas. In these areas–known as "hot spots" of crime–a very large amount (in relative terms) of crime occurs. In this chapter, we examine whether police statistics show that hot spots exist on one university campus. However, before we present our evidence, we first discuss the concept of "hot spots" of crime.

Hot Spots of Crime

Criminological research has identified places that host a disproportionate amount of crime (Brantingham & Brantingham, 1999; Sherman, Gartin, & Buerger, 1989; Sherman & Weisburd, 1995). A significant amount of research exists concerning hot spots of crime and their impact on criminal victimization. Specifically, research on hot spots has dealt with the crimes of burglary (Robinson, 1998a), auto burglary (Cochran & Bromley, 2002), liquor-related crime (Block & Block, 1995), homicide (Block & Christakos, 1995; Block & Block, 1998), street gang violence (Block & Block, 1995), gun violence (Sherman & Rogan, 1995), disorderly behavior (Koper, 1995), and drug activity (Green, 1995; Weisburd, 1995; Weisburd & Green, 1995).

Common hot spots of crime include street blocks near bars (Roncek & Maier, 1991), entertainment districts (Cochran, Bromley, & Branch, 2000), casinos (Stitt, Nichols, & Giacopassi, 2003), some street segments in cities (Weisburd, Bushway, Lum, & Yang, 2004), and bus stops (Loukaitou-Sideris, 1999).

Only a few published studies exist within educational institution settings that explore physical environmental features of crime hot spots. For example, O'Kane et al. (1994) found that about 40 percent of all auto-related crime occurred on only 12 percent of campus street segments, which were easily accessible to major thoroughfares. Astor et al. (1999) showed that the majority of violent events in high schools were concentrated in spaces with no guardians, such as hallways, dining areas, and parking lots. Rengert and Lowell (2005) showed that hot spots even exist within buildings on a university campus.

These hot spot studies are limited in terms of crime type and study setting. This is a particularly glaring omission in hot spot research considering the amount of crime–especially crimes against property that are most amenable to prevention efforts–that occurs on college campuses in any given year. It is likely that there are hot spots of campus crime because the environmental factors that may account for hot spots are prevalent on college campuses (e.g., a large amount of targets that are often unguarded in some locations, making those targets more attractive to offenders).

There are at least three kinds of hot spots, each of which potentially has a separate explanation (Clarke & Eck, 2006). First, crime generators attract "large numbers of people . . . for reasons unrelated to criminal motivation" (e.g., shopping areas, transportation hubs, festivals, and sporting events).

Here, crime is attributable to the "large number of place users and targets." Second, crime attractors are places that provide "many criminal opportunities that are well known to offenders" so that those "with criminal motivation are drawn to such locales" (e.g., prostitution and drug areas, entertainment spots). Third, crime enablers provide "little regulation of behavior at places" so that "rules of conduct are absent or are not enforced" (e.g., a parking lot with no attendant).

Several theoretical perspectives can explain these three types of hot spots of crime: rational choice theory, routine activity theory, and crime pattern theory. According to rational choice theory, offenders engage in criminal acts only when they believe that the potential benefits outweigh expected costs by their criminal behaviors (Cornish & Clarke, 1986). Circumstances, situations, and opportunities heavily affect the decision-making process because the offender considers these factors in such a way as to produce the maximum net benefits expected from committing crimes.

Routine activity theory posits that crime requires three elements: motivated offenders, suitable targets (potential victims), and an absence of capable guardians (Cohen & Felson, 1979; Felson, 2002). The risk of crime increases when these three elements converge at the same place at the same time. In contrast, eliminating any one element results in no crime occurring. Routine activity theory has been mostly used to explain property crime when the property is a suitable target and when it not protected by a capable guardian.

Finally, crime pattern theory combines rational choice theory and routine activity theory to explain the geographic distribution of crime (e.g., Brantingham & Brantingham, 1993; Eck & Weisburd, 1995). Crime pattern theorists assume that most offenders seek their crime targets within areas that are familiar to them. Serious offenders, like the rest of us, engage in noncriminal activities in their daily lives. As they engage in their daily routines, they come to recognize desirable targets for crime. It is in these areas that crime will most frequently occur.

According to crime pattern theory, triggering of a criminal event occurs by the presence of an opportunity that an offender comes upon in the course of a search (minimal or broad) depending on such factors as how well the offender knows the area. Nodes refer to where people travel to and from, paths are the main areas of travel in-between these nodes, and edges are the boundaries of areas where people engage in their activities (Clarke & Eck, 2006).

There have been numerous studies to explain campus crime with routine activity theory (Fisher & Wilkes, 2003; Mustaine & Tewksbury, 1998; Schwartz et al., 2001; Tewksbury & Mustaine, 2003; Volkwein, Szelest, & Lizotte, 1995; Wooldredge, Cullen, & Latessa, 1995). However, most of these studies focus on vulnerability to crime by focusing on victims' lifestyles rather than crime-prone spatial characteristics. This, too, can be conceived as a limitation to the body of literature on campus crime because physical features of the built environment play a large role in explaining where crime can cluster in hot spots, consistent with the crime prevention approaches of Crime Prevention Through Environmental Design (CPTED) and Situational Crime Prevention. In the next section, we discuss these two approaches to crime prevention.

Crime Prevention through Environmental Design and Situational Crime Prevention

Alterations to the physical environment, such as increasing lighting, are examples of CPTED, which aims to "[identify] conditions of the physical and social environment that provide opportunities for or precipitate criminal acts . . . and the alteration of those conditions so that no crimes occur. . ." (Brantingham & Faust, 1976, pp. 289–292). CPTED thus involves the management, design, or manipulation of the physical environment to prevent crime (Crowe, 1991; Robinson, 1999b). On the university campus, CPTED most commonly takes the form of blue-light trails, increased lighting and security mechanisms, and other target hardening devices (e.g., locks, alarms) (Robinson, 1999b).

CPTED is similar to "situational crime prevention." Situational crime prevention is aimed at eliminating opportunities for crime. It includes opportunity-reducing measures that are targeted at specific forms of crime and aimed at increasing "the effort and risks of crime and reduce the rewards as perceived by a wide range of offenders" (Clarke, 1992, pp. 3–4).

There are at least 16 different ways to reduce opportunities for crime through situational crime prevention. The four major categories of situational crime prevention include, (1) increasing the difficulty of crime; (2) increasing the risks of crime; (3) reducing the rewards of crime; and (4) removing excuses for crime (Clarke, 2001).

While CPTED and situational crime prevention generally involve changing the environment to reduce the opportunity for crime, they are aimed at other outcomes as well. These include reducing fear of crime and perceptions of crime risk, increasing the aesthetic quality of an environment (e.g., by reducing conditions of incivilities), and increasing the quality of life for law-abiding citizens, especially by reducing the propensity of the physical environment to support criminal behavior (Robinson 1999b).

On many university and college campuses, where the risks of victimization by serious violent crimes may be remote, relative to large and mid-size cities, CPTED and situational crime prevention strategies may still be useful. Since alterations to the physical environment of campus may make people

feel safer and less fearful, as well as increase the aesthetic quality of the sur-
roundings, CPTED and situational crime prevention have a place on campus. Further, crime prevention efforts directed at hot spots of crime on campus should greatly reduce the amount of crime on campus, given that most
crimes on campus (like off campus) likely occur in certain areas regularly. We
believe that focusing on hot spots of crime will reduce the majority of crime
on campus.

Hot Spots: A Campus Case Study

The current study examines the most recently available university police
statistics (2004–2005) for the most common crimes occurring on the campus
of a major comprehensive university in the southeastern United States. The
goals of the study are to determine which places generate the most crimes
known to the police and develop potential explanations as to why. We relate
the findings to those from the previous studies of the same university campus and pay special attention to violations of drugs and alcohol, since they
are related to other forms of criminality. The study's explicit focus on the
spatial aspects of the campus crime, make it unique.

About the University

The university under study–Appalachian State University–is located in
Boone, North Carolina, a town with only approximately 14,000 residents
(not counting students). The university is located in a county with only about
45,000 residents. Given these population figures, it is not surprising that the
town and the county have below average crime rates and especially very little violent crime. This is because rates of street crime tend to be much higher in large and mid-size cities (Paulsen & Robinson, 2004). Thus, there is a
wide perception that students at "Appalachian" are not threatened by the
possibility of serious criminal victimization, either while they are on campus
or while traveling throughout the town or county. Indeed, police statistics
show that serious street crime is rare relative to larger towns and counties in
the state and region.

This perception was recently shaken when, only 13 months apart, two
Appalachian students were murdered in off-campus drug deals that had gone
wrong. The murders caused great concern on campus and significant attention was focused on criminal victimization of university students and the
crime prevention techniques that could be implemented on campus to protect students and put people's minds at ease. This study was motivated, in
part, by these murders.

Appalachian State is a major comprehensive public university with approximately 14,000 students, and is one of 16 campuses of the state of North Carolina's university system. As Appalachian is located in Blue Ridge chain of the Appalachian Mountains, its campus is surrounded by mountains, trees, and park-like features (e.g., streams, boulders, etc.). Previous studies of the campus show that users of the campus generally rate the campus as highly attractive. The university is more than 100 years old and serves mostly residential students from the surrounding counties and larger state of North Carolina.

Study Methodology

We contacted the University Police Department and requested the most recent campus crime statistics. The available data included the past two years of data (2004–2005) of calls for police service and police-initiated services for various types of crimes. The data were stored in police logs that were not computerized; not searchable; nor organized by crime type, location, date, time of day, or any other meaningful category. Thus, we had to sort through each daily log of crimes known to the police—hundreds of pages each with between one and as many as 20 crimes per page.

We then made a list of campus crimes for each major crime indicated in the data. For example, going chronologically through the data, we listed each theft by location, date, and time. Then, we counted the total number of each type of crime to determine which types of crimes were most common on campus. This process introduces the possibility of error, as some crimes were listed more than once (often to update the case with new evidence or the passage of time as cases were solved or closed due to a lack of evidence). It is also possible that we did not receive every page of data from the department. Because of this, our counts of campus crimes may not perfectly match those ultimately compiled by the University Police Department.

Police often combined counts of alcohol and illicit drug violations. For example, at one police response at a dorm, five citations were issues for alcohol use and illicit drug use. Since the police log did not specify how many citations were given for alcohol violations and how many were given for illicit drug violations, we were forced to count these violations as five alcohol violations and five illicit drug violations. We suspect this will tend to inflate the numbers of these offenses (although the data will still likely underestimate the true number of alcohol and illicit drug use violations on campus since most are not known to the police).

An additional limitation of the police data is that most criminal victimizations are not included in police data. Nationwide, less than 40 percent of serious criminal victimizations are captured in police data (Robinson, 2005). Thus, this study of crimes known to the police does not likely capture the majority of criminal victimizations on campus. However, in the absence of a university-wide victimization survey that addresses location of offenses, police data are the only data available for a study of campus crime locations. Further, most studies of place and crime utilize official crime statistics from police departments (Paulsen & Robinson, 2004).

With these limitations in mind, we next plotted campus crimes on maps of the university campus in order to identify those areas on campus that generated the most crimes as reflected in police statistics. Given that we did not have addresses for any of the crimes, including those that occurred inside dorms, academic buildings, and in parking lots, we could not plot exact locations of where the crimes occurred. Further, it was impossible to plot crimes that occurred on streets since the police data did not indicate where on streets the crimes occurred. The police data merely indicated from which streets calls originated (or on which street the offense occurred). The most common crime on streets was driving while intoxicated (DWI), and most of these were likely discovered by the police rather than initiated by a telephone call for service.

Given the nature of criminal victimization on campus, it was impossible to calculate criminal victimization rates based on the number of potential victims in each location. This is because there is no way to know how many potential victims and targets there were in each location during the 2004 and 2005 calendar years. For example, one dorm may have had more criminal violations than another dorm, simply because there were more people there, and/or because there were targets that were more suitable. We did contact the university's Department of Housing and Residential Life and learned that the average number of occupants in each dorm is 267 students, with very little variation in this number across the 19 living centers. Only five dorms had substantially less than the number of average students in residence (these dorms housed 109, 128, 172, 215, and 221 students), and only one dorm had substantially more (371 students). We discuss the implications of these numbers in the findings section. It was impossible to calculate crime rates based on the number of students living in each dorm, since this is not a suitable indicator of the number of potential victims and offenders in any given location.

Data included crimes known to the police on campus, on noncampus buildings or property, on public property, and in on campus residential facilities. We did not consider noncampus buildings outside town limits. Public property includes roads, thoroughfares, streets, sidewalks, and parking facilities. Those that are off campus were also not considered. Thus, we only examined crime statistics on campus, in on-campus residential facilities, and in public property located on campus.

Results and Discussion

Most Common Crimes on Campus

The most common crimes according to the police data in the two-year period of study (2004–2005) were theft, alcohol violations, drug violations, and vandalism. Table 12.1 shows the numbers of recorded offenses for each type of crime in 2004–2005.

These top four crimes on campus in 2004–2005 are similar to those from

Table 12.1
CRIMES KNOWN TO THE POLICE (2004–2005)
AT APPALACHIAN STATE UNIVERSITY

Type of Offense	2004	2005	Total
Alcohol Violations	163	221	384
Arson	4	2	6
Assault	13	15	28
Breaking & Entering	17	13	30
Child Neglect	1	0	1
Communicating Threats	14	12	26
Disorderly Conduct	20	30	50
Domestic Dispute	0	6	6
DWI	31	29	60
Forcible Fondling	2	0	2
Forgery	1	1	2
Fraud	6	5	11
Hacking	1	0	1
Harassment	12	21	33
Harassing Phone Calls	17	17	34
Hit and Run	14	22	36
Illicit Drug Violations	116	139	255
Inappropriate Behavior	2	1	3
Indecent Exposure	1	0	1
Motor Vehicle Theft	7	3	10
Peeper	0	1	1
Possessing Stolen Property	3	3	6
Property Damage	15	10	25
Sexual Assault	3	2	5
Solicitation	5	2	7
Soliciting Sex	0	1	1
Theft	159	148	307
Trespassing	9	13	22
Vandalism	101	145	246
Weapons	10	14	24

previous studies conducted on the same campus from 1997–2000. For example, findings from victimization surveys of space users on the same campus suggested that the most common crimes on campus were crimes involving legal and illegal drugs. Further, the most common self-reported form of criminal victimization on campus was for someone to offer the student some illegal drugs while on campus, followed by burglary, theft, and threats of violence (Robinson & Mullen, 2001).

Police data also show that there were almost no violent crimes reported to the police for the past two years. In 2004 and 2005, there were no murders or robberies, only five sexual assaults, and 28 reported assaults (two students were murdered in 2005, but both were murdered off campus, as noted above). This, too, is nearly identical to the findings of the victimization surveys from previous years.

It should be pointed out that while the police crime data have consistently revealed less than ten sexual assaults per year on campus (and typically less than five), two previous victimization studies conducted on campus estimated the number of sexual assaults to be far higher (Mullen, Robinson, & Paulsen, 2001; Robinson & Mullen, 2001). Thus, consistent with any town or city—and heightened by the fact that there is also a town police department that may take criminal complaints related to sexual assaults—the number of calls for service for the crime of sexual assault is likely a vast underestimate (Abbey et al., 2001). It is likely that many other crimes also go unreported, including some assaults, much theft and vandalism, and probably the vast majority of alcohol and illicit drug use.

Hot Spots of Crime on Campus

With these additional limitations in mind, we plotted crimes known to the campus police on campus maps to demonstrate visually, which areas of campus were most likely to host criminal activity. Figures 12.1 through 12.6 show the campus crime maps.

In looking at the spatial distribution of crimes known to the police on campus, some important findings are evident. First, crime locations for illicit drug violations, alcohol violations, breaking and entering, assault, communicating threats, harassment, sexual assault, forcible fondling, vandalism, and theft are all concentrated largely at or near student dormitories. This finding is not unexpected as most student activity is centered around dormitories and thus victimization would also be expected to center around these dorms, consistent with routine activity theory and crime pattern theory (Brantingham & Brantingham, 1993; Cohen & Felson, 1979; Eck & Weisburd, 1995; Felson, 2002; Rossmo, 2000).

Previous studies of student lifestyles show that students spend most of their time at or near their residences (Robinson, 1999a). Thus, it is generally at student dorms–their main nodes of activity–where most opportunities for crime exist. We consider all university dorms as "crime generators" because large numbers of students congregate there for a variety of reasons, including criminal behavior.

Second, high-traffic areas between main parts of campus, such as near educational buildings and parking areas near pedestrian tunnels, also experience a moderate amount of crime, including thefts, vandalism, and crimes against automobiles (e.g., hit and run, property damage). This is also consistent with routine activity theory and crime pattern theory, as there are higher opportunities for crimes here due to the automobile and pedestrian traffic patterns at these places (Brantingham & Brantingham, 1993; Cohen & Felson, 1979; Eck & Weisburd, 1995; Felson, 2002; Rossmo, 2000). Essentially, it is reasonable to expect that the paths students and other users of campus space use to travel to and from their regular nodes of activities will host higher amounts of crime.

Third, there are three major places where crime clusters on campus for the crimes of illicit drug violations (Figure 12.1), alcohol violations (Figure 12.2), breaking and entering (Figure 12.3), and assault, communicating threats, harassment, sexual assault, and forcible fondling (Figure 12.4). The crimes of assault, communicating threats, harassment, sexual assault, and forcible fondling were grouped together because of the infrequent nature of each crime on campus and the similar nature of those crimes. That is, each is a crime that rarely occurs on campus and typically involves violence that is related to relationships between students (Carlson, 2005; Gover, 2004; Griffing et al., 2005; Lauritsen & Schaum, 2004; Thompson & Kingree, 2006).

The three places where these various crimes cluster are the main "hot spots" of crime on the campus. Another crime that tended to cluster in these same places, but far less frequently, was disorderly conduct. The three areas are dorms located around potential crime-generating environments. The first two areas are groups of dorms located across from the football stadium, its parking lots, and an open field known as "Duck Pond field." Duck Pond Field is an area that is used by students for recreational and sporting activities, including drinking alcohol associated with football games, playing sports, and hanging out, as well as some illicit drug use associated with parties. As such, these two areas can also be considered crime attractors since they will regularly draw in students looking to use and abuse alcohol and other drugs as part of social gatherings.

Hot Spots of Crime on Campus: A Closer Look. The first area (labeled Area #1 in the figures) is the "Yosef Hollow Community," and is comprised of five dorms. One of these dorms is all-male, whereas the rest are

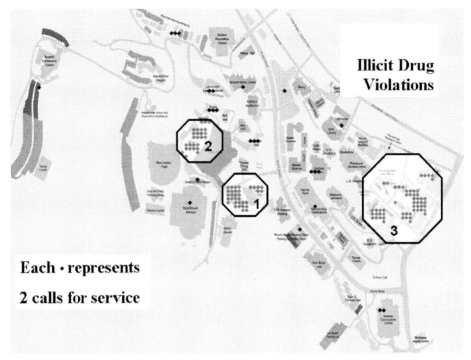

Figure 12.1. Hot spots of drug violations known to the police, 2004–2005.

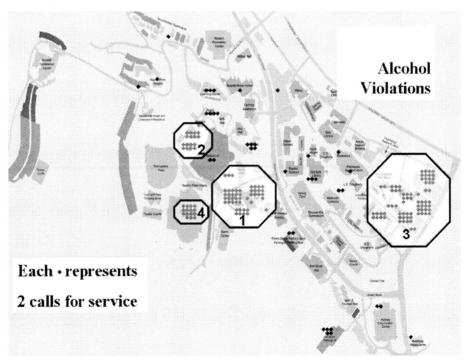

Figure 12.2. Hot spots of alcohol violations known to the police, 2004–2005.

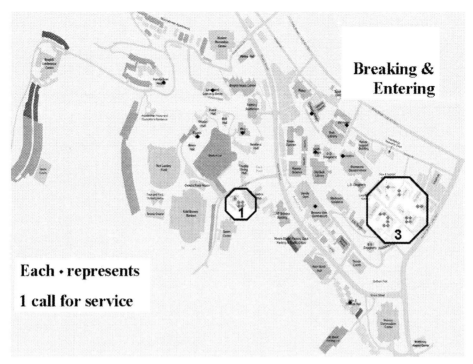

Figure 12.3. Hot spots of breaking and entering incidents know to the police, 2004–2005.

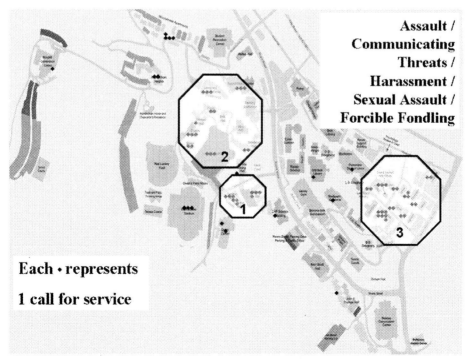

Figure 12.3. Hot spots of breaking and entering incidents know to the police, 2004–2005.

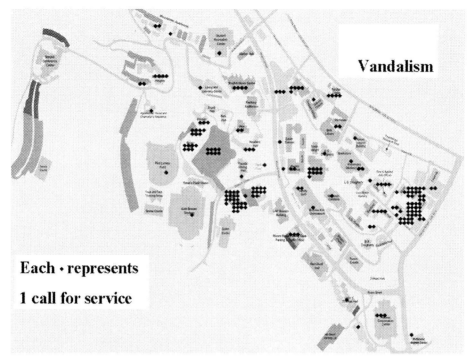

Figure 12.5. Acts of vandalism known to the police, 2004–2005.

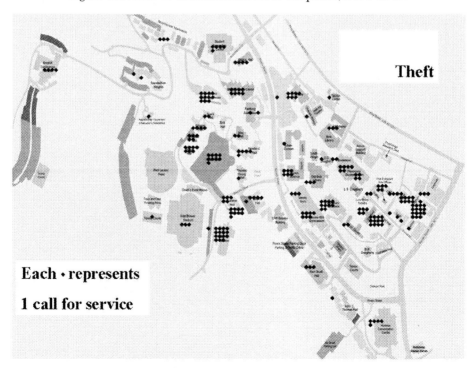

Figure 12.6. Thefts known to the police, 2004–2005.

co-ed. One of the dorms houses the "Wellness Community" where use of drugs, alcohol, or tobacco products will result in removal from the dorm. The Wellness Community could possibly act as a social control on the behavior of those in this dorm. Interestingly, both the all male dorm and the adjacent dorm housing the "Wellness Community," had a large amount of alcohol and drug violations, as well as acts of vandalism, theft, and disorderly conduct violations. None of the smaller dorms appeared in this group.

The second area (labeled Area #2 in the figures) is the "Stadium Heights Community," and is comprised of five dorms. One of these dorms is all female, whereas the rest are co-ed. Interestingly, the all-female dorm had no alcohol or drug violations, and only a few acts of vandalism or theft. Similarly, the "Living Learning Center," which houses some academic "learning communities," had very few crimes known to the police, with the exception of theft, which fell within a campus hot spot. The Living Learning Center could also serve as a social control on the behavior of students in the dorm. The Stadium Heights Community is a hot spot of crime, even though three of the smaller dorms on campus are located in this cluster. The rate of crimes known to the police in these smaller dorms is likely roughly equivalent to those large dorms in Area #1.

The third area (labeled Area #3 in the figures) is the "Eastridge Community" and is comprised of five co-ed dorms. The community is located on the other side of campus, near a major thoroughfare and a university-owned social club–an area that is also used by students for recreational activities, including concerts, dances, and other events where students 21 years and older are permitted to possess a six-pack of beer for each event (as such this can be considered a crime attractor). These dorms are closest to this club facility and to other establishments off campus where students frequently hang out for social purposes (e.g., restaurants and bars).

Three other nearby dorms, part of the "Pinnacle Community" (which also includes an apartment complex located on the other side of campus up a mountain that houses married, single-parent, graduate, and nontraditional students), are also near enough the university social club house a large number of alcohol and illicit drug violations, as well as acts of theft and vandalism. The largest dorm on campus is found in the Pinnacle community, which hosts a large amount of crimes known to the police.

Yet, the one dorm in this area that houses university honors students (which is also the smallest dorm on campus) had no alcohol or illicit drug violations, no reported acts of vandalism, and only two reported thefts in a two-year period. Similarly, the apartment complex that houses older and married students had very few crimes known to the police relative to other housing locations on campus (despite being of average size relative to all dorms on campus). The small number of crimes known to the police at the small honors dorm is due in part to the relative size of the dorm; yet, its lower incidence of crimes known to the police (as well as those at the apartment complex which houses older and married students) is likely due to the nature of student population there. These places serve as social controls on potential maladaptive behavior.

The crimes of assault, communicating threats, harassment, sexual assault, and forcible fondling occurred most often in the three hot spots of crime as well. Alcohol violations also clustered at these places, in addition to a fourth place. This fourth place (labeled Area #4 in Figure 12.2) is the football stadium itself, another crime attractor. Almost all the incidents here occurred on game days inside the stadium, and thus this hot spot is situational rather than static.

Theft was most prevalent in the above four areas, but also occurred frequently at a few others places. Given the widespread nature of theft on campus, it was impossible to neatly identify hot spots and thus none are indicated in Figure 12.6. The location of theft on campus is the most unique, primarily because it appears to occur occasionally all across campus. The same is true for vandalism, which is why no hot spots of vandalism are indicated in Figure 12.5. The dispersal of theft and vandalism across the campus likely reflects the numerous opportunities that are present across university buildings.

The primary difference between the location of theft and vandalism from other crimes on campus is that they tend to occur more frequently in academic buildings on campus (e.g., classroom buildings) and student support buildings (e.g., student union), as well as at some athletic facilities (e.g., university gym). These are places where opportunities for crime abound and where guardianship is lower (especially at night) than in student residences. Alcohol and illicit drug violations tend to occur almost exclusively at and around certain dorms and the football stadium. Part of this owes itself to opportunity factors–students spend more time in their dorms and socializing at certain places than they do in class, and alcohol and illicit drug use are obviously more accepted at these places than in academic buildings on campus (Robinson, 1999a).

Other Findings

We found some additional outcomes that are of interest to our study of campus hot spots. First, not all student dormitories were characterized by a high level of crime, as newer student dormitories built farther from the center of campus experienced less reported criminal activity. The relative lack of criminal activity at these newer dormitories is probably due to their distance from the center of campus, making them both socially and physically isolated from the center of campus. Crime pattern theorists would say these dorms are out of the awareness space of most campus users, and are thus less prone to victimization.

Second, the crime of DWI almost universally occurred on one street. The street is a main thoroughfare through campus (the primary path used by students driving cars) that connects nearly every dorm with restaurants, bars, and other student-centered locations. It is safe to say that this street stands out as a DWI hot spot because it is the only main thoroughfare through campus and thus is the main area where police officers will look for intoxicated drivers.

Third, there is a high degree of consistency between findings from the previous studies of student fear of specific campus areas, perceptions of students of where crime occurs, and the location of reported crime on campus in the current study. In general, areas identified by students in previous studies of the campus involving where they were afraid to go because of criminal victimization are consistent with areas where reported crime is highest on campus, although campus tunnels under streets (a place where some students feared going) host literally no reported criminal activity, except the occasional act of vandalism (Mullen, Robinson, & Paulsen, 2001; Robinson & Mullen, 2001).

In the earlier studies, 88 percent of students surveyed felt that most crime occurred in dorms and parking lots, areas where the spatial analysis of reported crime shows have high concentrations of crime (Mullen, Robinson, & Paulsen, 2001; Robinson & Mullen, 2001). On the campus of study, students have an accurate understanding of where street crimes occur, at least based on police data.

Hot Spots of Crime on Campus: Potential Explanations

As for the hot spots on campus, it is not clear whether they occur because of enduring characteristics about targets which make them attractive or suitable to multiple offenders (the risk heterogeneity argument), or if they occur because of factors related to the initial victimization (the state-dependent argument). Is it because certain people and places are different in some way that attracts offenders, or is it because initial victimizations result in the reinforcement of offenders' behaviors (e.g., Everson, 2003; Farrell, Phillips, & Pease, 1995; Robinson, 1998b)?

In the case of the campus, it is likely that the answer to each of these questions is yes. That is, it is likely that some places on campus are hot spots of crime because of factors related to criminal opportunities and student lifestyles that are consistently present, meaning criminality will likely occur there consistently over time. These are probably crime generators. Some of these places might also be more likely to host criminality due to a "legend" or "reputation" as the "party dorm" or a "cool hang-out," regardless of who lives there. These are better understood as crime attractors. Clearly, a handful of dorms on campus, including the largest dorm, the all male dorm, and the dorms that border the football stadium and the social club, have the largest number of crimes known to the police. Appropriately, these are also the dorms on campus that are known to be the "party dorms."

Applying community level factors that explain why some neighborhoods have higher crime rates than others to the issue of hot spots may also provide some explanation as to why some areas of a university campus have higher occurrences of crimes than others. Such factors include:

- Community composition (with higher rates of some types of people living in a community, crime rates are found to be higher);
- Community social structure (crime rates are also affected by the way in which inhabitants of an area interact);
- Oppositional culture (high crime neighborhoods are thought to be characterized by an "oppositional culture" or subcultural values that stem from frustration arising out of financial strains);
- Criminogenic commodities (rates of youth violence tend to be associated with the presence of places where alcohol use, drug use, and gun ownership are prevalent); and
- Social and physical disorder (high crime rate areas tend to be characterized by incivilities, which are signs that a neighborhood is in disarray) (Paulsen & Robinson, 2004; Sherman et al., 1998).

Social and physical disorder is not problematic anywhere on campus. Again, the campus is highly attractive and rated as aesthetically pleasing by space uses. Further, there is no evidence that some places on campus are characterized by different levels of oppositional cultures, although this is possible (some dorms may attract different types of people than others). Again, the all-male dorm tends to have a higher level of crimes known to the police than many other dorms. Community composition factors may explain higher crimes known to the police on some areas of campus, as may community social structure factors. That is, some dorms on campus, for whatever reason, have a more pronounced reputation for partying behaviors.

Criminogenic commodities may very well vary by campus location, as alcohol, illicit drugs, and weapons possession may simply be higher in some locations than others based on who lives there. As noted earlier, part of this owes itself to the proximity of dorms to criminogenic locations such as the football stadium and university-operated social club.

Implications for Crime Prevention

The findings of this study–based on crimes known to the police–show that there are some unique areas on campus that are most crime prone. Specifically, there are a few groups of dorms that generate the most known offenses for larceny, vandalism, breaking and entering, alcohol and illicit drug violations, assault, communicating threats, harassment, sexual assault and forcible fondling, as well as disorderly conduct.

Interestingly, the places on campus indicated by 2004 and 2005 police data as the most crime-prone–the three main hot spots on campus–are the same places found to generate the most fear and perception of crime risk by previous studies of the university campus that utilized victimization surveys of students, faculty, and staff. If this means, as we think it does, that the location of criminality on campus is relatively stable, this offers some unique opportunities for prevention strategies aimed at breaking the cycle of crime in some locations on campus. That the place of crime has remained stable from 1997 to 2006 is important, especially considering that new students have come to campus and that the campus has been significantly developed (i.e., built up).

The crime of sexual assault, which is likely vastly underreported on campus, is not spatially clustered due to any particular environmental conditions, and it is likely that it occurs in the same locations that alcohol use and illicit drug use is most prevalent. Sexual assault and alcohol use are clearly linked (Abbey, 2002; Abbey et al., 2001; Fisher et al., 1998; Testa & Livingston, 1999; Robinson, 2004; Wechsler et al., 1995; Wechsler & Wuethrich, 2003). That the crimes of assault, communicating threats, harassment, sexual assault, and forcible fondling all occur with the greatest frequency in places where alcohol use is most widespread should lead to preventive action in these dorms.

The most significant problem on the campus appears to be alcohol and illicit drug use. Since it appears that the same places that generate these offenses also generate the most incidents of other types of crimes, it is logical that alcohol and illicit drug use are driving these other criminal events, especially considering the student lifestyle (Robinson, 1999a). Young people often commit acts of stupidity–including disorderly conduct; vandalism; theft; assault; communicating threats; harassment; and more seriously, sexual assault–under the influence of drugs, especially alcohol (Robinson, 2004).

Alcohol is the one drug that would most likely lead to a psychopharmacological effect on criminality (Robinson & Scherlen, 2007). Because of the effects of the drug on the brain, as well as because of how it is consumed by young people and the setting in which it is consumed–alcohol is the one drug that is most likely responsible for the clustering of criminality at particular locations on campus. This warrants serious investigation into the effects that alcohol consumption has on criminality on this particular campus. Further, it warrants dedicated action on the part of the university administration to combat irresponsible alcohol use–especially by underage students–on the campus. This is not meant to de-emphasize the issue of illicit drug use on campus, which is the one crime that is likely most prevalent based on previous student surveys. Further, it is the illicit drug market that led to the murders of two students just more than one year apart.

Yet, even the Office of National Drug Control Policy has noted that when it comes to drugs and crime and mayhem, alcohol leads the pack (Robinson & Scherlen, 2007). At the university of study, there is no evidence showing that students drink more alcohol than on other campuses, or that they drink any differently. Still, this is the one drug that is most responsible for antisocial behavior and alcohol use clearly plays a meaningful role in the lives of a sizable portion of the student body throughout the year. Thus, one logical crime prevention strategy would be alcohol awareness campaigns directed at all students, and especially those who live in the particular dorms that comprise the hot spots of crime on campus.

Finally, other crime prevention strategies should be developed and implemented at the hot spots of crime on campus. Given that displacement is not likely to result, and that there is likely to be a diffusion of benefits, it makes very good sense to focus efforts on the areas that are most likely to host alcohol and illicit drug violations, theft, and vandalism (Clarke, 1998; Clarke & Weisburd, 1994; Cohen & Tita, 1999; Paulsen & Robinson, 2004). This would include the many well-tested efforts aimed at CPTED and situational crime prevention.

The strategies that would most likely be successful to reduce these crimes vary by type of crime. For example, a large number of thefts could be prevented by increasing student awareness of problem areas (e.g., the library, the gym) and encouraging students to maintain guardianship of their property at all times. A large amount of vandalism could be prevented by better securing construction sites on campus and increasing surveillability of other locations at night. And as noted above, much alcohol and illicit drug violations could be prevented by educating students about the dangers of irresponsible use and abuse, as well as giving students more opportunities for alternative forms of entertainment. Given the relationships between alcohol and illicit drug use and criminality, reducing alcohol and illicit drug use would likely reduce some thefts, acts of vandalism, disorderly conduct, assaults, communication of threats, acts of harassment, sexual assault, and probably breaking and entering.

REFERENCES

Abbey, A. (2002). Alcohol-related sexual assault: A common problem among college students. *Journal of Studies on Alcohol, 14,* 118–128.

Abbey, A., Zawacki, T., Buck, P. Clinton, A., & McAuslan, P. (2001). Alcohol and sexual assault. Alcohol Health and Research World, 25. Retrieved June 3, 2006, from http://www.athealth.com/Practitioner/ceduc/alc_assault.html

Appalachian State University. (2006). Annual Crime Report: 2004–2005. Boone, N.C.: Appalachian State University.

Astor, R., Meyer, H., & Behre, W. (1999). Unowned places and times: Maps and interviews about violence in high schools. *American Educational Research Journal, 36,* 3–42.

Block, C., & Block, R. (1995). *Street gang crime in Chicago: NIJ Research in brief.* Washington, D.C.: National Institute of Justice.

Block, C., & Block, R. (1998). Homicides in Chicago, 1965–1995 [Computer file]. 4th ICPSR version. Chicago, IL: Illinois Criminal Justice Information Authority. Ann Arbor, MI: Inter-university Consortium for Political and Social Research.

Block, C., & Christakos, A. (1995). *Major trends in Chicago homicide: 1965–1994.* Washington, DC: National Institute of Justice.

Bohm, R. (2000). *A primer on crime and delinquency theory.* Belmont, CA: Wadsworth.

Brantingham, P., & Brantingham, P. (1993). Environment, routine, and situation: Toward a pattern theory of crime. In R. Clarke & M. Felson (Eds.), *Routine activity and rational choice Vol. 5: Advances in criminological theory.* New Brunswick, NJ: Transaction.

Brantingham, P., & Brantingham, P. (1994). Surveying campus crime: What can be done to reduce crime and fear? *Security Journal, 5,* 160–171.

Brantingham, P., & Brantingham, P. (1999). A theoretical model of crime hot spot generation. *Studies on Crime and Crime Prevention, 8,* 7–26.

Brantingham, P., & Faust, F. (1976). A conceptual model of crime prevention. *Crime & Delinquency, 7,* 284–295.

Brinkley Jr, W., & Laster, D. (2003). Campus crime in Missouri: An analysis and comparison of crime in four-year colleges and universities. *Journal of Security Administration, 26,* 1–15.

Bromley, M. (1994). Correlates of campus crime: A nationwide exploratory study of large universities. *Journal of Security Administration, 17,* 37–52.

Carlson, B. (2005). The most important things learned about violence and trauma in the past 20 years. *Journal of Interpersonal Violence, 20,* 119–126.

Clarke, R. (1992). *Situational crime prevention: Successful case studies.* Albany, NY: Harrow and Hest.

Clarke, R. (1998). The theory and practice of situational crime prevention. Retrieved June 5, 2006, from http://www.edoca.net/ Resources/ Articles/ Clarke_the_ theory_and_practice_of_situational_crime_prevention.pdf.

Clarke, R., & Weisburd, D. (1994). Diffusion of crime control benefits: Observations of the reverse of displacement. *Crime Prevention Studies, 2,* 165–184.

Clarke, R. (2001). *Rational choice.* In R. Paternoster & R. Bachman (Eds.), Explaining crime and criminals. Los Angeles: Roxbury.

Clarke, R., & Eck, J. (2006). Crime analysis for problem solvers in 60 steps. Center for Problem Oriented Policing. Retrieved June 5, 2006, from http://www.pop center. org/learning/60steps/index.cfm?stepNum=17.

Cochran, J., & Bromley, M. (2002). Auto burglaries in an entertainment district: Patron perceptions of risks and precautionary behaviors. *Journal of Security Administration, 25,* 1–18.

Cochran, J., Bromley, M., & Branch, K. (2000). Victimization and fear of crime in an entertainment district crime "hot spot": A test of structural-choice theory. *American Journal of Criminal Justice, 24,* 189–201.

Cohen, J., & Tita, G. (1999). Diffusion in homicide: Exploring a general method for detecting spatial diffusion processes. *Journal of Quantitative Criminology, 15,* 451–493.

Cohen, L., & Felson, M. (1979). Social change and crime rate trends: A routine activity approach. *American Sociological Review, 44,* 588–608.

Cornish, D., & Clarke, R. (Eds.) (1986). *The reasoning criminal: Rational choice perspectives on offending.* New York: Springer-Verlag.

Crowe, T. (1991). *Crime prevention through environmental design: Applications of architectural design and space management concepts.* Boston: Butterworth-Heinemann.

Eck, J., & Weisburd, D. (1995). Crime places in crime theory. In J. Eck & D. Weisburd (Eds.), *Crime prevention studies: Crime and place.* Monsey, NY: Willow Tree Press.

Everson, S. (2003). Repeat victimization and "prolific" offending: Chance or choice? *International Journal of Police Science & Management, 5,* 180–194.

Farrell, G., Phillips, C., & Pease, K. (1995). Like taking candy: Why does repeat victimization occur? *British Journal of Criminology, 35,* 384–399.

Felson, M. (2002). *Crime and everyday life* (3rd ed.). Beverly Hills, CA: Sage.

Fisher, B., & Sloan III, J. (1993). University responses to the *Campus Security Act of 1990:* Evaluating programs designed to reduce campus crime. *Journal of Security Administration, 16,* 67–80.

Fisher, B., Sloan, J., Cullen, F., & Lu, C. (1998). Crime in the ivory tower: The level and sources of student victimization. *Criminology, 36,* 671–710.

Fisher, B., & Wilkes, A (2003). A tale of two ivory towers: A comparative analysis of victimization rates and risks between university students in the United States and England. *British Journal of Criminology, 43,* 526–545.

Fox, J., & Hellman, D. (1985). Location and other correlates of campus crime. *Journal of Criminal Justice, 13,* 429–444.

Gover, A. (2004). Risky lifestyles and dating violence: A theoretical test of violent victimization. *Journal of Criminal Justice, 32,* 171–180.

Green, L. (1995). Cleaning up drug hot spots in Oakland, California: The displacement and diffusion effects. *Justice Quarterly, 12,* 737–754.

Griffing, S., Ragin, D., Morrison, S., Sage, R., Madry, L., & Primm, B. (2005). Reasons for returning to abusive relationships: Effects of prior victimization. *Journal of Family Violence, 20,* 341–348.

Henson, V., & Stone, W. (1999). Campus crime: A victimization study. *Journal of*

Criminal Justice, 27, 295–307.

Johnson, I., & Sigler, R. (1996). Forced sexual intercourse on campus: Crime or offensive behavior? *Journal of Contemporary Criminal Justice, 12,* 54–68.

Koper, C. (1995). Just enough police presence: Reducing crime and disorderly behavior by optimizing patrol time in crime hot spots. *Justice Quarterly, 12,* 649–672.

Langhinrichsen-Rohling, J., Palarea, R. E., Cohen J., & Rohling, M. L. (2000). Breaking up is hard to do: Unwanted pursuit behaviors following the dissolution of a romantic relationship. *Violence and Victims, 15,* 1–17.

Lauritsen, J., & Schaum, R. (2004). The social ecology of violence against women. *Criminology, 42,* 323–357.

Loukaitou-Sideris, A. (1999). Hot spots of bus stop crime: The importance of environmental attributes. *Journal of the American Planning Association, 65,* 83–95.

Moriarty, L., & Pelfrey, W. (1996). Exploring explanations for campus crime: Examining internal and external factors. *Journal of Contemporary Criminal Justice, 12,* 108–120.

Mullen, K., Robinson, M., & Paulsen, D. (2001). Crime on campus: Repeat criminal victimization and hot spots of crime. Paper presented to the annual meeting of the American Society of Criminology, November.

Mustaine, E., & Tewksbury, R. (1998). Predicting risks of larceny theft victimization: A routine activity analysis using refined lifestyle measures. *Criminology, 36,* 829–857.

O'Kane, J. Fisher, R., & Green, L. (1994). Mapping campus crime. *Security Journal, 5,* 172–179.

Paulsen, D., & Robinson, M. (2004). *Spatial aspects of crime: Theory and practice.* Boston: Allyn & Bacon.

Rengert, G., & Lowell, R. (2005). Combating campus crime with mapping and analysis. *Crime Mapping News, 7,* 1–5.

Rengert, G., Mattson, M., & Henderson, K. (2001). *Campus security: Situational crime prevention in high-density environments.* Cullompton, Devon, UK: Criminal Justice Press.

Richards, G. (1996). The security survey: Creating a proactive foundation for campus crime prevention. *Journal of Contemporary Criminal Justice, 12,* 45–53.

Robinson, M. (1998a). Accessible targets, but not advisable ones: The role of "accessibility" in student apartment burglary. *Journal of Security Administration, 21,* 29–43.

Robinson, M. (1998b). The time period of heightened risk for repeat burglary victimization. *British Journal of Criminology, 38,* 76–85.

Robinson, M. (1999a). Lifestyles, routine activities, and residential burglary victimization. *Journal of Crime and Justice, 22,* 27–56.

Robinson, M. (1999b). The theoretical development of crime prevention through environmental design (CPTED). *Advances in Criminological Theory, 8,* 427–462.

Robinson, M. (2004). *Why crime? An integrated systems theory of antisocial behavior.* Upper Saddle River, NJ: Prentice-Hall.

Robinson, M. (2005). *Justice blind? Ideals and realities of American criminal justice* (2nd ed.). Upper Saddle River, NJ: Prentice-Hall.

Robinson, M, & Mullen, K. (2001). Crime on campus: A survey of space users. *Crime Prevention and Community Safety: An International Journal, 3,* 33–46.

Robinson, M., & Scherlen, R. (2007). *Lies, damned lies, and drug war statistics.* Albany, NY: State University of New York Press.

Roncek, D., & Maier, P. (1991). Bars, blocks, and crimes revisited: Linking the theory of routine activities to the empiricism of "hot spots." *Criminology, 29,* 725–753.

Rossmo, K. (2000). *Geographic profiling.* Boca Raton, FL: CRC Press.

Schwartz, M., DeKeseredy, W., Tait, D., & Alvi, S. (2001). Male peer support and a feminist routine activities theory: Understanding sexual assault on the college campus. *Justice Quarterly, 18,* 623–649.

Sherman, L., Gartin, P., & Buerger, M. (1989). Hot spots of predatory crime: Routine activities and the criminology of place. *Criminology, 27,* 27–55.

Sherman, L., Gottfredson, D., MacKenzie, D., Eck, J., Reuter, P., & Bushway, S. (1998). *Preventing crime: What works, what doesn't, what's promising.* Retrieved June 5, 2006, from www.ncjrs.org/pdffiles/171676.pdf.

Sherman, L., & Rogan, L. (1995). Deterrent effects of police raids on crack houses: A randomized, controlled experiment. *Justice Quarterly, 12,* 755–781.

Sherman, L., & Weisburd, D. (1995). General deterrent effects of police patrol in crime "hot spots": A randomized, controlled trial. *Justice Quarterly, 12,* 625–648.

Siegel, D., & Raymond, C. (1992). An ecological approach to violent campus crime. *Journal of Security Administration, 15,* 19–29.

Sloan, J. (1992). Campus crime and campus communities: An analysis of crimes known to campus police and security. *Journal of Security Administration, 15,* 31–47.

Sloan, J. (1994). The correlates of campus crime: An analysis of reported crimes on college and university campuses. *Journal of Criminal Justice, 22,* 51–66.

Sloan, J., Fisher, B., & Cullen, F. (1997). Assessing the *Student Right-to-Know and Campus Security Act of 1990:* An analysis of the victim reporting practices of college and university students. *Crime and Delinquency, 43,* 148–168.

Stitt, B., Nichols, M., & Giacopassi, D. (2003). Does the presence of casinos increase crime? An examination of casino and control communities. *Crime and Delinquency, 49,* 253–284.

Testa, M., & Livingston, J. (1999). Qualitative analysis of women's experiences of sexual aggression: Focus on the role of alcohol. *Psychology of Women Quarterly, 23,* 573–589.

Tewksbury, R., & Mustaine, E. (2003). College students' lifestyles and self-protective behaviors: Further considerations of the guardianship concept in routine activity theory. *Criminal Justice and Behavior, 30,* 302–327.

Thompson, M., & Kingree, J. (2006). The roles of victim and perpetrator alcohol use in intimate partner violence outcomes. *Journal of Interpersonal Violence, 21,* 163–177.

Volkwein, J., Szelest, B., & Lizotte, A. (1995). The relationship of campus crime to campus and student characteristics. *Research in Higher Education, 36,* 647–70.

Warr, M. (1990). Dangerous situations: Social context and fear of victimization. *Social Forces, 68,* 891–907.

Wechsler, H., Dowdall, G., Davenport, A., & Castillo, S. (1995). Correlates of college student binge drinking. *American Journal of Public Health, 85,* 982–985.

Wechsler, H., & Wuethrich, B. (2003). *Dying to drink: Confronting binge drinking on college campuses.* New York: Rodale.

Weisburd, D., Bushway, S., Lum, C., & Yang, S. (2004). Trajectories of crime at places: A longitudinal study of street segments in the city of Seattle. *Criminology, 42,* 283–321.

Weisburd, D., & Green, L. (1995). Policing drug hot spots: The Jersey City drug market analysis experiment. *Justice Quarterly, 12,* 711–735.

Wooldredge, J., Cullen, F., & Latessa, E. (1995). Predicting the likelihood of faculty victimization: Individual demographics and routine activities. In B. S. Fisher & J. J. Sloan (Eds.), *Campus crime: Legal, social, and policy perspectives.* Springfield, IL: Charles C Thomas.

Part III:

THE SECURITY CONTEXT
OF CAMPUS CRIME

Part III

THE SECURITY CONTEXT
OF CAMPUS CRIME

INTRODUCTION

One of the key components of the *Clery Act* is the requirement that post-secondary institutions develop and then publish policies and procedures relating to campus security, which include identifying where victims are supposed to report their victimization, the jurisdictional and operational characteristics of campus police/security departments, and the services available to sexual assault victims. Meeting these requirements creates issues and opportunities for postsecondary administrators who must design and implement programs and policies to help make college campuses safer.

After campus administrators identify the social context of their on-campus crime, among the first issues they confront involves developing and successfully implementing effective programs and strategies to *prevent* these crime. For example, they may implement strategies based on crime control through environmental design or proactive policing strategies, common to community-oriented policing. They may also emphasize educating students on the benefits of increased guardianship and target hardening of both themselves and their property. Administrators must also confront the growing menace of *high-tech crimes,* like identity theft, in which students are often involved as both offenders and victims. Further, administrators face both operational and organizational issues when their attention turns to policing the campus community. Finally, because no known strategy is 100 percent effective at preventing on-campus victimization, administrators must also design and implement policies or programs that provide *victim assistance* to those unfortunate enough to experience a crime, particularly those who experience any form of sexual assault.

Part III of the book presents three chapters that examine the security context of campus crime. These chapters include discussions of not only "traditional" issues, such as the professionalization of campus law enforcement and strategic and operational aspects of that process, but also how campuses must now address high-tech crimes.

In Chapter 13, John Sloan and Mark Lanier examine the prospects of Community-Oriented Policing (COP) on college and university campuses. The chapter describes the underlying philosophy of community policing as well as its administrative and tactical aspects. The chapter also suggests that the mission of campus police agencies makes COP particularly attractive for them. The chapter concludes by arguing the benefits of COP for campus police agencies.

Chapter 14, "The Evolution of Campus Policing: Different Models for Different Eras," by Max Bromley, traces the history of campus policing from Colonial America to the present. He presents a solid case for why the 24/7 college campus with its youthful, multiracial and ethnic identity and multiple functions–education, residential, and entertainment–requires that campus law enforcement move beyond traditional, rapid-response-oriented policing and toward proactive, problem-solving COP. His case study of the University of South Florida's efforts to implement COP as a new organizational model for the campus police department shows both the problems and the successes inherent in fundamentally altering both the organizational structure of a campus police department, but its culture as well.

Finally, Samuel McQuade authors Chapter 15, titled "High Tech Abuse and Crime on College and University Campuses: Evolving Forms of Victimization, Offending, and Their Interplay in Higher Education." In the chapter, McQuade focuses attention on "new" types of campus victimization–those involving technology. He explains how computing and telecommunication advances, including the Internet and cell phones, have created opportunities for campus personnel and computer networks to be vulnerable to victimization. McQuade shows how different types of attacks pose new security challenges for campus information technology (IT) departments, as well as campus police. In conclusion, he discusses how campuses can address high tech abuses and crimes through a variety of strategies such as active sanctioning of offenders, educating and training the campus community to protect information systems, and using technological advancements to prevent or countercomputing and telecommunication abuses and attacks.

The chapters in Part III provide both historical and contemporary insight into how the changing dynamics of campuses and opportunities for crime have influenced the operational and organizational structures of twenty-first century campus security operations. Chapter authors educate us about how and why changes occurred while reminding us that the campus police are not the only perspective needed to understand (and hopefully reduce) campus crime, especially as campuses also have to address high-tech abuse and crime among their community members.

Chapter 13

COMMUNITY POLICING ON UNIVERSITY CAMPUSES: TRADITION, PRACTICES, AND OUTLOOK

JOHN J. SLOAN, III AND MARK M. LANIER

INTRODUCTION

For most of the past 50 years, American policing has clung to a "professional model" that stressed random and reactive patrol, rapid response to calls for service, and an emphasis on law enforcement and crime control (see Fogelson, 1977; Maguire, 1997; Monkkonen, 1981; Reis, 1992). Since the 1980s, however, a major paradigm shift has occurred in the philosophical, operational, and tactical orientation of American policing that involves replacing the professional model with a new organizational model known as Community-Oriented Policing (COP) (e.g., Cordner, 1996, 1997; Maguire & Mastrofski, 2000; Rosenbaum, 1994).

Born from criticism arising in the 1960s of the professional model's apparent failure to reduce crime and its tendency to alienate citizens, particularly those in minority communities, proponents of COP argue this new "model" of policing not only helps control crime but also addresses the alienation from police commonly felt by members of urban communities (Skogan & Hartnett, 1997). COP represents a radical departure from the past, because it emphasizes decentralization and despecialization of organizational functions, officer empowerment, community partnerships, and problem solving, among others (Cordner, 1996; Maguire, 2002).

As discussed more fully below, COP involves multiple levels of reform, beginning with the underlying philosophy of the role of the police in the community and ending with specific tactics used by officers on the beat. COP has found favor with both academic police researchers and many

261

municipal police departments, both large and small. For example, in a 1999 survey of local law enforcement agencies, the U.S. Department of Justice found that 64 percent of departments, representing 86 percent of the U.S. population served by local police, had full-time officers engaged in community policing activities. COP has arrived and is unlikely to go away any time soon, despite its critics (see Bayley, 1988; Manning, 1984, 1988, 1989). Importantly for the present discussion, in recent years campus police departments have begun adopting COP (Bromley, 2003, 2007) and it appears to be the "new" paradigm for these agencies as well.

This chapter examines COP as an organizational model for campus police departments. We begin the chapter by presenting an overview of COP and discussion of its key components. Next, we examine the extent campus agencies have begun adopting COP, including case studies of its implementation on various campuses and a review of a national-level study of the extent campus police agencies have adopted COP. We conclude the chapter by arguing that, given its history and unique context, COP is a reasonable model for campus police departments to adopt.

Community-Oriented Policing: An Overview

The origins of COP can be traced to two publications occurring several years apart but which have become linked as forming COP's foundation: Goldstein (1979) and Wilson and Kelling (1982). Goldstein presented a strong argument that urban police needed to focus less on quickly responding to calls for service and more on neighborhood and community problems giving rise to crime, disorder, and fear. Instead of being reactive and focusing on rapid response to calls for service–as had been the dominant theme in policing since the 1950s–Goldstein called on the police to be more proactive and "problem oriented." This shift in orientation, argued Goldstein, would result in greater interaction and cooperation between the police and the community. In turn, generous benefits would accrue the police, such as enhancing its legitimacy in the public eye, individual officers developing stronger ties to the communities they were policing, and making departments more effective and efficient.

Wilson and Kelling (1982) presented the now (in)famous "broken windows" thesis which suggests that crime, neighborhood disorder, and citizen fear of victimization worked in combination to devastate communities. They used the example of a broken window left unrepaired in a building; soon, they argued, more broken windows would appear signaling prospective offenders that "no one in the community cared" enough to fix them. This "lack of care" opens the door for offenders to engage in even greater levels of lawlessness, fueling greater levels of neighborhood disorder and fear. If the police were to have any chance of making a difference, Wilson and Kelling argued, they had to work with the community and attack the "broken windows." In other words, before the police could address high levels of crime, they first had to address the problems that plagued high-crime neighborhoods and could only do so by collaborating with the community (see Skogan, 1990).

While approaching the same problem from different angles, the two articles reached the same conclusion. Both argued traditional, reactive-based, calls-for-service-oriented police strategies had failed and advocated for a new model of policing. Importantly, this model would need to bring together the police and the community to address the problems that give rise to crime, disorder, and fear and create partnerships between the police and the community to address these problems.

During the 1980s, academic researchers and police practitioners debated what Zhao, Lovrich, and Thurman (1999) call the "promises and challenges" of COP, particularly whether it represented something "real" or was mere "rhetoric" (Greene & Mastrofski, 1988). Helping to fuel this debate was the publication of several case studies alleging COP successes in Flint, Michigan (Trojanowicz, 1985); Houston, Texas (Brown & Wycoff, 1987); and Newport News, Virginia (Eck & Spelman, 1987). The National Institute of Justice furthered debate by disseminating the results of these experiments (Zhao, Thurman, & Lovrich, 1997; Zhao et al., 1999). For critics, however, the case studies merely showed the benefits of "foot patrol" or other changes in specific tactics used by beat officers, not the utility of COP in achieving its alleged promises (Greene & Mastrofski, 1988).

Zhao et al. (1999) suggest the 1990s marked a "third wave" of COP development where widespread acceptance and implementation of COP occurred. The Clinton administration played a crucial role because it strongly supported COP and pressed Congress to pass (which it did) the *Violent Crime Control and Law Enforcement Act* in 1994, which authorized subsidized funded for hiring 100,000 new community police officers by local law enforcement agencies and created the federal Office of Community Oriented Policing Services (the "COPS Office"). The Justice Department charged the COPS Office with coordinating and supervising community-oriented policing programs nationwide, which it has now done for over a decade.

Moving into the first decade of the twenty-first century, Cochran, Bromley, and Swando (2002, p. 508) suggest that COP initiatives now "are the preferred form of quality management strategies employed" to address issues such issues as productivity, responsiveness, and quality in the provision of police services to the public. Supporters claim it addresses these issues because it involves multifunctionality, coproduction, partnership, decentralization, a flat organization hierarchy, despecialization, and proactiveness (see Skogan & Hartnett, 1997).

Despite its widespread acceptance, confusion remains as to what COP actually *is*–a philosophy, an operational model, or a tactic–or something else entirely. In the next section, we address this key question.

The Components of COP

There is no consensus definition of COP (Eck & Rosenbaum, 1994). This is one avenue of criticism levied against supporters: if you cannot define it, how do you know if a department is implementing it and evaluate its effectiveness? Cordner (1996) answered this criticism by presenting a comprehensive explanation of COP, including its key dimensions–the philosophical, the strategic, the tactical, and the organizational–and various subcomponents of each dimension.

CORDNER'S DISCUSSION OF COP. Cordner's discussion begins by exploring the philosophical dimension of COP. According to Cordner (1996, p. 2), the philosophical dimension of COP ". . . includes the central ideas and beliefs underlying community policing. Three of the most important . . . are *citizen input, broad function,* and *personal service.*" *Citizen input* involves citizens having a say in how the department operates and how it responds to the community's security and safety needs. Cordner suggests departments can use specific methods to enhance citizen input including advisory boards (e.g., agency, unit, and beat); community surveys; creating Internet homepages and using email communication; and town meetings. Each technique is designed to bring together individual officers, department administrators, and citizens, and creates specific opportunities for citizens to have input into department operations at a variety of levels, from a specific beat to the entire agency.

Broad function points to the fact COP views policing as a broad-based activity that involves officers:

> . . . working with residents to enhance neighborhood safety. This includes resolving conflicts, helping victims, preventing accidents, solving problems, and fighting fear as well as reducing crime through apprehension and enforcement. Policing is inherently a multi-faceted government function; arbitrarily narrowing it just to call handling and law enforcement reduces its effectiveness in accomplishing the multiple objectives that the public expects police to achieve. (Cordner, 1996, p. 3)

The broad function component includes such activities as departments pursuing traffic safety through enforcement and engineering efforts; reducing drug abuse through public education and enforcement; reducing fear of victimization (particularly when it is not justified by actual victimization risk) through high-interaction patrols and enforcement of nuisance statutes relating to public panhandling or urban camping; providing services to domestic violence victims and implementing mandatory arrest policies (if appropriate); and participating in zoning/rezoning decisions to address public safety and traffic issues.

According to Cordner (1996, p.4), the *personal service* component emphasizes that police are not bureaucrats, nor should they behave like them:

> [Personal service] is designed to overcome one of the most common complaints that the public has about government employees, including police officers–that they do not seem to care and that they treat citizens as numbers, not real people. Of course, not every police-citizen encounter can be amicable and friendly. Nevertheless, whenever possible, officers should deal with citizens in a friendly, open, and personal manner designed to turn them into satisfied customers. This can best be done by eliminating as many artificial bureaucratic barriers as possible, so that citizens can deal directly with "their" officer.

Cordner (1996) suggests officers can enhance personal service by issuing business cards to victims, complainants, and witnesses and using pagers and voice mail so citizens can directly contact them. Cordner also suggests that departments can adopt slogans and symbols (e.g., mission statements, value statements) to reinforce the importance of providing personal service to the public.

THE STRATEGIC DIMENSION OF COP. The strategic dimension links the philosophical beliefs and values of COP to the specific programs and policies related to implementation. Three important strategic elements are *reorienting operations, emphasizing prevention,* and *focusing on geography.*

Reorienting operations involves departments (and officers) relying less on motorized patrol and more on face-to-face interaction with citizens. An important objective is to replace "ineffective or isolating operational practices (e.g., motorized patrol and rapid response to low priority calls) with more effective and more interactive practices" (Cordner, 1996, p.4). Additionally, as part of reorienting their operations, departments can find more efficient ways of performing necessary traditional functions (e.g., handling emergency calls and conducting follow-up investigations) to save time and resources that are then redirected to more community-oriented activities (Cordner, 1996). Examples of reorienting operations include increased reliance on foot and other forms of patrol (e.g., bicycle or mounted); differential patrol (e.g., delayed response, telephone reporting, walk-in reporting); and different investigative responses tailored to meet the needs of different types of cases, rather than automatically assigning detectives to follow up on all cases.

Emphasizing prevention focuses on making crime prevention a routine part of every officer's daily activities. Cordner (1996, p.5) suggests the following as activities geared toward prevention:

- *Situational Crime Prevention*–the most promising general approach to crime prevention is to tailor specific preventive measures to each situation's specific characteristics.
- *CPTED*–many departments have become involved with CPTED– Crime Prevention Through Environmental Design–which focuses on changing the physical characteristics of a location that make it conducive to crime.
- *Community Crime Prevention*–many departments now work closely with individual residents and with groups of residents in a cooperative manner to prevent crime (e.g., block watch).
- *Youth-Oriented Prevention*–many departments have implemented programs or collaborated with others to provide programs designed to prevent youth crime (e.g., recreation, tutoring, and mentoring programs).
- *Business Crime Prevention*–many departments work closely with businesses to recommend personnel practices, retail procedures, and other security measures designed to prevent crime.

Finally, Cordner (1996, p.6) states, "Community policing adopts a geographic focus to establish stronger bonds between officers and neighborhoods . . . to increase mutual recognition, identification, responsibility, and accountability." Cordner points out that while departments have traditionally assigned officers to beats (a geographic area), their accountability has been exclusively temporal (during their shift). COP shifts the focus from the temporal to the geographic by having departments use methods such as permanent beat assignments for officers; creating "lead officers" responsible for problem identification and coordination of the efforts of all officers assigned a specific beat during a 24-hour period; implementing "cop of the block" where a beat is subdivided into smaller areas of individual accountability so that although every officer has general responsibility for a beat, each officer also has special responsibility for a smaller area within it; creating mini-stations or store-front stations; and assigning detectives as "area specialists" to handle all investigations in a particular area, rather than specializing in one type of case (e.g., burglary) arising throughout the department's jurisdiction.

THE TACTICAL DIMENSION OF COP. According to Cordner (1996, p.6), the tactical dimension of COP "ultimately translates ideas, philosophies, and strategies into concrete programs, tactics, and behaviors," and suggests that the three most important tactical elements of COP include *positive interaction, partnerships,* and *problem solving.*

While policing inevitably involves negative contacts between officers and the public (e.g., traffic stops, stopping citizens on suspicion, or issuing orders to desist), COP seeks to offset these negative contacts as much as possible with positive contacts between officers and citizens. As Cordner (1996, p.6) puts it:

> Positive interactions have several benefits, of course: they generally build familiarity, trust and confidence on both sides; they remind officers that most citizens respect and support them; they make the officer more knowledgeable about people and conditions in the beat; they provide specific information for criminal investigations and problem solving; and they break up the monotony of motorized patrol.

Departments seeking to enhance positive interactions between officers and citizens can use a variety of methods to achieve that goal. For example, when handling routine calls for service, rather than officers rushing to clear the call and return to patrol, they spend extra time with citizens to create a more positive experience for them. Officers can also attend neighborhood association or block association meetings to show their commitment to the neighborhood. Such interaction can also provide additional benefits to officers, such as information from citizens on problems with which the officer is unfamiliar. Finally, instead of concentrating patrol on "public places or spaces," officers can stop and talk with people so their patrol now focuses less on *watching* people and more on *interacting* with them.

Key to the success of COP are active *partnerships* between police and other agencies, and citizens, in which the parties work together to identify and solve problems. Cordner (1996) suggests citizens can take a greater role in public safety than has been typical over the past few decades, and other public and private agencies can leverage their resources and authority toward solving public safety problems. While mindful of the fact there are legal and safety limitations on how extensive a role citizens can play in "coproducing" public safety, Cordner (1996, p. 6) argues ". . . it is a mistake for the police to try to assume the entire burden for controlling crime and disorder." Using "citizen police academies" to train citizens to patrol their neighborhoods; enforcing building codes; being involved with nuisance abatement; and working with landlords and tenants are just a few of the ways that officers can partner with citizens to address problems.

The final component of the tactical dimension of COP is *problem solving,* which Cordner (1996, p. 7) explains as follows:

> Community policing urges the adoption of a problem solving orientation toward policing, as opposed to the incident-oriented approach . . . Naturally, emergency calls must still be handled right away and officers will still spend much of their time handling individual incidents. Whenever possible, howev-

er, officers should search for the underlying conditions that give rise to single and multiple incidents. When such conditions are identified, officers should try to affect them as a means of controlling and preventing future incidents. [O]fficers should strive to have more substantive and meaningful impact than occurs from 15-minute treatments of individual calls for service.

Cordner (1996, p. 7) offers the following as "promising approaches" to problem solving:

- *The SARA Process*–many departments use the SARA model (scanning, analysis, response, assessment) as a guide to the problem solving process for all kinds of crime and non-crime problems.
- *Guardians*–when searching for solutions to problems, it is often helpful to identify so-called "guardians," people who have an incentive or the opportunity to help rectify the problem (e.g., property owners or school principals).
- *Beat Meetings*–some departments utilize meetings between neighborhood residents and their beat officers to identify problems, analyze them, and brainstorm possible solutions.
- *Hot Spots*–many departments analyze calls for service to identify locations that have disproportionate numbers of calls arising from them and then do problem solving to try to lower the call volume in those places.
- *Multi-Agency Teams*–some jurisdictions use problem solving teams comprised not just of police, but also of representatives of other agencies (public works, sanitation, parks and recreation, code enforcement, etc.) so that an array of information and resources can be brought to bear once problems are identified.

THE ADMINISTRATIVE DIMENSION OF COP. The final dimension of COP, according to Cordner (1996, p. 8), is the administrative. He describes this dimension as follows:

It is important to recognize an Organizational Dimension that surrounds community policing and greatly affects its implementation. [T]o support and facilitate community policing, police departments often consider a variety of changes in organization, administration, management, and supervision. The elements of the organizational dimension are not really part of community policing *per se,* but they are frequently crucial to its successful implementation.

Cordner suggests the three most important elements of the administrative dimension of COP are *structure, management,* and *information.*

Cordner (1996, p. 8) argues that restructuring police agencies to facilitate and support implementation of the philosophical, strategic, and tactical elements is one of the most important aspects of COP. Departments can facili tate this restructuring by using the following processes and activities:

- *Decentralization*–departments can delegate authority and responsibility more widely so that commanders, supervisors, and officers can act more independently and be more responsive.
- *Flattening*–departments can reduce the number of layers of hierarchy to improve communication and reduce waste, rigidity and bureaucracy.
- *De-specialization*–departments can reduce the number of specialized units and personnel so that more resources are devoted to direct delivery of services to the general public.
- *Teams*–A department's efficiency and effectiveness can improve by getting employees to work together as teams to perform work, solve problems, or look for ways of improving quality.
- *Civilianization*–Departments can reclassify positions currently held by sworn personnel so non-sworn personnel may hold them. Doing so allows both cost savings and better utilization of sworn personnel.

Management, according to Cordner (1996, p. 9), involves styles of leadership and supervision that emphasize organizational culture and values over written rules and formal discipline. Although COP does not advocate abandoning formal rules, its orientation is such that managers resort to them much less often to maintain control over subordinates. Practices consistent with this new orientation include mission statements guiding departments' decision making. Departments would also make continuous use of strategic planning to insure resources and energy remain focused on achieving the department's mission and adhering to its core values. Supervisors spend more time "coaching" and mentoring subordinates than simply reviewing their paperwork or enforcing rules. The department empowers subordinates by rewarding them for reasonable risk-taking behavior that furthered larger organizational goals. Superiors use selective discipline, whereby disciplinary processes distinguish intentional from unintentional errors and between employee actions violating core values versus those that merely violate technical rules. By using these methods, departments can successfully integrate a new style of management that facilitates the type of organizational change necessary for implementing COP.

Finally, Cordner (1996, pp. 9–10) suggests that "doing" COP and managing it effectively require departments to compile and then use certain types of *information* that have not traditionally been available in most, if not all, police departments. In the never-ending quality vs. quantity debate, for example, community policing tends to emphasize quality. This emphasis on quality reveals itself in many areas, such as avoiding traditional "bean-counting" procedures (such as arrests made or tickets issued) to measure success, and focusing on how well officers handle calls, rather than how quickly they are handled. Further, the geographic focus of community policing increases the need for detailed information based on neighborhoods (or even blocks) as the unit of analysis. The emphasis on problem solving highlights the need for information systems that aid in identifying and analyzing a variety of community-level problems.

Several aspects of police administration under COP that have implications for information include:

- *Performance Appraisals*–individual officers can be evaluated on the quality of the their community policing and problem solving activities, and perhaps on results achieved, instead of on traditional performance indicators (tickets issued, arrests made, calls handled, etc.).
- *Program Evaluation*–police programs and strategies are evaluated more on their effectiveness (outcomes, results, quality) than their efficiency (effort, outputs, quantity).
- *Departmental Assessment*–the police agency's overall performance can be measured and assessed on the basis of a wide variety of indicators (including customer satisfaction, fear levels, problem solving, etc.) instead of a narrow band of traditional indicators (reported crime, response time, number of arrests, etc.).
- *Information Systems*–an agency's information systems need to collect and produce information on the whole range of the police function, not just on enforcement and call-handling activities, in order to support more quality-oriented appraisal, evaluation and assessment efforts.

In summary, Cordner (1996) addressed the "devil in the details" of COP by comprehensively discussing what he views as the key dimensional aspects of COP and the subcomponents of each dimension. He also provided specific examples of methods departments can use to implement the key philosophical, strategic, tactical, and organizational dimensions of COP. Cordner's description provides a sound foundation to understanding what COP is, the changes that must occur to implement it, and the strategies and activities that will bring COP to the community.

Importantly, Cordner (1996, p.1) also describes what COP is not. He argues, for example, that COP is *not* a panacea, the answer to all the problems facing any one department. He does suggest that COP is one possible answer to *some* of the problems modern police agencies face, and that it may be *an* answer to *some* of the problems facing any one department.

He also argues that COP is not completely new, that some departments or individual officers report that they are already doing it or even that they have *always* practiced COP. While this may be true, there are specific aspects of community policing that *are* new and very few agencies can factually claim they have fully adopted the entire gamut of COP.

Third, Cordner argues that COP is not "hug a thug"–it is not antilaw enforcement or anticrime fighting. COP does not seek to turn police work into social work, but is in fact even more serious about reducing crime and disorder than has been the superficial brand of incident-oriented "911 policing" that most departments have been doing for the past few decades.

Finally, Cordner argues that COP is not a "cookbook" that contains an ironclad and precise definition of community policing, nor a set of specific activities that *must* always be included. Rather, COP sets forth a set of universally applicable principles and elements, but is flexible enough to realize that their implementation must vary because jurisdictions and police agencies have differing needs and circumstances.

Given this review of the components of COP, the immediate question becomes the extent COP "makes sense" for campus law enforcement agencies, given their history, organizational characteristics, and general mission. We address that question in the next section.

COP on the Campus:
A New Model for Policing College and University Campuses

One could argue that compared to municipal police, the campus police are better positioned to implement community policing. Compared to major municipal police forces, for example, campus agencies have traditionally relied to a larger degree on a proactive, crime-prevention-oriented approach. Bordner and Peterson (1983), Gelber (1972), and Peak (1995) have all argued that campus police traditionally overemphasized their "service-related" duties compared to their law enforcement duties and relied more on foot patrol, resulting in greater interaction between them and students, faculty, and staff. These historical forces are certainly favorable to the development of a new model like COP that actually formalizes their importance.

Chief Eric Jackson at the University of North Texas Police Department has presented what he sees as the "key" aspects of traditional law enforcement, community policing, and campus policing (Jackson, 1992). Table 13.1 presents his schematic, showing how the police mandate, police authority, the police role, police/community relations, and political considerations operate to place campus police in a favorable position to implement COP.

As shown in Table 13.1, Jackson sees major similarities between COP and campus policing, including such keys as the role of the community in crime control, department accountability, and in the authority granted the agency. Indeed, Jackson's point is that because of its context, the issues campus law enforcement face are far similar to those relating to community policing than to the traditional, reactive-based law enforcement of the 1950s and 1960s and thus make it easier for campus agencies to formally adopt the tenants of

Table 13.1
A COMPARATIVE ANALYSIS OF POLICE MODELS

Philosophy	Traditional Law Enforcement	Community Policing	Campus Policing
Police Mandate	Control crime via rapid response deterrence, apprehension	Control crime as means to insure community order, peace, and security	Law enforcement and disciplinary actions as means of control to insure campus order, peace, and security
	Reactive policing	Preventive policing	Preventive & reactive policing
Police Authority	Authority from law	Authority from society & community granted through law	Authority primarily from faculty, staff and students; granted through regulations and law
	Agency of the criminal justice system	Agency of municipal government and community	Agency of the university administration and campus community
Police Role	Legally defined/ limited by law	Socially defined, expanded role	Environmentally defined
	Distinct and separate from citizens	Legal and social agencies	Legal, educational, and social agencies
	Law enforcement officers/professional crime fighters	One of a number of agencies of order	Peacekeeping/educational professionals
	Addresses crime only	Addresses crime and social problems that affect crime	Addresses crime and environmental problems that affect crime
Relationship Between Community & Police	Passive role	Active role	Active role
	Supportive but adjunct to police	Shared responsibility for crime and social order	Shared responsibility for crime and social order
	Community as system of support	Community as client	Community as client
Politics	Apolitical	Political: mediate interests	Political: mediate interests & take advocacy role

continued

Table 13.1
A COMPARATIVE ANALYSIS OF POLICE MODELS

Philosophy	*Traditional Law Enforcement*	*Community Policing*	*Campus Policing*
Politics *(continued)*	Police and political issues kept separate	Responsible to community and political representatives	Responsible to community and board of trustees
	Fiscal accountability primarily	Policy and operational accountability	Total accountability

Source: Adapted from Jackson (1992) as cited in Lanier (1995).

COP.

As Bromley (2007) and others (Bordner & Peterson, 1983; Gelber, 1972; Peak, 1995; Sloan, 1992) have reported, campus police agencies have undergone a metamorphosis during the past 30 years, adopting organizational and operational characteristics that echo those used by local police agencies. The question is to what extent have campus police agencies adopted/begun adopting COP as their "new" organizational model in the same way that municipal agencies have done? What evidence is there that "COP on campus" is becoming widely used?

Evidence for COP on the Campus

Several case studies reveal that major universities in the U.S. have adopted COP. For example, the Director of Public Safety at Michigan State University (MSU) strongly endorsed the community policing concept for campus police back in the late 1980s and fully implemented COP with all Department of Public Safety (DPS) officers in 1987 (Trojanowicz, Benson, & Trojanowicz, 1988). The plan involved dividing the MSU campus into three large segments and assigning "teams" comprised of command and line officers to specific districts in each segment. The teams actively recruited students and staff to assist with the program. They also set up "mini-stations" in the larger dormitories, conducted surveys and needs-assessments to determine the most pressing problems in each area, and jointly developed strategies and solutions with students and campus employees.

The University of Washington at Seattle has also implemented community policing. Unlike Michigan State University, officers at the University of Washington make extensive use of bicycle patrols as part of their community policing strategy. The department reported successes with improved public relations, decreased response time, increased patrols of secluded areas, lowered operating expenses, and a boosting of officer morale while improving officers' physical health (Espinosa & Wittmier, 1991).

Virginia Commonwealth University (VCU) implemented community policing in the early 1990s involving its nearly 50 sworn officers (Carlson, 1991). The plan called for officers to organize Local Management Groups comprised of university members who regularly met to devise ways to increase positive interaction between students and the police, and who developed and distributed a survey to help identify specific problem areas. Second, the department revised patrol officer job descriptions and hiring criterion to reflect COP principles. The department recruited student volunteers to staff a Corps of Preventive Specialists (COPS) and serve on a campus watch program. Training in the principles of COP and officer evaluation based on those principles also became central to the VCU community policing effort. Finally, similar to the MSU model, the department divided the VCU campus into eight sectors with officers assigned to specific areas on a permanent basis. Officers are responsible for "designing, initiating, and maintaining various crime-prevention programs within their assigned sectors" (Carlson, 1991, p. 23).

The University of Alabama at Birmingham (UAB) is another university that implemented a community policing strategy on its campus during the 1990s. As part of the implementation process, the department created multiple "precincts" housed in the large, on-campus hospital and in two dormitories. Officers routinely patrol the campus on foot and using bicycles and they organized a "campus watch" program, led by a crime prevention specialist and staffed by volunteers drawn from the ranks of students, faculty members, and staff.

Finally, Bromley (2007) chronicles a near decade-long initiative to implement COP on the campus of the University of South Florida. Included in his analysis is discussion of how the department addressed the various philosophical, strategic, tactical, and administrative dimensions of COP and overcame multiple implementation hurdles. While a "case study," it nonetheless offers insightful commentary on the inherent difficulties associated with organizational change.

Anecdotal evidence thus suggests that COP is "catching on" among campus police agencies. However, until recently, no large-scale study of the extent campus agencies have adopted COP had been done. Bromley's (2003) analysis was the first such undertaking, wherein he compared campus agencies with their municipal counterparts to explore the extent the two groups either had begun implementing or had completed implementation of COP.

In his study, Bromley (2003) sought to answer two key questions: what is the current level of campus involvement in COP and how does that level of involvement compare to COP efforts undertaken in municipal agencies? To answer these questions, Bromley (2003) used data collected by a Bureau of Justice Statistics survey (the Law Enforcement Management and Administrative Statistics, also known as the LEMAS project) that included over 1,100 municipal police departments and nearly 150 campus police departments. Bromley (2003) then explored the presence of three aspects of COP in the two groups of agencies: (1) administrative support and department leadership (e.g., extent a written COP plan was created; whether officers were assigned to COP-related tasks, whether officers were evaluated using COP principles, and the extent of COP training officers received); (2) community outreach (e.g., the extent community members had been trained in COP and whether community partnerships had formed to address specific problems); and (3) operational strategies (e.g., assignment of patrol officers and detectives to specific geographic areas and use of foot and bicycle patrol).

ADMINISTRATIVE SUPPORT AND DEPARTMENT LEADERSHIP. Bromley (2003) found that about 25 percent of the campus agencies and 20 percent of the municipal agencies surveyed had a written community policing plan in place, while just over 50 percent of each agency type indicated it had "unwritten" COP plans in place. Further, an equal percentage of campus and municipal departments (72% and 73%, respectively) indicated they had officers assigned full-time to COP-based activities (e.g., problem solving or creating partnerships with citizens). About one-half of the agencies (50% of city agencies and 52% of campus agencies) provided at least eight hours of COP-based training to new recruits and about 28 percent of campus agencies and 32 percent of municipal agencies indicated they provided in-service training in COP for officers. Just over one-third of both groups of agencies (36% of municipal agencies and 32% of campus agencies) encouraged their officers to become involved in problem-solving partnerships with the community, while 22 percent of agencies in each group indicated they included collaborative problem solving projects in officers' annual evaluations.

COMMUNITY OUTREACH INITIATIVES. The survey also asked agencies about their involvement in community outreach projects, including whether the agency had formed problem-solving partnerships with citizens and/or other agencies, and whether the agency had trained citizens in COP. Bromley (2003) reported that 31 percent of the municipal agencies and 34 percent of the campus agencies had done the former, while 33 percent of the municipal agencies and 20 percent of the campus agencies had done the latter.

AGENCY OPERATIONAL STRATEGIES. Finally, Bromley (2003) assessed the extent municipal and campus departments had implemented operational strategies that supported COP. Here, he found that 53 percent of city agencies and 56 percent of campus agencies assigned patrol officers according to specific geographic locations and 10 percent of city agencies and 11 percent of campus agencies assigned detectives to specific geographic areas. Further, 55 percent of municipal agencies surveyed and 94 percent of campus agencies routinely assigned patrol officers to foot patrol, while 47 percent of city agencies and 75 percent of campus agencies routinely used bicycle patrol.

Bromley (2003) indicated the most salient results of his study were the general similarities between municipal police agencies and campus agencies in the extent they had implemented COP-based activities. He also found varying levels of commitment to key aspects of COP, indicating that both sets of agencies had (in general) failed to fully implement the organizational, strategic, and tactical changes necessitated by COP. Thus, while certain aspects of COP were common in both groups, variability in commitment indicated that campus and municipal agencies continue to "tinker" with COP, rather than fully implement it on a wholesale basis.

In summary, while anecdotal evidence shows a commitment to COP by campus police agencies, Bromley's (2003) larger-scale study shows that such a commitment is far from absolute and the level of commitment to COP by campus agencies roughly parallels the level found in municipal agencies. In some areas, such as the use of foot patrol or bicycle patrol (which would be a tactical component of COP), both sets of agencies routinely use these tactics. However, when evaluating the work of officers, few agencies included COP-based principles as a component of that evaluation. As other studies have shown (e.g., Bromley & Reaves, 1998a, 1998b; Reaves & Goldberg, 1996), parallels between campus and municipal police agencies exist not only in their organizational structure, policies, and procedures, etc., but also in their levels of commitment to COP.

Conclusion

Community policing is seemingly the new "paradigm" in American policing fueled in part by the U.S. Justice Department adopting it as the "new" model for policing and making funds available for local agencies to hire more community policing officers. Further, various experiments in some of the tactical aspects of COP such as problem solving partnerships, foot patrol, and other components generally show positive results, which has created optimism in proponents. Finally, efforts by proponents to adequately conceptualize and define COP helped further implementation by showing that it can be more "reality than rhetoric."

Concurrently, one could also argue that based on contemporary as well as historical factors, campus police are in an excellent position to implement community policing successfully. First, campus police have already relied on more proactive, preventive measures than have their municipal counterparts. Second, campus police are more readily in a position to interact more with their "clients," again compared to major municipal departments. Third, by their proximity to an environment of higher education they should not only be more flexible and innovative, but exposed to the most current philosophical and pragmatic police practices. Additionally, campus police have good success with utilizing paid and volunteer students (Brug, 1984).

Partly because increasing numbers of municipal police agencies are at least experimenting with COP, we expect increasing numbers of campus agencies will also do so as we move further into the twenty-first century. Because of the flexibility that COP offers, departments adopting it should be able to address such issues as officer empowerment; partnering with faculty, staff, and students to address crime and crime-related issues; more efficient use of resources; concern among members of the campus community with such issues as fear of victimization and disorders on campus; and the philosophical appeal of individualized and personalized police services.

As Carlson (1991:22) noted, the "university environment may be particularly receptive to such an approach" primarily due to "its inherent community cohesiveness." COP would seem to represent the next logical step in the evolution of campus policing and with it, the opportunity to show the campus context is the perfect "laboratory" for experimenting with innovative ways to police the community.

REFERENCES

Bayley, D. (1988). Community policing: A report from the devil's advocate. In J. Greene & S. Mastrofski (Eds.), *Community policing: Rhetoric or reality*. New York: Praeger.

Bromley, M. (2003). Comparing campus and municipal police community policing practices. *Journal of Security Administration, 26,* 37–50.

Bromley, M. (2007). The evolution of campus policing: Different models for different eras. In B. S. Fisher & J. J. Sloan (Eds.), *Campus crime: Legal, social, and policy perspectives* (2nd ed). Springfield, IL: Charles C Thomas.

Bromley, M., & Reaves, B. (1998a). Comparing campus and municipal police: The human resource dimension. *Policing: An International Journal of Police Strategies and Management, 21,* 534–546.

Bromley, M., & Reaves, B. (1998b). Comparing campus and city police operational practices. *Journal of Security Administration, 21,* 41–52.

Brown, L., & Wycoff, M. (1987). Policing Houston: Reducing fear and improving service. *Crime and Delinquency, 33,* 71–89.

Bordner, D., & Peterson, D. (1983). *Campus policing: The nature of university police work*. Lanham, MD: University Press of America.

Brug, R. C. (1984). Cal Poly maximizes use of students. *Campus Law Enforcement Journal, 14,* 45–46.

Carlson, W. (1991). Community policing at Virginia Commonwealth University: Designing strategies for a campus environment. *Campus Law Enforcement Journal, 21,* 22–25.

Cochran, J., Bromley, M., & Swando, M. (2002). Sheriff's deputies' receptivity to organizational change. *Policing: An International Journal of Police Strategies and Management, 25,* 507–529.

Community policing impacts 86 percent of U.S. population served by local police departments (2001). Retrieved September 11, 2006 from http://www.ojp.usjog. gov/bjs/pub/press/cplp99pr.htm.

Cordner, G. (1996). *Principles and elements of community policing.* Washington, DC: National Institute of Justice.

Cordner, G. (1997). Community policing: Elements and effects. In R. Dunham & G. Alpert (Eds.), *Critical issues in policing: Contemporary readings.* Prospect Heights, IL: Waveland Press.

Eck, J., & Spelman, W. (1987). Problem Solving: Problem Oriented Policing in Newport News. Washington, DC: Police Executive Research Forum.

Eck, J., & Rosenbaum, D. (1994). Effectiveness, equity, and efficiency in community policing. In D. Rosenbaum (Ed.), *The challenge of community policing: Testing the promises.* Thousand Oaks, CA: Sage.

Espinosa, G., & R. Wittmier. (1991). Police bicycle patrols: An integral part of community policing. *Campus Law Enforcement Journal, 21,* 10–13.

Fogelson, R. (1977). *Big city police.* Cambridge, MA: Harvard University Press.

Gelber, S. (1972). *The role of campus security in the college setting.* Washington, DC: United States Government Printing Office.

Goldstein, H. (1979). Improving policing: A problem-oriented approach. *Crime and Delinquency, 25,* 236–258.

Greene, J., & Mastrofski, S. (1988). *Community policing: Rhetoric or reality.* New York: Praeger.

Jackson, E. (1992). Campus police embrace community-based approach. *The Police Chief, 59,* 63–64.

Lanier, M. (1995). Community oriented policing on college campuses: Tradition, practices, and outlook. In B. Fisher & J. Sloan (Eds.), *Campus crime: Legal, social, and policy perspectives.* Springfield, IL: Charles C Thomas.

Maguire, E. (1997). Structural change in large municipal police organizations during the community policing era. *Justice Quarterly, 14,* 547–576.

Maguire, E. (2002). *Organizational structure in large police organizations: Context, complexity, and control.* Albany, NY: SUNY Press.

Maguire, E., & Mastrofski, S. (2000). Patterns of community policing in the United States. *Police Quarterly, 3,* 4–45.

Manning, P. K. (1984). Community policing. *American Journal of Police, 3,* 205–227.

Manning, P. K. (1988). Community policing as a drama of control. In J. Greene & S. Mastrofski (Eds.), *Community policing: Rhetoric or reality.* New York: Praeger.

Manning, P. K. (1989). Community policing. In R. Dunham & G. Alpert (Eds.), *Critical issues in policing.* Prospect Heights, IL: Waveland Press.

Monkkonen, E. (1981). *Police in urban America.* New York: Oxford University Press.

Reaves, B., & Goldberg, A. (1996). Census of state and local law enforcement agencies, 1996. Bulletin. NCJ 164618, United States Department of Jusitce. Washington, DC: United States Department of Justice, Office of Justice Programs.

Reis, A. (1992). Police organization in the 20th century. In M. Tonry & N. Morris (Eds.), *Modern policing.* Chicago, IL: University of Chicago Press.

Rosenbaum, D. (1994). *Community policing: Testing the promises.* Thousand Oaks, CA: Sage.

Skogan, W. (1990). *Disorder and decline: Crime and the spiral of decay in American cities.* New York: The Free Press.

Skogan, W., & Hartnett, S. (1997). *Community policing: Chicago style.* New York: Oxford University Press.

Sloan, J. (1992). The modern campus police: An analysis of their evolution, structure, and function. *American Journal of Police, 11,* 85–104.

Trojanowicz, R. (1982). *An evaluation of the neighborhood foot patrol program in Flint, Michigan.* East Lansing, MI: Michigan State University, National Center for Community Policing.

Trojanowicz, R., Benson, B., & Trojanowicz, S. (1988). *Community policing: University input into campus police policy-making.* East Lansing, MI: National Neighborhood Foot Patrol Center.

Trojanowicz, R., & Bucqueroux, B. (1990). *Community policing: A contemporary perspective.* Cincinnati, OH: Anderson.

Wilson, J., & Kelling, G. (1982). Broken windows: The police and neighborhood safety. *Atlantic Monthly, 243,* 29–38.

Zhao, S., Thurman, Q., & Lovrich, N. (1997). Community policing in the U.S.: Where are we now? *Crime and Delinquency, 43,* 345–357.

Zhao, S., Lovrich, N., & Thurman, Q. (1999). The status of community policing in American cities. *Policing: An International Journal of Police Strategies and Management, 22,* 74–92.

Chapter 14

THE EVOLUTION OF CAMPUS POLICING: DIFFERENT MODELS FOR DIFFERENT ERAS

MAX L. BROMLEY

INTRODUCTION

College campuses in America have undergone tremendous change over the last 50 years. This change has resulted in some observers suggesting that campuses today are often "cities within cities" (Bromley & Territo, 1990). Smith (1995) noted that it is not surprising that, as campuses have changed and grown, so too have the number of serious crimes occurring on them. While there is evidence suggesting that property crimes far outnumber violent crimes on campuses (Bromley, 1992; Fernandez & Lizotte, 1995; National Center for Educational Statistics, 1997), institutions of higher education (IHEs) must still be prepared to provide a high level of security for their communities. Therefore, today's campus executives recognize the necessity of having campus police forces available to provide most of the same services rendered by police departments in similar-sized municipalities (Atwell, 1988). Additionally, like their municipal counterparts, campus police agencies are increasingly adopting Community-Oriented Policing (COP) as their organizational model and basing their practices on COP principles.

Before discussing campus-based community policing efforts, it is first useful to review the development of campus police from a historical perspective. The next four sections of the chapter undertake that task by describing the various eras of campus policing from their humble beginnings to becoming "a part of the fabric of higher education" (Sloan, 1992). Subsequently, the chapter identifies and discusses the challenges facing campus police arising from the complex nature of the modern college campus. Later the chapter describes how campus police agencies have incorporated COP into their common practices. The chapter concludes with a case study of one university police department's experiences with implementing COP.

The Evolution of Campus Policing

The Watchman Era: 1700s–1800s

In early colonial times, various personnel, ranging from college presidents to faculty members, and sometimes even janitors, performed security functions at American colleges and universities. These individuals were responsible for enforcing often-lengthy lists of rules and regulations developed in an attempt to govern student lives while at school. Additional concerns with respect to security on campus included "the avoidance of fires and the protection of property from straying animals and irate town folk" (Gelber, 1972:16). Some IHEs used college professors to monitor student behaviors in dormitories and sometimes in the dining halls (Rudolph, 1962; Proctor, 1958). Brubacher and Willis (1968) cite examples from the mid-1800s where colleges used students to help enforce discipline and policies. Late in the nineteenth century, Witsil (1979: 7) noted, "some colleges created an 'Office of Proctor,' a designation for a university police officer, who was responsible for helping discharge disciplinary duties at the university."

It was not until 1894, however, that the first "official" campus police officers appeared when Yale University hired New Haven police officers to patrol its campus. The institution had experienced a series of bloody confrontations between students and townspeople and irate citizens demanded the campus do more to police student behavior. Following the recommendations of a committee composed of campus and city officials, two New Haven police officers began patrolling the Yale campus on a routine basis (Powell, 1981). Powell (1981) noted that these officers were so successful in their endeavors that the Yale campus eventually accepted them as part of its institutional setting.

The Campus Security Era: 1900–mid–1960s

The primary focus of campus security departments and their officers during the early part of the twentieth century continued to be on two primary areas: (1) student misconduct and, (2) property protection. According to Esposito and Stormer (1989), officers during this era wore the two hats of "campus watchman" and assistant deans of students. Powell (1981) writes that alcohol consumption was a campus problem, as it was elsewhere in the United States in the late 1920s and 1930s and that much of the property destruction and other student disturbances during the 1940s and 1950s on campus were often alcohol related. Thus, the role of "monitoring" student conduct by campus security officials continued well into the twentieth century.

Following World War II, American colleges experienced tremendous growth in student population and institutional size. The G. I. Bill made it possible for large numbers of returning veterans to attend college for the first time and created great impetus for the extension of higher education throughout the United States. According to Shoemaker (1995), this growth in campus population led to other typical community problems including crime. The existing campus security departments were often ill prepared for the rapidly changing college environment (Shoemaker, 1995).

During the 1950s and early 1960s, campus security departments remained organizationally attached to physical plant departments, reflecting the continued emphasis on their role in protecting campus and personal property. According to Kassinger (1971), this administrative arrangement failed to recognize what was needed in terms of professional law enforcement on the growing college campuses. Sloan (1992) notes that, during this time, many campus security directors and campus security officers were former city or military police and thus had professional law enforcement experience. Hiring ex-municipal police officers would be one of several steps taken by university administrators in an attempt to upgrade the quality of campus security services.

A second organizational approach used by some IHEs was for them to have security departments organizationally linked to the Dean of Students office (Powell, 1981). This reflected another emphasis often placed on the security department's role, that of student conduct enforcer. It was also during the 1950s and early 1960s that the Higher Education Section of the Campus Safety Association and the International Association of Campus Security Directors would be formed (Gelber, 1972). The International Association of Campus Security Directors would later evolve into the International Association of Campus Law Enforcement Administrators (IACLEA) recognized today as the primary professional organization for campus police chiefs and other high-ranking officials.

The Era of Professionalization: Late 1960s–Early 1980s

Events of the late 1960s and 1970s, including major civil disturbances and the anti-Vietnam war movement, led to dramatic change in the organizational structure and role of campus security departments in higher education. Social change related to the civil rights movement and protests, both violent and nonviolent, often created problems for college presidents who frequently found their existing campus security departments ill prepared to deal with these serious issues. While some IHEs summoned local law enforcement agencies to assist during these times, the approach often led to an exacerbation of the conflict (Skolnick, 1969). McDaniel (1971) suggests that university officials' failure to handle campus disorders was because they lacked a professionally trained campus police department.

Leaders seeking to change the role of the campus police recognized that for campus law enforcement to be truly effective, it would have to have a assume a role consistent with the educational expectations of higher education while simultaneously adopting the best practices of law enforcement. Individuals such as Bill McDaniel of Wayne State University, Ed Kassinger of the University of Georgia, Richard Bernitt of Michigan State University, and Bill Tanner of Florida State University were part of the leadership seeking professionalism in campus policing (Sims, 1971). These emerging leaders recognized that campus policing needed a new model, one that would eventually find a home in the higher education community and one that became what Sloan (1992) referred to as the "birth of the modern campus police department." Key to this model was training off campus officers by local and state police academies; such training would provide legitimacy to campus law enforcement.

During the 1970s and through the 1980s, the professionalization of campus policing would further accelerate. The 1970s new state statutes passed that granted to public colleges and universities the right to have sworn officers on their staff (Gelber, 1972). During the 1980s, experts explicitly recognized campus police departments were operating as professional law enforcement organizations. They found these agencies: (1) had become more organizationally autonomous; (2) resembled municipal departments in structure and operations; (3) enhanced education and training levels for their officers; (4) developed career paths for personnel; and (5) had become an accepted part of campus life at American colleges and universities (Peak, 1988, 1995; Sloan, 1992).

Experts noted other similarities developing between campus and municipal police agencies. Jacobs and O'Meara (1980) observed the equipment and technology (e.g., handguns, riot helmets, and tape recording devices) that campus police routinely used was comparable to that used by city police. The 1980s saw the introduction of nonlethal weapons, such as pepper spray to campus police (Sloan, 1992). Peak (1988, 1989) found many campus departments during the 1980s had rank structures and organizational hierarchies that closely resembled those found in local police departments. Likewise, membership in national police organizations, achieving accreditation status, and supporting professional growth of campus police officers through additional training were also indicators of the continued professionalization of campus police. When Bromley and Reaves (1998) compared campus and municipal police departments on a variety of operational and human resource issues using U.S. Justice Department data, they found additional evidence supporting the notion that strong parallels exist between campus police and their municipal counterparts.

The Community Era of Campus Policing: Late 1980s–Present

During the 1980s and 1990s, the evolution of campus police continued because of influences both internal to, and outside of higher education. The sheer growth in the number of students enrolled in IHEs and ever-increasing number of colleges and universities were obvious influences. According to the Digest of Education Statistics (1991), by 1990, there were approximately 14 million students attending college (triple the number of students that attended college in 1960) and almost 3,500 IHEs (up approximately 1,500 institutions since 1960). Today, the largest of the campuses, (those with enrollments of 25,000 students and above) often have daily on-campus populations that exceed 50,000 people; usually have large special events centers and/or football stadiums on their property; often have medical centers or hospitals on campus; and nearly half have a nuclear facility on its campus (Reaves & Goldberg, 1996).

Given this growth, it is not surprising that reports of serious crimes occurring on college campuses were common during the last few decades (see Lederman, 1994, 1995). If the 1970s saw the development of campus policing as a profession, the 1980s saw its maturation as a profession (Bordner & Petersen, 1983; Peak, 1988; Sloan, 1992). Some authorities have even suggested that by the 1980s, campus communities had come to expect full service policing from campus departments (Atwell, 1988). Legal scholars, such as Smith (1991), noted that the threat of serious campus crime had become very real and thus gave impetus to insuring that campus police had full law enforcement authority and responsibility.

In addition to the growing recognition that a full-service campus police agency would be the best choice to handle crime and security challenges brought about by the growth and increasing complexity of IHEs, forces outside the campus boundaries would further influence the changing campus police model. The legal arena would provide a two-pronged impetus for the evolving campus police profession.

During the 1980s, victims of their families filed a series of well-documented, highly publicized, and successful lawsuits against colleges and universities alleging that inadequate campus security contributed to the death or injury of the victims. Smith (1988, 1995), Bromley (1992), and others documented the impact these high-profile civil lawsuits had on college and university executive decision makers. Rightly or wrongly, litigants viewed the campus police department as the primary organizational entity charged with insuring a safe and secure campus. Therefore, the courts would exert pressure on campus executives to have adequate security programs in place, starting with a professional full-service police agency.

Congress and state legislatures also played a role in the continued professionalization of campus police. At both the federal and state levels of government, more attention than ever was focused on campus crime. Although research suggested many campuses are actually safer than their surrounding communities (Bromley, 1992; Fernandez & Lizotte, 1995), when a homicide or a rape occurs on a college campus, citizens, the courts, and even lawmakers have strong reactions. Congressional passage of the *Student Right-to-Know and Campus Security Act of 1990* (now known as the *Jeanne Clery Disclosure of Campus Security Policy and Campus Crime Statistics Act*) and enactment of statutes in 14 states (Seng, 1995) resulted in new policies requiring institutional disclosure of campus crime and arrest data and security policy information (Seng, 1995; Smith, 1995). These statutory requirements, in turn, had a direct impact on campus police organizations; legislative mandates gave additional emphasis to the responsibilities of the campus police.

One could thus argue that given the successful lawsuits brought against IHEs combined with "campus crime" statutes enacted by a variety of legislative bodies, the standard of "adequate security" on the college campus became much higher than that required of a municipality. If that argument is accurate, the role of campus police should continue to evolve to meet those expectations. There is simply no municipal parallel to the legal and legislative mandates now required of campus police agencies.

Given the relatively high expectation of providing adequate security, coupled with the increasing complexity of IHEs, campus police have continued to evolve in the mid 1980s and beyond. It was simply not sufficient to adopt a professional/crime control model within the campus community. Since the 1980s, many police agencies in America have been reshaping their philosophy and direction toward "community policing" (Goldstein, 1987). While many definitions exist for this new model, Trojanowicz and Carter (1988) observed that two key aspects of COP are that it is proactive and looks to reduce not only crime but also fear of victimization. Other characteristics of the COP model include a closer degree of cooperation between police and community members in finding ways to mutually deal with crime. In this evolving model, the police actively are involved with the community and often assign officers to specific locations for long periods to work closely with community members.

As previously noted, campus police have traditionally served a unique role within the campus environment. Not only are the campus police expected to provide professional law enforcement services, they also routinely interact with law-abiding campus community members such as students, staff, and faculty. Peak (1995) suggests the campus police view campus community members as "clients" who are served. Clearly, this relationship between the campus police and its community clients provides a framework for the development and implementation of community-oriented policing practices. Later in this chapter, examples of these practices will be described in some detail.

The preceding sections identified the various eras in the continuing evolution of campus policing. Each era reflected the role of the campus police at a particular historical point. To understand the currently evolving campus-policing model, it is first necessary to examine the uniqueness of the contemporary campus community. As Peak (1995) suggests, because the campus community is relatively small geographically and inhabited by a somewhat transitory but educated population, the context presents campus police an opportunity to experiment with and be innovative in their practices. The following section examines the uniqueness of the campus community and explores whether campus policing will evolve using a more flexible, adaptive approach to fulfill its role—namely COP.

The Modern College Campus: A Challenge for Campus Police

While the nature and extent of crime on college campuses is an important factor in determining the provision of campus police services, there are other major factors to consider when assessing how campus police are organized, as well as their tactics. This section provides an overview of the various features of a typical residential college or university campus, such as population demographics, its structural characteristics, and activities that individually and collectively affect the delivery of campus police services. Campuses may also vary according to utilization of campus facilities, and by whether people consider the location a "main" or "branch/satellite" campus. The following subsections describe these factors and the challenges they present to campus police.

The Nature and Extent of Campus Crime

Over the past several decades, there has been a growing body of research regarding the nature and extent of crime occurring on college campuses. Media sources have highlighted the most serious types of violent crime, such as sexual assault and homicide, occurring on campus (Lederman, 1993, 1995; Lively, 1996, 1997; Ordovensky, 1990; Palmer, 1993). While such violence does occur, and law enforcement should aggressively investigate such incidents and should be publicly reported, other authorities note that campuses are not necessarily as dangerous as portrayed in the media (see Brantingham, Brantingham, & Seagrave, 1995).

The majority of crimes reported to campus police are property-related offenses (Bromley, 1992; IACLEA, 1997; Lizotte & Fernandez, 1993; Reaves & Goldberg, 1996; Sloan, 1994). With respect to sexual assault, research has long shown this crime is often unreported to police officials (Territo et al., 1998). Hart (2003), using National Crime Victimization Survey (NCVS) data, found that between 1995 and 2000, only 12 percent of college women who were victims of rape/sexual assault reported the crime to police. Hart (2003) also found that nonstrangers committed 74 percent of the rapes/sexual assaults perpetrated against college students, a finding with obvious implications for campus police. Hart (2003) did find, however, college students experienced a lower rate of violent (rape, robbery and aggravated assaults) victimization compared to nonstudents ages 18–24. Finally, Hart (2003) reported that most student victimization occurred off campus.

The results of studies such as Hart's are important to the campus police in their efforts to educate campus community members regarding potential violence. It is also important for campus administrators to know as much as possible about the nature and extent of crime on their respective campuses. Data from crime reports, victimization surveys, and from campus departments such as student health services and victims' services can be useful in developing proactive police services shaped by extent victimization patterns revealed (Bromley & Fisher, 2002).

Demographic Features of College Campuses

The modern American postsecondary education institution's complexity is partially due to factors such as the size of enrollment and the number of facilities present on campus. Its complexity is also a function of additional variables such as the demographics of its community members, structural aspects of its campus, and the nature of ongoing activities on that campus. Understanding these factors and projecting future changes in them will have an impact on the ability to provide adequate police services to the university community.

A comprehensive campus security program must take into account a student population containing more women than men or a rapidly growing minority population. It must also consider an expansion in international student enrollment or an increase in "nontraditional" students coming to campus to start or continue their education. Additionally, the number of "night students" and the division of full-time and part-time students on the campus will be important considerations in determining overall security plans for a campus. According to Fernandez and Lizotte (1995), the diversity of a campus population directly affects security resources and potential risk.

Physical Features

A comprehensive security policy must also take into account the physical characteristics of a campus. For example, some campuses are public and therefore are relatively "open" to campus community members as well as nonaffiliates. Other institutions are privately controlled and more restrictive in allowing public access to facilities and limiting hours of operation of those campus facilities. Whether a campus is "residential" in nature or predominantly "commuter" would likewise be of importance in campus policing issues and will certainly influence an institution's security planning.

Lizotte and Fernandez (1995) note that security strategies and crime prevention education and programming efforts must take into account the previously mentioned demographic and physical factors. For example, Lizotte and Fernandez (1995) suggest that certain common crimes, such as rape and larceny, occur more frequently on residential campuses than on commuter campuses. On the other hand, commuter campuses have higher rates of motor vehicle theft (Lizotte & Fernandez, 1995).

The geographic location of a college is also important in underscoring the diverse nature of many campuses. Brantingham et al. (1995) have noted that specific campus locations directly affect a campus's overall crime rate. Because urban campuses often border large neighborhoods, the pool of prospective offenders would be large and thus such campuses might have higher crime rates than campuses located in rural settings. Research by Fox and Hellman (1985) supported this hypothesis. They found crime rates of urban campuses were higher if the campus was located adjacent to a lower socioeconomic demographic area within a city (see also Brantingham et al., 1995).

Campus Utilization

Brantingham et al. (1995) suggested IHEs can be described based on the degree students, faculty, and staff utilized the campus and its facilities. Brantingham et al. (1995) hypothesized that utilization of the campus and its facilities will be associated with daily macro-movement patterns of campus community members. The campus "user" categories they developed included "major," "moderate," and "minimal" user. At one end of the user-continuum, "major users" are students who make daily use of the campus as a residence or class/study facility and who attend many extracurricular activities there. A "major user" campus would be one with a large residential population, a significant number of classroom facilities, sports complex for football or basketball, and a multipurpose facility for concerts and plays. Brantingham et al. (1995) suggested the "major user" type campus should experience higher crime rates compared to the other categories of college campuses. At least one study supports associating the "major user" type of higher rates of campus crime. Specifically, in a study of college faculty victimization at a single urban institution, Wooldridge, Cullen, and Latessa (1995) found faculty members increased the risk of victimization when they were frequently on campus at night and on weekends making use of facilities.

At the other end of the user category continuum, the "minimal user" campus is one where students or staff members come to campus only when attending class or working and engage in few other on-campus activities. Brantingham et al. (1995) suggested less victimization would occur on a "minimal user" type campus. Therefore, in security planning for an institution, the campus police should take into consideration how people use a campus and its facilities on a typical day.

Campus Facilities

As campus police develop their security plans, they need also consider the number, complexity, and function of different facilities on the campus. As noted earlier, Reaves and Goldberg (1995) found that some of the largest campuses have medical centers/hospitals and special events centers attracting thousands of visitors/patrons. These facilities also draw on- and off-campus clientele. Similarly, a large sports stadium or basketball arena also draws on- and off-campus visitors. Hosting numerous large-scale public events or serving large numbers of medical patients requires customized police responses that go well beyond normal day-to-day police operations.

Persons unfamiliar with today's college environments might be surprised to see the number of nonacademic facilities providing essential daily services to campus constituents and guests. For example, today's college campuses have retail food service operations such as Subway® or Burger King®, credit unions serving as comprehensive banks, and convenience-type stores providing round-the-clock service for on-campus residents. ATM machines are often located on college campuses and large parking garages accommodate parking needs and save valuable horizontal campus property. While each of these facilities provides useful services to campus community members and visitors, they also represent potential risks as crime targets.

Main vs. Branch/Satellite Campuses

Lanier (1995) suggested an additional consideration in campus security planning involves accounting for sites in addition to a "main campus." One example would be the University of South Florida (USF) whose main campus is located in the suburbs of Tampa and enrolls 37,000 students, including 4,000 on-campus residents. A second, smaller, nonresidential campus is located in a downtown St. Petersburg business district. US Highway 41 (a major north/south corridor) divides a third campus located in Sarasota. This campus is located immediately adjacent to a regional airport and has a small residential population. Finally, USF has another campus that shares physical facilities with a community college in Lakeland, Florida. Security planning for USF thus must not only consider the general needs of the campuses, such as selecting security systems for buildings, but must also consider the unique needs of each campus.

When considering the appropriate level of police services for a "main" or "branch/satellite" campus, decision makers need to consider virtually all of the previously mentioned factors (e.g., population demographics, structural features, types of facilities). For example, if a "branch" campus offers primarily evening classes to older students, this presents a different challenge to the police than a "main" campus that has several thousand residential students. The demographic and physical characteristics of the "main" or "branch" campus will also drive, to some extent, the nature and delivery of crime prevention/public education programs.

The Evolving Community-Oriented
Policing Model on College Campuses

The diverse and complex nature of the current college environment contributes to the challenge of providing appropriate police services. As described below, many campus police agencies either have adopted or are adopting COP due to its flexibility and adaptability to the campus context. Successful municipal police agencies recognize that there may be considerable variation between the crime rate and quality of life issues in different neighborhoods and COP practices allow them to "tailor" their responses according to specific needs. Campus police must likewise recognize various factors, such as those identified in this section, that influence the nature and variety of campus police services.

For example, if a campus slowly changes from primarily a "minimal user" category institution to one that adds several thousand resident students, the change has serious implications for the police in terms of types of crimes, educational outreach efforts, and crime prevention efforts. Should a campus decide to extend its programs in an effort to offer more evening or weekend courses, build more 24-hour recreational facilities, or add an on-campus day care center, the campus police will face additional challenges. As change in higher education is continuous and inevitable, so too will be subsequent challenges confronting campus police officials. Anticipating and planning for the changes and using creative approaches to policing on campuses will be major contributors to the continuing evolution of campus policing. The strength of COP as a model for campus police is that its flexibility allows departments to change to meet the changing safety and security needs of the campus.

Viewing the Campus as a Community

We have seen that the complexity of the contemporary campus community has implications for both campus law enforcement planning and practice. Further, modern campuses may be viewed as "communities within communities" or as distinct entities. Sloan (1995) has argued that while there may be some differences between a campus community and a typical nonacademic community, they are similar in a number of ways. For example, most campuses have a fixed geographic location (Sloan, 1995). Fences, distinctive entryways, and signage delineate campus-specific property and create boundaries (even if only symbolic) between the campus and surrounding communities. Even in downtown, urban campuses, there is usually an effort made to separate the campus property from the surrounding area.

Additionally, the campus community members have common ties in a level of social interaction (Sloan, 1995). Residential students live and often eat in common areas. Commuters may belong to student organization or honor societies or attend extracurricular events on the campus. Faculty members usually have offices arranged according to their discipline or department; they work together on committees; belong to university governance groups; and attend cultural or sporting events with fellow faculty members and students. Support staff members frequently work in teams, socialize in break rooms, and likewise take advantage of campus special events. Students often stay at a given college four or five years, while some staff and faculty members spend their entire careers at one institution. The investment of time, mental and physical energy on the part of campus community members also contributes to a sense of "community."

An Overview of Community-Oriented Policing

If the "typical" college campus is a community, then campus police must adopt appropriate philosophical, organizational, and tactical orientations. COP affords campus departments the opportunity to do so. According to Peak and Glensor (1999), in the mid-1980s, many municipal police departments began moving from a reactive, incident-driven approach to policing to one that demonstrates a greater willingness to work in collaboration with key community stakeholders in order to reduce crime and to improve the quality of life. Thus, the police become "problem solvers" working in collaboration with neighborhood residents to address not only crime but quality of life issues, at least some of which are also tied to levels of crime in the community (e.g., abandoned buildings serving as "crack houses"). This change in the overall philosophy of policing has been steadily evolving for the last 20 years.

While it is not without its critics (e.g., Zhao, Lorvich, & Thurman, 1999), there is a growing body of research demonstrating COP practices are prevalent in many police agencies across the country. For example, according to the Bureau of Justice Statistics, the majority of police agencies serving cities of all population categories had full-time community policing officers and these numbers have increased since 1997 (Reaves, forthcoming). Almost 50 percent of local police departments provided in-service training in COP, and 31 percent provided COP training to new recruits in the academy (Reaves, forthcoming).

In addition to noting that municipal police agencies practice community policing, Cochran, Bromley, and Landis (1999) suggested many sheriffs' departments might be well suited for involvement in community policing. As elected officials, most sheriffs understand the need to work effectively with community members. If the Office of the Sheriff is an "open system," there is a continuous flow of information between the agency and the community. Sheriffs must be concerned with both crime and quality of life issues important to citizens, thus making a COP philosophy almost a necessity. Discussion now turns to the applicability of a COP philosophy on a college campus.

Beyond Traditional Policing for Campuses

Some authorities suggest that in order to provide adequate security consistent with the overall mission of an institution of higher education, the campus needs more than the traditional practices of a professional police department. Jacobs and O'Meara (1980:293) emphasized the need to include community members in providing safety on campus, ". . . students, faculty, and employee involvement in the issues of crime and deviancy should be emphasized. Security forces should articulate the special norms and institutional patterns of the university." Early in the professional development of campus policing, leaders such as McDaniel (1971), Kassinger (1971), and Sims (1971) also emphasized the importance of the "service" role of campus police. These individuals felt campus police should emphasize their service role over that of their law enforcement role to gain long-term acceptance within the academic setting.

To underscore the service role, some campus departments combined police, traffic/parking and environmental safety services under the organizational title of a Public Safety Department. Michigan State University, the University of Georgia, Pennsylvania State University, Florida State University, and the University of South Florida are examples of major universities that developed the "department of public safety concept" in the early days of the professionalization of campus policing. One could view the concept of a public safety department as an important predecessor of today's COP efforts on college campuses in much the same way "team policing" practiced in the 1970s preceded today's municipal COP operations. Gelber (1972), and Bordner and Peterson (1983) noted the emphasis placed by campus police on crime prevention efforts and similar community service. Providing public education programs and having officers routinely interact with campus community members while engaged in foot patrol were a part of campus police actions long before the term COP was formally instituted in city departments (Jackson, 1992).

Campus police agencies can initiate crime-prevention efforts, a major part of the COP philosophy, by utilizing nondepartmental resources. For example, to enhance controls over certain campus facilities, departments such as physical plant, housing, and student services can work with the police to achieve that end (Stormer & Esposito, 1988). Bromley and Territo (1990) suggested that creating a "team approach" that includes departments such as the General Counsel's Office, the Provost, the Vice President for Business, the physical plant, facilities planning, and residence life, in addition to the police, is a preferred way to develop a comprehensive plan with respect to campus security. COP principles emphasize just such a collaborative approach to creating a safer campus.

Brug (1994), Greenburg (1987), and Peak (1995) have all noted that the college campus environment provides a fertile environment for the initiation of COP efforts. Given the general openness to change and willingness to try new ideas found on most college campuses, it is reasonable that a COP model of policing would be a good fit.

Operationalizing COP on Campus

COP appears to offer to campus police the opportunity for continued professional development in an environment–the college/university campus–that encourages innovation and creativity. This approach goes beyond simply responding to calls for service in a professional and timely manner but seeks to involve community members in mutually identifying problems and solutions. In a survey of local chiefs and sheriffs, the National Institute of Justice (1995:2) identified common operational practices that are part of community policing:

- Permanent neighborhood-based offices or stations.
- Designation of "community" or neighborhood police officers.
- Foot patrol as a specific assignment or periodic expectation.
- Regularly scheduled meetings with community groups.
- Specific training and interagency involvement in problem identification and resolution.
- Use of regulatory codes to combat drugs/crime.

As the following examples illustrate, campus police can operationalize virtually all of these practices in a college community. Bromley (2006), in a survey of campus police departments, found that 56 percent of the departments assigned officers to permanent geographic locations, while 72 percent had one or more designated "community officers" on staff. Officers assigned to foot patrol were found in almost 94 percent of the departments, while bike patrol assignments were found in nearly 75 percent of the same agencies (Bromley, 2006). Territo et al. (1998) suggested that placing officers on foot patrol and on bicycles "humanizes" the police and enhances communication between officers and the community; walking or riding the campus creates numerous opportunities for officers to have positive interaction with members of the campus community.

Regarding practices such as routinely meeting with community members and training citizens in identifying problems and resolving them, Bromley (2006) found campus departments were involved in these practices. For example, approximately 31 percent of the departments surveyed had formed "problem-solving relationships" with community members and close to 21 percent had actually trained faculty, staff, and students in problem-solving techniques.

Using existing regulatory codes and involving nonpolice agencies in crime prevention and quality of life issues are also recognized practices on many college campuses. Stormer and Esposito (1988) and Bromley and Territo (1990) noted that a close relationship can be developed between the campus police and other departments, such as physical plant, student life, residence life, and the general counsel's office, to develop an overall strategy of crime prevention. Further, student governments on many campuses also work with campus police on making campuses safer by establishing student escort programs and installing emergency phones throughout the campuses (Bromley, 1995).

To expand COP practices, campus police departments may develop mutually satisfying relationships academic departments at the institution. Brantingham et al. (1995) and Sloan and Fisher (1995) have provided detailed descriptions of how academic departments can assist campus police in assessing campus security and the perceived risk/fear of victimization among their community members. Academic departments can assist campus police in conducting campus security surveys, including assessing, locks, lighting in public spaces, landscape design, and building architecture. These departments can also assist the campus police department in developing public education/crime prevention materials and a mechanism for timely release of news regarding campus crime and related information. Multiple academic disciplines (e.g., criminal justice, sociology, architecture, urban planning, and mass communication) may be involved with the campus police in these efforts. University provosts, administrative vice presidents, and deans of students can further foster community policing on a campus in much the same way that a city manager or city mayor can do so at the local level of government.

According to Peak (1995), the campus environment uniquely allows the campus police to try philosophical and tactical innovation. While it seems natural that campus police would continue to evolve in the new era of COP, the question remains of how a campus police department brings about planned change. The following section describes how one campus developed and implemented its COP efforts.

Community-Oriented Policing on the Campus: A Case Study

The University of South Florida

The University of South Florida (USF), located in Tampa, Florida, opened in 1960 and had an enrollment of 30,000 students in 1991 prior to the implementation of COP at U.S.F. The University currently has 200 degree programs at all levels: bachelors, masters, specialty, doctorate, and doctor of medicine. It is the principal public university for the Tampa Bay region.

Today the student population is quite diverse with students coming from every state in the nation and more than 100 foreign countries. Approximately 29 percent of the student body consists of members of minority groups (e.g., African American, Hispanic, and Asian). Approximately 60 percent of the students are women. Located on over 1,700 acres, USF has a major outpatient clinic, two hospitals, an elementary school, a hotel, and a 10,000-seat multipurpose facility in addition to its traditional academic and general-purpose buildings. It also has 25 miles of roads within its boundaries and nine public entry points R. Staehle (personal communication, October, 2003).

The University Police Department

The University of South Florida Police Department provides a full range of public safety services to the community 24 hours a day, seven days a week on the Tampa Campus. The State of Florida certifies all University Police officers after completing minimum standards training from the Regional Police Training Academy. General services provided by the University Police include car, foot, and bicycle patrol, investigation of all misdemeanors and felonies, traffic enforcement, accident investigation, special events management, and crime prevention programs.

The Development and Implementation of COP at USF

The University Police Department long had a reputation for professionalism and being community oriented. However, in 1992 department officials made a conscious decision to take additional steps to strengthen the relationship between the department and the campus community. They established a formal goal within the department's five-year plan to "develop and implement community-oriented policing (COP) throughout the university police department." The department took a number of subsequent steps to achieve that goal, as described below.

COP Training

In the Spring of 1992, the department hired professors from Anthropology and from African American Studies to conduct to series of two-day workshops on cross-cultural communication for all university police personnel. Prior to facilitating these workshops, the two professors spent a significant amount of time reviewing COP materials in order to develop their sessions within the context of the COP philosophy. Participants suggested creating a quality management committee composed of representatives of all university police operational sections. This group became instrumental in enhancing internal communication, reviewing new policies, and developing a revised mission and value statement for the Department that are consistent with COP efforts.

During the summer of 1992, the Associate Director and the Captain for Police Operations attended a COP workshop conducted by the International Association of Chiefs of Police (IACP). The workshop provided attendees an overview of national COP trends and helped attendees formulate additional plans of action for their departments.

Three law enforcement trainers from Michigan, including Chief Bruce Benson of the Michigan State University Campus Police who had considerable experience with community policing in the campus context provided specialized COP training for all university police personnel. These sessions provided participants concrete examples of how COP was being used in other agencies. The trainers also provided leadership training for all first-line supervisors within the department.

Community Survey

Next, the department developed a community survey to identify perceptions held by university community members regarding university police services and to assess the priority assigned to such services. The department also planned to survey its personnel to determine the priority they would assign to same services. Subject experts from the University Counseling Center, University Office of Resource Analysis and Planning, and the Office of Student Affairs previewed and evaluated the survey instrument; based on their input, the department revised the instrument and then conducted the survey. The racial/ethnic composition of the respondents paralleled the overall demographics of the university at that time.

Information gained from the survey helped university police command staff in implementing COP. In-service training sessions and public education programs addressed significant differences in the expectation of service delivery between the police officers and community members.

Department Reorganization and Geographic Deployments

The department then reorganized itself with a more decentralized management structure, consistent with COP principles. The department selected new patrol shift lieutenants who directly supervised their individual units. The department selected the lieutenants based primarily on their knowledge of and commitment to COP principles and their recognized ability as problem solvers. Further, the department revised not only its employee performance evaluation standards to reflect COP principles, but standardized questions used for applicants during the selection process to be more consistent with COP.

The department also assigned its uniformed patrol officers to specific geographic areas of the campus for them to become more familiar with the people living and/or working in the area. The department expected the officers would be more involved in problem solving and not merely respond to calls for service within their geographic areas.

Additionally, the department assigned two full-time university police officers as "community policing specialists" in student residence halls for a one-year period. One of specialist's goals was to work closely with residence hall staff and to serve as in-house liaisons to residents on a daily basis. The Department of Residence Hall Services actually provided office space for the officers in the residence halls.

Finally, all police personnel, in conjunction with their immediate supervisors, developed an individual "community policing project" for the following year. The department's management team reviewed these projects to insure that they met one of two COP criteria: (1) they sought to improve the quality of life within the university or (2) they sought to reduce crime on campus.

Responding to the Challenges: The COP Experience at USF

Described above were some of the unique challenges confronting campus police administrators. Since the early 1990s, the USF Police Department met many of these challenges but was able to remain flexible and adaptive in its approach to providing police services by continuing its COP practices.

For example, today the USF main campus has over 5,000 resident students compared to approximately 3,000 in 1992. The Residential Officer Program, which assigns a full-time officer and other rotating patrol officers to residence halls, has received office space, administrative support, and other resources from the Division of Residence Life which now sees the officers as an integral part of student resident hall life.

Another example of the value of practicing a COP philosophy occurred immediately following the terrorist attacks of September 11, 2001. By this time, the student body had experienced a significant increase in nonnative students who had arrived from over 100 foreign countries. COP officers from the University Police Department worked very closely with the Office of International Student Life in the days after 9/11 to provide information and reassurance to foreign students. Because of COP efforts, a partnership developed between the two departments that resulted in enhanced communication.

Presently, 60 percent of the students at USF are women, another example of a potential challenge regarding safety on the campus. Once again, working within the COP framework, the department initiated the nationally recognized *Rape Aggression Defense* (RAD) system. RAD is a comprehensive safety course for women, which combines the elements of awareness, prevention, and risk reduction with hands-on self-defense training. The proactive program has become so popular that the Physical Education Department, a COP partner, now offers it as a two-hour credit course.

One other example involves the vast growth in facilities on the USF campus. Today the campus has over 200 academic and support facilities. As part of the "team approach" used in community policing, a police department representative in consultation with the university's Facilities Planning Division, reviews all new building proposals and major renovation projects at USF. This process helps to identify possible security concerns and allows security enhancements before construction ever begins.

Conclusion

While a campus department can implement COP in a variety of ways, the foregoing example illustrated the comprehensive approach that a department must take to accomplish that end. As today's campuses grow in size and complexity, change will be inevitable and challenges will be formidable. Within the context of providing a broad-based, service-oriented approach to policing and security on a twenty-first century campus, campus police departments already practicing COP may best be positioned to anticipate and prepare for further change. The college campus setting that fosters innovation and changes would seem a good environment for campus policing to continue its evolution. Long before the concept "community-oriented policing" was invented, forward thinking campus police leaders understood the need to be proactive, community-involved, and service-oriented in their approach to providing police services. These same overarching principles are just as important in today's complex higher education environment and, as such, provide a framework for COP initiatives, both now and in the near future. Paoline and Sloan (2003) note that campus police are among the most numerous forms of specialized police and, therefore, it is important for researchers to continue their systematic study of the profession's evolution. This is a reasonable recommendation certainly worth pursuing.

REFERENCES

Atwell, R. (1988). *Memorandum regarding campus security.* Washington, DC: American Council on Education.

Baum, K., & Klaus, P. (2005). *Violent victimization of college students, 1995–2002.* (NCJ Publication No. 206836). Washington, DC: United States Department of Justice, Office of Justice Programs, Bureau of Justice Statistics.

Bess, W., & Horton, G. (1988). The role of campus law enforcement. *Campus Law Enforcement Journal, 19,* 35–36.

Bordner, D., & Petersen, D. (1983). *Campus policing: The nature of university work.* Lanham, MD: University Press of America.

Brantingham, P., Brantingham, P., & Seagrave, J. (1995). Crime and fear of crime in a Canadian university. In B. S. Fisher & J. J. Sloan (Eds.), *Campus crime: Legal, social, and policy perspectives.* Springfield, IL: Charles C Thomas.

Bromley, M. (1992). Campus and community crime rate comparisons: A statewide study. *Journal of Security Administration, 15,* 49–64.

Bromley, M. (1993). The impact of recently enacted statues in civil lawsuits on security policies at postsecondary institutions. *The Journal of Police and Criminal Psychology, 9,* 46–52.

Bromley, M. (1995). Securing the campus: Political and economic forces affecting decision makers. In B. S. Fisher & J. J. Sloan (Eds.), *Campus crime: Legal, social, and policy perspectives.* Springfield, IL: Charles C Thomas.

Bromley, M. (1996). Policing Our Campuses: A National Review of Statutes. *American Journal of Police, 15,* 1–22.

Bromley, M. (2006). Comparing campus and municipal police community policing practices. Forthcoming. *Journal of Security Administration.*

Bromley, M., & Fisher, B. (2002). Campus policing and victim services. In L. Moriarty & M. Dantzker (Eds.), *Policing and victims* (pp. 133–158). Upper Saddle River, NJ: Prentice-Hall.

Bromley, M., & Reaves, B. (1998a). Comparing campus and city police operational practices. *Journal of Security Administration, 21,* 41–54.

Bromley, M., & Reaves, B. (1998b). Comparing campus and municipal police: The human resource dimension. *Policing: An International Journal of Police Strategies and Management, 21,* 534–546.

Brubacher, J., & Willis, R. (1968). *Higher education in transition.* New York: Harper and Row.

Brug, R. (1984). Cal-Poly maximizes use of students. *Campus Law Enforcement Journal, 14,* 41–42.

Cochran, J., Bromley, M., & Landis, L. (1999). Officer work orientations, perception of readiness and anticipated effectiveness of an agency-wide community policing effort within a country sheriff's office. *Journal of Police and Criminal Psychology, 14,* 43–65.

Digest of educational statistics (1991). Washington DC: United States Department of Education.

Esposito, D., & Stormer, D. (1989). The Multiple Roles of Campus Law Enforcement. *Campus Law Enforcement Journal,* 19, 26–30.

Fernandez, A., & Lizotte, A.J. (1995). An analysis of the relationship between campus crime and community crime: Reciprocal effects? In B. S. Fisher & J. J. Sloan (Eds.), *Campus crime: Legal, social, and policy perspectives* (pp. 79–102). Springfield, IL: Charles C Thomas.

Fisher, B., Sloan, J., & Wilkins, D. (1995). Fear of crime and perceived risk of victimization in an urban university setting. In B. S. Fisher & J. J. Sloan (Eds.), *Campus crime: Legal, social, and policy perspectives.* Springfield, IL: Charles C Thomas.

Fox, J., & Hellman, D. (1985). Location and other correlates of campus crime. *Journal of Criminal Justice, 13,* 429–444.

Gelber, S. (1972). *The role of campus security in the college setting.* Washington, DC: United States Department of Justice.

Goldstein, H. (1987). Toward community oriented policing: Potential, basic requirements, and threshold questions. *Crime and Delinquency, 33,* 6–30.

Greenburg, M. (1987). Harnessing campus humanism for sake of public safety. *Campus Law Enforcement Journal, 17,* 41–42.

Hart, T. (2003). *Violent victimizations of college students.* Washington, DC: United States Department of Justice, Bureau of Justice Statistics.

International Association of Campus Law Enforcement Administrators (1995). *Campus crime report, 1991–1993.* Hartford, CT: IACLEA.

Jackson, E. (1952). Campus police embrace community based approach. *The Police Chief, 59,* 62–64.

Jacobs, J., & O'Meara, V. (1980). Security forces and the transformation of the American university. *College and University, 31,* 283–297.

Kassinger, E. (1971). Alternative to chaos: The need for professionalization of campus law enforcement. In S. Sims (Ed.), *New directions in campus law enforcement: A handbook for administrators.* Athens, GA: The University of Georgia Center for Continuing Education.

Lanier, M. (1995). Community policing on university campuses: Tradition, practice, and outlook. In B. S. Fisher & J. J. Sloan (Eds.), *Campus crime: Legal, social, and policy perspectives.* Springfield, IL: Charles C Thomas.

Lederman, D. (1993, January 20). Colleges report 7,500 violent crimes on their campuses in first annual statements required under federal law. *The Chronicle of Higher Education,* pp. A32–A43.

Lederman, D. (1994, February 2). Crime on the campuses: Increases in reported robberies and assaults. *The Chronicle of Higher Education,* pp. A31–A41.

Lederman, D. (1995, February 3). Colleges report rise in violent crime. *The Chronicle of Higher Education,* pp. A31–A42.

Lively, K. (1996, April 26). Drug arrests rise again. *The Chronicle of Higher Education,* p. A37.

Lively, K. (1997, March 21). Campus drug arrests increased 18 percent in 1995: Reports of other crime fell. *The Chronicle of Higher Education,* p. A44.

Lizotte, A., & Fernandez, A. (1993). *Trends and correlates of campus crime: A general report.* Albany, NY: Consortium of Higher Education Campus Crime Research.

McDaniel, W. (1971). Law Enforcement: The Officer as the Educator. In O. Sims (Ed.), *New directions in campus law enforcement: A handbook for administrators.* Athens, GA: The University of Georgia, Center for Continuous Education.

National Center for Educational Statistics. (1997). Campus Crime and Security at Post-Secondary Institutions. Washington, DC: U.S. Department of Justice.

National Institute of Justice Research Review. (1995). *Community policing strategies.* Washington, DC: United States Department of Justice.

Nichols, D. (1987). *The administration of public safety in higher education.* Springfield, IL: Charles C Thomas.

Ordovensky, P. (1990, December 3). Students easy prey on campus. *U.S.A. Today,* p. 1A.

Palmer, C. (1993, April 21). Skepticism is rampant about the statistics on campus crime. *The Chronicle of Higher Education,* p. B1.

Paoline, E., & Sloan, J. (2003). Variability in the organizational structure of contemporary campus law enforcement agencies: A national-level analysis. *Policing: An International Journal of Police Strategies and Management, 26,* 612–639.

Peak, J., & Glensor, R. (1999). *Community policing and problem solving: Strategies and practices.* Upper Saddle, NJ: Prentice-Hall.

Peak, K. (1988). Campus law enforcement. A national survey of administration and operation. *Campus Law Enforcement Journal, 19,* 33–35.

Peak, K. (1989). Campus law enforcement in flux: Changing times and future expectations. *Campus Law Enforcement Journal, 19,* 21–25

Peak, K. (1995). The professionalization of campus law enforcement: Comparing campus and municipal law enforcement agencies. In B. S. Fisher & J. J. Sloan (Eds.), *Campus crime: Legal, social, and policy perspectives.* Springfield, IL: Charles C Thomas.

Powell, J. (1981) *Campus security and law enforcement.* Woburn, MA: Butterworth.

Powell, J. (1994). The beginning–Yale campus police department–1894. *Campus Law Enforcement Journal, 24,* 2–5.

Powell, J., Pander, M., & Nielsen, R. (1994). *Campus security and law enforcement* (2nd ed). Boston: Butterworth-Heinemann.

Proctor, S. (1958). *The University of Florida: Its early years.* Unpublished doctoral dissertation, University of Florida, Gainesville, FL.

Ray, G. (1991). Campus police: A different view. *FBI Law Enforcement Bulletin, 60,* 14–15.

Reaves. (1996). Personal correspondence regarding a forthcoming Bureau of Justice Statistics Report.

Reaves, B., & Goldberg, A. (1996). *Campus Law Enforcement Agencies, 1995.* Washington, DC: United States Department of Justice.

Rudolph, F. (1962). *The American college and university: A history.* New York: Random House.

Seng, M. (1995). The *Crime Awareness and Campus Security Act:* Some observations, critical comments, and suggestions. In B. S. Fisher & J. J. Sloan (Eds.), *Campus crime: Legal, social, and policy perspectives.* Springfield, IL: Charles C Thomas.

Shoemaker, E. (1995). Non-traditional strategies for implementing community oriented policing. In *Community policing on campus.* Hartford, CT: International Association of Campus Law Enforcement Administrators.

Sims, O. (1971). *New directions in campus law enforcement: A handbook for administrators.* Athens, GA: The University of Georgia Center for Continuing Education.

Skolnick, J. (1969). *Politics of protest.* Washington, DC: United States Government Printing Office.

Sloan, J. (1992). The modern campus police: An analysis of their evolution, structure, and function. *American Journal of Police, 11,* 85–104.

Sloan, J. (1994). The correlates of campus crime: An analysis of reported crimes on university campuses. *Journal of Criminal Justice, 22,* 51–62.

Sloan, J., & Fisher, B. (1995). Campus crime: Legal, social, and policy perspectives. In B. S. Fisher & J. J. Sloan (Eds.), *Campus crime: Legal, social, and policy perspectives.* Springfield, IL: Charles C Thomas.

Smith, M. (1988). *Coping with crime on campus.* New York: Macmillan.

Smith, M. (1989). *Campus crime and campus police: A handbook for police officers and administrators.* Ashville, NC: College Administration Publications, Inc.

Smith, M. (1995). Vexations victims of campus crime. In B. S. Fisher & J. J. Sloan (Eds.), *Campus crime: Legal, social, and policy perspectives.* Springfield, IL: Charles C Thomas.

Territo, L., Halsted, J., & Bromley, M. (1998). *Crime and justice in America: A human perspective* (5th ed.). Newton, MA: Butterworth-Heinemann.

Trojanowicz, R., & Carter, D. (1988). *The philosophy and role of community policing.* East Lansing, MI.: National Center for Community Policing.

Witsil, J. (1979). Security at Princeton is low-keyed. *Campus Law Enforcement Journal, 9,* 6–7.

Wooldridge, J., Cullen, F., & Latessa, E. (1995). Predicting the likelihood of faculty victimization: Individual demographics and routine activities. In B. S. Fisher & J.

J. Sloan (Eds.), *Campus crime: Legal, social, and policy perspectives.* Springfield, IL: Charles C Thomas.

Zhao, J., Lorvich, N., & Thurman, Q. (1999). The status of community policing in American cities: Facilitators and impediments revisited. *Policing: An International Journal of Police Strategies and Management, 22,* 74–92.

Chapter 15

HIGH-TECH ABUSE AND CRIME ON COLLEGE AND UNIVERSITY CAMPUSES: EVOLVING FORMS OF VICTIMIZATION, OFFENDING, AND THEIR INTERPLAY IN HIGHER EDUCATION

SAMUEL C. McQUADE, III

INTRODUCTION

A book that focuses on campus crime presupposes that places like colleges and universities matter a lot. I agree. This is especially true in the area of computer science, computer engineering, and the more recent field of information technology (IT) where, since World War II, colleges and universities have been at the forefront of research and development into computers. Partnerships between postsecondary institutions and both private sector corporations and various agencies of the federal government have resulted in tremendous advances in such areas as the military, business, manufacturing, and engineering. Many of these advances had profound effects on society and literally transformed our everyday lives, particularly in the area of information access, dissemination, and use. The problem is that these innovations also have a dark side that involves criminal victimization of individuals at postsecondary institutions—students, faculty, and staff alike—and the institutions themselves.

Because computer science- and engineering-based activities occupy such a key role at colleges and universities in this country, they also present unique opportunities for individuals to both perpetrate and be the victims of "high-tech" crime. It is now possible for a college student to sit in her dormitory and systematically steal the identities of fellow students, deface corporate or government websites, or crash networks of computers. This possibility underscores the reality that cybercrimes, defined as "use of computers or other electronic information technology devices via information systems . . . to facilitate illegal behaviors" (McQuade, 2006, p. 16) cause real harm not limited to the cyberspace. In reality, people occupying physical space on college campuses use tangible devices to access and use information for illicit purposes and commit cybercrimes, such as computer hacking; identity theft; and pirating of software, music, or movies. Arguably, no physical or computing environment offers more opportunity for perpetrating cybercrimes than college and university campuses in the United States.

This chapter provides a "high-tech" perspective to new forms of crimes occurring on American college and university campuses. I begin by providing a brief history of computing on college campuses and describe how this work fueled early forms of computer-enabled crime. I then explain how evolving crimes, enabled by information technology (IT), inevitably drive our conceptions and labeling of what constitutes "crime," as well as how society is organizing for the investigation, prosecution, and prevention of these new forms of crime. The essential point in this section is that the development and adoption of technology for innovative and harmful purposes and as criminal justice system responses co-evolve. Therefore, so must our understanding and prevention of high-tech crimes on campuses and throughout society.

In the second section, I focus on ways in which high-tech crime occurs on campus. I begin by briefly describing predominant forms of campus crime enabled with IT. I then explain technological aspects of attacks to information systems leading to victimization. I also discuss in this section the interplay between off- and online victimization and offending–how students and others increasingly interact with and learn to use IT for righteous and offending purposes even as technology may cloud moral clarity about committing crime. This discussion provides the foundation for considering the extent and impact of IT-enabled crime on campuses, albeit based on a very limited number of empirical studies.

In the third and final section of the chapter, I discuss implications for academic reforms, specifically the need to consider the effects of IT in every aspect of human activity and in relation to traditional campus security and crime prevention. I argue that because physical and cyber aspects of campus safety and security are inextricably linked, college and university officials must rethink how they organize and provide for these in off-to-online computing environments. Needed reforms in academia also include greater monitoring of information systems for evidence of abuse and crime, sanctioning of offenders, and using IT to increase prevention of cybercrime. The chapter concludes with my thoughts regarding the fundamental challenge facing higher education: How should we deliver high-tech education amidst evolving IT-enabled abuse and crime?[1]

A Brief History of IT-Enabled Abuse and Crime on Campus

Early Computing and Computer Abuse on Campuses

Colleges and universities have always been at the forefront of computer-related and enabled research and education, as well as computer-related abuse, crime, and victimization. Especially since WWII and the Space Race that followed, computers have had increasing prominence on college and university campuses as a subject of academic study and a means of both research and education. University electrical engineering researchers funded by the military developed first generation (mainframe) computers during the 1940s and 1950s to design computerized rocket, missile, and other weapons guidance systems. Industry funding to universities followed during the 1960s for development of computerized accounting and banking technologies. By the early 1970s, super computers of the day, housed principally at major research universities such as MIT, supported increasingly complex data analysis in military, space flight, and health care research, as well as in support of banking and financial services management. Throughout these periods, early forms of computer abuse and computer crime, such as computer hacking, also emerged on or from within college campuses and throughout society as college graduates, increasingly competent in using computers, entered the workforce.

Since the 1980s, many computing and telecommunications inventions and innovations, including the Advanced Research Projects Agency Network (ARPANET), the Internet, and the World Wide Web, progressively transformed every aspect of society. Technological changes created new opportunities for imaginative and computer savvy offenders who tended to be bright young males, usually without criminal records, who were curious about and drawn to computers. Many of these individuals enrolled in increasingly popular computer science programs offered by two- and four-year colleges and universities. A few of these students helped establish a computer "hacker" subculture that espoused technological creativity and exploration through free and unlimited access to information (Levy, 1984).[2] This subculture affected computing norms on campuses across the country then and now, especially at technological institutes and involved mischievous computing pranks played out on college campuses all over the United States, in Europe, and in other places. As computing continued to expand during the 1980s, governments began to enact computer crime laws that specifically prohibited trespassing into computer networks; exceeding permissions to access areas within computer networks; and the unauthorized copying, altering, or destroying of electronic data.

Throughout this history, computers were transforming higher education in fundamental and profound ways. Like many other sectors in society, colleges and universities across the country steadily adopted information systems to support aspects of their business operations. Computers enabled the creation of distance learning and high-tech classrooms featuring integrated technologies providing dynamic visual and audio displays, recording, and interactive learning experiences, combined with Internet connectivity for accessing all types of subject matter content, and a variety of real-time teaching methods. Meanwhile students, staff, and faculty increasingly carry their own electronic devices, forever and radically changing the technological, social, and cultural environments of higher education.

Today thousands of colleges and universities, occupied by millions of young adults who often grew up as the primary users of computers in their homes, are the equivalent of candy shops of ubiquitous technological delights integral to virtually every aspect of campus life and operations. Increasingly dependent upon IT are classroom instruction, research and development, resident life and extracurricular student activities including Web accessible entertainment like electronic gaming and music/movie downloading services, as well as academic and human resources administration, media and alumni relations, and community outreach. Indeed, various publications rate and compare campuses partly based on technological capabilities available to support these functions. Campus administrators point to such rankings with pride and use them as a means of recruiting promising students and faculty. An institution deemed among the "most wired" in the country has now become almost as important as the size of its endowment.

Conceptual Evolution and Labeling of High-Tech Crime

With technological advances in society comes the recognition of new forms of criminality, conceptions of social constructs for them, and subsequent labeling, defining, and categorizing of these crimes. These changes are necessary to update methods of investigation and prevention, and formulate policies and legislation needed for administering criminal justice systems. Elsewhere (McQuade, 2006, pp. 10–18), I paralleled contemporary understanding of cybercrime with Sutherland's (1940) conceptualization and later diffusion of the concept "white-collar crime" which now encompasses a host of illegal behaviors involving the victimization of consumers, employees, and corporations. Like white-collar crime, constructs of IT-enabled crime evolved over 50 years, from approximately 1945–1995, and interested observers sequentially labeled them as: "computer abuse," "computer crime," "computer-related crime," "high-tech crime" and "electronic crime." Other constructs such as "corporate crime," "economic crime," and "transnational organized crime" also developed as computing, telecommunications, and transportation technologies radically changed illicit activities committed with computers and interoperable electronic devices Each new form of crime resulted in not-so-distinct forms of victimization, exacerbating conceptual confusion surrounding IT-enabled abuse, crime, and victimization. By 1995, overlapping conceptions of increasingly high-tech crime raised concern in academic and policy circles about definitional dilemmas surrounding IT-enabled crimes (National White Collar Crime Center & West Virginia University, 1996). Ensuing debate occurred over whether labeling crime constructs was even useful, given that deviancy and crime evolve technologically and in the process are naturally conceived in more or less accurate ways.

Debate notwithstanding, recognition, labeling, and responding to new forms of high-tech crime continue. I believe this process to be both useful and inevitable, although it challenges researchers, practitioners, and policymakers to recognize, accept, and work around this reality as they attempt to better understand, respond to, and prevent crimes on college and university campuses and elsewhere. As progress is made, we ought not be overly concerned about general labels for IT-enabled abuse and crimes, although elsewhere I have advocated adoption of "cybercrime" to represent illegal behaviors facilitated with computers or other electronic devices via information systems (McQuade, 2006, pp. 10–18). However, I also use the term "high-tech crime" for variation of expression to mean the same thing and simply note history has always regarded all forms of innovative abuse and crime as relatively "high-tech" in their day.

What is also important is that our current conception of IT-enabled offending on college and university campuses is not limited to behaviors prohibited by law. This is because laws eventually change with innovations in technology-enabled abuse and as people experience new and more devastating forms of harm. Historically, IT-enabled abuse periodically increased in seriousness, leading to widespread recognition of a societal problem and criminalization of the behaviors involved. Distributing spam, for example, was originally annoying, abused information systems' capacity by consuming bandwidth needed by workers, and frequently contained adware and spyware that exposed unwary users to various types of attacks. Now, with certain exceptions, sending spam is illegal in most states. Just as in the past, we now conceptualize and label offending and victimization according to the technological underpinnings that made the behaviors possible. As technology advances, new conceptions, constructs, and terms will likely be needed to capture the essence of innovative, harmful, and interrelated sets of behaviors occurring in society, inclusive of those that occur on college and university campuses.

High-Tech Crime and Abuse on College Campuses

Predominant Forms of High-Tech Crime on Campuses

Currently, there are seven predominant forms of IT-enabled abuse and cybercrime occurring on college campuses and via campus computer networks. In no particular order, these include: (1) writing and distributing malicious code (e.g., viruses, worms, Trojans, adware/ spyware, or spam); (2) disrupting computer services such as excessive unauthorized use of network resources, or launching denial of service attacks; (3) computer spying and intrusions, including hacking into networks or exceeding authorized permissions; (4) fraudulent schemes and data or devise theft, including credit card fraud and identity theft; (5) unauthorized and illegal file sharing (e.g., piracy of software, music, movies, and electronic games); (6) academic and scientific misconduct, including using computers to plagiarize, buy/steal papers, fake research findings, or post inappropriate content to websites, chat forums, or blogs; and (7) online harassment, including threats and cyber stalking. Note that this is not a comprehensive list and that within each of the seven general categories are several technologically distinct types of abusive/criminal behaviors.

Technological Aspects of Attacks Leading to Victimization

Understanding and managing IT-enabled abuse, crime, and victimization occurring on college campuses requires recognizing several technological aspects of appropriately using or misusing information systems and devices capable of processing, exchanging, and storing data. By *systems,* I mean wired/wireless computer controlled telecommunications networks (such as campus intranets that connect servers or the Internet, upon which rests World Wide Web), which allow computers and other types of electronic devices to send and receive data. *Devices* include desktop, laptop, and mini-computers, as well as combination scanner/copier/fax machines, cell phones, personal digital assistants (PDAs), pagers, and a menagerie of other devices. Such devices are increasingly smaller, more affordable, interoperable, have greater processing speed and memory capacity, and are capable of supporting more extensive multitasking (e.g., simultaneous Web browsing, listening to music, watching movies, playing electronic games, and sending or receiving text messages and other forms of data such as digital photos and real-time video streams via wired or wireless networks).

Let us now consider ten technological aspects of high tech abuses and crimes that complicate understanding and managing them both on campuses and elsewhere in society. First, consider that IT-enabled abuse and/or cybercrime occur as the result of someone using systems and devices to invade and possibly damage technology and/or other property of another inclusive of their computerized data. Generally, this plays out as technological competitions involving the capabilities of offenders versus those of potential victims. This state of affairs is consistent with basic principles of routine activities theory—motivated (and capable) offenders who have identified suitable targets without capable guardians (Cohen & Felson, 1979). These competitions have more generally to do with the theory of technology-enabled crime, policing, and security that explains evolutions in crime as the result of technology inventions and innovations, adoption of these for illicit purposes, and for diffusion of systems, tools and techniques throughout society (McQuade, 2006, pp. 176–178).

Second, college campuses create physical environments in which illicit use of electronic devices can be easily concealed and detected (if at all) usually only with electronic monitoring. A person using a cell phone to send a text message may be returning a friendly note or sending a threat, but in either case, may do so in public in an unsuspicious manner that causes no one to notice that abuse or crime is occurring in their midst. Consequently IT-enabled crimes are difficult if not impossible to notice using conventional means, and more difficult to prevent using ordinary crime prevention strategies like neighborhood, business, or campus watch programs. After all, nearly everyone on college campuses possesses portable electronic devices and can use them, under any number of circumstances, to facilitate high-tech abuse or crime.

Third, cybercrime often damages student, faculty, or staff software or hardware. Attacks of systems and devices may result in destruction, manipulation, and/or copying of confidential or personal data and allow for additional abuse or crimes. For example, after losing personal data, victims of identify theft typically have their financial accounts drained and their credit ruined. Victims may also be revictimized in other ways stemming from loss of their personal data, money, and credit rating (e.g., denied jobs requiring security clearances, housing and additional credit, or even being improperly arrested on warrants issued for crimes committed in their names) (Synovate, 2003). Subsequent crimes and victimization continue as long as offenders can tap funds through electronic means; unless and until victims correct their financial records; and until their names are cleared. Inadequately protected computer databases containing confidential information owned, controlled, or accessed by individuals, academic institutions, and government agencies often allow identity theft and other types of high-tech crime to occur.

Fourth, it follows that possessing and using confidential digitized data is central to committing IT-enabled abuse and cybercrime. However, data also exists in hardcopy and analog forms that scanners can change into digital form. Computer hackers learn about their human or technological targets, such as particular users or servers on a college or university network, through ongoing intelligence-gathering of security-related, personal, or other confidential information (e.g., identification of system administrator root account information, user names and passwords, contact lists, social security numbers, and financial account data). Armed with valuable data, offenders then perpetrate various high-tech crimes against people or organizations, whose physical facilities and/or IT systems they access using information acquired in prior attacks.

Fifth, different IT-enabled abuse and cybercrime, like traditional crime, often occur together in the course of a single event or through ongoing criminal activity. These offenses differentially affect students, staff, and faculty, as well as groups and organizations, depending on the relative strength of available defensive information security technologies. Each additional system identified, targeted, and successfully attacked likely contains different kinds and amounts of information. In turn, the value of this information varies depends on attackers' combined knowledge, skill, available resources, and access to technological systems and motivations (Parker, 1998). Personal information such as financial, health, and academic records are all potentially valuable sources of intelligence for committing abuse or crimes against data owners, as well as targeting other individuals, information systems, and facilities.

To illustrate, on March 11, 2005, an intruder stole a laptop computer from an office on the campus of the University of California at Berkeley. University officials were extremely worried because the device contained personal information for nearly 100,000 students, student applicants, and alumni. In 1994, Berkley experienced a hacking incident resulting in the loss of confidential information for hundreds of thousands of California residents being used for research commissioned by the state's Department of Social Services (Liedtke, 2005). Because many other colleges and universities have experienced similar thefts and hacking incidents along with other types of high-tech crimes, leading observers have concluded college campuses may be the most vulnerable organizations in society to breaches of information security (Marklein, 2006a).

Sixth, cybercrimes always involve physical actions combined with cyber transactions. Regardless of the IT used and types of assets targeted, there are tangible aspects to what perpetrators do—cybercrimes do not occur solely within the amorphous realm of cyberspace. Rather, human beings occupying physical space and using tangible devices connected to wired or wireless devices, perpetrate cybercrime, including sophisticated hacking, the release of malicious software programs, and denial of service attacks involving remotely controlled "bots."[3] In accordance with classic crime investigation theory, law enforcement officials can collect, analyze, and trace physical and cyber-based clues left by high-tech offenders. The challenge for investigators is to place a specific offender in control of a keyboard or other input device within the timeframe and location from which they initiated an attack. Fortunately, trained investigators employing computer forensic techniques in combination with traditional evidence collection methods can achieve this goal. This assumes such resources are available to colleges and universities, which unfortunately is not always true. Very few campuses currently have dedicated information security officers, much less those capable of under-taking computer forensics investigations.

Seventh, offenders using any number of IT systems and devices can launch attacks, sequentially or simultaneously, against targets located in many on- or off-campus locations. Offenders can launch attacks in relatively high-to-low-tech ways, from within particular facilities or network environ-ments that are co-occupied by victims or launch attacks from outside a facil-ity or computer network by defeating firewalls and password protections intended to keep intruders out. In other words, cybercrimes can be commit-ted by insiders such as students or campus employees or by outsiders, such as people who do not attend a given college or university, are not authorized to access or use a campus network, and live halfway around the world. It is also true that offenders can make it appear as though the attack came from halfway around the world when, in reality, the attacks originated from with-in a victim's geographic and network environment.

Eighth, as with traditional crime, victims are often targeted, manipulated, and fooled by offenders who know them personally or come to know enough about them through intelligence gathering to establish a relationship based on trust. In the world of high-tech crime, major examples of "social engi-neering" include: (a) *baiting* someone with jargon and facts into doing what is requested; (b) *name-dropping* to convey the existence of relationships to people in authority and thereby entitlement to access secure information; (c) *mixing fact and fiction* in order to confuse targets about an attacker's true goals; and (d) *intimidating, threatening, and shocking* individuals into spontaneously providing otherwise secure information (Parker, 1998, pp. 148–150). Several other technical methods of manipulating people to provide access to facili-ties, systems, devices, and data are also used (McQuade, 2006, pp. 114–117).

Ninth, the social engineering integral to intelligence gathering for carrying out high-tech abuse or crime underscores the reality of human factors relat-ed to offensive and preventative aspects of cybercrime. As previously indi-cated, cybercrimes are committed by people using IT, which is analogous to the expression that "Guns don't kill people, people kill people." Even so-called automated crimes carried out by self-morphing bots are, in reality, programs coded by individuals who make mistakes and are vulnerable to all the usual human entrapments that trip up criminals (e.g., bragging about their exploits, indiscreetly spending large amounts of illicit money, and leaving physical or cyber clues to their identity, etc.). From a preventative standpoint, most users, despite increasing consumer awareness regarding the many types cybercrime that now regularly occur throughout society, remain ignorant or naïve about their vulnerability because they do not understand the computing and technical aspects of information security. The Rochester Institute of Technology (RIT) employs very sound technical password management strategies, rendered largely useless by the fact that 55 percent of students randomly surveyed revealed that within the previous year they shared their system username and password with other system users or individuals not authorized to access the campus network. Of the 861 students who reported sharing this information, 70 percent said they never changed their password. Hence, high-tech abuse or crimes can be easily committed with their usernames and potentially even with their electronic devices by anyone who subsequently learns their network access data. Students' naivety is also exemplified when they post personal information to social computing sites like MySpace, XANGA, or FaceBook, thinking only their "Internet friends" can read the content or would access the information. Students also overestimate the level of security that such sites provide (see Angwin, 2006). In May of 2006, the badjocks.com website received national media attention after posting photos depicting partially nude male and female athletes from numerous colleges or universities who were allegedly participating in hazing rituals. Students involved were enrolled in schools including Princeton, Michigan, Wake Forest, and UC-Santa Barbara, among others. Members of Northwestern University's women's soccer team, included in the photos, later reported they were surprised and embarrassed by the media coverage (Armour, 2006).

Finally, being victimized does not necessarily mean being harmed only as the result of behaviors proscribed in computer crime statutes or other types of law, or even by college and university policies, all of which must continually be updated to keep up with innovative forms of high-tech offending. Rather, high-tech victimization appropriately includes abusive behaviors that cause any harm to individuals, groups, or organizations. This applies especially to campuses where computing is ubiquitous and technology-enabled culture and deviance are often on the fringes of society. For example, student plagiarism of someone else's copyrighted work may not rise to the level of violating state or federal copyright laws but can cause considerable harm to the original author, especially if the violating student's paper finds its way onto the Web without proper attribution thereby exposing the intellectual property (IP) to theft by third parties. Even if a violation of IP law did not occur as the result of the plagiarism, the behavior harmed the original author who could easily experience financial or another type of loss through additional unauthorized acquisition and distribution of their material. At a minimum they may feel stressed and need to expend time and other resources to protect their material if possible. Similarly, a faculty member who uses his/her college-issued computer during business hours to email family pictures to coworkers is not violating law but may well be violating institutional computer use policies by denying other users of the network needed bandwidth for legitimate school purposes. This situation is analogous to victimless crime, where theoretically, harm accrues to the community at large by willing participants' actions. Other forms of cyber abuse, such as Web page defacement and online harassment (also known as cyber bullying when adolescents are involved), may not constitute crimes per se, but nonetheless can and do harm victims in various ways (Swartz, 2005).

Off-and-Online Victimization and Offending Interplay

Thousands of potential victims and hundreds of perpetrators in ways that are technologically and behaviorally intertwined simultaneously use campus computer networks. This makes it difficult to neatly separate high-tech offending from victimization occurring on college campuses. For example, students who illegally pirate software, music, or movies via peer-to-peer (p2p) networks are violating federal (and probably state) copyright laws. But they are periodically also victimized as a result of unwittingly downloading malicious code embedded in the downloaded files that may damage their systems, their data, or lead to other crimes being committed against them such as when the embedded code is spyware. If not detected and quarantined, their now infected computers or other electronic device(s) will potentially further expose an entire campus of networked devices to infection, infiltration and other forms of harm, thus extending victimization through technology.

Consider the following hypothetical scenario:

Scott slides open his Palm Treo 650 as his computer crime professor continues a lecture on social penetration theory. The smart phone connects to the campus wireless network through an SD adaptor, allowing him to sign onto an instant messaging service without using his free cellular service subscriber minutes. Pretending to take notes, he silently starts a chat session with his friend Mike, joking about the pornographic videos of Mike's ex-girlfriend Sally that Mike previously posted online without her knowledge as revenge for their breakup a week earlier. Later, back in the dorm, Mike begins downloading the latest *Family Guy* TV episode through BitTorrent while resuming his chat with Scott who is now in a sociology class still pretending to take notes. Down the hall from Mike, Amy, who is also online with Scott, helps seed the *Family Guy* episode that Mike just sent to several friends. In the process, she posts the link to the torrent along with her course schedule to her MySpace page which is automatically sent to Brian's laptop via an RSS feed. Amy does not know Brian, but he certainly knows a lot about her, and he smiles at his luck as he reads her course schedule and plans his next social engineering move.

On campuses replete with systems and devices, the forgoing scenario is not far fetched. Recent research indicates a majority of students on campuses periodically misuse computers or other electronic devices to (1) buy papers, cheat on exams, or plagiarize the works of other people; (2) post onto websites or chat forums derogatory information about their classmates or professors; (3) harass, threaten, or solicit sex online; or (4) pirate and also redistribute copyrighted software, music, and movies (McQuade & Castellano, 2004). Obviously some of these abusive and criminal behaviors result in primary, secondary, or tertiary harm and thus contribute to overall victimization that occurs on campuses and via campus computer networks. This effectively extends and amalgamates social interactions and social computing on campuses and within surrounding communities to physical *and* cyber spaces occupied by students, staff, and faculty. In short, possible "locations and spaces" in or through which high-tech abuse and crime can occur are boundless, and yet geographic locations still matter because people necessarily live, work, study, or otherwise occupy facilities, grounds, or vehicles whenever they are using systems and devices.

Evidence for technological and behavioral interplay between high-tech offending and victimization by and among college students in particular has much to do with social learning theory (Fream, 1993; Rogers, 2001). This further underscores the importance of off- and online interactions. What students do not know about high-tech abuse and crimes from which they can benefit personally, they often find out shortly after arriving on campuses filled with IT, technologically well-informed peers, and unprecedented ability to access information about innovative offending methods. This situation is likely being exacerbated by media coverage of innovative high-tech crimes (Fream, 1993), which now effectively include a multitude of websites, chat rooms, and blogs specializing in high-tech offending content. The result is that high-tech victims and offenders on campuses frequently know each other personally in the flesh, or at least through social computing interactions. Indeed, one in three of 873 college students randomly surveyed in a 2004 study conducted at the Rochester Institute of Technology (RIT) reported that they knew the offender prior to the high-tech attack, abuse, or crime in which they were victimized (McQuade & Schreck, 2005).

The Extent and Impact of IT-Enabled Crime on Campuses

By now, you may be wondering how much high-tech abuse and crime occurs on campuses, and what are their social and economic impacts. Unfortunately, a dearth of empirical studies reveals relatively little about the extent of high-tech offending in society, much less the social, psychological, and economic impacts experienced by victims. What we know about the extent and impacts of IT-enabled crime on campuses is even more limited. Lack of knowledge stems from: (1) inconsistent conceptualizations and flawed research methodologies; (2) victims not being aware they have been attacked, or reluctance to report crimes for any number of reasons including easy treatment of cybercriminals by courts even when prosecuted; (3) violent and traditional property crimes being prioritized in the minds of campus officials; (4) insufficiently trained and equipped campus security or police officers who may also be indifferent about high-tech crimes or intimidated by technical aspects of cybercrimes; (5) noninclusion of even common computer crimes in police reporting systems such as national and state crime reporting systems and reports (e.g., the National Incident Based Reporting System–NIBRS) that colleges and universities may voluntarily contribute crime data to; and (6) continually changing IT and associated threat capabilities available to those who would use computers or other types of electronic devices for illicit purposes.

Despite these obstacles and the near absence of federal funding throughout the twentieth century for computer crime research, studies designed to measure the nature and extent of high-tech offending on college campuses have been undertaken. While most of these have usually involved convenience samples of students, a few have employed large random samples, rigorous data analysis, and testing of specific theories to determine causes and correlates of illicit, unethical, abusive, and/or criminal use of computers. The first of these studies was by Hollinger (1989), who surveyed 1,774 undergraduate students at a southern university about software piracy and computer hacking. Hollinger found a relatively large number of students admitted to participating in various types of computer offending behavior. Specifically, during a 15-week-long semester, 10 percent of respondents reported they pirated software and 3.3 percent of students surveyed reported they had violated another person's account/files/privacy. Fifty percent of those respondents said they did so only once during the semester in question, 11.1 percent reported they had committed one of these two offenses at least once, and 2.1 percent reported doing both activities. Skinner and Fream (1997) expanded Hollinger's study by asking 581 students about their lifetime, past year, and past month behavior involving: (1) software piracy, (2) guessing passwords, (3) gaining unauthorized access merely to browse data, (4) gaining unauthorized access to change data, and (5) writing/using virus-like programs. Skinner and Fream concluded that aspects of Social Learning Theory (e.g., differential reinforcement/punishment, definitions, and sources of imitation) were significant explanations for computer crime.

In 2004, McQuade and Castellano built on these and other studies with another self-report survey of 873 randomly selected students at the Rochester Institute of Technology. The survey examined perceptions, attitudes, and experiences, including 20 types of IT-enabled offending. Table 15.1 and Table 15.2 below summarize some of the victimization and offending data from this study.

McQuade and his colleagues conducted additional self-report surveys of randomly selected college students between 2004 and 2006 including: (1) an online survey of 574 incoming first-year RIT students; (2) a comparative study of 509 SUNY Brockport students that used the same instrument used at RIT in April, 2004; and (3) a program evaluation survey of 449 RIT students, split evenly between individuals who used and did not use a free music downloading service provided by the university. Although detailed findings from these studies have not yet been published, highlights further reveal the nature and extent of high-tech abuse and crimes committed by

Table 15.1
SELF-REPORTED VICTIMIZATION BY
COLLEGE STUDENTS IN YEAR PRIOR TO STUDY

Type of victimization	Number of Student Victims	Percent of Respondents
Harmed by malicious code	435	48%
Denial of service	115	13.8%
Online harassment	149	17.1%
Received online threat(s)	68	7.9%
Cyber stalking	52	6.1%
Hacking	99	12.3%
Stolen equipment	23	2.7%
Identity theft	55	6.5%
Other fraud	27	3.2%
Other	20	2.4%

Table 15.2
PERCENT OF SELF-REPORTED OFFENDING BY COLLEGE STUDENTS

Offending in 12 months prior to survey:	*Never*	*1–10 Times*	*11–30 Times*	*31+ Times*
Unauthorized music file sharing	24.5%	14.6%	7.4%	53.5%
Unauthorized movie file sharing	42.1%	22.2%	11.4%	24.4%
Unauthorized software file sharing	39.9%	36.9%	9.2%	14.0%
Obtained someone's credit card # without their knowledge	99.5%	.5%	0%	0%
Used credit card without permission	99.8%	0.2%	0%	0%
Plagiarized	92.9%	6.6%	0.2%	0.2%
Copied and inappropriately used someone else's computer code	93.1%	6.4%	0.2%	0.2%
Purchased paper and turned in as an assignment	99.0%	1.0%	0%	0%
Used a computer or other IT device to cheat on school assignment	94.2%	5.3%	0.2%	0.2%
Used a computer or other IT device to cheat on an exam	96.9%	2.8%	0.2%	0.1%

and among students:

- Offending behavior and victimization experiences of students at large private technological institutes versus small-to-medium sized general education colleges do not vary to any appreciable extent (McQuade, Gorthy, & Linden, 2006);
- Social learning theory is a powerful explanation of IT-enabled offending; campus alternative education sanctions and other disciplinary actions less than academic suspension have little deterrent effect on students' illegal file sharing (McQuade & Fisk, 2006);
- Students who engage in IT-enabled offending may specialize in specific types of abusive or illegal behavior (McQuade & Castellano, 2004);
- Students vary considerably in their ethical attitudes towards IT-enabled abuse and crime. For example, students regard using a computer or other electronic device to facilitate academic dishonesty or violate copyright laws as being less wrong than harassing or threatening someone online, and much less wrong than using IT to commit fraud (McQuade & Linden, 2006)

These and other studies confirm the need for greater attention to on-campus,

IT-enabled abuse and crime and suggest new avenues of research for investigators. Readers should understand that empirical evidence about the true nature, extent, and impacts of high-tech campus crime remains very limited. Fortunately, a growing number of researchers are paying attention to these issues and the day may soon come when government agencies or foundations sponsor funded research into behavioral aspects of high-tech offending on college and university campuses.

Implications for Academic Reforms

Amalgamated Offices for Information Security, Policy Development, and Training

Prior to computerization, campus security consisted almost entirely of uniformed officers protecting the institution's physical assets through installing and monitoring locks, lighting, and alarm systems; promoting pedestrian, vehicle, and personal safety; and conducting preventative patrols while making students and campus employees more aware of crime possibilities. Campus police officers commissioned with arrest power also investigated crimes occurring on college and university property and traditionally maintained close working relationships with law enforcement agencies in surrounding jurisdictions. These and many other functions remain extremely important in the tradition of physical security and policing.

In recent years, some 200 campuses throughout the U.S. have created Information Security Offices and organized these within Information Technology Services (ITS) divisions (J. Moore, personal communication, June 15, 2006). Analogous to traditional campus security offices, these "infosec units" concentrate on installing technological safeguards; monitoring network environments; and generally preventing, detecting, and responding to situations that threaten information systems. Depending on designated mission responsibilities, available resources and expertise, infosec units may also participate in procurement activities for system upgrades; provide cybercrime prevention training for students, faculty, and staff; investigate system abuses and cybercrimes; and support development and enforcement of campus policies and procedures pertaining to responsible use of IT and systems.

Given the apparent prevalence of IT-enabled abuse and crimes occurring on campuses, combined with institutional dependence on IT for every aspect of campus life and business operations, infosec units now provide essential services of equal importance to traditional physical security and policing services. The fact that crime on campus now runs the gauntlet from low-to-high tech and involves both the physical and cyber worlds, amalgamating the functions of traditional campus security offices with dedicated infosec units makes sense. Typically, however, postsecondary institutions continue to separate these functions, both organizationally and operationally: "cops" do their thing while "cyber sleuths" theirs. There is little, if any, recognition that IT-enabled abuse of systems and devices frequently occurs over time by students, faculty, and staff both on- and offline, and from on- and off-campus locations. For better organizing and operational purposes, it is useful to conceptualize a new campus security paradigm as a Venn Diagram in which illicit activities may occur strictly via networks or in physical places without using IT systems, or that crossover into the cyber and physical realms simultaneously. To put it another way, innovative and traditional crime increasingly involves illicit use of IT and related networks. Therefore, both the organization and its delivery of traditional security and policing functions must similarly evolve to address human behaviors that play out via physical and cyber realms. To remain effective, campus security and policing must become as seamless as the IT systems that enable illicit behaviors to be committed in increasingly high tech ways.

Sanctioning and Technological Solutions to Network Security and Prevention

Institutions must address IT-enabled abuse and cybercrimes on college campuses through active sanctioning of offenders and with technological solutions. Historically, colleges and universities have used administrative offices and programs to address student academic and nonacademic misconduct involving inappropriate physical, mental, emotional, or sexual abuse. Institutions seek to prevent such problems by developing written policies that specify inappropriate behaviors and sanctions the institution may impose for the behavior. Institutions address such misconduct, including that involving inappropriate use of IT, through mediation services, disciplinary hearings, and alternative education courses required of students who violate rules. Institutional sanctions, including academic suspension and expulsion, for unacceptable use of IT devices and network resources including online harassment, unauthorized downloading via p2p networks, copyright infringement, and violations of privacy proscribed in laws such as the federal Family Education Rights and Privacy Act (FERPA) and the Digital Millennium Copyright Act (DMCA) are designed to educate, prevent, and deter future violations.

Campuses also rely on a variety of information security and network monitoring technologies to prevent, detect, and respond to misconduct involving IT. These include contracting for services that automatically update operating systems, software applications, and malware definitions; hardware and software firewall and network traffic monitoring programs; and other programs that filter, block, or otherwise quarantine suspicious files or access to particular Web content, such as p2p sites known to facilitate the illegal downloading of software, music or movies. IT administrators assign unique Internet Protocol (IP) addresses to fixed or portable computers authorized to connect to campus networks (e.g., those located in computing labs, libraries, or owned by students, etc.), which allows officials and investigators to monitor and/or analyze computing activities accomplished with specific devices. Virtual privacy networks (VPNs) now allow authorized users from off-campus locations to connect securely to campus networks over the Internet. Institutions can configure technology-enabled password management processes requiring using strong passwords to access campus networks (e.g., those consisting of 12 or more randomly selected alphanumeric characters) and changing passwords on a regular basis. Many campuses are also eliminating social security numbers as a basis of student identification, encrypting data stored or transmitted over its networks, rapid fire email alert systems to warn of new malware releases, and restricting access to data based on authorized user security levels (Marklein, 2006b). And they are increasingly coordinating to stay abreast of emerging threats to information security and best practices for its protection with government agencies, private sector firms, and nonprofit organizations such as EduCause whose mission is "to advance higher education by promoting the intelligent use of information technology" (EduCause, n.d.). However, as previously indicated, human factors (i.e., knowledge and capabilities of campus IT professionals, offenders, and potential victims) have much to do with the effectiveness of passwords and other technological solutions to high-tech misbehavior.

Conclusion

The huge challenge facing today's colleges and universities is to combine high-tech education with intervention strategies to combat high-tech abuse and crime that continues to evolve and which is possibly increasing in both incidence and prevalence on college campuses. Two and four-year institutions in the U.S. commonly offer programs of study in computer science, software engineering, IT systems administration, and similar specializations.

Increasingly, academic institutions are also offering courses, if not entire programs of study, that focus on information security, computer/cyber crime, and computer forensics. This is rather paradoxical given that the computer-related inventions and innovations that have benefited society enormously have also led to new forms of criminality. Now, the founding institutions that made those advances possible are not only undertaking new research but also providing education and training to protect information systems. It seems that society has come full cycle.

Several academic institutions since the mid 1990s have been working to become certified as Centers of Academic Excellence in information security education.[4] These schools aim to help strengthen national critical information infrastructure protection against would be cyber-offenders and even so-called "cyber-terrorists." The National Colloquium for Information Security Education (NCISE), the National Security Agency (NSA), the National Science Foundation (NSF), and the Department of Homeland Security (DHS) are behind this movement and in full recognition of the vital role colleges and universities must play in strengthening the nation's IT capabilities through research and education.

Ironically, such research and education are geared towards a generation of students who grew up using computer devices, often without adequate supervision or training in information security or cyber ethics. In the series of computer use and ethics studies described earlier, my colleagues and I at RIT found most of today's college students not only grew up with computers in their homes, they were usually the primary users of those devices at ten years of age. In general, they were strongly encouraged and supported by parents who, although encouraging the use of computers for a variety of activities, failed to supervise adequately the use of IT devices. Lacking systematic cyber ethics and information security/safety-related education or training, today's college students are generally prone to IT-enabled offending and victimization. For many students, this reality may be exacerbated given powerful computers and high-speed Internet connectivity available on most campuses and combined with youth cultures that embrace actively using electronic devices for almost every imaginable activity—certainly for coursework, research, and chatting with friends, as well as for online shopping and various forms of entertainment such as watching/viewing downloaded music/movies, playing electronic games, and viewing of legal pornography—in some extreme cases the latter activities reportedly having detrimental effects on students' grades, employment responsibilities, and personal relationships (McQuade, 2006, pp. 153–155).

Higher education officials and faculty, working collaboratively across academic departments and campus services offices must embrace a new national education and workforce training imperative to raise awareness, knowledge, understanding and skills for enhanced Internet safety, information security and cyber ethics among students, faculty, and staff. It is the combination of education and training for all campus IT users in these subject areas, combined with efficacious technology solutions that will ultimately lead to prevention of cybercrime on campuses and their social computing environments.

Notes

1. Space constraints severely restrict the depth of my discussion and incorporation of examples. Readers should therefore regard this chapter as an overview of high-tech crime issues affecting colleges and universities. Nonetheless, I am hopeful the information contained in this chapter will be interesting, useful, and perhaps provocative. After all, IT-enabled crimes on college and university campuses are a subset and extension of innovative and harmful behaviors increasingly occurring throughout the modern world. These behaviors threaten users of computers and other types of electronic devices, are routinely and sensationally reported by the media, and criminal justice scholars, practitioners, and policymakers, including those on college and university campuses, who are struggling to better understand and prevent.

2. The term "hacker" is controversial. Among computer programmers in good standing with the technical community, the words "hacker" and "hacking" are used more often in the admiring or awed sense of a skilled software developer. People favoring this usage typically look with dismay on the usage of the term as a synonym for security cracking. In the nontechnical community, the word "hacker" most often describes someone who "hacks into" a system by evading or disabling security measures (retrieved August 6, 2006 from, http://www.en. wikipedia.org/wiki/Hacker_definition_ controversy#Quotations,).

3. A "bot" is common parlance on the Internet describing a software program that interacts with other network services intended for people, as if it were a person. Derived from the word "robot," the term reflects the autonomous character in the "virtual robotness" of the concept. The most common bots are those that covertly install themselves on people's computers for malicious purposes and that act as remote attack tools. More generally, they are web software agents that interface with Web pages. Web crawlers or *spiders* are Web robots that recursively gather Web-page information, as does the bot used by Google ("GoogleBot"). They may be used to interact dynamically with a site in a particular way, as by exploiting or locating arbitrage opportunities for financial gain (retrieved August 7, 2006 from, http://en.wikipedia.org/wiki/ Internet_bot).

4. Currently over 60 academic institutions have been certified by NSA as Centers of Academic Excellence in information security education.

REFERENCES

Angwin, J. (2006). Parental guidance: How safe are the top social networking sites for teens? We take them for a test run. Retrieved July 25, 2006 from, http://online.wsj.com/public/article/SB115333833014811453-LjMFsXTCUjSig Iarp2FhC0Y_TSs_ 20060822. html?mod=tff_main_tff_top.

Armour, N. (2006). Blogs, photo sites give everyone a peek at athletes' lives. Retrieved May 27, 2006 from, http://sportsillustrated.cnn.com/2006/more/ wires/05/26/2080.ap. bad.jocks.adv27.1331/index.html.

Cohen, L. E., & Felson, M. (1979). Social change and crime: A routine activity approach. In Joseph E. Jacoby (Ed.), *Criminological theory*. Prospect Heights, IL:

Waveland Press.

EduCause, EduCause home page. Retrieved August 6 from, http://www.edu-cause.edu/con tent.asp?PAGE_ID=720&bhcp=1.

Fream, A. Unpublished master's thesis. University of Kentucky, KY.

Hollinger, R. C. (1993). Crime by computer: Correlates of software piracy and unauthorized account access. *Security Journal, 4,* 2–12.

Hollinger, R. C., & Lanza-Kaduce, L. (1988). The process of criminalization: The case of computer crime laws. *Criminology, 26,* 101–126.

Levy, S. (1984). *Hackers: Heroes of the computer revolution.* New York: Doubleday.

Liedtke, M. (2005). Stolen UC Berkeley laptop exposes personal data of nearly 100,000. Retrieved April 6, 2005 from, http://www.detnews.com/2005/tech nology/0503/30/tech-132193.htm.

Marklein, M. B. (2006a). Colleges are textbook cases of cybersecurity breaches. Retrieved August 3, 2006 from, http://www.usatoday.com/tech/news/computer security/hacking/ 2006-08-01-college-hack_x.htm.

Marklein, M. B. (2006b). The new learning curve: Technological security. Retrieved August 3, 2006 from, http://www.usatoday.com/tech/news/computersecurity/ hacking/2006-08-01-college-security_x.htm.

McQuade, S. C. (2005). IT-enabled offending and victimization by and among RIT students: Implications for student services, education and training. Presented to the Student Affairs Division at the Rochester Institute of Technology, August 17.

McQuade, S. C. (2006). *Understanding and managing cybercrime.* Boston: Pearson Education.

McQuade, S. C., & Schreck, C. (2005). Correlates of high tech crime victimization. Paper presented at the 2005 Annual Meetings of the Midwest Criminal Justice Association, Chicago, IL.

McQuade, S. C., & Castellano, T. (2004). Computer aided crime and misbehavior among a student population: An empirical examination of patterns, correlates, and possible causes. Paper presented at the Annual Meetings of the American Society of Criminology, Nashville, TN.

McQuade, S. C., & Fisk, N. (2006). Social interactions for learning high tech crime: An empirical analysis of social learning and deterrence theory correlates. Unpublished manuscript. Rochester Institute of Technology.

McQuade, S. C., & Linden, E. (2006). College student computer use and ethics: An empirical analysis of self-reported unethical behaviors. Unpublished manuscript. Rochester Institute of Technology.

McQuade, S. C., Gorthy, M., & Linden, E. (2006). High tech crimes on college campuses: A comparison of offending and victimization at RIT versus SUNY Brockport. Unpublished manuscript. Rochester Institute of Technology.

National White Collar Crime Center & West Virginia University (1996). *Proceedings of the Academic Workshop.* Washington, DC: Bureau of Justice Assistance.

Parker, D. B. (1998). *Fighting computer crime: A new framework for protecting information.* New York: Wiley.

Rogers, M. K. (2001). A social learning theory and moral disengagement analysis of criminal computer behavior: An exploratory study. University of Manitoba,

Winnipeg, Manitoba.

Skinner, W. F., & Fream, A. M. (1997). A social learning theory analysis of computer crime among college students. *Journal of Research in Crime and Delinquency, 34,* 495–519.

Sutherland, E. H. (1940). White-collar criminality. In J. E. Jacoby (Ed.), *Criminological theory.* Prospect Heights, IL: Waveland Press.

Swartz, J. (2005, March 20). Cyberbullies: Intimidation lurks online in form of a young, faceless force. *The Wall Street Journal,* pp. A1, A5.

Synovate (2003). *FTC identity theft survey report.* Washington, DC: Federal Trade Commission.

POSTSCRIPT

In 1990, Congress passed and President George H.W. Bush signed into law the *Student Right to Know and Campus Security Act of 1990*. Hailed by some as an effective tool in the fight against campus crime, the legislation forced postsecondary institutions participating in Title IV federal financial aid programs to finally "come clean" with their crime statistics and security policies and "do something" about campus crime. Additionally, during the 1990s several states passed their own "campus crime" legislation and passed legislation that enabled colleges and universities to create campus police departments staffed by sworn peace officers.

Both federal and state legislation during the 1990s sparked much interest and activism in campus crime and security. During this time, the first edition of *Campus Crime: Legal, Social, and Policy Perspectives* was published–making it among the first edited collections of scholarly works devoted to examining different aspects of campus crime and security issues. Further, research on campus crime that began in the late 1980s gained momentum as social scientists increasingly became interested in, and funding became available to study, campus crime and safety. Scholars from a variety of disciplines regularly published peer-reviewed studies that described and explained the magnitude and the dynamics of on-campus and student victimization, and began critically questioning the effectiveness of both state and federal campus crime legislation.

Other parties were also actively engaged in furthering the safety interests of college students. For example, Security On Campus, Inc. quickly became the leading national advocate and watchdog for "doing something" about campus crime and helped student victims and their parents find "justice." To accomplish these goals, it began providing free advocacy and referral services for the victims of violent campus crime, and created a website providing a plethora of campus crime-related information to the public. Further, the U.S. Justice Department funded three large-scale, national-level studies of college student victimization experiences and one national-level study of postsecondary institutional compliance with federal legislation; reports and scholarly articles arising from these studies were also published. In 1998,

Congress renamed the statute the *Clery Act* while states continued to pass their own *Clery*-style legislation. Finally, in 2005, the U.S. Department of Education published a handbook for schools to assist them in complying with *Clery* stipulations. By any standard, these examples represent a great deal of activity geared toward "doing something" about campus crime.

Yet, over 15 years later, many of the same issues that activists, legislators, postsecondary administrators, and social scientists began addressing during the early 1990s either remain unresolved or the solutions implemented have been shown wanting. As a result, the legislative and judicial branches of government, social scientists, and security officials continue to focus their attention on campus crime. Concurrently, over 6,000 Title IV participating postsecondary institutions in this country address ongoing challenges involving compliance with state and federal legislation, civil lawsuits filed by crime victims, and other emerging campus crime issues such as stalking, high-tech abuse and crimes, and information technology security. Nearly two decades after congressional passage of the *Campus Security Act,* the center of attention continues to be "doing something" about crime occurring at postsecondary institutions. However, as several of the contributors to this volume point out, first and subsequent attempts at "doing something" resulted in either the passage of "symbolic" legislation and/or the implementation of policies or programs that had little substantive impact on campus safety and security.

The collected works in this volume present an early twenty-first century picture of the three contexts of campus crime—legal, social, and security—and some of the policy issues associated with them. While answers to basic questions asked during the early 1990s such as "how much crime is there on college campuses?" and "to what degree have postsecondary institutions complied with federal campus crime legislation?" have appeared, sometimes lacking from the "doing something" momentum are questions about the *effectiveness* of what is "being done." Simply put, answers to the question "what works?" are much needed to move from "doing something" about campus crime to "*effectively* doing something" to address campus crime.

Postsecondary institutions have "come a long way" in their efforts to address campus crime. Yet, as the chapters show, they still have a ways to go. While postsecondary institutions have at least made an effort to "come clean" with their crime statistics, have developed and implemented security policies that, at least on the surface, attempt to address some of the problems they face, and continue to work to address compliance and other issues arising from federal and state legislation, half way through the first decade of the twenty-first century many tasks remain unfinished. Questions concerning the extent, nature, causes, and effects of campus victimization and fear of victimization remain largely unanswered. Legislation, both at the federal and state level, may be more symbolic than real, and continues to be criticized by academics and advocacy groups alike. Decisions have only partly been made concerning the implementation of community-oriented policing (COP) in university police departments. Finally, new issues in security involving the use and abuse of information technology–issues that few could have imagined in 1990–threaten to supplant "traditional" security concerns on college campuses.

As we argued in the first edition of this volume, "campus administrators must realize that addressing the problem of crime on their campuses involves interdepartmental cooperation." More than ten years later, at best, evidence of such cooperation is mixed. The need for advocacy groups, such as Security On Campus, Inc., as well as developers and evaluators of crime prevention and education programs, is perhaps as great today as it was then. While progress has occurred, we hope that administrators quicken the pace with which they use the expertise and data available on their campuses to address the legal, social, and security contexts of campus crime and safety. By doing so, they can develop and implement policies and programs that are both evidence-based and routinely evaluated (and revised accordingly), rather than developing responses that are politically expedient but largely ineffective in addressing campus crime and security.

NAME INDEX

A

Abarbanel, Gail, 192, 194, 204
Abbey, Antonia, 74, 84, 160, 162, 177,
    179–180, 184, 200, 204, 232, 240,
    249, 251
Adams, A., 192, 194, 204
Adams-Curtis, L. E., 199, 206
Aizenman, M., 188, 204
Allbritten, W. L., 195, 200, 205
Allgeier, E. R., 151, 159, 164
Alvi, S., 203, 205, 254
Amar, A. F., 195, 201–204
Amick, A. E., 195, 202, 204
Andreoli Mathie, V., 85
Angwin, J., 313, 323
Appalachian State University, 251
Armour, N., 313, 323
Astor, R., 233, 251
Atwell, R., 280, 284, 299

B

Bachar, K., 177, 180, 184
Banyard, V. L., 190, 192, 196, 204
Barberet, R., 129, 145, 149–150, 160, 162
Bardsley, M., 46, 61
Bath, Catherine, v, 7–8, 18, 27, 47, 61, 66,
    68, 84, 118, 120, 184, 224, 227
Baucom, 57
Baum, K., 135, 144, 150, 162, 168, 185, 299
Bausell, C. R., 151, 162
Bausell, R. B., 151, 156, 162
Bayley, D., 262, 277
Behre, W., 251
Belknap, Joanne, v, 9, 18, 65, 69, 75, 84,
    144–145, 188–191, 195, 201, 204, 227

Bell, L. C., 115, 120
Benedict, J., 151, 158, 162–163
Benson, B., 273, 279
Benson, D., 196, 201–202, 204
Benson, D. J., 193, 197, 203–204
Berger, R. J., 195, 201, 204
Bess, W., 299
Bjerregaard, B., 216–217, 219–223, 227
Black, T., 190, 198, 204
Blair, K., 129, 146
Blevins, Kristie R., vi, 12, 19, 65, 118, 120
Block, C., 233, 251
Block, R., 233, 251
Bogal-Allbritten, R., 195, 200, 205
Bogle, Kathleen, 184
Bohm, R., 231, 251
Bohmer, C., 71, 84, 200, 202–203, 205
Bondurant, B., 70, 74–75, 84
Bordner, D., 271, 273, 277, 284, 293, 299
Boswell, A. A., 190, 205
Boyd, G. M., 183–185
Branch, K., 233, 252
Brandenburg, J. B., 190, 201–203, 205
Brantingham, P., 232–235, 240–241, 251,
    287–289, 294, 299
Brantingham, P. J., 144–145
Brantingham, P. L., 144–145
Brewer, R. D., 172, 183, 186
Brinkley, W. Jr., 232, 251
Britton, G. M., 199, 209
Bromley, Max L., vi, 15, 18, 116, 120, 129,
    134, 138, 145–146, 159, 165, 200, 205,
    232–233, 251–252, 262–263,
    273–278, 280, 284–285, 287,
    292–294, 299–300, 302
Brooks, C. I., 75, 86
Brown, L., 263, 277

SUBJECT INDEX